1992 Fordham
Reprint 20.00

1st h 5c

STEAMBOATS COME TRUE

Other Books by James Thomas Flexner

WILLIAM HENRY WELCH
and the Heroic Age of American Medicine

AMERICA'S OLD MASTERS:
First Artists of the New World

DOCTORS ON HORSEBACK:
Pioneers of American Medicine

Steamboats Come True

AMERICAN INVENTORS IN ACTION

By James Thomas Flexner

New York : The Viking Press : Mcmxliv

Copyright 1944 by James Thomas Flexner

First Published by The Viking Press in September 1944

Published on the Same Day in the Dominion of Canada
by The Macmillan Company of Canada Limited

Printed in U.S.A. by The Haddon Craftsmen

Acknowledgments

I am, of course, primarily indebted to the host of scholars, writers, and librarians who have plowed the field of steamboat history before me. Without their assistance, my labors would have come to nothing. Many libraries have accorded me hospitality and co-operation, particularly the Yale University Library where most of my research was done. Helen Whitall Flexner, Sidney Withington, and Marshall A. Best have kindly read the manuscript and made many valuable suggestions. Finally I must thank the members of my family and particularly my wife, who, in addition to helping me in many other ways, have patiently listened to me rambling on about steamboats until, I am sure, they wished the darned things had never been invented.

Contents

Illustrations

ix

Most of the decorations in the text are based on woodcuts by Alexander Anderson, 1775-1870, taken from his scrapbooks in the New York Public Library. One of the steamboats represents Fulton's first American vessel; the others are later ships, showing the next generation of development. They have been redrawn for this volume by RAYMOND LUFKIN.

PROLOGUE

In Pursuit of Paradox

SOMEWHERE overhead the sun shone, but it was strained and mottled by high foliage until the world was a perpetual twilight of dim greens. Silent and strange as the bottom of the ocean, the floor of the forest was unmindful of man. All his works, all the majesty and ingenuity of the human race, had shrunk to a narrow trail, insignificant as an insect's track, that wound endlessly through underbrush and fallen trees. And even this alien streak was less the product of Indian feet than of the sharp hooves of deer.

Now, in the 1780's, a new type of intruder traversed the ancient path. Dark and straight and moving with effortless speed on silent feet, John Fitch might have been mistaken for an Indian; but the thoughts in his brain belonged to another age and time. Already in his mind's eye the forest had vanished; fields, houses, cities stretched around him more substantial to his vision than the trunks of trees. From the pack on his back hung the chains that marked him as that first messenger of civilization, a surveyor.

On and on he walked swiftly; he could cover 40 miles in a day, moving, as he himself boasted, faster than any horse. For a long time the wilderness was unchanging: the same dim aisles of green, the same primeval silence. Then a murmur arose as if wind blew through the motionless trees, and suddenly sunlight struck down like an avalanche to blind his dark-accustomed eyes. The tall man stopped, blinking.

When his vision cleared, he looked out over a different world. Gone were the trees that impeded sight and motion, gone the tangle that clogged his feet. He stood on a bluff, and there below smoothness stretched a mile wide before him, smoothness disappeared into the horizon on his left and right. Beyond, he could see the forest rising once again, but below him an even plane of water flowed irresistibly toward the sea.

The surveyor sat down on a log to watch the Ohio River roll past. Perhaps as he lingered there a raft floated downstream, keeping to the center of the flood for fear of Indians, the armed men and their cattle tiny in the distance. His heart would have leapt at the apparition; men like these would people the cities his fancy built. But he knew that he might wait a hundred years and not see settlers or goods or any object move upstream, except an occasional barge or keel boat propelled so laboriously that the trip was an economic failure before it started.

Years later, an acquaintance remembered John Fitch to have said that "while engaged in surveying on the banks of the Ohio River, . . . he took his seat and for some time contemplated that beautiful river, it then rolling a full tide toward the ocean; and reflecting upon its immense length from its head to the ocean, he thought it impossible God had in His wisdom created a river with such length and irresistible current, without giving to man some power of overcoming the force of the water, and being able to navigate it up as well as down."

This was the vague imagining of a poet. John Fitch, "inventor of steamboats," as he was later to call himself, did not as yet realize that the properties of steam could be used to create motion. Steam engines existed in Europe, and a few had been brought to North America, but the surveyor did not know about them. He was allowing the clouds of fancy to form strange shapes within his mind; soon they would be dispelled by the necessity of carrying out his work in the wilderness. But something remained, some dim afterthought of dream that was to play its part in changing the history of the world.

During April 1785, several years after his vision on the Ohio, Fitch was again walking, this time with a very different stride. Afflicted with rheumatism, he hobbled down a country road in Bucks County, Pennsylvania. The wilderness had vanished; around him stretched well-cultivated farms, each with its substantial homestead. Fitch was returning from a religious meeting. As he struggled painfully on through the heat and dust, the crisp sound of hooves arose behind him, and in an instant a local gentleman and his wife moved effortlessly by him in a chair pulled by a spirited horse. Their dust choked the nostrils of the limping man. Fitch looked after them for a moment in irritation, and then his brow clouded with thought. How agreeable it would be, he pondered, if a poor man could ride in a conveyance without the expense of keeping a horse. And then in a flash of inspiration he decided that carriages could be propelled by the force of steam.

Fitch was delighted with the originality of his idea. When several weeks later the local minister, to whom he confided his secret, convinced him that steam engines already existed by showing him a drawing of one in a book, he was "amazed and chagrined"; it seemed as if fate had resolved that he would never think of anything new.

Five years passed and then rustics on the banks of the Delaware were pulled upright from their hoeing by a strange sound; there was a shriek in the air accompanied by an unnatural medley of chugging and splashing. Below them the farmers saw an odd something moving among the many sailboats in the river. It was shaped like a dory, but it had no sail and the men inside it were not rowing; they seemed to be sitting with amazing coolness in the very center of a cauldron that belched noise and smoke and sparks. Any Bible reader was instantly reminded of Shadrach, Meshach, and Abed-nego. Behind the intrepid voyagers, extending from the stern of the boat, were three large paddles like coal scuttles that, for no apparent reason, kicked the boat along so violently that it rushed past all the sailboats in the river.

After years of failure, misery, and derision, after a multitude of false attempts, Fitch had realized his dream of building a boat that would go upstream with certainty and speed. For months during that summer of 1790 the vessel moved on schedule between Burlington, N. J., Trenton, and Philadelphia, traveling 2000 or 3000 miles, sometimes, so excellent evidence indicates, at the rate of 8 miles an hour. Since Philadelphia was the intellectual capital of America and in close contact with the capitals of the Old World; since all of

America's leaders, from Franklin and Washington down, knew of Fitch's vessel, you would expect that the invention of the steamboat was now a reality. Yet after its single season of triumphant operation, the world's first successful mechanical boat lay rotting and forgotten in a cove of the Delaware, while its inventor wrote long arguments to prove he was not mad, took to drink, and died at last by his own hand.

A whole generation was to pass before the boon that Fitch offered was accepted by mankind. Other attempts made by many other inventors lit up the sky like slow fires, or like rockets, only to sink back one and all into darkness. England and France were in the race, but all their entries too were failures. Seventeen years elapsed before Robert Fulton's successful experiment on the Hudson.

Popular history tells us that August 17, 1807, was the date of the invention of the steamboat, and the voyage of the *Clermont* to Albany was the occasion. It is perhaps typical of popular history that the boat is incorrectly named; Fulton did not call her the *Clermont*. If we agree that this vessel was the first successful steamboat, we find ourselves faced with a group of contradictions. Fulton's boat was not the most mechanically perfect vessel built up to that time; it was much slower than Fitch's boat of seventeen years before; and not one of its component parts was original with Fulton.

Recognizing these facts, many writers have stated that it is ridiculous to call Fulton the inventor of the steamboat. The favorite rival candidate is Fitch, but there are many others: the Frenchman Jouffroy, the Englishmen Hulls and Symington, the Americans Henry, Morey, Roosevelt, Livingston, Stevens. Yet in opposition to the claims of these men, every one of whom preceded Fulton in date, some stubborn facts remain. Although Fulton came late in the development of steamboats, although he was unoriginal and by no means as brilliant an inventor as some of his rivals, he was the first inventor to have more than one boat operating at the same time, or to keep his ships moving for longer than a season or two. Before Fulton, there were periods of years when no steamboat puffed on any waters anywhere; after him, the line of steam navigation stretches unbroken to the present day.

The reader must be beginning to see that in entering the world of steamboat invention he is entering a world of paradox. Indeed, the seeming contradictions become more numerous the deeper our investigation goes. In the development of a mechanical invention, we would expect the determining considerations to be mechanical; that this was not the case with the steamboat is easily shown. Not only was the invention completed by a ship that was inferior in engineering to at least one of the failures that preceded it, but the basic technical problems were solved a generation before steamboats became a reality. When by 1782 Watt had developed a double-acting, separate-condensing, rotary steam engine, every one of the engineering difficulties presented by the steamboat had been resolved separately. All that was necessary was to mount an established engine in an efficient manner on some kind of vessel and connect it by one of many known means with a device that went back to darkest antiquity—the paddle wheel. Yet it took the human race thirty-five years to take this apparently obvious step. An account of the invention of the steamboat, then, cannot be limited to a study of technology.

If we tried to decide by reason in what country the steamboat was invented, we would be unlikely to hit on America, which was still a mechanical and scientific backwater; England would be the obvious place. Not only was Britain the home of the most skillful steam-engine builders in the world—Watt was the leader of a long-established and growing profession—but, as the cradle of the industrial revolution, it boasted a hundred skilled mechanics to every one in the United States. While America was an agrarian country where cash was extremely scarce, England had already entered the age of capitalism; funds were available for financing new projects. Nor must we forget that England was then as now the greatest maritime nation in the world. It should have been easy for a British inventor to secure the backing of some rich industrialist used to mechanical enterprise, to buy an efficient engine from

James Watt, to have his boat built and his machinery forged by leading artisans, and thus to produce a steamboat far beyond the mechanical and financial possibilities of America. How then can we explain the fact that the first practical steamboat was created by a Philadelphia surveyor and silversmith, fresh escaped from months of Indian captivity, who not only relied for financial support on tavern and shop keepers, but employed a watchmaker as his principal mechanic, and was forced by his ignorance to invent much of the Watt engine over again? And why was it that Fulton too was an American, who launched his invention on American waters?

Of course, in history as in science everything happens for a reason. The steamboat paradox could not have been a paradox at all, or it would not have taken place. In this book we shall try to find the logic in events that are particularly interesting because they seem so illogical.

In our search for answers, we shall follow the clues wherever they lead us, and like the detectives of fiction we shall find ourselves in some unlikely places. Primarily, we shall be concerned with the biographies of two very different men: Fitch the pioneer and Fulton the promoter. No aspect of their lives will seem so far away from steamboat invention that we may safely ignore it in our quest. If Fitch had not been a misfit—marvelously skillful yet impractical as a mad man; brilliant, visionary, quarrelsome, wild, and strange— the result of his labors would have been very different. Thus his perpetual rebellion against his environment; his tragic, frustrated childhood; his disastrous marriage which made him a homeless wanderer for life; his ludicrous adventures in the American Revolution; his arduous years as a wilderness surveyor and his terrible months as an Indian captive; his great manual skill that made him successively brass founder, clockmaker, silversmith, map maker, and engine builder; the strange compulsion that forced him to set himself up as the Messiah of a new religion, rival of Christ and Mohammed: all these are part of our story.

Nor can we overlook the poverty of Fulton's childhood after his tailor father died in the wilderness metropolis of Lancaster; his success as a portrait painter in provincial Philadelphia and his failure in more sophisticated London; his long search through poverty and obscurity for some justification for his feeling that he was born to make the world over in a new pattern; his unwillingness, as he dreamed of millions, to earn pence, and his resulting dependence, despite his pride, on the charity of his friends; his canal inventions which he hoped would bring a new era to mankind; his lifelong obsession with the development of submarine warfare, during which he capitalized on another man's discovery so successfully that he was able to sell the same "secret weapon" successively to Napoleon, Napoleon's enemy Pitt, and then the government of the United States. We shall note that he took up the steamboat as a minor activity, something of secondary importance which would make money to enable him to continue with his favorite scheme of placing all the navies of the world on the bottom of the ocean.

Fulton is one of the select group of American figures that has passed out of the realm of history into historical legend. His name appears in jokes on the radio and in the definitions of cross-word puzzles; he is a national hero. There is always a tendency to paint such figures as spotless and all-wise, perhaps to make them suitable models of virtue for inclusion in third-grade readers.

Of course, thus the flesh-and-blood Fulton has been transformed into a statue; book after book has presented him as a lay saint. If we wish to find the truth about him, we shall have to be wary and open-minded, seeking under the face-paint of myth the true features of life. The thoughts and deeds of our characters cannot be separated from the great impersonal forces which shape the pattern of history. To deal with an inventor as a unique individual operating independently of his environment would be like trying to describe the achievements of a swimmer without any reference to the water in which he moved or the currents that bore him in their own impersonal directions. Every gesture of our characters was impeded or altered or speeded ahead by forces more vast than the efforts of ten thousand men.

The steamboat was the first American invention of world-shaking importance; unlike the cotton gin, which was a simple gadget that could be built by any blacksmith, it required a new technology and a new attitude toward the world. That steamboat building was the foundation of our whole tradition of practical invention is shown by the fact that the American patent law was passed to take care of steamboat pioneers. Thus, as we pursue our quest, we shall explore the headwaters of a great stream that was to flow irresistibly through all subsequent American history; perhaps we shall gain some insight into the nature of American inventive genius. Now, in 1944, one of our nation's greatest assets in fighting cataclysmic war is our skill in building machines, the skill which Fitch and Fulton brought to its first major fruition.

The implications of their story go far beyond national boundaries, for the steamboat was one of those crucial inventions that change the whole cultural climate of the human race. Although mechanically less fundamental than the steam engine which preceded it, the steamboat brought the era of applied science for the first time in contact with the common man. The engine itself, used to pump water and at long last to turn factory wheels, did not enter into everyday life; a man might drink from a corner pump or wear machine-spun cloth without being aware of the fire-eating monster that made these things possible. But if he traveled on a steamboat, he had to entrust his life to something that his own eyes could see was new and strange.

One of man's fundamental attributes was being tampered with. Through centuries, human beings had learned to supplement their legs by using other natural forces: animals or the wind or the current of a stream. They had learned to apply these forces to advantage through sails and wheels and levers. But always the prime movers had been supplied by man's environment; he directed the energies they gave, but did not create them out of materials that were in themselves motionless. Preceding by years the introduction of the railroad or mechanical carriage, the steamboat was indeed something new under the sun. And when this invention had been accepted, a gap was made in the dike of human inertia and fear that let through the flood waters of the industrial revolution, those waters that buoyed up and engulfed man, and with which we are yet struggling.

Thus we find ourselves face to face with one of the basic questions of history; we are asked to define the forces that advance or retard a major shift in the civilization of the human race. Thousands of men have beaten out their brains on this problem, each arriving at a different, partial answer; probably the fundamental truth will not be determined until that far off but not impossible day when evolution creates a real science of history. Yet the struggles of our early American inventors, who attacked the forces of nature with spears of lath, may give us a glimpse or two into the nature of invention, which is nothing less than the mechanics of human change.

I. *Magic and Prophecy*

SAILORS on storm-battered seas, kept by contrary gales from home and safety, traveling through months and years in directions in which they did not wish to go, have always dreamed of magic boats that would travel against wind and tide. Of such star-crossed mariners Odysseus was the type. Homer drew a visionary picture of a mechanical boat:

> So shalt thou instant reach the realms assigned,
> In wondrous ships, self-moved, instinct with mind . . .
> E'en the stern God that o'er the waves presides,
> Safe as they pass and safe repass the tides,
> With fury burns; while careless they convey
> Promiscuous every guest to every bay.

But the dreamers who longed for an automatic boat knew that what they desired, being contrary to the laws of nature and God, could only be achieved by magic. Since in the Christian world magic was evil, a barque that sailed against the blasts of Heaven became in the imagination of mariners a symbol of terror. The Ancient Mariner, becalmed and dying of thirst, saw a speck in the distance:

> I bit my arm, I sucked my blood,
> And cried, "A sail! A sail!"

"Horror follows," the author continues. "For can it be a ship that comes onward without wind and tide?" Indeed, the boat proved to belong to Death and his mate. Even on our own Hudson River, so Washington Irving tells us, the ghost of Henry Hudson and his phantom crew were sometimes seen in storms sailing into the face of the tempest.

Magic also took into its domain man's dream of a machine that would move by itself, and if the machine belched steam like a dragon, that only made its supernatural origin more certain. The first known steam engines were used by priests to awe their worshipers. In the public square before a temple in ancient Alexandria, a crowd pushes and fidgets uneasily. The doors of the edifice are shut, for the gods are angry and will not speak to the people. But a burnt offering has been made; from a fire on the altar that stands before the temple, a sweet savor is ascending to the nostrils of the gods. Suddenly a gasp of awe rises from the waiting multitude as, untouched by human hands, the great doors of the temple open. Men throw themselves on the ground with joy; the gods are appeased; it is a miracle. Actually, the miracle was greater than the worshipers understood. A mighty power of nature had been harnessed, for the portals had been moved by the power of expanding gas.

Under the altar there was a hollow space filled with imprisoned air and communicating with a vat of water. When the heat of the votive fire expanded the air, its pressure drove the water through a pipe into buckets, and when the buckets became heavy enough, their weight opened the doors. This device had in it all the elements of the earliest practical steam engines, which were not to be built for fifteen hundred years.

After the awed worshipers had found courage to enter the temple at last, they may well have seen another wonder that filled them with equal amazement. Over another altar hung a strange ball from the opposite sides of which short pipes extended, one bent to the right and the other to the left. A fire having been lit, steam suddenly issued from the pipes. With a terrible hissing the ball began to spin, propelled by the reaction of the vapor as it rushed out of the narrow apertures. This device is known as Hero's engine, because it was described with other items of temple magic by Hero in his manuscript, *Pneumatica*, written in Alexandria probably during the first century A.D. Although it cannot be proved that Hero did not invent his devices, it seems likely that they came from ancient Egypt, or from civilizations of even greater antiquity.

The Romans were concerned with moving boats against the wind, but they did not give a thought to Hero's engine. As the human race had done for so long, they used the power of man and animals. Yet they applied some devices that steamboat inventors were to find valuable. It is said that the legions of Claudius Caudex were taken to

Sicily in boats propelled by paddle wheels driven by oxen. Although as late as the nineteenth century the invention was claimed by many men, the employment of paddle wheels as an alternate to oars seems to go far back into antiquity, as would be expected from the close analogy between their use for boats and their use to drive mills.

The dark ages swept over Europe, but here and there in old manuscripts there are indications that the power of steam had not been completely forgotten: in isolated instances it was used to move clocks or blow through organ pipes. Yet no concerted effort was made to develop a steam engine; indeed, had one been invented, it could have come to nothing. There was not metal enough in all Europe to fashion more than a few machines, and the inventor would not have found a mechanic anywhere on the face of the earth capable of keeping his device in repair. Furthermore, there would have been no work for his engine to do. A spinning wheel was turned easily by foot, and the well bucket served to raise water. On the sea, the existence of slaves who could be chained to oars by the hundreds made a new prime mover unnecessary. A steam engine could no more have appeared in the Middle Ages than an orchid can blossom in a snowstorm. A complete change in the economic, social, and cultural climate of man was necessary.

However slow the movement may seem, the seasons advance; myriads of seemingly insignificant changes in the minds and deeds of millions of men amassed through centuries to bring the age of enlightenment. Philosophers began to speculate on the meaning of natural phenomena: during the sixteenth century several writers pointed out the properties of steam and the ease with which a vacuum might be achieved by its condensation; it was demonstrated once and for all that steam and air were not the same. Inventors also appeared. One who applied Hero's engine to turning a spit may have been an American advertising man translated into the past like Mark Twain's Connecticut Yankee; his device, he wrote, "would eat nothing, and giving withal an assurance to those partaking of the feast, whose suspicious natures nurse queasy appetites, that the haunch has not been pawed by the turnspit in the absence of the housewife's eye, for the pleasure of licking his unclean fingers."

In the seventeenth century, civilization suddenly found itself face to face with a serious mechanical problem. During the millenniums in which man had used iron, he had gradually exhausted the surface deposits and dug deeper and deeper underground. For endless generations, the known pumps, propelled by water wheels or windmills, sufficed to keep the shafts clear of water, although they differed little from those that had been used in ancient Egypt; then the pits became so deep that the apparatus inexplicably ceased to function. Failure of vacuum pumps in wells 100 feet deep was called to the attention of Galileo and others; it was soon established that the weight of the atmosphere was responsible for pushing the water upward, and that the atmosphere could not handle a column of water heavier than itself. The whole problem was worked out in detail by Pascal in 1648.

To answer the need of miners, Edward Somerset, Marquis of Worcester, invented the first practical steam engine more than a century before the achievements of James Watt. Beginning his experiments as early as 1628, Worcester received in 1663 a patent for a "water-commanding" engine; thirty-six years later another English inventor, Thomas Savery, patented a second steam engine, which he called "the Miner's Friend." Whether Worcester's engine was similar to Savery's has been much debated, but the evidence remains inconclusive. The apparatus that Savery used can, however, be accurately described.

This so-called "fountain engine" was a steam pump and could be used for no other purpose than raising liquids. A large cylinder was filled with steam in such a manner that all the air was expelled; the steam was then cooled until it "condensed"; that is, changed back from vapor into water. Since it shrunk mightily in this process and no further air was admitted, a vacuum was produced. This vacuum drew water upward into the cylinder through a long pipe. The fountain engine had gone through one half of its cycle.

Now valves closed the descending pipe, and opened another that extended upward. When fresh steam was allowed to rush into the cylinder, its pressure forced the water to rise through this second pipe out of the top of the pump. Savery used two cylinders that worked alternately. Although his engine was extremely inefficient, consuming vast quantities of steam to raise a little water, it was so great an advance that it was widely used in mines and elsewhere.

Worcester and Savery, the two first steam-engine inventors, both concerned themselves with mechanical boats. It is highly significant that Worcester did not even suggest the use of steam; he urged on the British Navy paddle wheels driven by a capstan. The brass hats replied, "What have interloping people, that have no concern with us, to do to pretend to contrive or invent things for us?" In 1698 Savery cautiously wrote that he believed steam might be used to move boats, but he preferred not to meddle in the matter.

Among the many workers of the period experimenting with machinery moved by steam or gunpowder we find Denis Papin, who designed the first engine with a piston. This device was capable of making only a stroke or two at a time; when Papin considered applying the power of steam to boats, he reverted to Savery's more elementary form. The fountain engine, he argued, could be used to raise water that would then be dropped on the paddle wheels that made the vessel go. But when he attempted to apply actual paddle wheels to a real ship, he turned them not with steam but with the force of men and animals. The steam engine was not ready for boats.

As the result of the efforts of many men, by the beginning of the eighteenth century every element of the modern steam engine had been developed separately and been practically applied. The nature of atmospheric pressure and the pressure of gases had been worked out, as had the properties of a vacuum and the method of achieving it through the condensation of steam. Several workers had shown that the great expansion undergone by water when turned into steam, and the tendency of steam to expand further when further heated, could be used as a source of power directly, without resort to condensation. Mechanics had made in the laboratory boilers capable of sustaining any necessary pressure, while Papin had invented the safety valve. Others had followed him in fitting cylinders with pistons.

Some but by no means all of these elements were brought together by Thomas Newcomen who, it was said in 1705, patented the first engine capable of transforming the properties of steam directly into mechanical motion. A simple English artisan familiar with fountain engines, he insisted, against the advice of the learned, in experimenting with a cylinder containing a piston which he intended to connect with a separate pump. The result was the atmospheric engine, the first full-sized example of which was erected near Wolverhampton in 1712.

Since the weight of the air was the actual motivating force of Newcomen's engine, the top of the cylinder was left open. A walking beam, hung from its center like a seesaw, was attached at one end to the piston rod and at the other to the pump. It was weighted so heavily at the pump side that when no other force intervened the piston was pulled to the top of the cylinder. While the piston was rising, steam at ordinary atmospheric pressure was allowed to run into the closed cylinder beneath it. A valve having been shut, this steam was condensed, creating a vacuum in the cylinder. The force of the air then pushed the piston down for the work stroke. When the piston was at the bottom of its course, the valve opened, allowing new steam to enter as the weight on the walking beam pulled the piston up. Relying for its power on steam's tendency to shrink when cooled, this engine made no use of the other half of the cycle: water's tendency to expand when turned into steam.

The atmospheric engine was an immediate success for the purpose for which it was invented, namely pumping, and naturally the dreamers of steamboats were not slow in trying to apply its force to motion on the water. They faced tremendous problems. The engine was so inefficient that one adequately powerful would have to be so large that it could hardly be carried by a boat, and the vast amount of fuel it consumed would present a second weight capable of swamping a ship. Furthermore, no good method had been developed to transform the up-and-down motion of the piston into the rotary motion necessary to turn a wheel. Indeed, the piston moved at irregular intervals and the length of the stroke varied, while some sort of weight, like that at the end of the walking beam, was necessary to pull the piston up again after its work stroke.

In 1736 Jonathan Hulls, a Gloucestershire clockmaker, patented a scheme for applying the Newcomen engine to a towboat by a system of weights and pulleys, strings and ratchets, which were supposed to turn a single paddle wheel at the stern. Whether or not he actually built a boat is a subject of controversy, but if he did, it could not possibly have worked, since the power of any Newcomen engine he could have floated would have been too small to move his complicated mechanism to any purpose. It is said that Hulls incurred so much derision because of his crazy scheme that he disappeared from his native village to London, where he died obscure and penniless. After his flight, the village urchins sang:

> Jonathan Hulls
> With his patent skulls
> Invented a machine
> To go against wind and stream;
> But he, being an ass,
> Couldn't bring it to pass,
> And so was ashamed to be seen.

Naturally many people in addition to Hulls suggested, in reports to learned societies or in pamphlets or in discussions with other savants or in patent applications, that the Newcomen engine be applied to boats; a vast amount of paper work turned out plans which included many means of applying mechanical force to the water: screw propellers and pumps and paddle wheels and mechanical imitations of the feet of ducks. The only flaw in this activity was that it was largely mental; no successful experiment was made.

During the year in which Hulls took out his patent, in a small Scotch seaport James Watt was born, the son of a prosperous artisan. He became an instrument maker and was given a workshop at the University of Glasgow. As a young man he was interested in the use of steam according to an entirely different principle from that of the Newcomen engine; instead of achieving power through the weight of the atmosphere acting on a vacuum caused by the condensation of the vapor, he wished to superheat the steam so that it would be confined at a high pressure, and then use the force of the vapor rushing powerfully through a narrow aperture to drive his machinery. However, like all other speculators whose imaginations ran in the direction of "high-pressure engines," he was discouraged by the fact that the machinery would probably explode; craftsmen were not ready to build practical boilers that could withstand forces much greater than one atmosphere. How exciting it would be, Watt remarked to his friends, to make a steam carriage that would move according to the high-pressure principle, but of course it was impracticable.

Then the natural philosophy class at the University of Glasgow was given a model of a Newcomen engine. It was shiny and efficient looking, but it would go for only a few strokes. Professor Anderson sent it to London to be mended; after it came back with a bill attached it went no better, so Anderson asked Watt to see what he could do. Knowing nothing about atmospheric engines, Watt, as he wrote, "set about repairing the model as a mere mechanician."

Soon he discovered that the boiler, although in perfect proportion for a large engine, was too small to work in miniature where the forces were different. If he were not to construct a new boiler, he would have to discover some way to make the engine move with less steam. Experiments revealed that the amount of vapor used for every stroke was several times the contents of the cylinder. Meditating on this, Watt decided the trouble was that during each stroke the cylinder had to be heated to the temperature of live steam, 212 degrees, and then cooled to produce condensation, say to 60 degrees. Naturally, much heat was wasted in this continual shift of temperatures, while the first steam that entered the cold cylinder condensed at that moment, and was thus lost in addition to putting water where it ought not to be. Furthermore, the continual heating and cooling took so much time that the engine could not be expected to make more than a few strokes a minute. The answer, of course, would be to keep the cylinder constantly above the boiling point. But how then would you achieve condensation? Although the problem seemed insoluble, Watt allowed his mind to wander over it.

On a Sabbath afternoon in May 1765 he was lured by the blue sky and gentle breezes to take a walk in the ancient Glasgow Green. He entered the gate at the foot of Charlotte Street, and had just passed the old wash house when he was struck with one of the most world-shaking revelations. Fellow-strollers saw nothing but a respectable gentleman taking his constitutional; the children playing around his feet did not even look up at the man whose stride interfered with their games; but that moment the human race had reached one of the great milestones of its history.

"The idea came into my mind," Watt remembered, "that as steam was an elastic body it would rush into a vacuum, and if a communication was made between the cylinder and an exhausted vessel, it would rush into it and might there be condensed without cooling the cylinder." In other words if a separate container were attached to the cylinder, and this container contained a vacuum, the steam would be sucked into it from the cylinder. The cylinder could then be kept hot, while the container or "condenser" remained cold. In his first flash of revelation, Watt also conceived of a pump, motivated by the engine and attached to the separate container, which would preserve the vacuum by sucking out the water created by condensation and any air that might have leaked in. "I had not walked further than the Gold-house when the whole thing was arranged in my mind." Now there existed, although still only in the imagination of the inventor, a mechanism efficient enough to move boats.

At the moment of Watt's inspiration, John Fitch, although only twenty-one years old, was already a failure; he had been apprenticed to a clockmaker but had failed to learn the trade. As for Robert Fulton, he was not yet even born.

II. *The Twig Is Bent*

ALL we know of John Fitch's youth and young manhood comes from an autobiography he wrote when old and embittered. Concerning his birth, he stated, "The night of the 21 of January 1743 old stile was the fatal time of bringing me into Existance at which time all nature seemed to shrink at the convulsed Elliments which seemed to forebode the destiny of the innocent infant then making its way into existence that dismal night my Father had to go about four miles for a Midwife and to worry thro' the Snow Banks on his return perhaps with nearly the same difficulties that I have gone thro' life but I was as obstinate at that time as at the Present when a new project takes me and could not be prevailed upon to pospone takeing a View of the World till the Rodes should be rendered any way passable."*

The Fitch homestead was half in the Connecticut township of Windsor and half in Hartford. "From the singularity of my shape, disposition, and fortune in this world, I am inclined to believe that it was the design of heaven that I should be born on the very line, and not in any township whatever, yet am happy that it did not happen also between two states, that I can say that I was born somewhere. Thus, sir, I have given you an account of the

---

* Quoted exactly as Fitch wrote it, this passage shows his phonetic spelling, his lack of punctuation, his erratic use of capitals. In the interest of clarity, I have in all subsequent quotations, not only from Fitch but from the other characters in this book, modernized the spelling and punctuation. There seems little to be gained in impeding the reader by demonstrating over and over again that the eighteenth-century standard of orthography was different from ours. Although Fitch, being entirely self-educated, was a worse speller than most, even as cultivated a man as Washington would write the same word two or three different ways in the same passage, and then toss commas around seemingly at random. The reader is guilty of anachronism if he regards such inconsistency from under the raised eyebrows of a twentieth-century school-marm. The modernization of spelling and punctuation, of course, in no way changes the sense of the passages quoted, which are in all other respects reproduced exactly as they were written.

birth . . . of one of the most singular men perhaps that has been born in this age."

John Fitch was convinced that from the opening moment of his life he had trod a very strange path. Yet the farmhouse where he spent his childhood was a typical New England farmhouse of its time, and his parents were very like their neighbors. Perhaps it was the death of his mother when he was four years old that brought a quality of nightmare to the house where her voice was forever silent. His earliest memories of his father and brothers are concerned with hardship, injustice, and cruelty.

One event which took place shortly after his mother's death symbolized to him his entire childhood. His smaller sister Chloe, who was his closest companion, by accident set fire to two bundles of flax stored in a corner of the kitchen. Although himself a little child, Fitch seized a burning bundle; by resting it against his knees, he managed somehow to drag it over to the hearth. His face was burned and, as the memory came back to him, his hair actually caught fire. Slapping out the fire with his bare hands, he returned for the other bundle, which he carried to the hearth in the same manner, again igniting his hair. Consciousness of heroism assuaged his pain as he hurried toward the barn to savor praises. But Chloe, who had rushed out before him, had said something which had been misunderstood. When in the dark yard the pitifully burned little boy met his brother, he received a series of blows. Nursing a deep sense of injustice, he complained on his father's return, but received no redress. "This, sir," he wrote, "being what I may call the first act of my life, seemed to forebode the future rewards I was to receive for my labors through life, which has generally corresponded exactly with that."

From his home where such injustice flourished, Fitch fled to school; the schoolhouse became his sanctuary from the world. As an old man, he still boasted that during his first summer there he learned to spell "commandment" and "Jerusalem" with facility. That a few years later he was able to repeat by heart the *New England Primer* from "Adam's fall to the end of the catechism" ranked in his memory with the building of steamboats.

When he was eight, however, the door of the schoolhouse was closed to him. Although he could swingle no more than two pounds of flax a day or thresh no more than two bushels of grain, to secure such "pitiful, trifling labor," his father called him home from the world of dream. "This piece of injustice I can never forgive him, and I think Heaven dealt very hard with me to give me such a mean, niggardly wretch for a father. Had He let me be born son to Paddy Colwine, I would revere my father as the most dutiful child. Yet, sir, there was a great deal to plead in excuse for him. He was educated a rigid Christian and was a bigot and one of the most strenuous of the sect of Presbyterians, and carried it to such excess that I dare not go in the garden to pick currants, or in the orchard to pick up an apple on the Sabbath, and I really believe that he thought that the extent of his duty toward me was to learn me to read the Bible, that I might find the way to Heaven, and when he had done that felt perfectly easy, and if I could earn him 2 d. a week it ought not to be lost."

Fitch so hated the farmwork that was his natural portion in life that he believed himself too weak to carry on the routine labors of planting and harvest. Describing how daily he almost fainted from exhaustion, he insisted that his elder brother made him over-tax his strength out of a sadistic desire to make him suffer. All through his autobiography, in describing periods of unhappiness he states that he was incapable of physical labor; yet in the next breath he would boast that he could out-walk any horse. Although he ascribed many of his later troubles to his "insignificant appear-ance," he was to stand more than 6 feet tall and give his con-temporaries an impression of great power.

Tied to the farm, barred from school, the little boy became, in his own words, "almost crazy after learning." He found in the attic a copy of Hodder's *Arithmetic*. If there was a respite in his labors, he disappeared with the book under his arm, and soon he was far away in a clean, impersonal world of numbers that moved according to immutable laws. Concerning this, he had a happy memory, one of the few his autobiography contains. A group of neighbors sit in the main room of the Fitch homestead. Spinning wheel and unswingled flax have disappeared into the dark corners; his father and his brothers are mute; and in the bright light of the fire stands the little boy. He is working out before everyone's eyes how many minutes old he will be when he is ten. After the correct sum is achieved, a murmur of admiration goes up from the neighbors. But even in his flush of triumph, the little boy feels guilty, for he is only nine years old, and he knows that he could not have done the multiplication by nine.

Fitch was afflicted with a conscience as stern as that for which he criticized his parent. It is significant that in his account of his childhood, the inventor makes no mention of personal communion with the Calvinist God who ruled over the tight-walled Connecticut fields and entered the boy's homestead in a shape very like his father's. Probably deep psychological compulsions made him ignore the religious part of his upbringing, although it had a profound effect on his subsequent career. Fitch's hatred for his parent and the environment his parent represented was based on something more frightening than difference; it was based on an aching similarity in many things. The father's avenging conscience that would not allow a single berry to be picked on the Sabbath haunted the son's every step, although it manifested itself in other ways. Perhaps in his boyhood rebellion against his parent's farm, Fitch convinced himself that he was rebelling too against his parent's God. Yet he never escaped from that stern deity. Even when he fled to the farthest wilderness, Jehovah traveled with him, inexorable and all-demanding. In building steamboats, Fitch may well have been forging a sword with which to slay or appease this terrible companion.

After he had mastered Hodder's *Arithmetic*, the boy taught himself geography and a little surveying, but finally he became discouraged; he abandoned his books and joined his contemporaries in the games of childhood. "This helped to sweeten life, and from the time I was between thirteen and fourteen years of age till I went apprentice, I enjoyed myself as much as most of the Virginia slaves who has liberty to go to a dance once a week." Fitch was allowing himself to drift with the tide and be happy, but as an old man he did not remember gratefully these years of joy. Clearly he felt that he had demeaned himself, been wicked even. Concerning this period of gaiety, he wrote that there was "nothing important to relate."

His story gathers tempo with an effort. Insulted that he had not been invited to help raise a church steeple, he took up arms against his environment once more. At the age of seventeen Fitch ran away to sea, but the future inventor of steamboats quickly decided that sailoring was not for him. Because of rough treatment accorded him by the mate, he deserted the first ship before it even left port. Stubbornly he signed on another vessel. Although this time he was treated humanely, he was continually miserable on the water, and gave himself up for lost in a storm. After five weeks of skirting the coast, he returned to his father's house and the drudgery of the farm.

Shortly thereafter, Fitch was sent to the mill with some grain, and he met fate at the crossroads. Fate, who rarely appears in heroic guises, was a little man with an immense head, who was sitting beside his wife in a buggy. Leaning forward with his whip in his hand, he appraised Fitch from small eyes that gleamed shrewdly under his exaggerated forehead. Then he introduced himself as Benjamin Cheney, master clockmaker, and said he needed just such an apprentice as John seemed to be. When their roads parted after 40 or 50 rods, Fitch trudged off behind his laden horse in a whirl of excitement. Clockmaking was a good trade.

It seemed a boon from Heaven, but when Fitch called on Cheney a few days later, difficulties began to multiply. As he sat in a room loud with ticking and talked with the somewhat evasive little man, John became convinced that Cheney intended to make him labor on the farm, not in the workshop. Perhaps he should have left indignantly; but there was a magic in all the brightly polished boxes around him, a magic of springs and wheels and gears moving together with mathematical precision. And the gnome-like artisan with his hands folded on his distended belly was the sorcerer who controlled the pendulums that swung so surely in unison. Oh, to be a sorcerer's apprentice!

Shrewdly Fitch bargained until Cheney agreed to write in the indentures that Fitch was to spend only six months in the fields; during the rest of the year he was to be taught the mysteries of clockmaking. "Being too conceited that I could learn a trade in a short time, if I only had the first principles of it," the young man was delighted.

Fitch, who could not peer into the future, had no conception of how important the opportunity he seemed to be offered might be to his future career. Clockmakers were the leading artisans in America primarily concerned with the manufacture of precision machinery from metal. Blacksmiths, it is true, made heavy goods of iron, but their technique was much less precise. Should a plow be several inches off center, it would still turn a furrow, but the wheels of a clock must be exact to a fraction of an inch. In addition, the machine had to be worked out as a whole, so that the pull of the weights would turn the hands at exactly the right pace. When an eighteenth-century American needed a tool that was too complicated for a blacksmith, he was likely to appeal to a clockmaker. Members of the trade made surveyor's and mariner's instruments, mechanical jacks and scales, bells, and even an occasional fire engine or printing press. Although his training would show him how to work on only a small scale, clockmaking was the best craft America offered to a future inventor of steamboats, assuming that he succeeded in learning it.

As he set off to join his new master, in his imagination Fitch felt the handles of the clockmaker's tool already firm in his hands. Instead, he found himself gripping the handle of a hoe. Every morning he was sent out to the fields; nor did his situation greatly change when winter came; there was always wood to chop or a chore to do around the house. Hourly, as he went back and forth on his tasks, Fitch passed the door of the workshop where clocks were made, but the door remained shut; he was not invited in. Clearly Cheney had no intention of setting up a business rival by teaching his apprentice any of the secrets of his trade.

After two and a half years, during which the only instruction he received was in "trifling, pottering brass work," Fitch struck. The two men got on so badly together that there was no possibility of compromise; Cheney suggested that Fitch move to the shop of his younger brother, Timothy Cheney. The new indentures, which were executed on June 8, 1763, specified "that he was to learn me the art of making brass and wooden clocks, and also watch work. . . . As my situation was changed, I set into work with high spirits, expecting that I was sure of getting a trade by which I might subsist myself in a genteel way."

At Timothy Cheney's, however, he was again ordered to "small brass work." While he cast buttons, his master cast parts for clocks; perhaps he was allowed to hammer the castings to give them the proper temper, but he was given no hand in the cutting and filing and fitting that was the hard part of the trade. There was a metal lathe in the shop, and probably a "clockmaker's engine" to cut the gears, examples of the only complicated metalworking tools that were common in America, but Fitch was not allowed to touch them. Timothy Cheney was as bad as his brother had been.

Terrified of his master, whom he considered "a wicked, unjust man and intolerably mean; a proud, imperious, hasty man," Fitch did not dare complain until he had passed his twenty-first birthday and was legally an adult. Then he demanded to be put at watch and clock work. Timothy refused. Fitch threatened to go to law, and they almost came to blows. After that the sensitive young man could not bear to stay in the house any longer; forgetting about lawsuits, he agreed to pay Cheney £8 if he could leave instantly, four months before his indentures were done.

On a gray winter day Fitch walked home to find somehow the

large sum needed for his release. "I saw the cruelties with which I was treated, the wickedness of the man, the dilemma which I had brought myself into by running myself in debt three years, to wear out them clothes for monsters, and a demand of £8 more added to it. I . . . cried the whole distance, and doubt not that nearly as much water came from my eyes that day as what I drank. I acknowledge this is an unmanly passion, but cannot to this day avoid such effeminacy."

After he had begged the necessary £8 from his relatives, Fitch was a free man; this meant he was obliged to take care of himself. He had, so he wrote, worn out his clothes slaving for "monsters," and he was more than £20 in debt. He did not dare seek employment as a clockmaker, "for fear I should show my ignorance in the business I professed." Fitch's first twenty-one years had been one continuous defeat; certainly they presaged for the future of the already warped young man nothing but failure and obscurity.

Yet when he set up as a brass founder, making buttons and other small objects for his neighbors, he was almost instantly successful. Now that he was his own master, now that no other personality cast its shadow across his work bench, the skill of his hands manifested itself; in two years he had paid all his debts and was worth £50 besides. He even covered much of the ground lost during his apprenticeship, teaching himself how to clean and make clocks. But the young man who had been so long an outcast was not satisfied with his lonely success; he craved companionship.

Soon a woman appealed to him, perhaps because there was nothing terrifying about her. Lucy Roberts, he remembered, was "in no ways ugly, but somewhat delicate in her make, but rather inclined to an old maid, and I believe her to be several years older than myself, but her age I never knew." They were married in December 1767, and a son was shortly born to them.

Fitch, who in his autobiography always dwells on misfortune, makes no mention of whatever happiness his marriage brought. That he dearly loved his son is clear, since that love haunted him all his life. Concerning his wife he wrote only that she soon became a terrible scold. We gather that she wished to settle down to the comfortable existence of a small-town artisan's wife; she was frightened by the whirlwind of energy and ambition to which she was tied. Successful at last, after so many years of failure, able to look his father and his brothers in the eye, Fitch felt that anything was possible for him now. Borrowing with confidence, he enlarged his brass shop, went into the potash business, speculated in many directions. When his wife inveighed against his rashness, he paid no attention. The last straw seems to have been when in his search for spiritual solace he deserted the sober Presbyterian fold for the evangelical splendors of the Methodist sect which was just invading Connecticut.

Unable by any other means to hew her husband down to a respectable, conventional shape, Mrs. Fitch gave way to shrill fury. Although, so Fitch tells us, he never talked back to her, each of her tantrums left its bitter residue in his mind. After a year and a half of marriage, he began saying in a very calm voice that if she did not control her temper he would desert her. Naturally, this threat only made her more voluble. The artisan started to put his affairs aright so that he would not leave her in debt, but before the time he had set for his departure came, physical passion got the best of him, and he was in terror lest he should be trapped. "Fearing an increase of my family urged my departure." Actually his wife was carrying another child, a daughter, when he fled, but he swears he did not know this; if he had, "I should never have left her but worried through life as well as I could.

"On the 18th January 1769 I left my native country with a determination never to see it again, and having no fixed place in my mind where to wander, I set out bare of money, not having more than seven or eight dollars with me. . . . This day, sir, was the most dismal of any I ever saw: to set off from home and leave my friends and relations, neighbors and acquaintance, and a child which I valued as much as my own life, and to go almost bare of money I knew not where, nor what distresses might come upon me when friendless and among strangers." His wife did not believe that he would really depart "till about an hour before I set out, when she appeared affected and distressed, and in a most humble manner implored my stay, and followed me about half a mile, where I stopped. This added double grief, and I really felt an inclination to try her once more; but my judgment informed me that it was my duty to go, notwithstanding the struggles of nature which I had to contend with."

Fitch wandered aimlessly for weeks over the frozen countryside, completely at loose ends. Several times he was on the point of returning to his family, but always some chance happening strengthened his resolution. One evening, for instance, in the taproom of a tavern outside Elizabethtown, New Jersey, he boasted of having deserted a tempestuous wife, and savored the admiration of his fellow-topers at such brave rebellion against petticoat government. Yet when he went to bed at last, the most terrible loneliness descended upon him. He arose the next morning determined to go home, but he was afraid that his acquaintances of the previous night would notice the direction he took and laugh at his irresolution. With a brave smile, he set out on the road to Philadelphia intending, when out of sight of the tavern, to return eastward by a circuitous route.

However, his irresolution returned until at last he became so exhausted with emotional stress that he was hardly able to carry his pack. He dragged himself to a farmhouse; knocking at the lower half of the Dutch door, he looked in through the upper half. An old man was sitting in a chimney corner smoking a pipe as he listened with a stolid expression to an old woman who stood over him, her tongue active in high wrath. As she expatiated on her husband's faults and her own long-suffering patience, Fitch continued to knock, but no one paid any attention. He opened the door and walked in.

When the enraged woman turned in surprise, he asked her why she treated her husband that way, and if she did not feel she could change her conduct. Too amazed to object to this intrusion, the woman replied that her husband was a villain who deserved everything he got, and more. Then Fitch said that if they were so unhappy together, the only sensible thing for them to do was to part. To this the woman acceded, saying she should have left her husband long ago, and the man with the pipe nodded his head. Then while the ragged stranger sat down to listen, the couple discussed terms of separation. Soon they came to an impasse, for the woman would go only if he gave her half his property, and to this he would not agree. Fitch at last felt called on to intervene; from what he had seen of the wife, he said, he thought the husband would be well rid of her even if he had to give her all his property.

Instantly the woman turned her fury on him. Picking a burning log from the fire, she hurled it with such accuracy that he saved himself only by using his pack as a shield. As she reached for another, he fled out the door, but she was after him at once, and he was forced to dodge a second flaming missile in the garden. Fitch ran down the street till the house was out of sight. He had lost all desire to return to his own termagant. Chance, that puppet-master of human destiny, had pulled a string, and John Fitch was a homeless wanderer for the rest of his days.

In Trenton an opportunity arose that temporarily brought Fitch's roving feet to a standstill. He secured employment with James Wilson, a silversmith. Although his new master was such a sot that he had practically no business, and was able to pay only about three pence a day, Fitch was delighted with his bargain. In Wilson's workshop he had discovered a great treasure, a first-class set of tools. From dawn till after sunset, while his master caroused, Fitch held the tools in his hands, working out their uses, asking his master questions when he seemed unusually sober. In about six months Fitch decided that he needed Wilson no longer since he had taught himself how to be a silversmith.

This involved amazing self-confidence, for silversmithing was the aristocrat of all Colonial trades. The artisan received the metal, usually in the form of coins, from his patron, and worked it up by a complicated technique into elaborate shapes that had to be almost perfect because they were designed for show. Not only utility was required, but beauty as well. How Fitch, who had been starved for loveliness all the long years of his life, must have revelled in the clear sheen of the metal and the feeling of creation as the forms grew under his hands!

Returning to his trade of manufacturing brass and silver buttons, Fitch earned enough money to buy Wilson's tools; then he gleefully announced that he was a silversmith. Soon patrons came flocking to his workshop. An account book shows that between October 1773 and November 1775 he employed seven journeymen, including his former employer Wilson, and that he made coffee and teapots, cream pitchers, tankards, spoons of every sort, buttons, "pin cushion hoops and chains," camp cups, sugar tongs, sword mountings, and gold brooches. He claims that he secured "a greater run of business than any silversmith in Philadelphia, at least it was the opinion of my journeymen I had." Fitch had achieved one of those lightning transitions from destitution to prosperity that were as typical of his career as his sudden dives back to misery.[1]

Despite his success, Fitch did not settle down to the conventional life of a master craftsman and man of property; his heart was still a wandering heart. Often he left the busy workshop of which he was master, and set out on foot to explore the roads of the unknown, "with my budget of silver on my back that has weighted not less than 30 pounds, and £200 worth." His spirit found surcease in the endless motion of new landscapes before his eyes, and the excitement that came before he knocked on a new door, for each house locked within its walls a separate world. When he stepped across the threshold into he knew not what, he was a stranger, that most blessed of all creation. The housewife who looked up from her spinning, or the farmer whittling a new handle for his plow, knew nothing of John Fitch, the man who was haunted by childhood memories, who had left his wife and children, whose nerves were continually playing him tricks. The stranger was what he seemed to be in that moment of entrance. If he wished, he could be a humble peddler who also cleaned clocks. As evening darkened without, he sat by the fire, while the life of these people whose worries he did not know rustled round him and gathered him into its folds. He showed the children how the clock wheels cogged together, and perhaps helped the mother lift a heavy iron pot.

Or else, if he wished, he could be a master silversmith engaged on business of importance. The domestic who opened the door under the fanlight and led him into a spacious central hall was obsequious; and while he waited for the mistress he appraised the carving on the stairs in which he recognized motifs he sometimes used in silver. Then he was crisp and businesslike with the lady who greeted him, presenting references, gathering into his hand at last some silver to be made into a teapot.

John Fitch, the master artisan, walked away down an alley of ornamental trees, and soon he was in a tavern; but he was a different man now, John Fitch the good fellow. If any of his companions in the taproom noticed the slight tremor of his hand or the nervous agony in his face, he was unconscious of it as the liquor bit his throat. He was a hero now, and he boasted of fabulous exploits until the lights were extinguished and, as he stood on the doorstep to breathe the cool air, the stars were tipsy in the sky.

But sometimes, even here on the open road, his father's conscience rose triumphant within him, as though he had never left the cramped farmhouse of his childhood. It was not right for a man to be happy; duty was the only thing that mattered, duty a thousand times compounded until it became a weight that crushed and an iron that seared. What had he done to fulfill the obligations he had undertaken; what had he done to his wife, to his son and the daughter that had been born after his departure? Haunted by such questions, Fitch wrote passionate letters to his children; he mourned their separation, begged them to join him in Trenton, offered to provide them with education and clothing. Once, in an agony of contrition, he promised to take in their mother as well, but the deserted wife spurned the proposition, and it was never repeated. Forever lonely, forever haunted with memories, Fitch learned that a man could never escape from himself, however fast he ran.

But he would show the fates; he would be himself, and yet a great man. He hurried back to Trenton where men bowed to him in the streets, and he had money out at interest. Was he not worth £800?

How long Fitch, if left to himself, would have continued his successful career as a silversmith, it is impossible to say. The American Revolution intervened, and in the resulting excitements he did everything wrong. Convinced that "if Heaven ever gave me any genius it was certainly in that science" of warfare, he petitioned for a commission, but as soon as he was elected first lieutenant in the militia, he was so overcome with shyness that he changed places with the second lieutenant. The first lieutenancy coming vacant again, he considered that he had a right to it, and when someone else was elected to the position, "I took my gun and knapsack on my back and marched back to Trenton alone, and wished to have my judgment convince me that Great Britain was right, but finally concluded not to resent my wrongs on my country." Yet he felt too affronted to attend muster, "which gave me much uneasiness, as I was the only active officer in Trenton."

Soon with twenty workmen at his command he was repairing guns for the New Jersey Committee of Safety. But in his enthusiasm he worked on Sunday, and for this heinous offense the local Methodist congregation, which he had helped organize, expelled him. Again he was punished for doing what he believed was right.

Next the British marched into Trenton and destroyed his workshop. He fled to Warminster in Bucks County, where he made many close friends, and then, after further enemy advances, to Washington's encampment at Valley Forge. Seeing that the troops needed tobacco and beer, he undertook to supply them, an enterprise that paid him $40,000 in continental paper. When inflation threatened to wipe out this munificent-sounding sum, he resolved to buy warrants for western lands and himself survey the most valuable tracts.

Having secured wealthy backers for his land speculations, Fitch was too eager to take the safe route to Kentucky through Virginia and the Cumberland Gap; he struck directly west to the Ohio and then drifted down the river whose far bank was occupied by hostile Indians. The flotilla of rafts on which he traveled was attacked, and several men wounded, but this did not dampen his ardor. Having spent the summer surveying in Kentucky, he hurried back to Bucks County to sell everything he owned so that he might buy more warrants, "knowing there was an immense fortune for me if I attended to it with what money I could raise." He even disposed of the silversmith's tools which had been his proudest possessions. The future inventor of steamboats had now, he thought, turned his back on the crafts forever. He would carve a fortune out of the wilderness.

The frontier had a natural appeal for men of Fitch's temperament. The textbook picture of pioneers as rugged individuals seeking danger out of an excess of nervous health is probably a fallacy; the men who fled civilization ever farther and farther into the unknown were likely to be misfits who could not support themselves in the complicated wilderness of society. A drawing room where women smiled and men boasted was much more terrifying to Fitch than the wildest forest. The ladies demanded graces which he was sure he did not possess; always he was overconscious of what he considered his "uncouth" face and figure. And suppose he did ingratiate himself with a woman, caught perhaps by her physical charm? He had learned that close emotional relationships lead to nothing but pain. As for the boasting males, Fitch felt inferior to them in all the arts of making an impression; yet he knew he was a better man than any of them, than all of them put together. Naturally, he had to assert his worth by saying something disagreeable. But if this made him unpopular, he was hurt and resentful, for he was hungry for the love and respect of the world. Above all else, his soul needed to banish its long, psychic loneliness, to feel united with the rest of mankind: with his family, with the citizens of his town or the members of his militia company, with the drunken loungers in a tavern. But never was he able to submerge a deep feeling that he was unique, different from all other men. In rare moments of exaltation, this sense of strangeness was a joy to him, made him believe that he was set apart for a special, glorious destiny, but usually he felt like a freak being exhibited to the snickers of a curious and scornful world.

He wrote, "My temper of mind, being so different from any man that I ever saw before, caused me many new difficulties. My natural disposition I find to be truly this; . . . it seems to be part of my existence and I cannot overcome it. When in easy circumstances, modest to excess and put up with almost any indignities, and resent them no other way than by a familiar levity. But when in wretchedness, haughty, imperious, insolent to my superiors, tending to petulance; yet exceedingly civil in both instances till indignities are first offered to me, and the greater the man the more sweet the pleasure in retorting upon him in his own way. And a man in this disposition to be in low circumstances, can never get through the world easy."

How changed was his environment when, leaving the last settlement behind him, he trod powerfully into the wilderness! The trees that rocked over his head, the animals he brought down with his rifle, the vast flowing of vast rivers, even the rains that wet him to the skin and the tempests that threw huge trees like javelins in his path; all these acted not by human whim, but by the "laws of the God of Nature" which no man could alter. All was impersonal; the movement of cloud and tree and water stemmed neither from affront nor favoritism; nature went its own way ignoring John Fitch. And so John Fitch did not need to resent the forest and the river; he took their moods as they came, happily, with an appreciation of their tremendous grandeur. And what if there were dangers to be faced? A man was on his own here and could rely on his own abilities. Fitch never doubted his abilities.

Of course there were human beings in the forest, Indians armed with gun and tomahawk. Fitch was soon to find out how he felt about these.

Since by selling all his effects he had been able to raise only £150, he decided that before he invested in land warrants, he would buy a cargo of flour and carry it down the Ohio to the settlers: a speculation dangerous because of the savages, but correspondingly lucrative. Having made a will in which he particularly remembered the children he had deserted, he walked to Pittsburgh, secured his flour, loaded it on a large flatboat, and with ten companions abandoned himself to the current of the Ohio on March 18, 1782. Three days later, the boat ran aground on an island slightly below the mouth of the Muskingum River.

All other expedients to dislodge the vessel having failed, the voyagers laboriously carried Fitch's flour ashore. When they were afloat again, it was almost dark; they decided not to reload until the next morning. Tying the painter to a sapling, they went below to sleep. Fitch suggested that they post guards. His words were received with jeers: was the big Easterner afraid? Again and again Fitch's caution produced this result among the careless bullies of the frontier, and each time, as now, he was hurt and indignant. "I have always thought that it is the worst kind of cowardice of being afraid that others should think us afraid," he wrote. "Therefore, have always expressed my apprehensions with freedom, for two reasons: first that others might be cautious, and second, to fortify their minds in case of an accident, as courage always increases in men as they are inured with danger."

Having jeered at Fitch to their hearts' content, his fellow-voyagers gave in to his wisdom; they posted guards. During his own watch, Fitch laid an axe beside the painter so that he might cut loose at the least untoward sound. He heard nothing.

At daybreak Fitch noticed that his axe no longer lay by the line; he searched for it all over the boat, but dared not ask where it was for fear of again being accused of timidity. Finally he joined the others in the caboose for a drink of hot buttered rum. He noticed that a scout they had sent ashore had been gone a long time, but no one else seemed to think this strange. The voices of the drinkers rose loud through the stillness, when suddenly all was drowned out by a burst of gunfire; the cup fell from Captain Magee's hand; blood spurted from his head; he lay motionless. Everyone dived below decks. Then Thomas Bradley, "a man of more courage than prudence," crept up to cut the fast; a rifle spoke; he sprang into the air and then was still. "As soon as that happened I got Bradley's gun and cartridge box, when there were nine of us under deck well armed." The Indians waited above, crouched behind a pile of driftwood; the white men cowered below; all that was needed for safety was to cut the line so that the boat would drift out into the stream.

Although the others, lacking "any stomach for such a breakfast," trembled in abject fear, Fitch and Houston stationed themselves at portholes with their guns ready cocked. For a half hour there was no movement on shore, no sound, just a terrible stillness. Then Fitch took a tomahawk and began to chop a hole through the bow so he could cut the line. He had made slight progress when a ball passed through the planking "so near that I felt the wind of it fresh in my left eye." Retreating, Fitch began to make a shield of planks with which to protect himself while he chopped. No one helped him. "If I ever felt myself angry and swore with a hearty good will it was at that time, and had the strongest temptation to tomahawk one Sigwalt who cringed down behind me that I ever had to do a wicked act."

The shield was almost finished when a familiar voice came from the bank; it was the captured scout bearing a demand to surrender. This at last produced movement among the cowering crew; while Fitch pleaded, assuring his companions that he would have the boat free in half an hour, the men stood up and marched ashore. Only Fitch and Houston remained. Fitch looked at his companion and said, "If it must be so, we may as well go, too." He went and Houston followed him.

"Thus, sir, we ran aground for want of judgment, and gave ourselves up prisoners to savages for want of courage, as nine stout men of us, all well armed, marched out to eight Indians, which was more than I expected there was, as I imagined they all fired at the first shot." Fitch blamed himself for not having asked for the axe that morning, so that he could have cut the boat loose without difficulty. He also mourned that he had not the presence of mind to continue the fight after the others surrendered.

It was Fitch's destiny to be a citizen of the future, to leap before his generation into a new age and time. Now, however, he fell backward through the centuries. When on March 22, 1782, he walked with hands upraised from his vessel onto the Indian shore, he entered the prehistoric past. As he stood sullenly with his companions, waiting to hear his fate, several of his painted captors went on board the boat and scalped the dead men; then they tied a war club to the steering oar and cast the vessel loose. Fitch had entered the age of stone.

III. *France Plays the First Card*

S O THE years passed, leaving Fitch still ignorant of the powers
of steam, powers that were known to thousands of men all
over Europe and America. James Watt, too, was having his
difficulties. After the revelation on the Glasgow Green, he had
hurried home, his mind full of visions, but he had to wait to test
them until the next day, for he could not work on the Sabbath. Then
he built a little model out of tinplate and solder, closing the top of
the condenser with a thimble taken from his wife's workbasket.
The model demonstrated to his satisfaction that he had solved the
problems of the condensing steam engine.

After this his efforts bogged down, as if he were waiting for
Fitch to grow older. He was not sure which of the many ideas he
had were best; he experimented with a complicated and impractical
wheel, on the inside of which the force of the steam acted directly.
When he got down again to his condensing engine, he thought of
many forms it could take, and each new experiment involved the
solving of new mechanical difficulties. He faced financial troubles
too, for he was a poor man who could not spare much time from
making his living. More than three years passed before he took out
a patent for his idea—it was granted January 15, 1769—and even
then he was far from building a practical engine.

From 1769 to 1774 Watt was so busily engaged in making surveys
of possible routes for canals and in other types of civil engineering
that it almost seemed he had forgotten his steam engine. Not until
he received the backing of a rich manufacturer and capitalist, Matthew Boulton, did he return to work on his invention. His first
actual full-size engine was not set up and put to work until March
8, 1776.

Designed solely to motivate pumps, the engines Watt now began
to build in quantity were not suitable for driving a boat. He had not
yet attempted to make the piston beat regularly by the application

of steam to both sides of the plunger, nor had he worked out any device by which the up-and-down motion of the engine could be made to turn a wheel. Watt was satisfied, however, since he could sell to mine owners as many of these single-acting engines as he could make. For years he resisted the urging of the more visionary Boulton to design an engine that could drive a mill. At last Boulton forced Watt's hand. In 1781 the inventor patented methods for achieving rotary motion, and in 1782, a double-acting engine. In listing possible applications, he spoke of a steam carriage, but he made no mention of boats. Yet he had finally created a motor that could achieve man's dream of moving against wind, current, and tide. All that was now necessary was the combination of known principles into an efficient mechanical boat.

While Watt tinkered with his engine, modifying it slowly into commercially effective form, other men continued to dream of applying the Newcomen engine to boats. Papers were written, a few actual attempts were made, but no practical results had been achieved when steamboat mania descended on two minor French noblemen, officers of Louis XIV's artillery. Le Comte Joseph d'Auxiron and le Chevalier Charles Monnin de Follenai whiled away the long hours in camp speculating on whether steam could drive a boat. In 1770 Auxiron became so fascinated with the idea that he resigned from the army and submitted to the government plans for a vessel which he insisted would carry heavy loads up the rivers of France more quickly than could be done with men and horses. For more than a year his crazy-sounding scheme wandered from desk to desk in the government offices; then, on May 14, 1772, he was formally promised that if he could make a steamboat work, the government would give him the exclusive right for fifteen years to use such appliances in France.

Within a week Auxiron and his friend Follenai had interested enough noblemen to form a company. Soon steam engine and boat were building on the Isle de Cygnes in the middle of the Seine at Paris. The boatmen of the river, rowing by in the craft men had used for a thousand years, jeered at the little workshop on the island, but as the hammering continued, as strange contraptions began to be visible on shore, fear gripped the hearts of the sailors. Supposing— of course it was an impossible idea—but just supposing the steam-propelled vessel really moved; what would happen to their trade, their livelihood? The jeers changed to threats, and Auxiron was forced to post a military guard to protect his workshop.

In December 1772 the boat was launched; soon a vast brick foundation was raised upon it, and then the boilers were installed. When a fire was lit, the water boiled satisfactorily, giving off a hiss-ing of steam that struck terror into the hearts of passing barge-men. Next two paddle wheels were swung over the sides, and in April 1773 the cylinders were placed on top of the boiler. The thing looked so peculiar and formidable now that enraged mobs gathered on the near-by quay. Auxiron decided even his military guards might not avail; he towed his craft down river to Meudon.

Now came months of tinkering while recalcitrant parts were made over and over by the blacksmiths and coppersmiths, medieval type artisans who had never before been asked to fashion anything even vaguely resembling this complicated monster. They sought to forget their failures at a near-by tavern, and it is said that they were approached by sinister characters who pressed money into their hands. Be that as it may, when Auxiron came to his workshop one morning in September, the boat had vanished. It was dimly visible at the bottom of the river.

Everybody accused everybody else. Auxiron stated that his work-men had been bribed into dropping the heavy counter-weight of the engine onto the bottom of the boat, thus opening the seams. The members of the company, on the other hand, insisted that Auxiron himself had sunk the boat to hide failure. Looking back from the vantage point of years, we may suspect that none of the charges were well founded: a Newcomen engine, with its tremendous brick foundations, was so heavy that it needed no outside assistance to open the seams of a boat. In any case a lawsuit followed. During 1775 the courts instructed the stockholders to pay for raising the boat and putting it in condition, but before this could be done Auxiron, worn out by battles and disappointments, died of apoplexy, one of the many martyrs to the steamboat.

His attempt, however, was only the first of a series that took place in France. The scene now shifts to an inland field; it is dawn. A colonel and one of his subordinate officers face each other with dueling swords in their hands; the blades strike together, gleaming in the early light, and then the picture fades out. We do not know who was wounded—perhaps the colonel was killed—the important fact for our story is that the younger man was arrested on a lettre de cachet, and, at the request of his family, one of the leading houses in Franche-Comté, immured in the military prison on the Island of Sainte-Marguerite, famous as the home of the man with the iron mask.

Claude-François-Dorothée, marquis de Jouffroy d'Abbans, sat in his prison window, a homesick exile. He saw in the distance the city of Cannes, where beautiful women walked on the shore and men lived normal lives; but it was all far off, a dim blur, as impossible to reach as the stars of midnight. Before him was the sea, changing in a thousand lights and winds, but impersonal, lonely. The movement of ships across his view was a bit of life that made his eyes sparkle. Sometimes he saw heavy men-of-war crawl by against the wind, ranks of oars extending from their sides, propelled, as he knew, by the anguish of prisoners less fortunate than he, poor devils who had been condemned to the galleys. He began to while away his time by writing a treatise on boats. Probably he had heard of Auxiron's attempt; in any case, steam began to figure in his imagination.

Released from jail in 1775, the provincial nobleman, who had never been to Paris, hurried there in the first high spirits of freedom. He threw himself into all the gaieties he had dreamed of so long, but even the brightest lady's eyes were dimmed by another vision of his prison years, the vision of a boat that moved by a mysterious power.

The French accounts of Jouffroy leap at this point into fallacy. They tell us that the brothers Périer, who had secured an exclusive right to pump water for Paris by steam, had bought from the firm of Boulton and Watt an engine which was a great inspiration to Jouffroy when he saw it chugging away in their workshop. Thus, we are told, the steamboat inventor learned about Watt's discoveries, which he is said to have used in his experiments. Actually, the Périers had not in 1775 even secured their exclusive right to pump water for Paris; they had no engine in operation for that purpose, nor, as irrefutable documents make clear, had they ever heard of Watt's invention.[1]

It was natural for Jouffroy to consult the Périers, however, since they were the leading manufacturers of machinery in France. Encouraged by what they told him about the Newcomen engine, Jouffroy interested the Marquis Ducrest, brother of Madame de Genlis, and like her an influential aristocrat interested in science. In the ornate gardens of Versailles, Ducrest spoke of steamboats to lords and ladies dressed, for a day's outing, like shepherds and shepherdesses. The ladies clapped their hands with enthusiasm at the thought of this marvelous new toy, and a few of the men listened gravely.

The upshot was an historic conference at Ducrest's mansion. Present were Jouffroy, an assortment of noblemen, A. L. Périer, and the projectors of the previous scheme, Auxiron and Follenai. Everyone agreed enthusiastically to build a steamboat. But then an argument developed about the amount of power to be used. Backed by the discredited Auxiron and Follenai, Jouffroy insisted that a boat would be much harder to drive than a wagon, since a wheel would take much less purchase in water than on land; Périer scoffed at this, insisting that any force that would move a cart would move a boat. His reputation as a mechanic was high; Ducrest and the other noblemen bowed to his opinion, and he was commissioned to build an engine that had exactly the power of one horse.

Certain that Périer would not succeed, Jouffroy returned to his native Franche-Comté. At the little village of Baume-les-Dames, on the River Doubs, in opposition to all the wisdom and wealth of Paris, he started to build a steamboat according to his own ideas. He took over the remains of Auxiron's company, Follenai worked hard to raise money, and from his death-bed Auxiron himself wrote, "Courage, my friend. You alone are right."

Was he glad or frightened when he heard that Périer had failed? In 1775 the one horsepower engine was put on board a boat in the Seine; the vessel was said to have moved in still water, but the power was not sufficient to carry it against any current whatsoever. The famous mechanic and his supporting noblemen gave up, agreeing that steamboats were a visionary dream.

Having like Auxiron been promised an exclusive right to use steamboats in France should his experiment succeed, Jouffroy persevered. Since he could not get a cylinder cast and bored in his provincial village, he commissioned the local coppersmith to make one of sheet copper; it was bent into shape, smoothed inside with a hammer as a teapot would be, and then reinforced like a barrel with iron rings. Authentic descriptions of its action show that the engine was not, as modern writers state, of the Watt type; it was a Newcomen engine.[2] A heavy counter-weight pulled the piston to the top of the cylinder, sucking in steam below; cold water was then sprayed into the cylinder, condensing the steam to produce a vacuum; the weight of the atmosphere forced the piston down for the work stroke. A system of pulleys connected the piston rod with the propelling apparatus. Published in France by Genevois in 1650, and probably thought of a thousand times by dreamers who had watched aquatic birds, this device was a mechanical web foot fastened to the end of a rod. At the work stroke, a paddle opened out like a fan, taking hold on the water; then a counter-weight pulled the rod toward the bow of the boat, the reverse effect of the water shutting the fan. Although it seems wild today, this device, which did not require rotary motion, was not badly suited to the Newcomen engine, the piston of which moved only a few times a minute, and then irregularly, the uneven condensation making some strokes slow, some fast, some short, some long. The boat into which the machinery was placed was 40 feet in length and 6 feet broad.

The trial, made in June 1776, was, in the words of a French writer, "not completely happy." When the boat got any way at all, or was aimed upstream against the current, the rush of water kept the duck's feet from opening even for the work stroke. Unable to think of a method to remedy this, Jouffroy admitted defeat for the time being.

Personal difficulties now crowded in on the young man. With few exceptions, the nobility of the châteaux, among whom Jouffroy belonged, felt superior to science, and regarded industrial pursuits as suited only to the lower classes. The inventor was subjected to family persecution. Indeed, the leaders of his clan hardly dared show their faces at Versailles, they were teased so unmercifully. The young inventor was referred to in the fragrant bowers as "Jouffroy-la-pompe," and, as they watched the cool tinkling of the fountains, the imitation shepherdesses laughed delicately as they repeated a stock joke. "Do you know," they asked, "that gentleman of Franche-Comté who floats steam engines on rivers? He pretends that he can mix fire with water." Jouffroy himself could hardly go into company; he was subjected everywhere to the ridicule "*qui blesse en tout pays et tue en France*."

Eager to continue his engineering, he wanted to join the artillery, because mechanical considerations were of importance there. But the members of his family knew that gentlemen fought with swords; the artillery with its grimy cannon and its wholesale method of warfare was suitable only for the sons of the bourgeoisie. Forbidden to enter so demeaning a service, the young man gave in to family pressure. But nothing could stop him from tinkering with steamboats.

In the meanwhile, an event that might have been of tremendous use to him took place in Paris. Finally given their exclusive right to pump water for the city, the Périers had investigated steam engines in England, learned of Watt's discoveries, and bought an engine with a separate condenser. The parts were imported in 1779, but the brothers, who considered themselves at least as clever as the English inventor, added improvements of their own which so slowed down their engine that, as Watt wrote Boulton in 1782, it made only four strokes a minute. If Jouffroy, still immured in the provinces, learned of the new principle on which his rivals' machine worked, he was probably kept from realizing its value by the fact that the doctored engine moved no faster than those of the old type. In any case, all recent published accounts to the contrary, Jouffroy continued to employ a Newcomen engine.

By 1783 he had a second boat ready for trial. It was 130 or 140 feet long and 14 feet wide, a big river boat for its period, which probably explains much of its success, since its size enabled it to carry a relatively powerful engine. The machinery had been made in 1780 at Lyons by MM. Frères Jean. Two cylinders, open at the top to the weight of the atmosphere, were arranged so that the work stroke of one synchronized with the recovery stroke of the other. Pulleys and ratchets connected the piston rods with the propelling apparatus which Jouffroy had substituted for the unsatisfactory duck's feet: a pair of paddle wheels.

The formal trial was made on June 15, 1783, fourteen months after Fitch had surrendered to his savage captors. Thousands of people crowded the wharves at Lyons to watch; by the very waterfront were the members of the local academy, who had been invited to testify to success or failure. The long boat wallowed dangerously under the weight of its engine but remained upright as a fire was lit under the boilers. To the intense excitement of the crowd, sparks began to fly from the chimney; Jouffroy waited with a cramped heart for the pressure to mount. At last the heavy pistons began to rise and fall slowly; slowly the paddle wheels turned. The boat was cast loose. It stood motionless for a moment in the gentle current of the Saône, the wheels slapping against the water, and then it began to move. At first imperceptibly, then faster but not as fast as a walk, the craft puffed upstream, the floorboards rocking under the impact of the engine. For fifteen minutes the gradual progress continued to the shouts of the multitude; then everything seemed to give way at once. The hull opened and water rushed in; the boiler opened and steam rushed out. Quickly Jouffroy eased the boat to shore. Imperfect as his experiment had been, he was the first man who can be proved to have made a boat move under its own power.

He returned to Lyons to receive the plaudits of the multitude.

Jubilantly he sent the government an affidavit signed by the members of the Academy of Lyons testifying that he had driven a boat weighing about 327,000 pounds against the current of the Saône. He felt that nothing could stop him now. He had clearly fulfilled the stated requirements for receiving a fifteen-year steamboat monopoly in France; and with this valuable right in his pocket, he would have no difficulty raising money to build a stronger boat; and with a stronger boat he would start commercial operation between river cities. One steamship would make enough to pay for another, and so on *ad infinitum*.

On receiving his documents, the government asked the Academy of Sciences in Paris to determine whether a discovery had really been made, and the Academy appointed a committee headed by Jouffroy's rival, Périer. So certain of his success that he did not even go to Paris to argue his case, the inventor remained in Franche-Comté, dreaming of wealth and glory. When he received a letter bearing the great seal of France, he opened it with an anticipatory smile on his face. He read: "It appears that the trial made at Lyons did not satisfy sufficiently the requisite conditions. But, if by means of a steam engine, you succeed in taking up the Seine for some leagues a boat carrying 300 milliers, and the success of this attempt is proved in Paris in an authentic manner, which would leave no doubt of the advantages of your method, you can count on receiving a privilege for fifteen years."

There had been an Homeric battle in the Academy of Sciences. L'Abbé d'Arnal, who was later to have a steamboat of his own, had supported Jouffroy, but most of the other members had refused to believe. The invention was so new and impossible—had not the great Périer himself shown it impossible?—that it would be madness to take the word of provincial savants like the academicians of Lyons. And who was this Jouffroy who pretended to do such marvelous things? He had no reputation of any sort; he belonged to no academy whatsoever. The experiment would have to be repeated in Paris, under the eyes of the national academicians themselves.

Poor Jouffroy looked at the minister's letter in blank despair. His boat and engine had been so flimsily built that fifteen minutes of activity had destroyed them altogether. Where was he to get the money to start again? He wrote Périer suggesting that a new boat be built in the Parisian's workshop; the famous mechanic replied that he would not touch so novel and hazardous an experiment unless a fund of 100,000 livres were put up in advance. Hoping to convince his rival, Jouffroy sent a little model of his invention to Paris. Périer did not even acknowledge its receipt.

Jouffroy had always been torn between the new world of mechanics and the old world of the aristocracy into which he had been born. Probably he had hoped that when his steamboat succeeded, his peers would admire him, and that thus he would be able to reconcile these warring elements. But under the discouragement of failure, he gave in to his environment. In his dreams, perhaps, he still moved upstream in a clanging boat, yet he devoted his waking hours to the conventional activities of his class. And when the French Revolution broke out, he took the side not of his interest but of his blood. Supporting the old against the new, the King against the bourgeoisie, he was forced to flee from France. As a disgruntled exile, he watched disapprovingly while a former corporal of artillery made over France into a nation ready to embrace the industrial revolution.

Even before the days of James Watt, the virus of mechanical boats crossed the Atlantic. James Kenny, a Quaker trader, noted in his diary during 1761 that William Ramsay, a young man at the forest outpost of Fort Pitt, had invented a vessel in which paddle wheels motivated by foot treadles "will make the boat go faster as if two men rowed, and he can steer at the same time by lines like plow lines."

It was natural that America's first boat inventors should appear not on the seacoast but far inland on the banks of wilderness rivers.

Sailboats moved easily on the ocean and in the tidewaters. But since settlement followed means of transportation, by the middle of the eighteenth century the territory thus accessible was pre-empted. Land-hungry pioneers were forced to surge westward into regions from which they could not export their products. This made little difference during the first stages of settlement, but when the farms in the isolated clearings began producing a surplus to sell, many minds turned to finding some means of navigating the back-country waterways.

An historian searching for early steamboat stirrings would naturally look to Lancaster, that westernmost city in Pennsylvania, which had already evolved the first important invention dictated by the wilderness: the Kentucky rifle. Lighter and much more accurate than any gun known anywhere else in the world, this weapon required extremely precise metalwork, and its manufacture was carried on at the very edge of the wilderness by men in daily contact with pioneers who roamed the banks of the Ohio. We need not be surprised that America's first recorded steamboat worker was a Lancaster gunsmith.

Born in Chester County in 1729, William Henry came at an early age to Lancaster, where he soon became the leading manufacturer of the Kentucky rifle. He served as armorer to Braddock and then to Forbes during the French and Indian Wars, and later played an important part in fitting the American troops for the Revolution. He invented labor-saving machinery for his gun works, is credited with the discovery of the screw auger, and made use of the properties of heated air in his "sentinel register," a device for automatically opening and closing furnace flues.

As is so often the case, his steamboat experiments have been exaggerated. Writers who should know better say that when he went to England in 1760, he found "the English mind much agitated by Watt's discoveries," and that he called on Watt. Of course 1760 was five years before Watt had even conceived of the separate condenser. After Henry's return, the story continues, he built a steamboat with paddle wheels which he launched near Lancaster in 1763 and operated until it was sunk by an accident. There is no good evidence to support this, and much to disprove it.

It is clear, however, that in 1775 Henry mentioned the possibility of steamboats to the mathematician Andrew Ellicott, and three years later to Thomas Paine. But as treasurer of Pennsylvania and the incumbent of a multitude of other posts, he was playing so active a part in the Revolution that it was not till well along in the 1780's that he found time to work on his scheme of driving a boat by turning a wheel with the force of high pressure steam. Hoping to submit them to the American Philosophical Society, he made some drawings, but soon laid the project aside, perhaps dissuaded from attempting high pressure, as Watt had been, by the structural difficulties involved.

Henry was not the only steamboat inventor to come from Lancaster. Among the ragged urchins who roamed the streets and even played sometimes in the great man's doorway, there was a poor widow's son in whose face, perhaps, a clairvoyant might have read amazing things. Born a few months after Watt had thought of a separate condenser, twenty-two years younger than Fitch, this lad had been christened Robert Fulton.

IV. *Stone Age Adventure*

WHEN we left John Fitch, he had just fallen down through centuries of evolution; he had become an Indian captive. This most mighty blow yet dealt him by the universe atrophied for the moment all the rebellion in him. Overcome with lassitude, he asked if he might lie down; Captain Crow, who spoke English, graciously accorded him permission. He wrapped his cloak around him and went to sleep. The Indians had been very civil and had "behaved with great coolness and deliberation," but while Fitch slept a major change came over them; they had found the white man's whiskey. Captain Buffalo became particularly excited. Suddenly, Fitch was pulled awake by a wild shout. "Teak! teak!" screamed Buffalo.

"I opened my eyes and rose up on end and shook my head and said, 'No!' and he said again 'Teak!' and drew his tomahawk a fair blow to sink it into my head. I looked him full in the face, and felt the greatest composure to receive it that I ever felt to meet death, unless it is since I began the steamboat." Crow caught Buffalo's descending arm.

The Indians divided their booty into bundles. Each swung a pack of about 60 pounds on his own back, but they gave the strongest prisoners only 30; Fitch, who was adjudged weak, was given less than 10 pounds to carry. The captives were tied, but only ceremoniously, with bits of bark that they could have snapped with one finger. Then the party turned their backs on the world of white men and plunged westward into the forest. The 2,000 miles that lay ahead between the Ohio River and the Pacific Ocean was alien land; white men had not cleared fields there or built cabins. As day after day the march continued, each step left farther behind the world into which Fitch had been born.

Rain fell and then sleet. His cap having been confiscated, Fitch took a severe cold, and his eyes became so sore he could hardly see.

50

Although the Indians divided their waning provisions equally with the prisoners, he was perpetually hungry. Physical misery vied with mental as he staggered ever onward toward a fate about which it was better not to think.

Yet under all his despair the mind of the surveyor and colonizer would not lie still. Where towering trees touched crowns over the shores of rivers, so that the broad flow ran sunlessly through a cavern of leaves, Fitch saw broad fields sweeping down to the banks, and heard the rumble of stones grinding the maize of his dream. He struggled to fasten the winding trail in his memory, so that he would not forget where the great commonwealths of the future would rise.

The helpless captive, who had always been in revolt against his own environment, studied his barbarous masters with a curiosity untouched by loathing. That they always kept scouts before and behind, while no one accused them of cowardice, he regarded as a vindication of his own cautious ways. He was interested, not horrified, when, as they sat around the campfire, Crow ceremoniously prepared the scalps of his two former companions, cutting them in circular form and stretching them on little red hoops. Buffalo, Fitch wrote, tended him a "piece of generosity [which] I believe exceeds the most Christian nations." Fearing the captive would be stripped of his clothing for the sake of his silver buttons, the Indian cut them off and allowed Fitch to put half in his own pocket.

On the twelfth day of the march, the party reached a Delaware village. It was almost empty, since the braves were attending a grand council at a neighboring town, but the women who had been left behind gave Fitch's captors a piece of news that struck terror into the prisoners' hearts. A hundred white men under the command of Colonel Williamson had induced a large body of Christian Indians, converts to the Moravian faith, to surrender by saying they would protect them from more savage tribes by taking them to Fort Pitt. Once the Indians had disarmed themselves, the whites tied them in groups—men, women, and children all together—and massacred more than ninety souls. Only two boys escaped to tell the story. Since Fitch and his companions were the first colonists to be captured after this outrage, reprisal seemed in order according to the Indian law.

That night the captives were treated more harshly than ever before; the next morning the party set out for the town where the grand council was deliberating the Williamson massacre. At the outskirts of the settlement, the Indians stopped. They took all bundles from the prisoners, gave them moccasins to take the place of their shoes, and explained that if any braves abused them, they were to run for the long house at the end of the village; once inside, they were safe. The party then proceeded till they reached the foot of a hill on the top of which they saw the council house with a crowd of savages around it. The captors gave the scalp hallow eleven times, one for each prisoner or scalp. As the last shout died into echo, a stout brave, painted black, and naked except for a breech cloth, ran like a deer to Crow, seized a pole from which the two scalps had been hung, and sprinted toward the council house.

The prisoners proceeded in single file up the hill. When they reached the summit, a vast war whoop shook the sky and the crowd rushed toward them like a tidal wave. The prisoners halted in dismay. The instant the crowd reached the first white man, he fell under a rain of blows; the other captives took to their heels. As Fitch sprinted for the sanctuary, he was struck many times, but always with an open hand. An Indian grabbed him by the hair and pulled him to the ground; he gave himself up for lost, but his attacker released him immediately he was prone. Scrambling up, he saw that now there were only women before him, but his relief was short-lived. The ladies were armed with sticks, and they struck with all their might, much harder than the men. "I scampered along as fast as I could, and a merry frolic they had." About 20 feet from safety, Fitch fell over a log; he thought it more expedient to proceed on hands and feet. Having got his head in the council house, he stopped thankfully, but several hearty whacks on his behind notified him that he had misinterpreted the statute. Quickly he drew this part too into the sanctuary.

Sixty feet long and 20 feet broad, with large doors at each end, the council house was packed with brightly colored chiefs and warriors.

Slinking with his companions to a corner, Fitch watched eagerly for the crowd to give some indication of his fate. But the braves merely squatted quietly on the floor. With much ceremony, women brought in kettles containing hominy; when the chiefs had partaken, the food was offered to all, the prisoners receiving an equal share.

"After a long silence, as still as a Quaker meeting," Fitch remembered, "the chiefs began to speak one after another, and in the most solemn manner, and from the observations I made from their manner of speaking, their gestures, etc., I became exceedingly alarmed, and if ever I was frightened it was at that time. The rest of the prisoners was no way alarmed, but received it more as a curiosity than anything serious." For hours the debate continued; then suddenly the Indians streamed out of the hall, leaving Fitch and his companions alone in the darkening ceremonial chamber. "I not knowing my fate felt much depressed in my spirits, with an inveterate resentment for the indignity offered me that day, with a full determination to resent my wrongs on them if I ever lived to get out of their hands."

Six small fires having been built on the earthen floor at equal distances, the Indians returned. Suddenly the oppressive stillness was rocked by a powerful rhythm coming from drums and calabashes filled with beans or pebbles. Three or four women started to circle around one of the fires; they took tiny steps, lifting their feet as if marching, and then with a graceful spring brought their feet together. Soon other women took up the beat, little girls mingling with crones of seventy, until there was a ring around each fire. As the steps grew faster, the women threw off their blankets which they dexterously twined around their waists. "Their collars and bosoms were open," wrote Fitch, the Puritan moralist, "but nothing appeared indecent. After about twenty women had engaged in it, it was begun by the men, who made the most laborious work of it they could, as if the greater extravagances they run into in cutting wild capers the better dancers they was, and some went so far as even to throw their heads into the fires, then jump up with a yell nearly half as high as a man's middle. I believe I may say quite every one of the men at the same time singing his own song. This appeared to me as a spectator was the most fatiguing, rough, and manly exercise which could be invented, and I am apt to conclude as rational as our dances from the Italian music. Every one of the prisoners except myself danced at this ball, but I felt as sulky as an Indian. I scarce ever felt such feelings before or since. It seemed as if I was allotted to die by the hand of savages, and that I did not care how soon, and did not wish to gratify them in any one thing, although in the afternoon I was amazing timorous, and would have given all my lands in Kentucky, or nearly all, to have saved my life."

Soon Fitch was the only motionless figure in the great room, where noise and motion were in a wild riot, and the uneven glow of flame caught on bare flesh that contorted in frenzy. Brought up on visions of hell fire and of Satan's devils, Fitch never doubted that the dance was a prelude to torture. He cursed Williamson, who had put him in such danger by massacring the Moravian Indians: "I hope it may not be the case, whether I go to heaven or hell, that I shall be where he is, and I write it now to be read after my death that I do not forgive him, but mean to affront him wherever I see him, . . . not for the injury he did me, but for exercising the quintessence of wickedness." As Fitch sat there sullenly, a chief took a fancy to his linsey-woolsey trousers, although they were broken at the knees. He offered a valuable breech cloth, richly decorated with wampum, in exchange, but the prisoner just shook his head; Fitch would rather be tomahawked today than burned tomorrow. The chief then sent his agent to another prisoner; although this time the breech cloth was not offered, the captive complied instantly.

The white men and the Indians danced side by side under Fitch's burning eyes. He waited for the frenzy to turn into a fury of attack against himself and his companions, but the night passed to the rhythm of pounding feet, and before dawn dancers began to disappear into the darkness. Little by little the hall emptied until the prisoners were again alone. Then a polite emissary appeared to offer them women for the night. Fitch refused.

The next morning the chiefs reassembled, bringing white persons to read the papers found on the prisoners, who were suspected of being involved in the massacre of the Moravian Indians; but the documents proved the captives were not warriors. "They might have known it before," Fitch commented. Then the debate went on. As Crow explained later, many chiefs called out for the execution of all the prisoners, but on the other side it was argued that the living men would bring a good price when turned over as American captives to the British at Detroit. Finally a compromise was arrived at: four prisoners were left behind—Fitch believed they were slaughtered—and the rest, including Fitch, marched out again into daylight.

One of five assigned to Buffalo, Fitch accompanied the old chief to his village, where the captives were ordered to build a house. Suffering from a pain in his chest, Fitch refused to work, but his fellow white men, Parkerson and Hopkins, dragged him to the task. "I told them that they, it was true, had courage enough to take hold of a sick, helpless man, but if they had only that much resolution at the time we were captured, I should not be in that situation. Nay, I told them, if I had only a half dozen old women with me at that time that had only resolution enough to keep their feet and not to lay themselves flat down in the bottom of the boat, I never would have been a prisoner." This tirade did not endear him to his companions, but Buffalo was sympathetic, doctored him with calmus root, and exempted him from labor.

Fitch, who was always interested in matrimonial matters, records that the brave was attended by "a likely young squaw." When some days later his wife appeared, carrying a fine child about eight months old, Fitch, remembering his own marriage, waited eagerly for the fireworks to start. The wife sat down beside her husband and his lady; for fifteen minutes nothing was said. Then they conversed in low musical tones. That night the young squaw left husband and wife together, lying down about 10 feet away. "But," adds Fitch, "she need not have slept alone had she come on our side of the fire." The next morning Buffalo killed a deer and gave half of it to his wife, who went away well pleased, leaving Buffalo to proceed to Detroit with his paramour. In this way, Fitch comments, the husband was kept happy and the wife saved an arduous journey.

Once more on the march, Fitch had his first view of the prairies; endless flat expanses from which clumps of hazel bushes rose like islands. It rained continuously, until the men were wading ankle and even waist deep; provisions became very scarce, since Buffalo could not leave the prisoners to hunt. The five white men were guarded only by the old chief, the squaw, and two children; Fitch's companions suggested that they overcome their captors and escape. To this Fitch objected, pointing out that they were far behind the Indian towns, did not know their way, and even if not recaptured would probably starve to death. He did not think the suggestion had been made in earnest, "but as soon as I gave them my opinion they grew very clamorous because I would not join them, and said many ill-natured things, till I got somewhat warm and damned them for a set of cowards, and told them I would not undertake anything with them but what I thought I could accomplish with my own hand; but if they was so desirous of doing it, I asked them what prevented? There was but one Indian, a poor little squaw that a man could lift with one hand, and two little Indian papooses, and I would remain passive, and there was four stout, hearty fellows of them, and they certainly did not want my help unless they wanted me to do the whole, and told them I was too well acquainted with them to join in such an affair or even to attack one single papoose."

Thus the captives wrangled along through hunger and wet until on the seventh day of march they reached the Maumee River, about 18 miles from Lake Erie, where there was an Ottaway town and a trading post kept by two white men, Saunders and Cochran. The prisoners were allowed to sleep in the kitchen of the store, while Buffalo encamped on a near-by hill. All went well until a band of Delawares, returning with money and whiskey from the English fort at Detroit, joined the old chief; soon there was the sound of violent revelry on the hill. Saunders' white servant, who had imprudently entered the Delawares' camp, staggered into the shop flowing with blood and fell dead from a tomahawk wound. The traders rushed out indignantly, but in a few minutes they were back, with "fear impressed in their countenances." Soon the incoherent shouts of the revellers turned to five scalp hallows, one for each prisoner. Seizing an axe, Fitch slipped through the kitchen window into a garden where he had seen some bean poles; he cut a club for each of his companions, but they merely "laughed at me for my frenzy."

The scalp hallows continuing, Fitch retreated with the axe "to a stable which had but one entrance, and being thus situated I knew that I could probably kill three or four before they could take me." Through a crack in the wall, he saw the Delawares come charging down the hill, brandishing tomahawks. When all seemed lost, the inhabitants of the Ottaway village rushed out to defend the white traders whom they had adopted into their tribe. The two groups of Indians faced each other—one sullenly determined, the other prancing drunkenly—and then the Delawares halted. They shouted to the prisoners to come out and be killed. Fitch, however, remained in the stable, and the others cowered in the kitchen, where Saunders stood over them, tomahawk in hand.

Finally the Delawares returned to their whiskey kegs on the hill. Fitch lay down to sleep in the barn, "but heard every hallow as plain as if I had been awake." The shout was given many times during the night, and always "equal to our number, that I had no expectation of living out the next day unless they should drink so much as to put them asleep, and about an hour before day they seemed to be quiet, but at daybreak were as noisy as ever and gave the scalp hallow again."

The only hopeful sign was that Buffalo had not taken part in the attack the night before. However, on the following morning he came wabbling down the hill. Through the crack in the barn, Fitch watched for some sign to show his owner's mood. When the old Indian stopped, steadied himself for a moment, and then gave a scalp yell for each prisoner, Fitch's nerves tightened sickeningly. Before the echoes had died, Buffalo had scuttled into the kitchen where the other captives cowered. Peering through a window, Fitch saw him point to the Indian encampment, as he shouted angrily at the prisoners and finally drove them from the room.

Then Buffalo sat down to talk to one of the traders. Fitch concluded "that I might as well submit to my fate as soon as late." He climbed in the window and said with great cheerfulness, "How do you do this morning, Captain Buffalo?" He secured a low stool, and placing himself at the chief's feet, laid an arm over his bare thigh and sat gazing in his face. When the old Indian finally rose to make another attempt to drive the prisoners to their death on the hill, he motioned Fitch to remain in the safety of the traders' kitchen.

Fitch's act of submission presents an interesting problem when we recall that a few weeks before he had been the only prisoner who had refused to dance for favor. On that occasion, he swore eternal vengeance against his captors, but we have his word that this "passion was moderated before I reached the United States." Indeed, he had come to feel much more friendly to the Indians than to his white companions. Since the Americans were representatives of his own world, at every instant he had to measure his courage and sagacity against theirs; much of his account of his captivity is given to proving his superiority over the other captives. But he felt superior to the Indians because of his race; he wrote that "the most exalted genius" among the savages could not command more than a thousand men, or be a Newton, Franklin, or Rittenhouse. Indeed, he believed the two races so different that they could not have had the same Savior.

Since because of racial separation he did not feel it necessary to prove himself a better man than the Indians, he could accept them as he accepted any other force of nature, study the laws according to which they moved, and bend before their wrath as a tree bends before the gales of autumn. Indeed, he found much in Indian life that appealed to him. When the white man's tricks and whiskey did not intervene, the savages moved unerringly according to an ethic that grew so naturally from their environment that, as he observed, it was not necessary for them to have written laws or a settled form of government. With them a man tortured by the contradictions of civilization could walk with assurance down paths clearly defined by custom and taboo. Cruelty existed, it is true, but it was the impersonal cruelty of an owl pouncing on a mouse; the Indians would offer their wives to cheer the nights of prisoners who were to be burned at the stake the following day. Captives and captors alike shared the same starvation and the same feasts: abstract justice was as profound an obsession among the Indians as it was to Fitch himself.

His contemporaries remember that Fitch came to resemble his captors; he is described as "straight, tall, and imposing; his hair, eyes, and complexion very dark; his gait rapid, his arms swinging to and fro as he walked. In fact, he had nearly acquired the external character of an Indian. Like him, in traveling he planted his feet straight with the path so that, with moccasins, the red man himself could not distinguish the track from one of his own race." It is quite possible that had Fitch been held for a while in an Indian village, he would have stepped from his own time not into the future but into the past; like other neurotics who fled white civilization to the frontier, he might have settled down happily to a savage life and become a member of a tribe. Instead of becoming a major prophet of the machine age, he might easily have walked the forest trails as companion and leader of men from the age of stone. And perhaps he would have been happier. Certainly during his struggles as a steamboat inventor he often looked back with nostalgia to his Indian captivity.

The trader Saunders intervened; afraid, after Buffalo's drunken orgy, of what might happen to the prisoners, he himself delivered them to the British at Detroit. The ragged scarecrows from the wilderness gave the commandant of that outpost a shock by telling him of Cornwallis' surrender. Although the victory that was to end the Revolution had taken place six months before, no word had reached England's most important western bastion. Thinking it would have been just as well if the news had never arrived, the Royal Major hurried his informants to cells where they were kept incommunicado. But Fitch shouted the intelligence out the window to passers-by on the street, and carefully told the sentries, many of whom, proving to be "good Whigs," enthusiastically agreed to spread the tidings.

After an arduous journey between British positions on the Great Lakes, the captives were finally deposited on a small island, opposite

Coteau du Lac, where many American prisoners were congregated. Fitch had not been there two hours "before Parkerson and Hopkins represented me as the damnedest Tory that remained unhung." And Fitch soon contributed to his unpopularity by his own actions.

He started a vegetable garden, thereby, so his fellow-prisoners charged, putting ideas in the minds of the guards who might force all to do likewise. "As soon as I had got my seeds in the ground, I began to think of carrying on my trade [of brass founder], for I could not endure the thought of being idle." However, "all the tools I had was my old graver, and no steel on the island to make any with. . . . My first thought was to make a vice, but before I could make that I must have a turning lathe to turn the screw." He managed to collect a saw, a chisel, a plane, an axe, and a shoemaker's hammer. To these he added an anvil by setting an iron wedge in a block of wood. He then made his lathe from an old ramrod, the blade of a jackknife, and an iron hoop. Using "our common fire, blown by my mouth or hat," he forged a file from the spring of the jackknife, and also a variety of chisels from an old razor blade. The screw for his vise was now easily turned. With improvised woodworking tools, he shaped blocks of wood for the ends and "put jaws to it with iron hoops nearly as nice as could be done in the City of Philadelphia." A blowtorch presented a difficult problem, but he made one by hammering the edges of a barrel hoop together lengthwise so accurately that there were no leaks. In ten days he had "a fine set of tools."

From a worn-out brass kettle he fashioned a quantity of buttons. After he had cut ciphers on them with his graver, they were, he declared, "but a little inferior in looks to a gold button." And they were easy to sell. Having taken on an assistant at wages and two apprentices, he erected a furnace for melting silver, and fashioned molds and crucibles from sheet iron, so that he could make silver buttons as well as brass. He employed a German coal burner among the prisoners to produce charcoal, and hired other prisoners to collect wood. During nine months on the desolate island, he made, so he tells us, three hundred pairs of brass and eighty of silver buttons, as well as nine wooden clocks. In his spare time, he improvised tools with which to repair watches, and put two or three in order.

Using the proceeds of his industry, he bought himself a "superfine suit" and a good hammock of Russian sheeting which he hung midway in the barracks, thus escaping from the filth and vermin of his fellow-prisoners. He also had five blankets and three cord of wood laid up for the winter. "I got to be as rich as Robinson Crusoe." A prisoner pent on a little island, he had accomplished a lifelong ambition. His hammock was a visible sign of eminence; as he lolled there in his fine clothes, looking down on the frowzy men stretched on the floor beneath him, he knew that he was the richest and most prominent man in all his little world. And this had been achieved through his own probity and skill.

One evening before roll call it was announced that the prisoners had been exchanged and would be returned to the United States. The captives danced with joy around Fitch's motionless figure. He was happy where he was; he begged to be allowed to remain. But the British officers merely laughed at so bizarre a request. Forced to leave his prosperity behind him, to return to freedom and the world of ordinary men, Fitch was at one blow reduced to the same level as his shiftless companions.

With the other prisoners from the middle colonies, he was scheduled to sail down the St. Lawrence and then through the open ocean to an Atlantic port. "I much dreaded the going round by sea," wrote the future inventor of steamboats, "as I was born a natural coward to the water, and solicited earnestly that I might be sent across with the Vermont people by the way of Crown Point, but to no purpose." He was so uneasy the first night on shipboard that "I had a great mind to desert, but could not get any to accompany me.

"We had nothing but storms, calms, and head winds till I had got such a disgust to the sea that I told the captain if he would once set me safe on shore again, I would sign any articles that he should produce if he ever catched me on the Atlantic any more." Fitch was seasick the whole passage, and whenever he could get on deck his bitterness drove him into acrimonious quarrels with the British officers and his fellow-passengers.

A great tempest blew up, and Fitch became convinced that the vessel would be cast on the New Jersey shore. "I went under deck and eat as hearty a supper as I could. After I had eaten all I could, I stripped myself of my long blanket matchcoat which would have entangled my legs in the water. . . . I also took off my overalls and put on breeches, stockings, and shoes, and then put on my fur cap, but finding the ears would fall down over my mouth . . . got needle and thread and sewed them up strong. . . . After which I took out a large pair of shoemaker's nippers out of my box of tools and put them in my pocket, thinking that if I should want to get through the surf that I could take hold of one handle and grab with the other in the sand to prevent it washing me off." As he awaited catastrophe in his weird costume, the shoemaker's nippers trembling in his hand, he may well have longed for a ship that could by its own power resist being blown on a lee shore. But no practical expedients occurred to him.

The boat rode out the storm and reached New York on Christmas day, 1782. Convinced, as always when he was unhappy, that he was very sick, Fitch wrote "two principal, leading men in the Methodist congregation of which at that time I was a member," asking them to bring him some supplies; they paid no attention. "It gave me such a disgust of Christianity that I thought if I ever could see their Master, I would tell Him plainly that I was both hungry and thirsty, sick and in prison, and two of His curst scoundrels would administer nothing for my necessities." All the old resentments of life among his peers had descended on Fitch once more.

After a brief period of idleness in Bucks County, during which he was increasingly haunted by thoughts of the children whom he had deserted, Fitch returned to the wilderness. The peace with England having made it clear that the United States would control the territory northeast of the Ohio, he formed a company to survey choice tracts so that warrants for them could be taken out the instant the land offices opened.

Paddling in a canoe up wild tributaries of the Ohio, Fitch was swayed again by dreams of empire. Once more each rich bottom land, where towering trees indicated fertile ground, whispered to him of riches; once more the high movement of the wind, patterning the sunlight through a vertical maze of green, brought such peace to his heart as his heart was ever to know. He had not yet thought of steamboats. No premonition reached him that also in the western country a drama was acting itself out that was to have a vital effect on his destiny. And one of the characters in that drama was the greatest hero of his age, George Washington.

V. *Enter a Soldier of Fortune*

THE instant the Revolution was over, a vast army of settlers started pouring into the central valley of America. Since mountains almost impassable to wagons separated the new territory from the original states, the Mississippi River system became the only logical means of carrying goods. Yet use of even the downward current was denied the pioneers by the Spanish who held New Orleans and would not let American ships through. On their virgin bottom lands, the settlers could grow an endless quantity of produce, but they could not get it to any market.

The natural solution was to bargain with Spain for the right to make use of the Mississippi, yet the leaders of the original colonies feared this step. Washington wrote Richard Henry Lee: "However singular the opinion may be, I cannot divest myself of it, that the navigation of the Mississippi at this time ought to be no object with us. On the contrary, until we have a little time to open and make easy the ways between the Atlantic states and the western territory, the obstruction had better remain. There is nothing that binds one country or one state to another but interest. Without this cement, the western inhabitants, who more than probably will be composed in a great degree of foreigners, can have no predilection for us, and a commercial tie is the only tie we have." Washington feared that unless trade routes were opened between the old colonies and the new, the new would become a distinct nation or even possibly join with Spain.

That great financial gain would accrue to any region that secured the western trade was by no means forgotten. In a letter to Washington, Jefferson expressed concern lest New York gain the advantage. He argued that the Potomac, separated from the Ohio River by only one narrow stretch of land, offered a much shorter route to the sea than did the Hudson. "Nature then has declared in favor of the Potomac, and through that channel offers to pour into our lap the whole commerce of the Western world. But unfortunately [the route] by the Hudson is already open and known in practice; ours is still to be opened."

Washington replied that some ten years before he had been struck by these facts, and had been the principal mover in an attempt to improve the Potomac and James Rivers. The plan was "in a tolerably good train when I set out for Cambridge in 1775. . . . With you I am satisfied that not a moment ought to be lost in recommencing this business, as I know the Yorkers will lose no time to remove every obstacle in the way of the other communication, as soon as the posts of Oswego and Niagara are surrendered."

On resigning from the Army, Washington had written his friends eloquent descriptions of how he was going to settle down to the peaceful life of an ordinary farmer, but the scheme of opening a waterway to the West through Virginia appealed mightily both to the patriotism of the statesman and the business instinct of the largest landowner on the Potomac. The project became Washington's major interest between his retirement as General and his election as President.

Seated on the porch of Mount Vernon, watching an occasional craft glide over the Potomac below him, in his mind's eye he saw the river crowded with boats bearing to eastern markets the rich produce of the West. But how were the manufactured goods of the East to return up river? Washington knew that in England, where canal building had become a fever, the waterways were kept completely level by the use of locks, and were thus equally navigable either way. This was practical in a small country, where neither the distances to be covered nor the differences of level were great, but the Potomac stretched for hundreds of miles, and often rushed through precipitous rapids or dropped over sheer cliffs in spectacular falls. To flank the river with a conventional canal would be a stupendous feat which, even if it were an engineering possibility, would be tremendously expensive. Washington knew that it had always been hard to raise capital in agrarian

America, and that at this time unresolved currency difficulties created by the Revolution were likely to frustrate the most modest business venture.

Never before in the history of the world had the time and place been equally ripe for a mechanical boat. The oceans had not created the need; sailboats crossed them so effectively and cheaply that they were not to be supplanted by steam until generations after it was used for inland trade. In Europe, those countries that possessed long, wild, turbulent rivers had been denied the blessings of the industrial revolution; a steamboat could not have been built on the Danube or the Volga because the necessary skills were unknown, and in any case the static medieval society had no great need to move men and goods in bulk. On the other hand, countries like England and France were small, and their rivers were little and flat; the old methods of transportation sufficed. The same had been true of the American Colonies as long as they did not penetrate beyond the Atlantic plateau; it was the settling of the West that called imperiously for a steamboat. And if one American were to become interested in mechanical boats and to try to put them over, what more influential American could be found than George Washington?

Now was Fitch's great chance, but he was surveying in a forest glade, still unconscious of the power of steam. Another inventor was to approach Washington first.

In September 1784 Washington mounted his horse and rode west to attend to business connected with his large land holdings, and, as he wrote in his diary, to "obtain information of the nearest and best communication between the eastern and the western waters, and to facilitate, as much as in me lay, the inland navigation of the Potomac." Since he enjoyed the gaieties of life, he stopped off at an imitation of the British resort town of Bath, which was being vigorously promoted far back in the mountains in what is now West Virginia. This settlement in the wilderness, which had been hopefully named for its elegant model, was thus described in the *Maryland Gazette*:

"In Berkeley County five bathing houses, with adjacent dressing rooms, are already completed; an assembly room and theatre are also constructed for the innocent and rational amusement of the polite who may assemble there. The American Company of Comedians, it is expected, will open there. . . . It is supposed that they will continue so acceptable to the bathers as to encourage the proprietor to renew his visits yearly. 'The Muses follow freedom,' says Socrates. From Greece and Rome they certainly fled when those mighty empires fell. Let us hail, therefore, their residence in America!"

Several years later a Methodist bishop testified in his diary to the gaiety of the new resort and the purgative quality of its waters. "My soul has communion with God even here," Francis Asbury wrote. "When I behold the conduct of the people who attended the springs, particularly the gentry, I am led to thank God that I was not born to riches; I rather bless God that I am not in hell, and that I cannot partake of pleasure with sinners. I have read much and spoken but little since I came here. The water has been powerful in its operation. I have been in great pain, and my studies are interrupted."

When Washington reached Bath, the malign fate which Fitch believed took a special pleasure in thwarting him made the General stay at a newly opened inn, whose advertisement, published a few months before, read, "James Rumsey and Robert Throgmorton propose opening a very commodious boarding house for the residence of ladies and gentlemen, who may honor the Bath, at the sign of the Liberty Pole and Flag. Every possible attention will be paid to render the situation of those who honor them with their commands perfectly agreeable."

Greeted by the innkeeper, James Rumsey, Washington saw before him an almost unbelievably good-looking man, with a large mouth bent into an extreme Cupid's bow, and handsome almond-shaped eyes under a broad brow. His big nose was beautifully molded, with fine nostrils. Courtly in the extreme, his manner was saved from effeminacy by an underlying ruggedness that bespoke the man of action; his hands, although protruding from lace ruffles, were calloused by labor. And if he was almost too suave, this was counteracted by a certain shy hesitancy of speech. James Rumsey always made a brilliant impression on everyone he met, and the General was no exception. Undoubtedly Washington was pleased to find so suitable a character presiding over the new inn in the embryo center of pleasure. Since Rumsey was also a builder, he gave him a commission to erect two houses on some land he owned in Bath.

As the talk proceeded between the General and the hotelkeeper, the beautiful man's illusory diffidence increased; finally he asked whether he might tell the General something in extreme confidence. This agreed to, Rumsey confided that he had invented a mechanical boat which would go up the most rapid streams with practically no manual assistance. Washington must have started at the words, for they promised a solution for his greatest difficulties; but in an instant he was skeptical. The thing was impossible, he insisted. Looking around again to make sure no one was listening, Rumsey said he had constructed a practical model whose operation he would be glad to show His Excellency.

Soon the two men slipped out of the boardinghouse to a secret nook where Rumsey had made a little flow of water run rapidly through a shallow, flat-bottomed channel. Then probably the young man left the General, and reappeared in a moment with a model in his hand. Two miniature boats, with poles reaching downward over the gunwales, were joined together side by side, with a paddle wheel between them. When this contraption was placed in the current, the water spun the paddle wheel which in turn actuated the poles, and the poles pushed on the bottom to move the boats forward. Before Washington's amazed eyes, the little model walked upstream.[1]

The delighted General gave Rumsey a certificate in which he testified: "I have seen the model of Mr. Rumsey's boats, constructed to work against the stream; have examined the powers upon which it acts; have been an eye-witness to an actual experiment in running water of some rapidity, and give it as my opinion (although I had little faith before) that he has discovered the art of propelling boats by mechanism and small manual assistance against rapid currents; that the discovery is of vast importance, maybe of the greatest usefulness in our inland navigation, and if it succeeds, of which I have no doubt, that the value of it is greatly enhanced by the simplicity of the works which, when seen and explained to, may be executed by the most common mechanic." Fitch was to write that this certificate was "one of the most imprudent acts" of Washington's life.

The statesman, however, remained jubilant. In summing up the results of his western journey, he wrote, "Rumsey's discovery . . . may not only be considered as an important invention for these states in general, but as one of those circumstances which have combined to render the present epoch favorable above all others for securing . . . a large proportion of the produce of the western settlements, and of the fur and peltry of the Lakes also." He continued his exploration of the Potomac Valley more than ever convinced of the utility of his scheme for binding the East and West in one indissoluble union.

Rumsey had already notified the Virginia House of Delegates that he had invented a mechanical boat capable of going upstream largely under its own power. Encouraged by Washington, he now applied for an exclusive right to use on the waters of the state "boats which are constructed upon a model that will greatly facilitate navigation against the currents of rapid rivers." On January 1, 1785, Virginia granted him a monopoly for ten years; Maryland soon followed suit, and South Carolina resolved that if the boat proved to be of public service, he should be rewarded.

With a passion for secrecy that was one of his outstanding characteristics, Rumsey had been careful to give away no mechanical details in his petitions; as a result all the documents dealing with his pole boat, including Washington's certificate, were so ambiguously worded that it was possible to believe the boat had been actuated by steam. This was to make much trouble for Fitch and to entrap many later historians. People who like to believe in the sanctity of the printed word would be horrified to see the number of standard histories which state that Rumsey built a model steamboat in 1784.

Contributing to the confusion is the fact that Rumsey had already conceived the idea of using steam, although he had made no experiments. Various persons were to testify that in 1783 or '84 Rumsey had stated in conversation that, as one witness phrased it, "he was of opinion that a boat might be constructed to work by steam, and that he intended to give it a trial, and mentioned some of the machinery that would be necessary to put it in practice." When he was in Richmond during November 1784 to see to his pole-boat monopoly, the inventor called on Washington and, as the General remembered, "spoke of the effect of steam and the conviction he was under of the usefulness of its application for the purpose of inland navigation. But," Washington continues, "I did not conceive, nor have I done so at any moment since, that it was suggested as part of his original plan, but rather as an ebullition of his genius."

Forced some years later by Washington's testimony to admit that his original boat had not involved steam, Rumsey said that, although he had long meditated on steam engines, he had not yet determined whether they "could be reduced to such simplicity and cheapness as to make them of public benefit. Not being certain of this, though perfectly convinced of the power, was my only reason for not mentioning this scheme also to the General at that exhibition."

The exact moment that Rumsey conceived the idea of a steamboat is of much less importance to history than the fact that through his pole boat he had succeeded in getting the ear and the support of the Virginia dynasty. Washington continued to believe enthusiastically in his mechanical genius; Jefferson was notified of his discovery, and John Marshall wrote that should the Potomac be opened and "should Mr. Rumsey's scheme for making boats to work against the stream answer the expectation of our sanguine gentlemen, the communication between us will be easy, and we shall have but little occasion to test the navigation of the Mississippi." Wherever the inventor showed Washington's ambiguous certificate, it worked wonders; he himself wrote, "It convicts [convinces] almost every person that sees it, and puts quite a new face on my scheme."

Rumsey was to be Fitch's greatest enemy in the invention of steamboats; indeed, the two men were to impede each other and hasten their common downfall. The passage of one hundred and fifty years has not succeeded in killing the rivalry between them. Only a few years ago a Rumsey supporter wrote an attack on Fitch entitled *A Brief Account of Last Century's Inventive Steam Pirate*, and the sentiment thus expressed would be echoed enthusiastically today in many a Southern breast.

Rumsey's early life belongs among "the short and simple annals of the poor"; he left no autobiography, and he was for many years too obscure to appear in records. We know he was born in Bohemia Manor, Cecil County, Maryland, during March 1743, about two months after Fitch. His great-grandfather, Charles Rumsey, came to South Carolina in 1665 and settled at the head of the Bohemia River before 1678. James's father, Edward, was said to be a farmer of limited means, but, it is added hopefully, "of good social standing." Probably Rumsey had little formal education and picked up his mechanical skill through the study of humble crafts. He is said to have been an expert blacksmith; later his principal trade seems to have been that of millwright. According to his admirers, he fought heroically in the Revolution, but his name does not appear in any of the official records. We know that he lived in Baltimore for a time, and owned some property there, which he sold before he bought land at Sleepy Creek, Maryland, in 1782, where he formed a partnership in the milling business with George Michael Bedinger. Bedinger's biographer says that Rumsey was too dreamy and absent-minded to be a good business man, but this is a statement automatically made about any inventor; Rumsey's later acts reveal that he was sharp, perhaps a little too sharp.

Somewhere along the line he married Mary Morrow, who came from a family of shopkeepers in Shepherdstown, now in West Virginia. Shepherdstown became his official home, but he did not spend much time there. In 1783 he was at Bath, where he managed a mill, and bought and sold goods, and built houses, and in 1784 opened his fateful boardinghouse.

Rumsey's early career was superficially very like Fitch's. Also an artisan from a farming background, he too tried his hand at many businesses, never staying in one trade or place long enough really to succeed. But there the similarity between the two men ends. Fitch would have shunned a town like Bath, with its gaiety, its social pretensions, and its craving after vice; he would have made the worst innkeeper in the world. He was afraid of his fellow-men, while Rumsey was always at ease. The Southerner sported the graces of a gentleman, and only his amusement at himself in this role, when writing to his shopkeeping relations, suggests that he was self-nominated to social eminence.

Fitch found life a terrible indenture which had been signed for him without his permission by his Creator, and which like his agreements with the Cheneys, contained many unfair clauses to begin with, and even then was not lived up to by his masters. To Rumsey life was a session at the gaming tables, where you took risks for the exhilaration of it; when you won, you spent your money like a gentleman, and when you lost, you had the added excitement of bluffing your opponents into thinking that your assets were not all gone. The two men would have hated each other at sight even if they had not met, with bayonets fixed, between the trenches of the first great steamboat war. For the moment, however, neither knew that the other one was in the world.

After exhibiting his pole boat to Washington, Rumsey became increasingly interested in the alternate project of using steam. "I applied myself with unremitting attention to perfect my steam engines," he wrote some years later, "and made such progress in that fall and the ensuing spring [1784-85] that my experiments assured me the perfection of such a machine was within my reach." One of his boarders gives us a very garbled account of an experiment he says the inventor tried in January 1785. We make out that by suspending in water the end of a square tube made of pine boards, and then pouring more water into the tube so that it rushed out of a little hole under the water level, Rumsey determined that the tube went forward of its own volition. He was trying to discover whether a boat could be made to move by the force of liquid driven out from its stern by a steam pump.

Rumsey, however, had not discarded his pole-boat scheme. On March 10, 1785, he wrote Washington that "many neat and accurate experiments" had convinced him it would be even more useful than he had formerly believed. The faster the stream, the quicker the ship would go, and he had worked out by mathematics that if he used a huge paddle wheel he could make the vessel ascend the stream twice as fast as the current that moved the wheel.

Continuing in the same letter, Rumsey made his first written mention of steamboats, although his phrasing was carefully designed to mean nothing to anyone but Washington himself. "I have taken the greatest pains to effect another kind of boat upon the principles I was mentioning to you at Richmond. I have the pleasure to inform you that I have brought it to the greatest perfection. It is true it will cost more than the other way, but when done is more manageable and can be worked by a few hands. The power is immense, and I am quite convinced that boats of passage may be made to go against the current of the Mississippi or Ohio River, or in the gulf stream from the Leeward to the Windward Islands, from 60 to 100 miles per day. I know it will appear strange and improbable, and was I to say this much to most people in this neighborhood they would laugh at me and think me mad, but I assure you, sir, that I have ever been very cautious have [how?] I assert anything I was not certain I could perform. Besides, it is no phenomena when known, but strictly agreeable to philosophy. The principles of this last kind of boat I am very cautious not to explain to any person as it is easily performed, and the method would come very natural to a Rittenhouse or an Eliot. The plan I mean to pursue is to build the boat with both powers [pole and steam] on board on a large scale, and then, sir, if you would be good enough once more to see it make actual performances, I make no doubt the [state] assemblies will allow me something clever, which will be better for the public as well as myself than to have the exclusive rights. I am astonished that it is so hard to force an advantage on the public."

This passage requires careful reading. It proves conclusively that before Fitch ever thought of a steamboat, Rumsey was conscious of the advantages that could be gained. However, although Rumsey states "I have brought it to the greatest perfection," the rest of the letter makes it clear that he was speaking only of his theoretical thoughts. He makes no mention of a model steamboat—nor did he ever claim to have constructed one—and he says he would not "assert anything I was not very certain I could perform"; in other words, he had not performed it. Puzzled as to whether steam would be more efficient than his wheel and pole device, he intended to put on a boat, which was not yet built, both types of machine so that they could be compared. His remark that the steamboat "is easily performed" is an amusing indication of his lack of experience with that complicated monster. Not only he and Fitch but a host of others were to learn better by actual trials.

Washington replied politely, "It gives me much pleasure to find that you are not less sanguine in your boat project than when I saw you last, and that you have made such further discoveries as will render them of greater utility than was first expected. You have my best wishes for the success of your plan."

The time had now come for Fitch to begin work on steamboats, but Rumsey had already staked his claim before the most influential man in America.

VI. *The Birth of an Obsession*

WHEN the curtain rises again on John Fitch, we find him on horseback resolutely fording a wilderness stream, holding aloft a handkerchief tied to the end of a pole. Behind him ride his companions, the marks of fear on their faces. An Indian squaw had seen the party across the water, and Fitch, certain that it was useless to flee, had determined to try a gesture of friendship. His assistants follow him sullenly until the horses climb the far bank and the Indian encampment comes in view. Its size terrorizes the backwoodsmen who whisper to Fitch that it would be better to run at whatever cost, since "if they was of the bad sort of Indians it might prove fatal to us." When Fitch proves resolute, the frontiersmen, hiding as best they can behind the trees, allow him to go on alone.

They watch as Fitch dismounts with great deliberation at the very rim of the camp, ties his horse, lays down his gun and his tomahawk, and then, with his saddlebags in his hands, goes onward. His gestures had been greeted with complete silence, and he finds no one in the camp but the squaw he had seen, yet he is convinced that many braves are hidden in the woods. Conscious every moment of invisible eyes squinting at him through their gun sights, Fitch sits down quietly. After a decent interval, he opens his saddlebags and loads the squaw with trinkets. When the gifts are graciously received, Fitch's companions walk into the camp and squat down next to their leader. The white men remain seated for a proper ceremonial period, and then leave the camp with great deliberation. But once out of sight, they hurry down river at a gallop.

Fitch had learned how to handle the problems of a stone-age world, but the time had come when he was to leap from the past to the future. Would he be as efficient there?

By the spring of 1785 Fitch was back in Bucks County. Since he was prepared to claim more than 200,000 acres of rich territory the instant Congress opened its land offices, he merely had to sit still to become rich. But he was incapable of sitting still. To keep his memory fresh, he copied Hutchins' and McMurray's maps of the Northwest Territory, modifying them where his experience told him they were inaccurate. Then it occurred to him that settlers would buy a cheap chart designed to be portable. He bought some copper, hammered it into a smooth sheet, polished it, and engraved his map. On a borrowed cider press, he printed copies which a local young lady colored. In an idle moment, Fitch had tossed off what is said by experts to be the only map known to have been drawn, engraved, and printed by a single person.

This unique feat accomplished, Fitch was again at loose ends. Prevented by rheumatism from much physical activity, he sat by the hour in Cobe Scout's wheelwright shop while his imagination sought hungrily for some hope to expand over, some injustice to lament. Then a Sunday morning dawned bright, and ignoring his infirmity, he decided to walk to church at Neshaminy. As he limped home, a carriage passed him swiftly, and in a thunderbolt of inspiration he conceived the idea of propelling a wagon by steam. At first the magnitude of the project frightened him, but then he asked himself, "What cannot you do if you will set yourself about it?"

Fitch soon realized that the rough, muddy, rutty roads of the period could not support a steam engine on a carriage; then it occurred to him that there was no similar objection to floating one in a boat. When this idea sprang into his mind, did it come in the guise of triumphant destiny, or did it seem just one more of his thousand schemes?

He made a rough drawing to show how steam could move a vessel, and he carried it excitedly to the local pastor, the Rev. Nathaniel Irwin. That gentleman walked to his bookcase and drew from the shelves Benjamin Martin's *Philosophia Britannica*. Turning the pages, he laid before Fitch descriptions of Newcomen's, Cowley's and Savery's atmospheric engines. "I was amazing chagrined, . . ." Fitch remembers. "I did not know that there was a steam engine on earth when I proposed to gain a force by steam." His first reaction was that he had been cheated out of a great invention, but on reflection he decided he should be encouraged, "as my doubts at that time lay in the engine only."

Fitch believed that he had conceived the use of steam entirely out of the blue; that he actually did so may well be questioned. His biographers tell us that he was inspired by watching the vapor issue powerfully from a kettle, but he himself makes no mention of such an incident, and the same story is told of Watt and others. Even should we accept this legend, the distance between a flow of steam on a kitchen range and a machine that would move carriage or boat is so great that it is hard to conceive a man's imagination spanning it at one jump. Since America's first successful Newcomen engine had operated a pump in a copper mine in New Jersey, not far from the region Fitch traversed as a peddler of brass and silver, he may well have heard it mentioned. He would not have been sufficiently interested then to remember specifically what he had been told, but the idea may well have lain dormant in his mind, until called up again by new associations. It is not uncommon for a conception to leap into the brain entirely shorn of its source and thus seeming an original inspiration.

Having studied the Rev. Mr. Irwin's book, Fitch threw his tremendous energy into working out the details of a steamboat. The problem fell naturally into two parts which Fitch for some time pursued separately. One aspect was the construction of an engine. This would have given no trouble to an English inventor, who could easily have purchased the most modern type from Watt. Fitch, however, had to work the mechanism out himself from a printed description of out-dated devices. The other half of the problem, that which was peculiar to steamboat inventors, was putting the engine in a boat in such a manner that its force worked on the water.

Although many writers state that he did so, and even give detailed descriptions of a miniature steamboat puffing under its own power on a local mill pond, it is certain that Fitch made no attempt at this time to build a model engine. He contented himself with making drawings of a machine very close to the Newcomen engine described in Irwin's book. There were two boilers and two cylinders. Alternately pulled upward by springs, the pistons drew steam into the cylinders; when the steam was condensed by the injection of water, the atmosphere pushed down the piston for the work stroke. No hint is given of how Fitch intended to link the force of the engine to the apparatus moving the boat.

Of the boat itself he made a model, a tiny skiff 23 inches long and 4¾ inches broad. Attached to one side only was an endless belt carrying a series of flat, broad paddles that were designed to push the boat forward by passing through the water, and then to return to the bow on the upper side of the belt. This model is deposited with the American Philosophical Society.

As yet Fitch had contributed absolutely nothing to steamboat inventing—indeed, he was far behind some of his predecessors—but in his ignorance he was delighted with what he considered his great discoveries. Even before he carved his model boat, he had carried his plans to Philadelphia, America's intellectual capital. In London he probably would have been laughed at, and perhaps the ridicule of the wise, at this early date, would have driven him from the steamboat to some other of the grandiose schemes that were always flying through his mind. But the local savants did not know enough to realize the depth of Fitch's naïveté. He showed his plans to Dr. John Ewing, provost of the University of Pennsylvania; Robert Patterson, professor of mathematics; "and other respectable characters in the city, from whom I met with no discouragement."

On August 20, 1785, Dr. Ewing, so Fitch tells us, "put the scheme afloat" by committing himself to what others had said but were afraid to write down. He wrote William C. Houston, who he mistakenly thought was still a member of Congress: "I have examined Mr. Fitch's machine for rowing a boat, by the alternate operation of steam and the atmosphere, and am of opinion that his principles are proper, and philosophical, and have no doubt of the success of the scheme if executed by a skillful workman. . . . The application of this force to turn a wheel in the water, so as to answer the purpose of oars, seems easy and natural by the machine which he proposes, and of which he has shown me a rough model. . . . He proposes to lay his invention before Congress, and I hope he will meet with the encouragement which his mechanical genius deserves."

Houston forwarded Ewing's letter to his successor in Congress with a covering note in which he said that he himself, "though not troubled with a penchant for projects, cannot help approving the simplicity of the plan. The greatest objections to most pretensions of this sort is the delicacy and complication of the machinery. This does not seem liable to such objections." Whatever may have been Houston's naïveté about the simplicity of steam engines, he raised here a question which we shall meet again and again because of its great contemporary importance. Nowadays, when trained mechanics abound, whether or not a machine is complicated makes little difference to its introduction, but in the eighteenth century the local blacksmith was likely to be the most efficient mechanic available. Anything that he could not fix would remain out of order for a long time.

Having secured a third letter from Dr. Samuel Smith, provost of the College of New Jersey, Fitch presented on August 29, 1785, the following petition to Congress:

"The subscriber begs leave to lay at the feet of Congress an attempt he has made to facilitate the internal navigation of the United States, adapted especially to the waters of the Mississippi.

"The machine he has invented for the purpose, has been examined by several gentlemen of learning and ingenuity, who have given it their approbation.

"Being thus encouraged, he is desirous to solicit the attention of Congress to a rough model of it now with him that, after examination into the principles upon which it operates, they may be enabled to judge whether it deserves encouragement. And he, as in duty bound, shall ever pray.

John Fitch."

Forever after, Fitch was to claim that this petition made him the only inventor of the steamboat, for in his ignorance he believed this was the first publication of the idea. An invention, he insisted over and over, should date from such first publication, since at that moment the author gave his discovery to the world. Other projectors who, as Rumsey was to do, kept their discoveries secret until the work was completed, deserved no consideration since, were they to die, their contribution would die with them. The question of which man finished his boat first or brought it closest to perfection was also irrelevant, since once an idea was announced, it was always possible for an imitator to out-hurry the original inventor, or to make small improvements on the first man's basic labor. No, publication was the only important consideration, and his own petition to Congress constituted the most conspicuous type of publication. Fitch himself was so absorbed in what he was doing that he was convinced all the rest of America must be equally absorbed. He wrote that his steamboat petition "was so new and rare a project that scarce anything was ever more talked of in this age, unless it was the battle of Lexington." Actually, Fitch's petition was not even entered on the records of Congress, and the committee to which it was referred did not take the trouble to consider it.

As amazed as he was indignant, Fitch wrote, "Determining to revenge myself on the committee of Congress and prove them to be but ignorant boys, I determined to pursue my scheme as long as I could strain a single nerve to forward it. I at that time did not look so much for the benefit, as to prove to the world by actual experiment that they were blockheads."

On September 9, 1785, Fitch wrote the Spanish Ambassador, asking permission to show him a machine for "promoting inland navigation, and particularly adapted for the Mississippi River. . . . Could said engine be put in practice, it would be of infinite utility to his Most Catholic Majesty's unlimited dominions." The Ambassador received Fitch graciously, listened with flattering interest, and promised to lay the matter before his sovereign. Glowing with delight, Fitch rose, but the Spaniard motioned him to sit down again; he had a few practical details to discuss. As the fine gentleman subtly outlined a plan that would turn the invention to the sole advantage of Spain, the artisan concluded that he was much too conversant with the wicked courts of Europe, "although I never saw one myself. . . . We found we had different views: mine were to serve the world of mankind in general, and his to serve his master." Curtly breaking off the conversation, Fitch walked out of the room.

Years later he was to write, "God forbid that I should ever be guilty of the like error again. . . . The strange ideas I had at that time of serving my country, without the least suspicion that my only reward would be nothing but contempt and opprobrious names, has taught me a mightly lesson in mankind—and to do it at the displeasure of the whole Spanish nation is one of the most impolitic strokes that a blockhead could be guilty of."

Poor Fitch was getting himself involved in international complications of which he had no inkling. All through his steamboat negotiations his mind remained fixed on the idea that his invention would be most valuable in navigating the Mississippi upward from the Gulf; he stated this in his petition to Congress and was to state it again and again. The advantages to the western country seemed so obvious to the artisan-surveyor that he felt everyone must consider them all important. He did not know that America's political leaders believed that the prosperity of their own states and the preservation of the union dictated keeping the Mississippi closed. And Spain, too, had her own global axe to grind. His Most Catholic Majesty did not want a powerful nation dominating North America. He was using his control of the mouth of the Mississippi as a lever with which to wrench the United States apart. Already his agents were circulating in the taverns at wilderness crossroads, whispering into influential ears that Spain would never open the Mississippi to the United States, but would be glad to do so if Kentucky declared itself an independent nation. Following the course of logic, of "natural law" as he himself would have called it, Fitch in all innocence was driving his invention against the current of national and international intrigue. Here he was less fortunate than Rumsey, whose steamboat had by chance become part of Washington's scheme for a Potomac canal.

Repudiated by the politicians, Fitch turned to the savants. Later in September, he presented his model and a written description to the American Philosophical Society. He called on Franklin, "who spoke very flatteringly of the scheme, and I doubted not his patronage of it."

Fitch then left Philadelphia to attend to his real estate holdings. The same session of Congress which had ignored his steamboat scheme had passed a law regulating the allotment of western lands which completely nullified the value of the surveys he had made since 1782. "Thus," he comments, "was an immense fortune reduced to nothing at one blow." However, the warrants he had laid down in Kentucky during 1781 were still good; he determined to visit his acres, stopping off first at the land office at Richmond, Virginia, to make sure his titles were not being contested.

But he could not get the steamboat out of his head. From his first stop, Warminster, he wrote Franklin that he was certain his invention would "answer for sea voyages as well as for inland navigation, in particular for packets where there should be a great number of passengers." The fuel could be kept in the space formerly used to carry drinking water, since the distillation of steam would supply this necessity. Not only would the engine drive the boat into the wind and keep it off a lee shore, but it would also man the pumps. "I expect to return from Kentucky about the first of June next, and nothing would give me more secret pleasure than to make an essay under your patronage, and have your friendly assistance in introducing another useful art into the world."

Since he felt the realization of his project "to be far beyond my abilities," Fitch was eager to get the opinion of every man of science he could reach. Passing through Lancaster, he called on William Henry. After the gunsmith had greeted him politely, Fitch received a terrible shock; he was given his first inkling that others had thought of steamboats before him. Speaking quietly, as if nothing awful were happening, Henry remarked that a while back he had proposed building a steamboat and had made drawings which he intended to submit to the American Philosophical Society. Fitch's incredulity appeared on his face. "Although I gave no hint of the kind, I believe he thought I suspected him, and went and hunted his papers and produced a draft to me, which was to propel a boat by a steam wheel." Picking up the drawing with trembling hands, Fitch saw that it clearly represented a steamboat. But even yet he could not believe that anyone had thought of the invention before he himself had presented it to Congress; it was obvious that his companion was lying, that the drawings must have been made since that time. It was not till considerably later that Fitch was convinced by Andrew

Ellicott's testimony that Henry had conceived of steamboats as early as 1775.

There in Henry's drawing room Fitch was kept tongue-tied by the conflict of emotions within him, and it was just as well that his suspicions did not burst out into speech, for now his host said, "Although I am many years before you in the scheme, yet as long as I have not brought it to the public view, . . . I will lay no claim to it, but will frankly give it to you as you are the first publisher of it to the world." So the conversation proceeded amicably, and Fitch eventually admitted that the idea of driving a wheel with the expansive power of steam was entirely new to him; in other words, he had never considered using high pressure. "When I informed him that I could have no conception of how a steam wheel could be made, he frankly offered to make a model at his own expense, and let me have it."

Treated with such generosity, Fitch could only depart with a cordial handshake and a smile, but underneath "it chagrined me considerably to find that I could think of nothing but someone would be before me in the thought." Yet he comforted himself with the realization that Henry had admitted that his petition to Congress had made him the real discoverer.

Next Fitch stopped at Frederickstown to call on Washington's intimate friend, Governor Thomas Johnson of Maryland. Since Frederickstown was the metropolis nearest to Bath, Rumsey had already been shopping there for machinery, and had even asked Governor Johnson, who operated an iron forge, to cast some cylinders for him. But the Virginia inventor had been very secretive, pretending that the apparatus was needed for his pole boat or for machinery connected with the warm springs, and in any case, despite Fitch's imaginings to the contrary, the idea of steamboats was considered too crack-brained to interest people much. As was his habit everywhere, Fitch talked enthusiastically about his idea at the tavern in which he stayed, and handed his model round—he was later to claim this inspired Rumsey—but he appears to have received no hint that his rival was concerned with steamboats. He undoubtedly knew about the pole boat, and Washington's certificate, and the monopolies Rumsey had received from various legislatures, but none of these seemed to conflict with his scheme. And Governor Johnson said nothing about the cylinders he had been asked to cast; he expressed interest in Fitch's plans and advised him to lay them before Washington.

This suggestion seems to have terrified Fitch. He suspected that Washington was "heart-sick of boat projects," but he felt that if he did not stop at Mount Vernon he would offend Governor Johnson. Later he was to write that his call on the father of his country was "the most fatal thing" that ever happened to him.

With a sinking heart Fitch walked up the curving road to America's most famous private residence; perhaps he stammered a little as he told his business to the impeccable colored butler, but in a moment he was ushered into a chamber where he found the General alone. The tall, graceful patrician received the ungainly artisan with matchless courtesy. Fitch wrote, "I had a most favorable opportunity of laying my plans before him, as no company intervened." While Fitch expatiated with his usual enthusiasm about his ability to serve the world, saying that he was the first and only inventor of steamboats, he noticed on Washington's countenance "some agitations of the mind that was not expressed." Finally, he interrupted his tirade to ask if his plan in any way conflicted with Rumsey's. The General seemed worried by the question; he said that he was under an oath of secrecy and "could not give Rumsey's plan by negatives." Then he seemed sorry for his curt reply, loaded Fitch with attentions, asked him to dine and stay the night.

Washington finally left the room, but suddenly he returned, "as if by design, and informed me that my plan was not the same as Rumsey's presented to him at Bath, but that some time after that, at Richmond, he had mentioned something of the sort to him, but he was so engaged in company that he did not attend to it, but made no mention of Rumsey's writing to him on the subject." The object of Fitch's visit had been to get a letter of introduction from Washington to the Virginia Assembly, but this the statesman tactfully refused to give him.

The momentum of Fitch's enthusiasm was so great that he was not disturbed by this interview. What if Rumsey, like Henry, had dreamed of steamboats before he did; he was sure that his petition to Congress still made him the true inventor. Fitch tells us that he left Mount Vernon with "all the elated prospects that an aspiring projector could entertain. . . . And was fully convinced that I could not interfere with Mr. Rumsey, otherwise the known candor of General Washington must have pointed out to me such interference."

Later Fitch was to charge that Washington, out of "a too great delicacy of his own honor," had behaved disingenuously. Their talk, the inventor assumed, had convinced Washington that he had made a grave mistake in giving a certificate to Rumsey; this realization "undoubtedly touched him in the tenderest part, and he must have been more than mortal if he see a hope of retrieving that imprudent step, and did not embrace it, if it was at the expense of an unnoticed, indigent citizen."

Certainly Washington had gone through an unpleasant half hour. The uncouth artisan, who combined social uneasiness with great aggressiveness while he made ridiculously exaggerated claims, must have been much less attractive to the General than the urbane innkeeper who spoke with a deprecatory smile and knew how to push without seeming to do so. But on the other hand, justice was the General's guiding star; he must be fair to all.

He was in an impossible situation. He had promised Rumsey complete secrecy, but this wild man in his parlor would interpret silence as meaning that Rumsey had never mentioned steamboats. After leaving the room to think the matter over, he decided that the fairest thing to do was to relax a little on his oath and state Rumsey's claim so that, as he later wrote, "whichever, (if either) of them was the discoverer might derive the benefit of the invention." But he still was not sure that he had acted fairly. He had told Fitch about Rumsey; should he not tell Rumsey about Fitch?

After hesitating two months, Washington wrote Rumsey on January 31, 1786: "Sir: If you have no cause to change your opinion respecting your mechanical boat, and reasons unknown to me do not exist to delay the exhibition of it, I would advise you to give it to the public as soon as it can be prepared conveniently. The postponement creates distrust in the public mind; it gives time also for the imagination to work, and this is assisted by a little dropping from one, and some from another, to whom you have disclosed the secret. Should therefore a mechanical genius hit upon your plan, or something similar to it, I need not add that it would place you in an awkward situation, and perhaps disconcert all your projects concerning this useful discovery, for you are not, with your experience of life, now to learn that the shoulders of the public are too broad to feel the weight of the complaints of an individual, or to regard promises if they find it convenient, and have the shadow of plausibility on their side, to retract them. I will inform you further that many people in guessing at your plan have come very near the mark; and that one, who had something of a similar nature to offer the public, wanted a certificate from me that it was different from yours. I told him that, as I was not at liberty to declare what your plan was, I did not think it proper to say what it was not."

Here indeed was a spur dug deep into Rumsey's side.

GALATEA, BY RAPHAEL

Although in the nineteenth century inventors fought over which of them had invented the paddle wheel, in 1514 a sea nymph had supplemented dolphin power with an auxiliary wheel.

FITCH'S FIRST CONCEPTION OF A STEAMBOAT
His own model, 1785

A STEAMBOAT ON THE ROCKET PRINCIPLE
Rumsey's Potomac Boat, 1787

TO MAKE A STEAM ENGINE PADDLE LIKE A CREW OF INDIANS
Fitch's crank and paddle scheme, 1786

BAXTER © HARLEY

FITCH'S TRIUMPH OF 1790
This vessel traveled thousands of miles seventeen years before Fulton's steamboat

JOHN FITCH
from a post-
humous engraving

JAMES RUMSEY
probably by
George W. West

RIVALS TO THE DEATH

MRS. JOHN WILKES KITTERA
c 1786

ELF-PORTRAIT
after a
large oil by
Benjamin West
c 1810

MINIATURES BY ROBERT FULTON

THE BIRTHPLACE OF ROBERT FULTON

A mid-century print in the Currier and Ives tradition

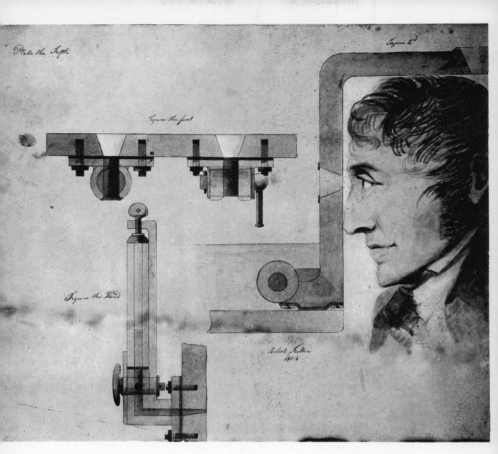

FULTON IN THE CONNING TOWER OF HIS SUBMARINE
An unconventional self-portrait

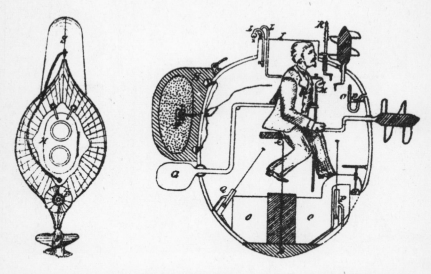

**WASHINGTON USED THE WORLD'S FIRST SUBMARINE
TO PROTECT NEW YORK HARBOR**
A reconstruction of Bushnell's *American Turtle,* 1776

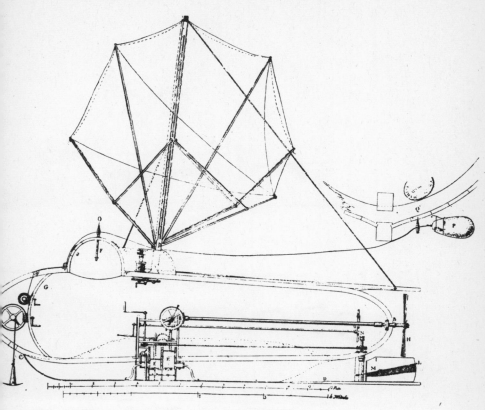

FULTON'S *NAUTILUS:* DESIGNED TO CREATE UTOPIA
Napoleon used this submarine against the British fleet

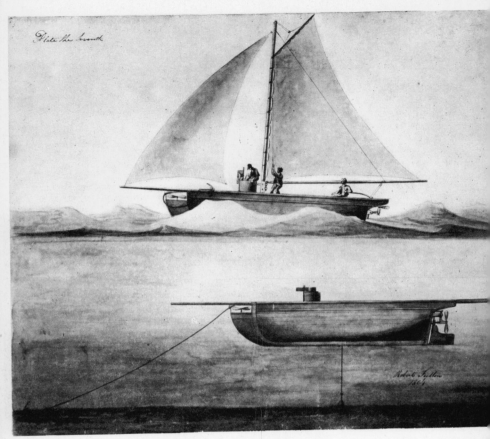

FULTON'S PROJECTED SECOND SUBMARINE CAMOUFLAGED AS A SAIL
His own drawing, showing it on the surface and submerged

FULTON HOPED HIS CAPTIVE MINES WOULD PUT AN END TO NAVIES
A scheme he tried to sell first to Napoleon, then Pitt, then Jefferson

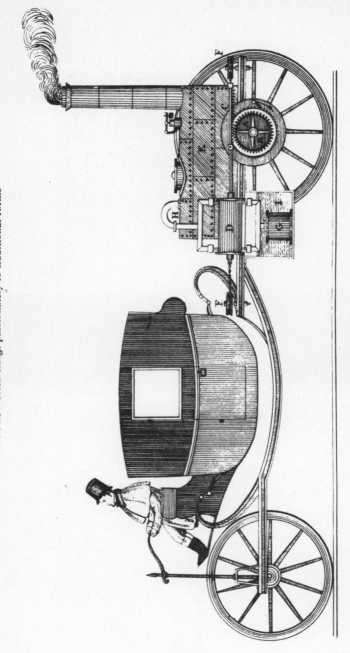

SYMINGTON'S STEAM CARRIAGE
The new often clings passionately to traditional forms

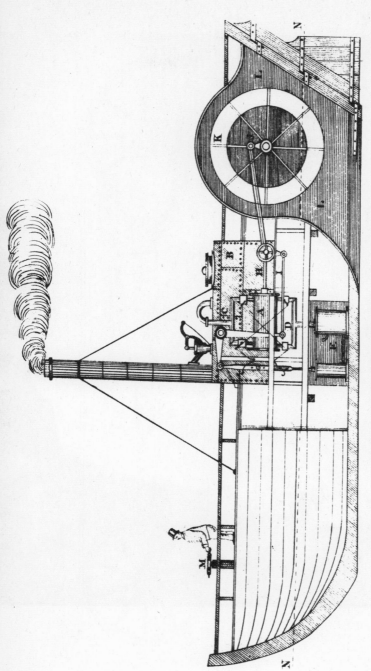

SYMINGTON'S CHARLOTTE DUNDAS

The vessel which English writers insist completed the invention of the steamboat

FULTON'S HISTORY-MAKING STEAMBOAT PASSING WEST POINT

Drawn from life by St. Memin

THE LAUNCHING OF THE FIRST STEAM WARSHIP

A contemporary print of Fulton's *Demalogos*, also known as the *Fulton the First*

VII. *The Race Is On*

Now it was a race, Fitch vs. Rumsey, and Rumsey had a head start. Not only was he the first to conceive the idea of steamboats, but by the time he received Washington's warning he was far ahead in attempting practical application. During the very month when Fitch was struck with his vision of steam, Rumsey employed his brother-in-law, Joseph Barnes, to build a boat on which he hoped to try both his steam and pole methods. But soon the Potomac Canal, which was giving him so great an opportunity, created an interruption.

Having pushed authorizing bills through the Virginia and Maryland legislatures, Washington had organized a company to make the Potomac and James Rivers navigable as far west as possible, and then to build good wagon roads across the divide to the Ohio River system. He wrote Edmund Randolph that although a few locks would probably have to be erected to circumnavigate waterfalls, for most of the distance the Potomac would merely be cleared of obstructions and a channel opened. He still relied on "the probable advantages which are expected to be derived from Rumsey's mechanical discovery" to take the boats upstream. He had "not the smallest apprehension" that Rumsey's project would fail, but if it did he intended to fasten to the rocks in the river a system of chains on which boatman could pull their craft upstream. Thus the expense of cutting an independent canal with locks and towpaths would be avoided.

When the Potomac Company advertised for an experienced engineer to superintend their works, they discovered there was no one in America with enough canal experience to dare even to apply. Washington then offered the post to Rumsey, writing, "I have imbibed a very favorable opinion of your mechanical ability, and have no reason to distrust your fitness in other respects." On July 14, 1785, Rumsey was appointed chief engineer of the most advanced transportation project of its time in America, a project which, we are told, created as much excitement as the Panama Canal was to do years later.

Leaving Barnes to carry on his boat projects in his absence, Rumsey joined the directors for a detailed exploration of the river; he rode in the same canoe with Washington, and undoubtedly let drop remarks about the brilliant future of his inventions.

Rumsey, however, soon found himself up to the ears in difficulties. No sooner had he made a beginning in cutting a channel than the rushing mountain torrent, swollen by rains, would wash all away. It became increasingly difficult to find laborers willing to struggle in the freezing water under wilderness conditions; only men unemployable for other jobs applied, jailbirds who terrified the entire countryside and made Rumsey fear for his life. He wrote Washington, "The complaints that was made to me was shocking, that no person could come on their lawful business but what got abused, and that the officers of justice durst not go on the grounds to execute their offices." The sheriff near Great Falls, wishing to arrest some workmen who had been in a tavern brawl, got up a posse of fifty armed men and marched on the camp in force; only Rumsey's intervention prevented what might have turned into a little civil war.

When the trouble-makers were discharged, it was impossible to hire anyone else. The company, under Washington's leadership, tried to overcome this difficulty by buying Negro slaves and the indentures of Irish immigrants who had agreed to a certain number of years of service in return for their passages to the New World. Soon Rumsey was advertising in the local press for the return of indentured workmen who had been driven to flight by the gruelling labor. If a fugitive was caught, his head and eyebrows were kept shaved, but even this conspicuous mark of disgrace did not keep him from slipping away again at the next opportunity. Attempting an almost impossible task with inadequate knowledge, poor tools, and the worst possible type of workmen, Rumsey was kept perpetually busy on the canal job, as his almost daily reports to the Potomac Company show.

His boat experiments were now entrusted almost entirely to

Barnes, who built a vessel near Bath which by the fall of 1785 was so far completed that it could be floated down to Shepherdstown. During October or November, Rumsey confided to Governor Johnson that he intended to move his boat by steam. Later Johnson was to charge that Rumsey had lied to him, implying that Washington's certificate had been for a steam, not a pole, boat, but Rumsey insisted that Johnson had misunderstood. In any case, he ordered a pair of cylinders from Johnson's iron furnace.

When the foundry proved unequal to the task of making such unusually large castings, Rumsey ordered Barnes to have the cylinders fashioned from sheet copper in Frederickstown. A wood-turner supplied models around which a coppersmith hammered the metal into the requisite shape; the seams were then fitted by a neighboring blacksmith, and the whole soldered and riveted together. When the wooden cores were removed, the result was two very handsome metal containers in the shape of cylinders; how strong they would prove was another matter. Hiding whenever possible the nature of the machines he was building, Barnes secured from local craftsmen the other apparatus he would need to apply not only Rumsey's steam ideas, but his pole-boat invention as well. The object, of course, was to compare the efficiency of the two devices.*

In December 1785 Barnes loaded his machinery on the boat Rumsey had bought, and drifted down to Shenandoah Falls, where the inventor was trying to cut a canal around the gigantic waterfall. According to the testimony of a neighbor, Rumsey and his assistant "continued adapting and suitably fixing" the machinery to the boat "until the seventh of January 1786, when the ice driving in the river obliged them to desist proceeding further for that season, and they accordingly that same day drew the boat in the mouth of the run, took off the machinery, and laid it in my cellar for and during the winter."

When, about a month later, Rumsey received Washington's letter

---

* Fitch later tried to prove that the work was not done in 1785, as Rumsey stated, but in 1786. The author's reason for disregarding this charge is outlined in Chapter XI.

warning him about Fitch, he was far ahead of his rival. Fitch had not yet attempted to build a steam engine, or for that matter even seen one, while Rumsey had actually begun to install on a boat an engine which Barnes insisted had been prepared "upon the plan used and improved in England."

Still unaware that Rumsey was tinkering with steamboats, Fitch had proceeded from Mount Vernon to the state capital at Richmond, where he petitioned the Virginia legislature for funds to help him put over his invention. James Madison supported the measure, but no action was taken. The governor, Patrick Henry, was so interested that he urged the members of the assembly to solicit subscriptions for Fitch's map of the western country. The inventor agreed that if one thousand maps were sold, he would either exhibit a steamboat on the waters of Virginia in nine months, or else forfeit £350. Gleefully, he gave up his western trip and hurried back to Bucks County to print more maps.

He stopped off at Frederickstown, where Governor Johnson took some subscription papers for the maps and wrote Governor Smallwood of Maryland, urging him to do the same. From this document we learn that Fitch's soaring imagination was no longer content with steamboats only; he was going to apply steam engines "to a variety of uses." Johnson added, "All that I have to request of you, sir, is that you give him an opportunity to converse with you; you will soon perceive that he is a man of real genius and modesty. Your countenancing him will of course follow." For once Fitch seems to have made a good impression on an aristocrat.

On December 2, he appeared before the American Philosophical Society to present his plan in person. Although he had never seen an actual engine, he was riding so high that, as he tells us, the discussion of the learned savants of the society filled him with delight; it impressed him with his own superior knowledge. Franklin was not there but, after Fitch had left the hall, Francis Hopkinson read a paper by the philosopher which was to have a profound effect on the development of our story.

The paper contains a dozen or more ideas about boats which had wandered through Franklin's mind during the weary days on shipboard when he was returning from France in 1785, some months before he had heard of Fitch. Concerning paddle wheels, the philosopher wrote, "this method, though frequently tried, has never been found so effectual as to encourage a continuance of the practice." The failure, he continued, was due to a waste of energy; only the bottom paddle drove the boat forward, for the one entering the water tended to lift it up and the one emerging to pull it down.

Next Franklin revived the suggestion made in 1753 by the Frenchman Daniel Bernouilli, that if a stream of water was driven out of the stern of a boat below the water line, its reaction on the body of water in which the boat floated would drive the vessel forward. Bernouilli's experiment had merely involved an L-shaped pipe stretching to the rear into which water could be poured; Franklin added a pump that drew water in at the bow and drove it out at the stern. "A fire engine might in some cases be applied to this operation with advantage," he concluded.

Thus in a single paragraph in the middle of a rambling list of suggestions Franklin had outlined a form of steamboat that appealed more strongly than any other possibility to citizens of the eighteenth century. Changing the reciprocating motion of a piston into the rotary motion that would be needed to drive a wheel or a chain of paddles still presented a serious problem in America, although in England it at last had been solved. Furthermore, steam engines had through all their history been used for nothing but pumps, and even Watt's new discovery was still largely employed for this purpose. Here was a scheme by which a pump could be made to drive a boat, and it was backed by the authority of America's greatest scientist. Furthermore, and this was very important at the time, the mechanism of application was simplicity itself: just a series of pipes. Nowadays we know that this early attempt to apply the rocket principle was impracticable for many reasons, not the least of them being that much energy would be lost by lifting the water into the pump and bringing it to a standstill there before it was driven out the stern.[1]

The pump scheme—a rudimentary form of jet propulsion—was instantly accepted by all Americans interested in steamboats. If we credit the evidence already given concerning Rumsey's experiments in January 1785, we must conclude that he had conceived the idea independently; in any case, it cannot be shown that during his entire career as a steamboat inventor he ever tried any other method. And Fitch, when he heard of Franklin's paper four days after it had been read, was seduced away from his own more advanced ideas; he resolved to build a pump boat, when he had secured enough money to build anything.

Raising money was Fitch's problem. He advertised his maps in several cities, promising to use half the purchase price to forward the steamboat, and he presented petitions for financial aid to the Pennsylvania, New Jersey, and Maryland legislatures. He wished, he notified the latter body, to procure an engine from Europe, and promised to expend any money received under the direction of the well-known Philadelphia mathematician, Andrew Ellicott. A committee reported: "However desirable it is for liberal and enlightened legislators to encourage useful arts, yet the state and condition of our finances are such that there can be no advance of public money at present."

Fitch was butting a postwar depression. The currency of the Colonies had been greatly inflated during the Revolution, promissory notes of every sort had been issued, and now no one knew what the financial future held. Each state was pursuing its own fiscal policies; there was talk of a federal union, but should this be accomplished, it was impossible to guess what would become of the states' obligations or their ability to tax. However friendly the legislators might be to Fitch's scheme, they were in no position to give him a cent. Even the sale of his maps languished; the members of the Virginia Assembly, for instance, despite all their fine promises, sold only twenty.

Turning to private persons, Fitch outlined his scheme to Arthur Donaldson of Philadelphia, who possessed both means and a reputation for ingenuity; he had been one of the contractors to remove from the Delaware the *chevaux-de-frise* put there during the Revolution, and he had invented a machine for cleaning docks, "the hippopotamus," for which the Pennsylvania legislature had granted him a monopoly. He listened to Fitch with interest, but said he would have to consult Levi Hollingsworth before giving an answer.

Fitch returned to Warminster to wait, and shortly thereafter met an old woman who had just come from Philadelphia. When, as usual, he burst into talk about his steamboat, she said that a man in Philadelphia had also invented one "and that they thought it would be the greatest thing in the world." She could not remember the man's name, but when Fitch suggested Donaldson, she said that sounded right. Fitch rushed to Philadelphia and was soon knocking on Donaldson's door. He was out, but his wife told Fitch coldly that he had indeed invented a steamboat, which was different from Fitch's, and that he intended to go ahead with it.

Fitch had long known that the various legislatures had granted to Rumsey, Donaldson, and others exclusive rights for the use of inventions within state borders for a number of years. There being no federal government and no patent office, these monopolies were the contemporary equivalents of patents. Fitch had not applied for such an act, since "the taking out of an exclusive right before I saw some ways to perfect the scheme appeared to me almost too serious an affair." Unlike other, less painfully conscientious, projectors, he regarded such a right as a two-sided contract in which he agreed to complete the boat, and felt that in case of failure, "I should put my reputation so hurt that I dare not attempt it. . . . The thought of faithless dealing with a state was more horrible to me than a common executioner."

However, Donaldson was now treading on his heels. Fitch was convinced that if he raised enough money he could not fail, and at this moment he met Colonel Cox of New Jersey, a rich man who had a rich son-in-law, John Stevens, Jr. Cox stated that if Fitch could obtain an exclusive right "I should not want for money to get my scheme through; that he, and his son-in-law, Mr. Stephens [sic], would enable me to perfect it." Thus encouraged, Fitch appealed for a monopoly to the Pennsylvania and New Jersey legislatures, sending the latter body the following statement: "We, the subscribers, having examined the principles of the steamboat constructed by John Fitch, are of the opinion that it may be the means of improving the navigation of these states to great advantage and therefore deserves the protection and encouragement of the legislature." Signed were the names of fourteen citizens, including Cox and Stevens. Thus importuned, the New Jersey legislature passed on March 28, 1786, a law securing to Fitch for fourteen years "the sole and exclusive right of constructing, making, using and employing, or navigating, all and every species or kinds of boats, or water craft, which might be urged or impelled by the force of fire or steam, in all the creeks, rivers, etc., within the territory or jurisdiction of this state."

Delightedly Fitch hurried to Cox, but the rich man seemed to have forgotten his promise. "My astonishment and distress when I found myself under such serious engagements, and forsaken by those whom I esteemed my only patrons, I will not attempt to describe. . . . However, Colonel Cox advanced $20 toward it, but never received a single sou from Mr. Stephens, although it was promised by Colonel Cox that he would take one, two, or more shares."

Fitch would have been even more astonished and distressed if he had realized the chain of events he set going by calling to John Stevens' attention the possibility of steamboats. Not only was the New Jersey landowner to become an important steamboat inventor in his own right, but he was to interest his brother-in-law, Robert R. Livingston, who in turn was to employ the services of Robert Fulton.

For the moment, Fitch was more worried by Donaldson, who had petitioned the Pennsylvania legislature that any right granted Fitch be limited to the use of paddles, while he, Donaldson, be given a monopoly on the use of jet propulsion, which he claimed to have discovered. Now for the first of many times Fitch argued that his invention could not be limited; that he had invented the use of steam for boats however employed. He had, he said, tried seven different modes for applying the energy to the water, and could produce four different models, but this was only a beginning; he had thought of fifty different modes. His monopoly would be worth nothing, he argued, if forty-nine other monopolies were granted for forty-nine other ways of applying steam. And in any case, Donaldson had not invented jet propulsion, but had lifted it from Franklin's paper. The committee of the Pennsylvania legislature deferred action.

But Fitch had the New Jersey monopoly in his pocket, and on the strength of this he resolved to form a company. First he called on Franklin. The philosopher listened to his excited caller with benign good nature and was complimentary about the possibilities of his plan, but when Fitch asked him a sign a certificate of merit, he became evasive. This only augmented Fitch's flood of passionate arguments and glorious prophecies. Finally, Franklin led the inventor into the next room, where he opened a desk, took out five or six dollars, and tried to present them to Fitch. Recoiling as if struck, Fitch said he would only take the money as a subscription to his company. Franklin shook his head and again held out the bills. "The indignation which inflamed my blood," Fitch wrote, "could hardly be suppressed, yet I refused it with all the modesty I was master of. . . . I esteem that as one of the most imprudent acts of my life that I had not treated that insult with the indignity which he merited, and stamped the paltry ore under my feet."

Charging at a later date that Franklin had wanted to steal the steamboat from him, Fitch went so far as to suggest that the philosopher had after their first interview surreptitiously added the reference to "fire engines" in his maritime paper. Even Franklin's biographers criticize him for lack of imagination in not having realized the importance of what Fitch was doing. Perhaps the truth was that alone among the Philadelphia savants Franklin was sufficiently well informed to realize that Fitch had contributed nothing.

The idea of steamboats was not new, and the confident wild man had never seen a steam engine.

Others were more sanguine. In one week, Fitch was able to organize a company. Of forty shares, he kept half, selling the balance for $300 to fifteen backers. They were on the whole an undistinguished group, although not poor: small merchants, shop and tavern keepers, and a sprinkling of gentlemen with moderate influence.[2]

It was typical of the times that many men had to combine to subscribe so small a sum. English laws had long prohibited the establishment of financial institutions in America, and the revolution which had swept away these restrictions had been followed by a depression which had not encouraged economic enterprise. Since capital was still largely in land, there were few men with sufficient fluid resources to back a speculative venture single-handed. Companies like Fitch's were often formed, in which a group of men agreed to co-operate for a specific end, but unlike modern companies they did not attempt to start out with sufficient capital to complete their efforts. A partner agreed to take a percentage of the risk in order to achieve a percentage of the gain; his purchase of a share involved more of a promise than an outlay. After the small sum subscribed to get the venture started had been expended, the company would vote whether to levy further contributions on its members. Thus the promoter was forced to return again and again to his backers, and if at any moment they refused to support him further, the work would be brought to a standstill. Even if the vote were favorable, an individual backer did not have to abide by the will of the majority; should he refuse to honor a levy, he would only lose his share in an enterprise which he had already decided was a lost cause. Worst of all was the fact that if the company as a whole decided to take no further risks, they kept their ownership of the original rights; the promoter was prevented from going elsewhere to raise the cash he needed. Thus the fifteen men Fitch had enlisted to help him could, simply by losing interest, bring to an end his whole career as a steamboat inventor.

Fitch, however, was jubilant. With the $300 he had raised, which

seemed to him a munificent sum, he set out confidently to build a
steamboat.

Rumsey had spent the winter working on a very important idea.
A major problem involved in putting a steam engine on a boat, particularly a small boat such as he had in mind for the Potomac Canal,
was the weight of the machine and the large amount of space it
occupied. One of the worst offenders on both scores was the boiler,
which, in addition to being bulky and heavy, contained many pounds
of water. Conscious of this, Rumsey decided to substitute for the
conventional large reservoir a grillwork of pipes through which
the flames of the furnace would pass. This compact device, then
known as a pipe boiler and now as a tubular boiler, contained at
one time no more water than was immediately necessary to supply
steam, and the weight of the pipes themselves was small.

Late in January or early in February, the necessary pipes were
made at the Ante Eatum (Antietam) Iron Works, and modified by
a craftsman at Bath; the result, however, was so crude that Rumsey
did not even try to put the device together; he proceeded with his
old boiler. When the weather moderated, he put the machinery back
on his boat. Barnes tells us that in April 1786, the very month in
which Fitch organized his company, an attempt was made to move
Rumsey's vessel under steam. "The boat went against the current of
the Potomac, but many parts of the machinery being imperfect, and
some parts rendered useless by the heat of the steam, he was obliged
to have it repaired, which was done at the Great Falls, and she was
tried again, but failed in the repaired work, though it made many
powerful strokes before it failed, and sent the boat forward with
such power that one man was not able to hold her."

A neighbor's diary gives March 14, 1786, as the date of the first
attempt, and makes it clear that Rumsey was not present. The in-

ventor was still immersed in a multitude of tasks. Whether he still kept his inn at Bath is not clear, but he was building houses there. His work on the Potomac Canal might by itself have been one of the labors of Hercules. In addition, his mind was continually throwing up ideas for inventions that had nothing to do with boats; a year later he was to announce two different improvements in the application of water power to mills. His mind was so fertile that Jefferson, that citizen of the world, was to characterize him as "the most original and the greatest mechanical genius I have ever seen." Unlike Fitch, he did not suffer from an *idée fixe*; indeed, he seemed unable to select the most important idea from among the multitude thrown up by what Washington called "the ebullition of his genius."

The race between Fitch and Rumsey was beginning to resemble the famous race between the hare and the tortoise. Rumsey now ordered Barnes to lay the steamboat aside and perfect the pole boat. And soon he was engaged in an absorbing battle with the canal directors. When they raised his first assistant, Richardson Stewart, to an authority equal to his, Rumsey threatened to resign unless his own "pay and emoluments" were increased. To his horror, the directors accepted his resignation on July 4, 1786, and appointed Stewart to his place. Rumsey then came forward with pages and pages of charges of malfeasance against his rival; the directors dismissed them all on the grounds, as Washington himself stated, that they were "malignant, envious, and trifling."

When on September 9 the pole boat was given its first public trial, the inventor was too busy with his other affairs to be present. Under Barnes's direction, so Rumsey wrote Washington, the vessel with three tons of stone and one ton of spectators on board went upstream about 200 yards. The spectators were delighted, but Barnes was not. The poles had been too light to take a good hold on the bottom, and the whole contraption was very unsteady, since the machinery had been mounted on a single hull, not on a double boat as Rumsey had at first intended. "The people on board shouting and running backward and forward," Rumsey complained, "added much to this inconvenience."[3]

A few days later Rumsey joined Barnes and was about to make

another trial, although the current was not really running fast enough, when a crowd of villagers appeared on the bank. Remembering that the previous experiment had been received favorably, and that "spectators generally give their opinion according to what they see without any allowance for accidents," he rowed to shore, determined not to risk the good impression his invention had already achieved. "Nor have I made any further experiments since."

Although he wrote Washington that his test had proved that the pole boat could not fail to go upstream 3 miles an hour under proper conditions, Rumsey switched back to steam, perhaps because he thought it more suited to a single hull. When he reinstalled his steam machinery, he included the pipe boiler he had invented almost a year before but had never used. During a trial made in December, the very property of the new device that was eventually to be its great advantage proved his undoing. After the use of high pressure steam became common on boats, such boilers were standard equipment, one reason being that they supplied the vapor at temperatures higher than the boiling point. Rumsey, however, like almost all his contemporaries, used steam at little more than atmospheric pressure; the increased temperatures generated by his boiler only served to melt the solder and make the device useless before the boat could be got in motion.

On December 17, 1787, Rumsey wrote Washington that his pole-boat scheme was blocked because he did not have the money to build a second hull; only his desire to back up Washington's certificate kept him from abandoning it altogether. As for steam, "nearly a new machine [would have] to be made before anything could be done, as my new constructed boiler made such hot steam as to melt all the soft solder, and news coming frequently that Mr. Fitch would soon come forth. Add to this that the ice carried away my boat, and broke 30 feet out of her middle, a large family to support, no business going on, indebted, and what little money I could rake together expended."

At least for the moment, the hare was brought to a standstill. What of the tortoise?

VIII. *Fitch Discovers a Friend*

His company formed, Fitch needed to build an engine. Since, as he wrote, he "never was vain enough to suppose myself equal to that task," he searched around for an expert to help him. Steam-engine building in America was in its infancy. As yet there had been little need for it; our mines were still shallow enough to be cleared by more simple pumps, and everywhere water power abounded. A few English mechanics experienced in building Newcomen-type engines had drifted to this country, but lack of demand had forced them to shift to other occupations. One, John Nancarrow, operated an iron foundry near Philadelphia; to him Fitch now turned.

Nancarrow was slow and Fitch impatient, but finally, after thirty days during which Fitch called on him every day, the engineer produced a drawing "which was to work upon the old-fashioned plan of engines, and to have a weight to raise the piston." This, of course, was a Newcomen engine; Fitch, who must have heard somehow of Watt's separate condenser, "had assurance enough," as he wrote, "to set up my opinion against the one who was esteemed the greatest engineer in America." He rejected Nancarrow's draft.

He was then advised to consult Josiah Hornblower and Christopher Colles in New York. Hornblower, member of a great Cornish family of engine builders, had crossed the ocean to erect the New Jersey Newcomen engine which, as we have speculated, may have been Fitch's first inspiration. Having married an American heiress, Hornblower set up as a gentleman and abandoned mechanics. Colles, an Irish engineer and architect, had in 1775 proposed building a Newcomen engine to supply New York City with water.

Nancarrow, Hornblower, Colles: these were the men in America who possessed experience. Fitch had repudiated one, and now he decided not to bother with the other two. Shortly before, he had met a German watchmaker, Henry Voight, to whom he had taken an instant fancy. On the eve of going to New York to consult the experts, he had called on Voight and "in that evening's discourse it was easy for me to perceive that he was the first genius ever I was acquainted with." As darkness paled toward dawn, the artisans talked and drank, drank and talked, their voices rising in enthusiasm. We can reconstruct the scene from our knowledge of the men involved. The clockmaker was handsome and husky, physically a perfect foil for the gangling and ungainly Fitch. There was more brute strength in him, less of the delicate balance of nerves that made Fitch so sensitive and unpredictable an instrument. Voight pounded on the table as he made his points in a German accent, and the assurance in his voice did not carry with it the undertone of self-doubt that gave an almost hysterical tone to Fitch's rantings. His laugh was gargantuan and sure. Although he had never made a steam engine, he was certain he could build one. Had he not learned how to handle metal and even invented some machines when he had worked in a mint in his native Germany? They were wonderful machines as he described them there in the roof filled with sweet scents of tobacco and alcohol. He suggested to Fitch that they build a model which, after their ideas had been proved correct, they could expand into a great machine that would speed boats through the water. When Fitch reeled out at last into the motionless streets of dawn, he felt that he could look up to Voight "with the pleasing assurance and confidence that a wife can to her husband."

Fitch had found something he needed even more than a collaborator; he had found a friend. Although he had been willing to work with the gentlemen who had been recommended to him, we may be certain that he feared that Nancarrow or Hornblower or Colles would treat him as a lackey. He greatly preferred collaborating with a simple artisan like himself, who enjoyed liquor and good-fellowship; a man, indeed, who did not know too much more than he himself knew. They would work things out together, sharing their ignorance and their wisdom, their failures and excitements and successes as two pals should do. Side by side they would face the hostile world Fitch had always dreaded to face alone.

And so the ignorant artisan cast aside the wisdom of the Old World, spurned the whole long tradition of steam-engine building. He was not interested in what had been achieved before him; indeed, each revelation of the knowledge of the past tore down his self-esteem by reducing the originality of his own ideas.

Voight's reputation has always been so over-shadowed by Fitch's that few biographical details about him have been preserved. He was born during 1744, probably in Germany. We have his own statement that he worked for a German mint "in his younger years, in which he flatters himself that he had introduced some valuable improvements"; he must have come to America as an adult. It is impossible, however, to identify him with any certainty as either the "Hans Vogt" or the "Johann Heinrich Voight" who landed at Philadelphia respectively in 1769 and 1772. By 1775 he was doing business under his own name as a watchmaker. He was, so he asserted, "not an unuseful citizen during the [Revolutionary] war as his various manufacturing machines will evince."

One of his advertisements tells us that Voight, whose shop was on Second Street above Race Street, "carries on the watchmaking business in all its branches. Such as making all sorts of new watches upon all principles which they can be made on in Europe, etc. He flatters himself . . . that he has made some improvements in watches which will be of great utility. He likewise carries on the watch-case and watch-hand making business in all sorts of metal. Watchmakers in the country or in any other part may be supplied on the shortest notice. Watches and watch-cases gilt; clocks, watches, and watch-cases repaired at the most reasonable rates."

Concerning Voight's character we have only Fitch's statements, written many years later after the two friends had quarreled. "Mr. Voight is a plain Dutchman who fears no man and will always speak his sentiments. . . . It is true he is not a man of letters nor mathematical knowledge, but for my own part I would depend on him more than a Franklin, a Rittenhouse, an Ellicott, a Nancarrow, a Matlock all combined, as he is a man of superior mechanical abilities and very considerable natural philosophy." And again: "He is a man of high passions, confident in his own abilities, flushed to excess with the prospect of success and equally depressed with a disappointment. I esteem myself the more cool and dispassionate [!], and it absolutely required two men of the same disposition as ours to complete the great undertaking. . . . He is also a handsome man, and a man of good address, and familiar, friendly, and sociable to all, and a truly honest man in his trade, but the most griping miserly wretch on earth for the honors of invention."

That Voight brought with him from Germany little knowledge of steam engines is indicated by the struggles through which he and Fitch were to pass. In 1790 Fitch wrote, speaking of himself in the third person, "The great length of time and vast sum of money expended in bringing the scheme to perfection have been wholly occasioned by his total ignorance of the improved state of steam engines, a perfect knowledge of which has not been acquired without an infinite number of fruitless experiments, for not a person could be found who was acquainted with the minutiae of Boulton and Watt's new engine; and whether your petitioner's engine is similar or not to those in England, he is at this moment totally ignorant."

In confidence and high spirits, the partners set to work to build an engine. Only scraps of evidence have come down to us about their early mechanical efforts, and these are somewhat contradictory; we make out that being unsure what was the best engine design, they contemplated many different modes. Their first plan, which they sent to Hornblower for approval, seems to have included a separate condenser. Hornblower, whose experience had been with Newcomen engines, could see no advantage in this new discovery; he thought the proposed engine "rather too complicated. . . . The well and pump which you propose for obtaining partial vacuum is certainly unnecessary."

"We began," Fitch tells us, "a small model of a 1-inch cylinder, which proved unsuccessful, it being too small to overcome the friction." This impractical miniature, which cost about £3, is important to history because, although the work of his own hands, it was the first steam engine Fitch had ever seen.

By August the partners completed a larger model with a 3-inch cylinder. They seem to have discarded the separate condenser; we gather that the so-called "injection water," a thin spray which cooled the steam to produce condensation, was thrown by a pump directly into the cylinder. However, the engine contained another of Watt's important improvements, for it was double-acting, the steam working on both sides of the piston. Since the inventors clearly had no detailed information of Watt's work, but only knew in the broadest general terms what he had achieved, we must credit them with great ingenuity in making a double-acting engine work at all. Watt himself had struggled for many years with the problems involved.

In September Fitch wrote Franklin offering his model engine to the American Philosophical Society; it had cost $100, but he would accept whatever the Society wished to give him. With amazing candor for a man eager to make a sale, he continued, "The principles upon which it operates are good, and will in every respect communicate a satisfactory knowledge of a steam engine, and in some measure of its power. Yet it has some defects, which are chiefly the following, viz.: First, the stove and boiler being small, the steam is not sufficient to move the piston more than about 20 strokes per minute. Second, the piston being worked both ways by steam, its rod soon becomes heated, that it cannot move home one way, by a space of from half an inch to 2 inches, by its then creating steam. Third, the pumps which alternately inject water into the cylinder cause too small friction. Yet, notwithstanding these difficulties, the piston moves with considerable velocity, when unloaded, and is supplied with steam."

As we have seen, Fitch had been overawed by Franklin into giving up in favor of pump propulsion his more advanced ideas of driving a boat with paddles; he had even ordered a hull with the necessary pipes. Now, under Voight's urging, he countermanded the order. The 45-foot skiff which was delivered to him in the spring of 1786 looked like any other boat. Although many writers tell us that the model engine was placed in this vessel and the whole thing steamed along, this could never have been intended, since the engine, with its 3-inch cylinder, was much too small. As the documents make clear, the inventors used the skiff as a proving ground for methods of propulsion which they manipulated by hand.

In July Fitch and Voight tried out several devices they had invented: "a screw of paddles," an endless chain bearing perpendicular boards, and some others. After each new contraption had been attached to the skiff, they pushed off into the Delaware hopefully. From the banks and from their own craft in the river, the professional boatmen watched with broad smiles. Determined to impress their mocking audience, Fitch and Voight sweated at the cranks which were supposed to drive their new-fangled paddles through the water. Their muscles ached and their breath came out in gasps, but the skiff barely moved. Delightedly, the boatmen jeered. When their last device had proved a failure like the others, Voight "as soon as we landed, stole off from me and let me alone to take care of our machinery and stand the scoffs and sneers of those who waited our arrival." Fitch was also distressed, and "to remedy that" hurried to a tavern where he consumed considerable "West India produce."

The next day he and Voight were ashamed to see each other, "and my study then was how I could get clear of the scheme with honor." He was glad when the arrival of night made it possible for him to go to bed, but he was too worried to sleep. As he tossed in anguish, a vision came to him of the canoes in which he had traversed half-explored western waters, and then suddenly he realized how to make a steam engine paddle like a crew of Indians. He would attach paddles, like those usually operated by men, to arms which were motivated unevenly by the turning of a crank. When the crank moved downward, the paddles would be pulled through the water to the stern, and when the crank went up, they would return toward the bow through the air.[1]

"About 12 o'clock at night the idea struck me, . . . and by the time the watchman cried one o'clock, grew too uneasy to keep my bed, thinking it to be a thing of such importance that I ought not to risk a single hour of my life for fear it might be lost to the world, but that it ought to be committed to paper." Once out of bed, he was too excited to return. Would day never come so he could tell

Voight? The instant the sun first peeped over the horizon, his foot-steps were loud in the silent streets as he ran to awake his friend.

Soon the scheme was applied to the skiff. When the surly boat-men rowed up and offered to race, Fitch and Voight delightedly agreed, and, so Fitch wrote, their clumsy-looking mechanism carried them first to the mark.

Fitch now felt his invention was complete: his cranks and paddles rowed and his model steam engine moved, despite defects he was certain he could remedy. It was only necessary to combine the two on a large scale. On July 28 he wrote his stockholder, Stacy Potts, "We have now tried every part, and reduced it as certain as any-thing can be that we shall not come short of 10 miles per hour, if not 12 or 11. I will say 14 in theory and 10 in practice. The com-pany is to meet tomorrow evening and I doubt not they will pursue it on a large scale and make a boat of 20 tons burthen, and a 12-inch cylinder. I have lately invented an easy, simple, and practical way of rowing a boat, applicable for an engine, where I am persuaded that the strength of two men will do the work of three. At any rate, with one man in our boat we fear no one man going before us not-withstanding our oars are not properly adjusted."

Fitch felt on the verge of success, but the members of his com-pany had lost interest. Potts used his enthusiastic letter as an excuse for bowing out. "I shall reflect with pleasure on the encouragement I have given" to an invention that would so benefit mankind, but now that it "is likely to be lucrative and interesting to the sharers," he wished to withdraw as he had not entered the scheme to make money. For whatever reason, not enough of the other members came to the company meetings to establish a quorum. "If a levy should be made, the absent members would esteem their money taken from them by me, and would much prefer seeing a common beggar come to their doors than myself."

The financial difficulties which were never again to leave him now descended on Fitch. All the hardships he had ever experienced—sickness, leaving his child, his Indian captivity—were nothing, he wrote, to his distress "in raising money from my best friends. Could money have been extracted from my limbs, amputation would have often taken place, provided the disjointed part could have been readily joined, rather than to make the demands which I have. I need not add to this the insults of populace, for none was felt by me excepting only those designed for my patrons, and those only that were offered by them." To give the finishing touch, the Philosophical Society showed no interest in buying his model engine.

In September 1786 Fitch notified the Pennsylvania legislature that he would gladly postpone the granting of the exclusive right he had petitioned for if they would lend him £150. "Mr. Voight and myself are sure that we can make an engine; nay, we are vain enough to believe that we can make one as good as they can in Europe," he wrote. "Since the scheme is approved by all men of science who have examined it, and there never has been one, even of my most bitter enemies, that has ever attempted to point out how it will miscarry," should the Assembly not support him, "what would be said of us in other countries? Would they not say that there was a poor fellow in America that proposed a plan that would enrich America at least three times as much as all that vast country North West of the Ohio . . . and this he demonstrated as clear as one of Euclid's problems; and not only that, but ascertained it in miniature, so as it could not admit of a doubt—and notwithstanding he applied to Congress and to each of the middle states, they would not give him a single sou to execute his plan, because they thought that he could do it by begging and save them the expense. May heaven forbid that such a stigma should be placed to the account of the country that gave me birth! . . .

"Could I by any means raise sufficient money, I would not ask it from the legislature; but there is such a strange infatuation in mankind that it seems they would rather lay out their money in balloons and fireworks, and be a pest to society, than to lay it out in something that would be of use to themselves and country." Even if the boat failed, he pointed out, "the state gets two engineers by it"; having taught themselves how to build steam engines, he and Voight would save "many hundreds of pounds from going to Europe for that very article."

The committee to which Fitch's petition was referred recommended the loan of £150, but the legislature disagreed by a close vote. Then Fitch renewed in several states his appeal for monopolies, which, since they cost nothing, were much easier to obtain than cash grants. Delaware gave him an exclusive right to all steamboats on February 3, 1787; New York on March 9; and Pennsylvania, after determining to ignore Donaldson's claim, on March 28.

Although Fitch was ignorant that Rumsey was also building steamboats, Rumsey knew all about Fitch; it is hard to understand why the Virginia inventor did not enter some objection to the laws being obtained by his rival, which were closing to him the waters of state after state. Rumsey's passion for secrecy must have had something to do with it; he was unwilling to proclaim publicly what he was doing. Clearly he hoped that the loosely worded monopolies granted him for his pole boat would be interpreted to include steam, thus giving him a prior right. Yet he should have been worried when Pennsylvania, which had passed his vague monopoly law, gave another to Fitch for the use of steam. It may be that Rumsey relied on the influence of Washington to pull him through when his boat was ready. None of these explanations, however, seem adequate.

Rumsey's strange inaction was to have a major influence on the development of the steamboat. Since his friends were more influential, and since he had actually got moving first, had Rumsey entered the battle at this time he would in all probability have blasted Fitch out of the water. And had Fitch failed to receive his monopolies, there seems little doubt that his backers would have deserted him, bringing his labors to an end.

As it was, Fitch was able to use his Delaware monopoly as a basis on which to reorganize his company in February 1787, doubling the number of shares and securing additional money with which to proceed.[2] He had already published in the *Columbian Magazine* a description of what he intended to do:

"The steam engine is to be similar to the late improved steam engines in Europe, those [the following] alterations excepted: the cylinder is to be horizontal and the steam to work with equal force at each end thereof. The mode of forming a vacuum is believed to be entirely new; also of letting the water into it, and of letting it off against the atmosphere without any friction. [No documents make clear the nature of the methods Fitch had in mind.] The undertakers are also of opinion that their engine will work with equal force to those late improved engines, it being a 12-inch cylinder. They expect it to move with a clear force, after deducting friction, of between 11 and 12 hundred pounds weight, which force is to be applied to the turning of an axle tree on a wheel of 18 inches diameter.* The piston is to move about 3 feet, and each vibration of the piston turns the axle tree about two-thirds round. They propose to make the piston strike 30 strokes a minute, which will give the axle tree about 40 revolutions.

"Each revolution of the axle tree moves 12 bars 5½ feet. As six oars come out of the water, six more enter the water, which makes a stroke of about 11 feet each revolution. The oars work perpendicularly, and make a stroke similar to the paddles of a canoe. The cranks of the axle tree act upon the oars about one-third of their length from their lower end, on which part of the oar the whole force of the axle tree is applied. The engine is placed in about two-thirds of the boat [a tremendous proportion], and both the action and reaction of the piston operate to turn the axle tree the same way."

Fitch began this description in the future tense, but soon turned unconsciously to the present, so sure was he that his boat would work as planned.

---

* This was done by means of chains attached to the piston rod and wrapped around a drum which worked ratchet wheels on the driving axle; a balance wheel, heavily weighted with lead, was to continue to turn during the slack periods of the engine, giving a semblance of even motion.

IX. A Miniature Painter

As he paced the streets of Philadelphia, Fitch must often have passed a younger man as tall as he. Fitch would have been carrying a tool or a casting or a peculiar shaped piece of wood; he would have been spotted with grease perhaps, and certainly his clothes would have been messy. The other man would have been neatly dressed, even if his coat was a little thin at the elbows, and in his hand would have been the neat wooden box in which he stored the chips of ivory, the colors, and the brushes of a miniature painter. Perhaps the artist paused to stare at the inventor of steamboats, whose crazy imaginings were well known and a general laughing stock, but Fitch would not have noticed, since he was used to being an object of curiosity. And what interest could he have in that obscure limner, Robert Fulton?

The painter, however, moved with a flourish; he was well pleased with himself. Although still under twenty-one, he had conquered much adversity and become a successful artisan; he hoped soon to be as substantial a man as his father had been before calamity altered the fortunes of that once prosperous merchant tailor.

Robert Fulton senior, we are told, was a Scotch-Irishman who emigrated from Kilkenny to Philadelphia, where for a few years he engaged in mercantile pursuits. Our first definite information about him, however, shows him in 1735 already a tailor in Lancaster, Pennsylvania, member of a frontier community that had been laid out as a town only five years before. That he did some trading on the side is indicated by the account books of a Philadelphia merchant from whom he bought in less than two years goods valued at £375.13.8¾. Once he purchased five hogsheads of rum in two months; he could hardly have drunk it all himself. A substantial citizen, the elder Fulton held several village offices, rising to assistant burgess of the borough. In 1765 he married Mary, daughter of Joseph Smith of Oxford township; she could not have been very rich since on her father's death she inherited only £5.

Lancaster grew with sensational rapidity, and the elder Fulton seems to have prospered. Yet in 1765 he gave up his trade and became a farmer. Raising the large sum of £965, partly in cash and partly through a mortgage, he bought 393 acres in Little Britain township near the outskirts of the city. He had hardly moved to the two-story stone farmhouse by a crossroads when on November 14 his patience in accepting a succession of three daughters was rewarded; his wife presented him with a son whom he gleefully named after himself.

Fulton was to tell his friends that he "attached no importance to the circumstances of his birth"; concerning his childhood, he was as reticent as Fitch had been frank. Thus few details have come down to us. It is clear, however, that as the baby's eyes were able to take in more and more of the world, he saw around him defeat and decay. His father had made a mistake in buying the Little Britain farm; until lime came into general use as a fertilizer during the 1830s, the land of the region was singularly unproductive. Year after year the elder Fulton plowed and harrowed, put in the seed, weeded, cultivated, and dreamed optimistically of the yield. But the plants that emerged in even rows were always scrawny. Harvest time, the traditional season of rejoicing, was a grim period when it was unwise to compare intake with outlay. There must have been long faces around the house, perhaps even hunger and want.

In 1771, when the boy was seven years old, his father's name no longer appeared on the tax list of Little Britain township; the mortgage on the farm had been foreclosed and the Fulton family evicted. They returned to Lancaster, where Robert senior tried to set up again as a tailor. Whether he could have achieved prosperity once more it is impossible to say, for three years later he died.[1] He made no will, probably having practically nothing to leave. His son, it is said, was sent to live with an uncle, but was unhappy there and insisted on returning home.

Now we enter the period of the inventor's life about which least can be ascertained. The court records, which have buoyed us up so far, are innocent of the Fulton name; we cannot even guess how Mrs. Fulton supported her brood of three daughters and two sons. Since biographers, like nature, abhor a vacuum, and almost a dozen lives of Fulton have been written, there are legends galore. At the age of fourteen, we are told, he propelled a boat by hand power on a local pond with a paddle wheel of his own invention. If this really happened, it is inexplicable that years later when Fulton was struggling to prove his right to the paddle wheel, he never mentioned this incident which would have given him priority over several of his rivals. The other tales of his miraculous childhood inventions, most of them first published in 1856, are equally improbable and will not be repeated here.

Much has been made of the fact that Fulton spent his childhood in the same small city with William Henry, the steamboat pioneer; we are given graphic descriptions of the interviews between the famous man and the eager boy. Yet it is unlikely that they ever discussed steam. Henry was one of the most prominent men in the province, Fulton an obscure and poverty-stricken child. Furthermore, shortly after Henry first spoke of steamboats in 1775, he was engulfed in the Revolution; an armed sentry stood in front of the house where he carried on business of national importance. And before Henry had put his ideas on paper, Fulton had left Lancaster for Philadelphia.

Yet legend is probably correct when it tells us that Fulton hung around the workshops of the gunsmiths, and was occasionally allowed to handle a tool. It is hard to believe that a boy who was to grow into a mechanical genius paid no attention to the opportunities of playing with machines that Lancaster offered. However, for the time being he was more interested in drawing pictures.

Having taught him how to read and write, his mother sent him when he was eight to a school kept by Caleb Johnson, a narrow-minded Quaker whose Tory leanings were to get him into trouble during the Revolution. One of Fulton's classmates brought to school some colors mixed in cockle-shells. Fascinated by the bright pigments, Robert begged and begged until he was given half. The two friends started to paint in rivalry, but Fulton's pictures were so much better that his companion was ashamed and gave him all the colors. After that, so a classmate remembers, he neglected his studies and was often beaten by the schoolmaster.

Lancaster boasted a tradition of painting as well as mechanics. More than a decade before Robert was born, Benjamin West, an innkeeper's son living two days' ride distant, had begun to draw without any instruction. His Quaker neighbors, who had been kept by their religion from seeing many pictures, considered the childish scribbles wonders of art, and soon his reputation had traveled so far that he was called to Lancaster, where he painted William Henry and other leading citizens. From Lancaster he went to Philadelphia, and from Philadelphia to Rome, and from Rome to London, making a sensation everywhere. By the time of Fulton's boyhood, the so-called "American Raphael" had become court painter to George III and perhaps the most admired artist in the Western world. Naturally writers have tried to establish some connection between West and the Fulton family; none of the evidence holds water.[2] Yet Robert may well have seen West's paintings and been inspired by the success of a local boy who had risen so far from circumstances somewhat like his own.

Fulton was ten when the American Revolution began to roll into Lancaster. It came as a bedraggled column of British sailors, marching forlornly under the bayonets of Yankee guards. The city was so far from the battlefront that it was made a leading depot for prisoners of war. The privates were lodged in the barracks, while the officers lived in taverns or private homes. British gentlemen on parole walked the streets like free citizens, among them the yet obscure John André. Since André was to become famous, and since he dabbled in painting, writers have postulated that he gave Fulton instruction; again no evidence transmutes legend into historical fact.

Daily the tempo of life in wartime Lancaster grew faster. The hammering in the gun shops echoed far into the night like rifle fire; Continental troops mustered in the square to protect the town from rumored Indian raids; the boom of cannon announcing important news from the battlefront brought the entire population to their doors. And always there was the arrival of more prisoners of war, thousands of men bringing with them fever and lice, squalor, poverty, and despair. On the evening of June 4, 1777, the prisoners in the barracks disarmed their guards. All the church bells sprang to life, drums pounded in every street, doors opened, disgorging militiamen. Was there excitement or fear in the twelve-year-old boy's heart; was he relieved or disappointed when the prisoners gave up after the first volley?

That fall the main British army landed at Elkton on the Chesapeake; soon dusty, terrified riders brought the rumor that Lancaster was to be invaded. The rich began packing their belongings; all night long the streets were loud with fleeing wagons. But the British took Philadelphia instead. Then the great men of the Revolution appeared in the Lancaster streets, for the Continental Congress had adjourned to that city. Fulton looked on the faces of John Adams and John Hancock, Thomas Paine and David Rittenhouse.

On October 20 a messenger brought the news that Washington had driven Howe back into his ships and retaken Philadelphia. That night and the next the town was almost as light as day, for everyone had illuminated his windows; if any person failed to do so, he was considered a Tory and his windows were smashed. Enthusiastic militiamen roamed the streets, drinking, singing, shooting in the air. Then the town was more dark and quiet than ever; the rumor had proved false.

Hardly had one sensation died before another appeared. Suddenly the town was loud with German voices; a fine Teutonic band played in the public square. More than two thousand Hessians captured at Saratoga had been marched into Lancaster. The barracks being already crowded, the privates lived in mud huts under conditions of the most terrible misery. The bewildered German peasants, who had been dragged by force into a war about which they knew nothing, were a perpetual butt for the jokes of the local youngsters; Fulton is said to have lampooned them in caricature.

Thus the alarms of war, its excitement, its miseries, its possibilities of glory were woven into the being of the boy who was to spend much of his adult life in the effort to invent new, more deadly instruments of battle. And three other aspects of Fulton's childhood were also through him to influence the development of the steamboat: his interest in art, the mechanical background supplied by Lancaster, and the searing poverty that left a scar on his soul.

Recent biographers have one after another said that Fulton did not go to Philadelphia until he was seventeen; as an example of how history gets scrambled, it might be amusing to trace the development of this mistake. Fulton's first biographer, his intimate friend Colden, said that by the time he was seventeen he was making money in Philadelphia as a miniature painter. Writing in the same year, Delaplaine enlarges on Colden's statement, stating that "while yet very young" Fulton was apprenticed to "a Mr. Andrews, a jeweler" in Philadelphia and that by the time he was seventeen "he was already in receipt of a tolerable income from the sale of portraits and landscapes." The next biographer, Reigert, ignoring Delaplaine and reading Colden carelessly, fixed on the year seventeen and stated that Fulton had gone to Philadelphia at that age. His version was repeated from book to book until Dickinson, Fulton's most modern biographer, coming again on Delaplaine's statement, spurned it because it conflicted with accepted fact.

Actually there can be little doubt that at an early age Fulton was apprenticed to Jeremiah Andrews, an English jeweler who reached New York from London in 1774, and moved to Philadelphia probably two years later. According to his advertisements, he carried "a neat assortment of jewelry of his own manufacture equal to any imported. Ladies' paste shoe buckles of the newest patterns, gentlemen's knee and stock buckles, garnet hoop rings and every other kind of rings, lockets and brooches, plain or with stone, hair worked in the neatest manner, mourning rings made on the shortest notice, with every other kind of jewelry by their humble servant, Jeremiah Andrews, living in Second Street, between Chestnut and Walnut Streets, Philadelphia."

Fulton had been very fortunate, for the trade of jeweler, a recent offshoot from silversmithing, was an aristocrat among eighteenth-century crafts. As he leaned over his master's work bench, the boy learned to shape objects with a delicate precision that would be of great value to either a painter or a mechanic. Indeed, it was no coincidence that so many early American artists—Fulton, Morse, Peale—were inventors as well. The arts and crafts had not become separated as they are today, when many a painter, his mind full of airy conceptions, can wield a brush but is likely to smash his finger with a hammer. Up to the middle of the last century, manually trained Americans, interested in the form, structure, and shape of actual objects, saw no basic difference between constructing a picture and constructing a machine.

Instead of following slavishly in his master's footsteps and doing the menial tasks assigned him, Fulton developed a specialty of his own. It was fashionable to commemorate the dead by carrying rings or lockets decorated with the hair of the deceased woven into an intricate pattern. Andrews advertised "hair worked in the neatest manner"; this extremely delicate work appealed to Fulton.

Often the hair designs were placed on the reverse of a locket on the front of which was a water color of a tomb with a vaguely Grecian figure weeping beside it. From painting such scenes it was a very small step to doing portraits in miniature. And there were many opportunities for a miniature painter in a jeweler's shop. The little likenesses on chips of ivory were worn about the person, usually in lockets whose chains and cases were made by the jeweler, sometimes even set in rings. A jeweler usually had a connection with a miniature painter; it was even better if the whole product could be produced in one shop. Little by little, such work was given to Fulton. Since there is no evidence that his master ever painted miniatures, the apprentice must have found elsewhere whatever instruction he received in this difficult craft. Critics have suggested that he may have studied with either James or Charles Willson Peale; perhaps he merely imitated the ivories of these leading miniaturists.

The earliest picture that can be assigned to Fulton is a pen-and-ink drawing made in 1783, a reproduction of a French print showing little but care in copying. Mutually contradictory miniatures have been attributed to his professional period in Philadelphia; the pair of portraits of Mr. and Mrs. John Wilkes Kittera are typical of the group that is most likely to be authentic. Unsophisticated in the extreme, showing the naïve freshness of self-taught artisan painters, they fall into the category commonly known as "American primitives." The drawing, although the result of aching care, is poor. Some parts of the faces are flat; other features, such as the ends of the noses and the points of the chins, have been modeled too heavily and stand out from the ivory like little hard round balls. Depicted with a network of clumsily crossed lines, Mrs. Kittera's hair resembles a bird's nest perched on her head. The coloring is neither bright nor very harmonious.

Such flaws exist in large numbers, but, as is often the case with naïve pictures, the whole effect is much more charming than the technical skill of the painter seems to warrant. Within their limitations, the miniatures are complete and serious works of art, a total and unself-conscious expression of the capacities of the painter. Most delightful perhaps is the pleasure he reveals in the exact depiction of little gay details: the pearls on Mr. Kittera's waistcoat which, although smaller than the head of a pin, are rendered with literal and loving care; the meticulously painted roses on his wife's bosom, which form the brightest touch of color in the whole composition.

What do these pictures promise for the artist's future development? It is as hard to say as to judge a child's ability from a high-school theme. Certainly no genius is indicated, but there is hard work here, and seriousness. If while gaining technical proficiency the painter can keep his sincerity, if without making use of half-felt traditional expedients he can change the clumsy freshness of the amateur into the deeply felt grace of the professional, then perhaps the artist will find a worthy rank among the professional painters of his time. But, so the history of American art continually reveals, it was extremely difficult for artisan painters not to discard their primitive virtues when they attempted to immerse themselves in the great current of European art. As in society the self-made gentleman is most likely to go in for artificial airs, so the self-made artist is most likely to pursue sophistication for its own sake alone. Yet if he can accept the brilliance of the metropolis without throwing over the simple sincerity of the provinces, he may well be a greater painter than those who never trod in humble paths.[3]

The Philadelphia directory for 1785 lists "Fulton, Robert, Miniature painter, corner of Second and Walnut Streets"; this is the first appearance of the inventor's name in any record. Since the address is the same as that given in Andrews' advertisements, we may assume that the young man was still working in close co-operation with his preceptor, probably in the same workshop.

Before he was twenty-one, Fulton was struck by a misfortune that might easily have stopped the career of a less resolute man. He contracted a racking cough; soon he was showing "other symptoms indicating a disposition to pulmonary complaints." His friends advised him to take the medicinal waters at Bath, in Virginia.

First, however, Fulton accompanied his mother to Washington County, Pennsylvania, an extreme frontier district where her brother was the Presbyterian minister. There, describing himself as "yeoman" and "miniature painter of the city of Philadelphia," he signed a deed buying his mother a farm for £80. His biographers say that he earned the money from his art, but this seems unlikely since miniature painting was not a lucrative trade and we have no reason to believe that his business was large. Documents show that part if not all of the sum was borrowed, and that the venture was regarded as a family liability; an argument developed later over which member should pay the debt.[4]

Fulton then went to Bath, probably arriving there in May 1786. The man who was to be credited with the invention of the steamboat had an uncanny way of turning up wherever steamboats were projected. Some of Rumsey's machinery was at that moment being built in the village, and the boat was on the point of its first trial. History is tantalizingly uncommunicative as to whether Fulton heard of the venture or was interested. We do know that some years later in London he was an acquaintance of Rumsey's; perhaps they met at this time.

His visit to Bath was, from another aspect, a turning point. At Philadelphia, the yeoman artist had associated with other artisans; if he painted a gentleman, it was only a business relationship. But "in the unrestrained intercourse of a watering place" he found himself talking as an equal with men in fine linen shirts who had been to Europe, and he succeeded in impressing them as he impressed everybody his whole life long. He was a tall and graceful man, probably not as heavy as he was later to become, with a definite gleam of genius in his face. From large and deep sockets, his dark eyes shone with the fire of excitement and energy, and the words came from his full lips in an impetuous stream. But unless he was very different from the person he became a few years later, all this flash and flare was well controlled; his energy seemed to be driving for specific purposes, toward a future he could see. And he was never one to underestimate his previous achievements or to let fact stand in the way of an impression he wished to make.

Setting themselves up, as all gentlemen must, as connoisseurs, Fulton's new friends admired his paintings, and told him that all he needed to be one of the greatest artists of the age was to study in Europe. The magic name of West was invoked; it is said that Fulton was given a letter of introduction to the King's painter. After a few weeks in Bath, he returned to Philadelphia, dissatisfied with all he had known before. How could he admire the paintings of his fellow provincial artists now that he had dreamed of European masterpieces; how could he be happy with his yeoman friends after he had bought drinks for gentlemen? Fulton, whose ambitions never knew any bounds, was poised for the flight that would carry him further than even he imagined.

But first there was the necessity of raising funds for the trip, an astronomical amount when compared to the earnings of a miniature painter. Fulton set to work even harder than before; he branched out into oil painting and pastels. At this time he moved from Andrews' address into a shop of his own, advertising on June 6, 1786:

"Robert Fulton, miniature painter and hair worker, is removed from the northeast corner of Walnut and Second Streets to the west side of Front Street, one door above Pine Street, Philadelphia." It is said that Franklin befriended him and that he painted the philosopher's portrait; the picture, if it ever existed, is lost. The granddaughter of a rich merchant, John Ross, was told that when Fulton was "young and poor" he came to her father with a letter from Franklin. The merchant suggested to the painter that he might make big money by drawing crayon likenesses of young ladies in society, and offered his daughter as the first subject. Many years later, when he was famous, Fulton remembered that he had been "unknown and friendless" and she "a beautiful young girl."

Fulton's new Front Street studio was within a short block of the Delaware. Outside his door, perhaps visible from his window, was the perpetual movement of ships. Sometimes as the pageant moved by, he must have found it hard to keep his mind on his painting and hair work. Since Fitch tried out his new method of propulsion shortly after Fulton had moved to Front Street, the painter may well have seen a strange craft pushed grotesquely up the river by mechanical antennae like a water spider's. If Fulton saw this wonder, did he curse himself for always running after distractions, and then return to his easel? Or did he hurry to the quay to get a better view? Of one thing we may be certain; we will not find the answer in any of Fulton's writings. He never admitted any connection with steamboats before his own.

While Fitch was building a full-sized engine so that he could make his first actual steamboat trial, Fulton was raising money to leave Philadelphia. Patriotic merchants, eager to lift the cultural level of their provincial homeland, had sent Benjamin West abroad, and the result had been so happy that financing European trips for promising painters had become an American habit. Thus Fulton was able to borrow the necessary funds, one Samuel Scorbitt being named as his principal patron. During the summer of 1787, he sailed for London. In his pocket he had only 40 borrowed guineas and a letter to West, but his mind was filled with a belief in his own special destiny. The poor widow's son who had for a few years been earning a competence as a hair worker and miniature painter had somewhere, somehow, acquired an awe-inspiring confidence in his own powers. He did not doubt that before his 40 guineas were spent he would be able to compete successfully with the English artists who had been represented to him as the greatest then alive. As for steamboats, if they had entered his consciousness at all, they existed only on the very periphery.

X. *Triumphs All Round*

Fitch was very happy during the spring of 1787 as he built his steamboat; all his dreams seemed on the point of fruition. Approaching a machine-age problem from the point of view and with the tools of an eighteenth-century craftsman, he had no conception of the vast number of elements that would have to be co-ordinated before a steamboat would function efficiently. He did not realize that in addition to forms, you had to deal with stresses and proportions and the properties of materials. Since he had decided to go back to his earlier idea of using a Watt engine, he needed, he knew, an air pump and a condenser, but to build them seemed easy. He did not understand that when you changed the shape or size of your condenser by a fraction, you actually had a different mechanism on your hands.

From a general idea of its principles, Fitch set out to reinvent the details of a Watt engine; we need not share his surprise when troubles began developing. No sooner was the machine put together in May 1787 than he discovered that the wooden caps to the cylinder admitted air, and more serious, that his idea of a horizontal cylinder was untenable, since the piston leaked. He had completely to rebuild the engine with a vertical cylinder, "a very tedious and expensive job. We also discovered that our steam valves were very imperfect, although they was ingeniously contrived by my friend, Mr. Voight, and which every man of science would have approved until the defects were discovered by actual experiment. In lieu of which, he then invented a double cock with the steam to pass and repass through said cock to the cylinder, . . . and although it is simple I esteem it as one of the most ingenious inventions."

The engine was again set up, but now the condensation was bad. Several condensers had been tried, each at an expense which irked the members of the company; "we were obliged to throw them away and to apply a pipe condenser, the production of Mr. Voight's teeming brain." Having persuaded their backers "to try one experiment more," the partners installed the new device. This time the steamboat actually moved over the waters of the river, but Fitch, whose eyes were always staring at perfection, did not regard this as a triumph. He wrote that the condenser "answered the purpose exceeding well, but produced a greater disaster. The engine worked so brisk that we could not find steam to supply it." After the boat had gone a short distance, they had to stop and wait for the boiler to generate more steam.

When Fitch went to the company to ask for money for a larger boiler, the members, who had been led to believe each change would bring perfection, expressed great unwillingness. "I am so unfortunate that I am not able to communicate my ideas by word of mouth," Fitch tells us; he wrote out a passionate appeal. The nervously tortured man, whose whole life had been a search for a logical path through the labyrinths of the world, expressed not discouragement but faith, for he felt he was dealing with an impersonal force that would yield once it was understood. "It is sure that the laws of God in mechanism have permitted a steam engine to work on board of a small boat equally as well as if it had been placed on land, and rowed the boat at the same time, under good way and notwithstanding we had frequently to stop and for no other reason than for the want of steam; and the same law will permit me to make steam sufficient on board vessel as on land, was my boiler properly constructed, unless nature should recoil so far as that the boiling of water would not produce it." His difficulties were due to a lack of knowledge of God's laws, which "are equally positive in every branch of mechanism, and in all sciences, as other things, and I do not know of more than one man on earth that perfectly understands them all, and would willingly give a thousand pounds, if I had it, to be made infallible and consecrated Pope for one year. I acknowledge I was vain in undertaking a business which I knew nothing about, that has taken near a century to bring to perfection—I mean the steam engine—especially when it was to be applied to a different purpose from any heretofor in use." Yet, since like causes produce like effects, and he had proved his engine and oars, he could not fail.

Then he launched into a series of financial arguments. A steamboat, he insisted, could compete with a stagecoach if it went equally fast, since it "would save a great expense of horse flesh and feed—travelers better accommodated than in wagons, their fare cheaper, and less fatigue." He presented figures to show that a steamboat could travel up the Mississippi more cheaply than a barge poled by manpower, and emphasized again the fact that the larger the boat the more easily it could be driven by steam.

Now he turned from his new vision of applied science to its exact opposite, to the old vision which had haunted him before: a savage paradise. "But why those earnest solicitations, to disturb my nightly repose, and fill me with the most excruciating anxieties; and why not act the part for myself, and retire under the shady elms on the fair banks of the Ohio, and eat my coarse but sweet bread of industry and content, and when I have done, to have my body laid in the soft, warm, and loamy soil of the Banks, with my name inscribed on a neighboring poplar, that future generations, when traversing the mighty waters of the West, in the manner that I have pointed out, may find my grassy turf, and spread their cupboard on it, and circle round their cheerful noggins of whiskey, with three times three, till they should suppose a son of misfortune could never occupy the place. . . .

"I thank my God for the perseverance he has given me, in carrying to such a length as I have, and for the tranquillity of mind which I feel at present, although in some respects I have thrown myself in very alarming circumstances, but should I once reach the fertile plains of Kentucky, and there enjoy my health, I would bid defiance to the blind, unguided frowns of fortune, and when once in calm retirement, the promise of riches or favor of courts will not be solicited, I have long resided in the state of Pennsylvania, and confess that I leave it with reluctance. . . . I now expect to become a citizen of another state. It would have given me a heartfelt pleasure, could I have rendered more and an immediate service to the state than I have, yet please myself with the idea, that when I am sleeping under the poplar in the lofty forests of Kentucky, my feeble attempts will be found to be of that use which I now wish them to be. Yet doubt not but I shall be censured by the giddy and unthinking, but if the number does not exceed those that could mend what I have done, I retire content fully satisfied to say farewell. . . ."

Here is a passage of such eloquence that it might well find its place in an anthology of American writing. Had fortune led him into different paths, Fitch might well have been a poet.

Moved by his words, the stockholders furnished enough money for the larger boiler and, when it was installed during August 1787, the various parts of the engine were at last in something approaching harmony. Fitch has given us no details of the first trial, but we can visualize the anxiety with which he and Voight lit the fire under the new iron vessel on its base of brick. They watched with eagerness as the steam pressure rose; and then at last came the moment for starting the engine. Soon the piston began to rise and fall of its own volition. Then the mooring was cast off and the power applied to the oars. With a delightful clanking, the cumbersome mechanism pulled the paddles through the water; the boat moved slowly away from the pier. So far so good, but would it keep on moving? The fire burned and the engine steamed and the oars rowed minute after minute without interruption, while the little craft with its long legs crawled like a water bug up against the tide. Elation must have flowered in the hearts of the inventors, but it was followed by disappointment.

The boatmen on the river had at first stared in amazement to see the peculiar creation actually go, but when they calculated the speed of the steamboat, the smiles returned to their faces. Undoubtedly some strong young man in a rowboat amused himself by racing the contraption, and although Fitch and Voight fired the engine higher and willed speed with all their might, the mechanical monster fell behind, for this boat of Fitch's never went faster than 3 miles an hour. It could not, he realized, be put into service on the Delaware, since it was much slower than the stagecoaches which galloped down the riverside roads, and as for the Mississippi, more power would be needed to stem that powerful current. Later Fitch remembered none of the elation, only disappointment. "When we had got the alterations made, we found ourselves more embarrassed than ever. We found our engine to work exceedingly well and plenty of steam, but not to go fast enough to answer a valuable purpose on the Delaware, which threw me into the greatest consternation."

However, the fact remains that Fitch's boat of August 1787 was not only the first steamboat to move consistently on American waters, but the most efficient steamboat that had ever been built by man. Its only rival was Jouffroy's vessel, which employed an old-fashioned Newcomen engine, which seems to have gone even more slowly, and which disintegrated so completely during its one trial that it could never move again. When Fitch brought his boat back to the wharf, it had sprung no leaks and was ready to set out once more.

Fitch's invention had achieved practical results at what would seem to have been a perfect moment, for the Constitutional Convention, attended by leading citizens of all the states, was meeting in Philadelphia. Fitch wrote, "There was very few of the convention but called to see it, and do not know whether I may except any but General Washington himself; the reasons why he omitted it, I do not pretend to say." The Virginia delegates, led by Governor Randolph, "were pleased to give it every countenance they could." On August 23, William Samuel Johnson, a leading Connecticut delegate, wrote him, "Dr. Johnson presents his compliments to Mr. Fitch, and assures him that the exhibition yesterday gave the gentlemen present much satisfaction. He himself, and he doubts not the other gentlemen, will always be happy to give him every countenance and encouragement in their power, which his ingenuity and industry entitles him to." David Rittenhouse, the famous astronomer, John Ewing and Andrew Ellicott gave Fitch certificates, while a delegate to the convention wrote home that he was "on board the boat and saw the experiment succeed."

Before he laid his vessel up for the winter, Fitch had taken it without serious mishap on numerous demonstration runs. Many of America's leaders had seen one of the most revolutionary sights the history of the world had ever afforded—they had seen a vehicle moving under its own power. But did they believe the evidence of their eyes?

Fitch was convinced that he could not fail of success if he had a larger engine, and he had no difficulty persuading his stockholders to advance the money for an 18-inch cylinder. Triumph seemed within his grasp when he heard a strange rumor. He was told that a Virginian named William Askew had said that Rumsey, the pole-boat inventor, claimed to be the inventor of the steamboat as well. Askew "told so many unaccountable and contradictory stories about it that he gained but little credit with our company as to the truth of the main story itself. For my own part, I could not credit it, but suspected him to be a man that wished to tell great stories; but could not get to see him myself."

The rumor spurred Fitch into applying at once for an exclusive right in Virginia, the state that controlled the Mississippi valley, where Fitch hoped to bring his steamboat to its greatest flowering. But Virginia was also Rumsey's home state, and the site of his objective, the Potomac Canal. At last the laggard Southerner entered the lists. However, instead of contesting Fitch's priority to the steamboat itself, he took the shaky ground that the law he had already received for his pole boat included the rights to steam. Since this contention was easily disproved, Fitch's law was passed on November 7, 1787, before the Rumsey forces could get fairly moving. The Philadelphian was granted a monopoly for fourteen years, but only on condition that by the end of three years he should have operating on the waters of the state at least two steamboats of 20 tons burden.

Fitch had triumphed for the time being. Yet he was now faced with a time limit, and, even more dangerous to his hopes, he had at last smoked out Rumsey, who lost no time in throwing aside the cloak of secrecy and appearing before the world as a rival steamboat inventor, an inexorable enemy.

We left Rumsey in the beginning of 1787 with his boat damaged by ice and all his money expended. Rumors of Fitch's activity kept streaming in to Shepherdstown, where Rumsey was now living. "There was no time to lose," he wrote, "for had I delayed a moment, all my time, which was several years with the closest attention; all my expenses, which had been very great, to the most of all I had, would have been irrevocably lost." In his great need for funds, he "mortgaged a few family Negroes," and sold to his brother-in-law, Charles Morrow, a percentage of his rights to the pole boat for £1,000, most of which was probably not paid.

One day in July the citizens of the quiet West Virginia village were startled by an unearthly screaming the like of which had hardly ever before assaulted the ears of man. If Irish immigrants thought of banshees, they must have realized at once that even the haunts of the Old Country had no such lung power. Probably the citizens rushed to their doors, and then down to the river front whence the sound came. Rumsey had had his pipe boiler repaired, and it was giving off so much steam that the sound could be heard at least half a mile. As his neighbors shook their heads and put their hands over their ears, they little realized they were having a preview of the machine cacophony that was to afflict their descendants every day of the year.

August, the month in which Fitch's boat went 3 miles an hour, passed to the sound of tinkering. The steam engine Rumsey was completing was roughly similar in principle to Watt's early single-acting engines. In order to reduce to a minimum the complication of the apparatus, Rumsey placed his steam cylinder on top of another cylinder which functioned as a pump. The two cylinders had a single piston rod, which passed through the division between them and carried the motion of the steam piston directly to the plunger of the pump. When the steam piston rose, the plunger of the pump, being pulled upward, sucked in water through valves placed in the keel. The force of the atmosphere then drove the steam piston down, and the pump plunger descended, driving water through a pipe out of the stern of the boat.

Although he used a separate condenser and an air pump, details of the apparatus show that Rumsey only partially understood the advantages of Watt's discovery. Thus he tried to keep his steam piston tight by shooting on top of it at every stroke a stream of water, an expedient which worked exactly counter to Watt's basic principle of keeping the steam cylinder always at the boiling point. Yet when we consider the disadvantages under which Rumsey worked, his scheme showed great ingenuity.

By September Rumsey was ready to make his trial. As Fitch and Voight had done a few weeks before, he fed fuel into the furnace with a constricted heart. Finally, the steam engine actuated the pump, and water rushed out of the stern, setting up a mighty eddying. "The boat," Barnes tells us, "moved up the river against the current with about 2 tons on board, besides the machinery, at the rate of 2 miles per hour." Rumsey had no such elaborate ideas of speed as Fitch; he was delighted. But suddenly the screaming that had so terrified the villagers broke out again like the cries of mocking imps in hell; the boat filled with steam and came to a standstill. The boiler had opened at several joints. Rumsey was forced to skull back to shore.

He was repairing the damage in a leisurely manner, when the disturbing news reached him that Fitch was applying for a Virginia monopoly. To Washington, Rumsey confided that he "should not have come forward publicly until spring had it not been for Mr. Fitch's stealing a march on me in Virginia." As it was, he set December 3, 1787, for a public trial.

The local great man, General Horatio Gates, was particularly invited, and the townspeople notified. Thirty-nine years later an old gentleman, who admitted his memory was feeble, described the occasion, and his account was after the passage of many more years embellished by another gentleman who was not even born till 1815; he claimed to have conversed with eye-witnesses "in his youth." This is the classic description which is repeated in most writings on Rumsey; indeed, it is hard to resist, as it is very picturesque.

We are asked to visualize a beautifully clear day, and crowds streaming to the river in a holiday mood. There is much laughter, and the words "crazy Rumsey" are heard falling from many lips, but the solid citizens of the community, towering figures like General Gates, are wearing thoughtful frowns as they meditate on the deep significance of what they are to see. The spectators come to a halt on the bluff and look down on the ferry landing where the little boat is moored, already giving off wisps of smoke and steam. Handsome as always, dressed, we may be sure, in the height of fashion, Rumsey is the center of attention. Now he is on the lower level seeing to the machinery; now on the bluff, greeting his guests. He is surrounded with a clamor of people, asking to be allowed to go on board to make the historic run. Faced with so many requests, Rumsey, the courtly, knows the perfect answer; bowing to a local charmer, he announces that the places of honor on the boat shall be accorded only to ladies. Amid squeals of appreciation, the local matrons stream out on the wharf. Here the picture blurs a little, as the ladies are described as carrying parasols in mid-winter, but we will not object: parasols give a colorful touch. One by one Rumsey helps the charmers on board and sees that they are comfortable; a lady who has brought her knitting along expresses the general confidence by clicking away on her needles. And the sun shines down on the parasols happily from a sky of perfect blue.

Captain Morrow steps to the helm, while Rumsey attends to the boiler and machinery. The ladies smile and wave and knit; the spectators lean eagerly over the edge of the bluff; willing hands push the vessel out from the wharf. Then Rumsey starts the engine; the boat moves slowly into the middle of the river, pauses for a moment as it meets the current, and begins to chug upstream. For an instant there is awed silence, and then the voice of Gates, that old campaigner, is heard to shout, "She goes, — by —, she goes!" We regret that history does not fill in the dashes, thus enabling us to report exactly what brand of profanity appealed to the hero of Saratoga. Hearing approval so forcefully expressed by the greatest Shepherdstonian of them all, the crowd breaks into cheers, while Gates, still holding the center of the stage, throws his hat into the air.

The boat is moving smoothly up the river, giving off just enough noise and steam to be impressive, but much too courtly to drop any soot on the immaculate ladies, who, under their parasols, are beaming and waving. Rumsey bows like an automaton. Thus cheerfully the world's first steamboat (for all repeaters of this tale thus characterize Rumsey's invention) goes half a mile or more to a point opposite Swearingen's spring, where it turns round and returns to a little distance below the town, urged on by the enthusiastic shouts of the townspeople who are now completely convinced. After plying to and fro for two hours, the boat pulls in to the ferry landing, and at that moment, the knitting passenger, to complete the effect of mankind's first steamboat trip, triumphantly turns the heel of her sock. The crowd rushes down to the wharf and Rumsey is inundated with congratulations.

So much for the traditional account which this writer, wishing to be in the fashion, has not hesitated to heighten a little in his turn. The known facts concerning Rumsey's successful trial are much more meager. We have a certificate signed by Gates, in which he says that he had been asked to see the experiment "and had no small pleasure to see her get on her way, with near half her burthen on board, and move straight against the current at the rate of 3 miles per hour." He was informed and believed that the machinery was very imperfect "and by no means capable of performing what it would do if completed." Furthermore, he did not doubt that the invention might be brought into common and beneficial use "as the machine is simple, light, and cheap, and will be exceedingly durable, and does not occupy a space in the boat of more than 4 feet by 2½." The Rev. Robert Stubbs, a teacher in the Shepherdstown Academy, signed an affidavit with the same wording, and eight substantial citizens signed another which adds the information that the boat had "2 tons on board, exclusive of her machinery."

On December 11, the boat took a second trip. This time the speed was given in copiously signed affidavits as 4 miles an hour, and the load as 3 tons. Six gentlemen added, "We think the machinery does not weigh more than six or seven hundred weight, and is not included in the burthen mentioned above." A letter published in a local newspaper reports with naïve optimism that the machinery would not cost more than 20 guineas for a 10-ton boat. "It is thought that if some of the pipes of the machine had not been ruptured by the freezing of water, . . . which ruptures were only secured by rags tied round them, that the boat's way would have been at the rate of 7 or 8 miles an hour."

᙭ After its second trial, Rumsey's boat was laid up, never to move again. The inventor sent copies of the eye-witness certificates to Washington and the Virginia legislature.

Now both Fitch and Rumsey had publicly demonstrated steamboats that moved with some regularity under their own power. Fitch had the priority by about three months. Although he claimed to have gone only 3¼ miles an hour while Rumsey claimed 4, no actual basis of comparison exists, since Rumsey's speed seems to have been estimated by eye while Fitch used a log line. Nor is definite information available concerning the distance traveled by either boat; probably all the runs were short. Fitch, however, took many trips, operating his vessel during several months, while Rumsey admittedly made only two trials.

From the standpoint of mechanism, each had advantages. Rumsey's pipe boiler lightened and reduced the bulk of his engine; indeed, it was an invention of considerable importance, since it became years later standard equipment for boats which were driven by high-pressure steam. However, like high-pressure engines themselves, it was beyond the engineering possibilities of Rumsey's own time. This most advanced of his ideas was, as is often the case, the weakest point in his machinery; the pipe boiler was continually burning out.

Fitch's oars were somewhat crude in application, but the principle involved, that of using solid paddles, was sounder than Rumsey's jet propulsion. However, in this particular the preconceptions of the time were likely to do Fitch an injustice. Rumsey's scheme had a greater contemporary appeal. Not only was it backed by Franklin's authority, not only did its reliance on a steam pump involve a much smaller break with the traditions of the past, but the mechanism was simpler and had fewer parts to get out of order, a fact which, in those days when mechanics were few, seemed greatly to increase its utility.

The two inventors, each with a concrete achievement to point to, were about to collide. In any arguments that followed, Rumsey was likely to be able to convince their contemporaries that his mechanism was the best, and he possessed a great advantage in having the ear of the Virginia dynasty; Washington, Jefferson, and the other Southern leaders were already predisposed in his favor. Yet Fitch had entered the public arena first: he had staked his claim everywhere and possessed monopoly laws from four states. Could the latecomer drive Fitch from the legal position in which he was entrenched? The test was at hand.

XI. *The Rivals Collide*

IN DECEMBER 1787 Fitch petitioned for an exclusive right in Maryland, which controlled part of the Potomac Canal, and Rumsey
sprang to his own defense. Caught in the cross-fire, ex-Governor
Johnson, who had had business with both men, found himself confused; he consulted Washington. The General's reply both advanced
and retarded Rumsey's cause. On one hand, his statement that Rumsey had mentioned steam to him in 1784 sufficed to keep Fitch from
getting the Maryland monopoly. On the other hand, Washington
distinguished so carefully between Rumsey's pole and steam plans
that the inventor, who had tried to bolster his position by pretending
that his vaguely worded pole-boat laws also covered steam, was
forced publicly to admit that the two inventions were different.
He did it with a bad grace, and usually contradicted himself in the
next sentence, as when he wrote that Fitch had fraudulently secured
exclusive rights from two assemblies (Pennsylvania and Virginia)
"which granted me the same in 1784." Although he had never mentioned steam to any legislator who had voted for his statutes, he had
been playing with the idea in his own mind; he refused to believe
that this could not somehow be made to have legal validity.

Determining to annihilate his rival in print, Rumsey published
during January 1788, in Berkeley County, Virginia, a pamphlet with
a long title beginning *A Plan Wherein the Power of Steam Is Fully
Shown*. He possessed the priority, he insisted, since he had mentioned
steam to Washington and others before Fitch, by his own admission,
had even dreamed of the idea. By quoting affidavits of two of his
friends, he tried to prove that his own boat was much better than
Fitch's. One of the gentlemen stated that Fitch's boat must have cost
£300 while he was "convinced" that Rumsey's could not have cost
more than £20. He added his belief that Fitch's machinery weighed
7 tons and Rumsey's not more than 800 pounds. The other gentle-

man made a different estimate, giving the weight of Fitch's machinery as 5 tons and Rumsey's as 500 pounds. That such vague and contradictory figures could be presented as evidence shows how far mechanics was from being an exact science in America.

Summing up, Rumsey wrote: "The difference there is in weight, machinery, and expenses between his steam engine and mine is enormous. . . . Now I can with truth assure the public that Mr. Fitch's boat, so loaded with machinery, complexity, and expense, . . . can never be useful, as his machine, by his own publications, allowing for frictions and the necessary slipping of his paddles through the water, will not propel his boat at the rate of more than 3 miles in an hour where no current opposes."

Rumsey argued that Fitch's monopoly laws should be reinterpreted to include not all steamboats but only those propelled by oars, and that he, Rumsey, should be given the right to jet propulsion. He wished that each state would appoint a "committee of experimental philosophers," so that he might convince them "of the practicability of all I have proposed, of the simplicity of my machines, and of the smallness of their expense."

On March 24 Rumsey wrote Washington, "Tomorrow morning I throw myself upon the wide world"; he was going to Philadelphia to raise money for his experiments. He had been forced to sell his boat to pay his debts, but had preserved his machinery, which he had loaded on a wagon. If he received encouragement in Philadelphia, Barnes was to follow with the wagon. "There is no period in my life," Rumsey continued to Washington, "that could give one greater satisfaction than to have it in my power to stop the mouths of the envious few (I might add ignorant) that has taken the liberty to cast reflections on the gentlemen that was so kind enough to give me certificates; one of this description would have got roughly handled by the gentlemen of this place if he had not made a very timely escape."

But at heart Rumsey was terrified at moving to the great city that was Fitch's stronghold. His departure, he later confided to his brother-in-law, Charles Morrow, "caused my philosophy and fortitude to totter, and I believe nothing short of desperate circumstances such as mine then was could have enabled me to pursue the precarious undertaking I had set out upon, and leave the once peaceful shades of Berkeley. You can have no idea, my friend, of the various scenes of anxiety and care that I have went through, attended with agitations both of body and mind that hope, fear, success, and disappointment merits in general occasions. Yet no retreat, except that of poverty and contempt through a wilderness of want, was left for me to attempt, and therefore a desperate pursuit became necessary. Conquer or fall was my motto."

Fitch was at work on a larger engine. Unforeseen expenses kept cropping up, and soon he found himself again in financial difficulties. Once more he made the modern gesture of turning to the government for support. In a petition to Congress he stated that he had "run out of the last shilling which I have." The members of his company who had supported him as a philanthropic gesture felt they had done enough, while others, who had hoped for a profit, were unable to pay their obligations "through the scarcity of cash, which brings money in such small sums I am continually embarrassed; and my demands being so much beyond what we ever expected, I am thrown into the greatest difficulties and distress. These inconceivable disappointments, delays, and expense has a tendency to relax the good intentions of my patrons." He hated to beg from them: "The thoughts of living on mean and base dependence destroys my thoughts from being employed where they ought to be; that is, in the execution of my business. . . . I know that the finances of Congress are small at present, of course; I know that they have not money to give, yet was they to give me land, I could turn that into money and complete my undertaking."

Since this was before the ratification of the Constitution, Congress was still made up of state delegations that voted as units; nine had to approve a bill before it was passed. But this number of delegations had not yet even arrived at the meeting place in New York.

While Fitch was waiting for a quorum, he met St. John de Crève-coeur, the talented French consul who had just written the famous *Letters of an American Farmer*. Before they had talked for many minutes, the Frenchman's eyes were shining with steamboat fever, and they were planning to put the invention over in Europe. On January 6, 1788, Crèvecoeur wrote the Duc d'Harcourt an exaggerated account of Fitch's boat, saying it had gone 5½ miles an hour, and that Franklin was president of a company to forward it. He asked that Louis XV empower him to commission a model to be sent to France. Although Fitch asked nothing "for the communication of his principles," Crèvecoeur hoped that His Majesty would make him a present of several hundred louis.

Next Crèvecoeur wrote Franklin, asking his opinion of Fitch's boat. On February 16 the philosopher replied, "I cannot get about readily, and therefore have not seen it. I have no doubt that the force of steam, properly applied, may suffice to move a boat against the current in most rivers, yet when I consider the first expense of a machine such as a steam engine, the necessity of always having a skillful mechanist at a high salary to manage and repair it, and the room it will occupy on the vessel, I will confess the fear I entertained lest the advantage should not be sufficient to bring the invention into common use; though the opinion you sent me of Mr. Rittenhouse, who is an excellent judge, gives me a more favorable opinion."

Franklin was still unimpressed by Fitch and all his works, but this did not cool the Frenchman's ardor; as his letters to the inventor show, he lobbied among members of Congress for Fitch's bill. And Fitch, who was counting his acres before they were granted, promised gratefully to name the first township set out in his new lands after Crèvecoeur.

Too impatient to wait for the dilatory Congressmen, Fitch had returned to Philadelphia. He was shocked when his usually enthusiastic patron, Colonel Wells, received him very coldly. Asked the reason, Wells handed him a copy of Rumsey's pamphlet. Fitch thereupon composed a pamphlet of his own, which was rewritten by Wells and published under a title beginning, *The Original Steamboat Supported.* . . .

If we read Fitch's effusion with the eye of an impartial contemporary who had no further knowledge of the controversy than this pamphlet and the one it answered, we can see that it did not carry much conviction. It was too smart by half. Determined to prove Rumsey had not started his steamboat in 1785, as he stated, but in the following summer, Fitch based his arguments on his opponent's wording, torturing the sentences to reveal verbal contradictions that were not necessarily in the underlying meaning. During two trips to Virginia—was he the man who, as Rumsey wrote Washington, would have got "roughly handled" if he had not fled?—Fitch procured certificates from craftsmen and spectators which purported to show that Rumsey was lying, but the certificates, which were themselves muddled, showed merely that people get easily confused on dates.[1]

Having attempted to prove that Rumsey's first practical experiments did not precede his, Fitch went on to say that it made no difference who had started first, since the only important consideration was who had made the first public announcement. Henry, he pointed out, had experimented with steamboats before Rumsey, but made no claim. Fitch insisted that his title to all steamboats rested on his having laid his idea before Congress on August 29, 1785.

His boat was more efficient than Rumsey's, Fitch argued, since although heavier, it went almost as fast. But "however faulty my work might be, and however perfect his own, it would have no force in the determination of our title to the invention." Only priority of announcement mattered.

He insisted that jet propulsion was not original with Rumsey, it had been suggested by Bernouilli and Franklin, and Fitch himself had experimented with it. Like his contemporaries, Fitch did not understand the advantages of his own use of paddles. He had only given up jet propulsion at Voight's insistence, and he was in danger of slipping back to it in an even more impractical form. "I am now," he wrote, "trying an experiment, and the machine is almost finished, to propel a boat not by expelling water but air." We gather the experiment was not successful, as we never hear of it again.

When Rumsey arrived in Philadelphia, Fitch, so Barnes tells us, read to him "the whole or part of his pamphlet previous to its publication." This is the only mention of a scene which must have reached epic proportions. What induced Fitch to carry the battle to his rival's very face? Probably he interpreted it to himself as the essence of fairness. He would give his enemy warning of the attack; he would demonstrate that he dared say every word in Rumsey's hated presence.

We can see Fitch, his face tight with nervous intensity, his coat out at the elbow and his shoes down at the heel, curtly greeting the fashionably dressed Southerner who must have been puzzled by the call. Fitch is brusque, Rumsey suave, and the manner of each irritates the other. Rumsey offers Fitch a chair; Fitch drops into it clumsily and without further words pulls the manuscript from his pocket. As he reads out loud, Fitch is carried away by his words, his voice taking on a rhythmical intonation. When he comes to a particularly devastating point, he looks up to see how Rumsey is taking it, but he gets no satisfaction, since the handsome face before him, long disciplined in the arts of the gambler, is expressionless. The calmer Rumsey remains, the more excited Fitch becomes, until at last his voice is shrill with emotion. Perhaps he skips a little at the end, to get the interview that is giving him no satisfaction over more quickly. At last he folds the manuscript, puts it back in his pocket, and with a curt bow stalks out of the room. And only when the door slammed shut does Rumsey give way to the rage that possesses him. As a result of the interview, Rumsey arranged to have his pamphlet republished in Philadelphia under the new title, *A Short Treatise on the Application of Steam.* . . .

Fitch and Voight were working on their boat. They had waited several months for the 18-inch cylinder to be cast, but the job had proved beyond the abilities of the Warwick Furnace, which had never before received such an order. The finished cylinder was

defective, and while the steamboat company debated whether to try
to fix it by lining it with copper, the proprietors of the furnace broke
it up for pig iron. Forced to use their old 12-inch cylinder, the
inventors determined to change the proportion of their boat from
45 by 12 feet to 60 by 8, hoping that the reduction in width would
give them more speed. Instead of the oars working at the sides, broad
paddles like snow shovels were attached to the stern; a crank mechanism connected with the engine pushed them against the water, and
then brought them back above the surface. Fitch continued to employ this method in all his experiments on the Delaware, sometimes
using three, sometimes four paddles. Although less picturesque in
appearance than the oars at the sides, it was undoubtedly more efficient.

The idea of a pipe boiler had occurred to Fitch and Voight entirely independent of Rumsey; indeed, before they knew that their
rival was working with steam. Fitch had cannily opposed its use, on
the ground that it could not be prevented from leaking. However,
Rumsey now made such a fuss about his pipe boiler that Fitch's
backers were determined to use the device. "Knowing ourselves to
have the priority," Fitch wrote, "and that he must have taken the
idea from Governor Johnson, who had seen my drafts, and not
knowing but he would gain the priority in one if we did not adopt
it, [I] gave my hearty consent."[2]

When Rumsey set to work to organize a company, in an amazingly short time he secured backers much more influential than
Fitch's had ever been. Franklin's predilection for jet propulsion induced him to buy a share; the Virginian was thus enabled to use his
name. William Bingham, one of the richest men in America, subscribed, as did several important firms of merchants and the London
banking house of Robert Barclay. Benjamin Wyncoop was so enthusiastic that he invested in twenty shares; as Rumsey wrote a
friend, "he has been propelled with great velocity through the streets
for several days by the force of steam alone."[3]

The company, which called itself The Rumsean Society, planned
to promote all Rumsey's inventions, not only his steamboat and pipe
boiler but his mills and his steam engine for raising water. Drawings

for these were submitted to the Philosophical Society, and Rumsey was soon elected a member, an honor which had never been accorded Fitch.

On May 15 Rumsey wrote Washington: "Have met with great opposition from Mr. Fitch's company who seem to stop at nothing to carry their point. By advice of several friends, we attempted an agitation [arbitration?] of the matter, and I was met several times by deputies from his company, in the course of which I offered to make an equal join of the matter with them, which they refused, and they offered me one eighth, which I refused, when all negotiation ceased."

Although there was still much ground to be covered, it is possible that if the two companies, which were systematically tripping each other up, had got together at this time, the invention of the steamboat might have been completed a generation before Fulton's triumphal voyage. Here we see how personality shapes events of overwhelming importance; the breakdown in the negotiations must be explained not by the historian but by the biographer. Rumsey was a relatively well-balanced individual with a matter-of-fact, realistic approach to the world. He made inventions because they came to him easily, and he wanted to put them over because that gave him money, reputation, and the satisfaction of achievement. His own personality was involved only as the personality of any business man is involved in his ventures. As long as he realized what the wisest course was, he could take it without any interference from inner voices.

Fitch on the other hand was a fanatic, always ill at ease with his fellow-men, his sense of superiority a rickety floor built over a deep well of uncertainty. His whole life was an attempt to vindicate himself in his own eyes as well as those of the world. His basic need was, in his own words, to demonstrate that "little Johnny Fitch can do something of importance." The steamboat was to be his justification; he had merged his personality with it to such an extent that he could as easily sign away half his own mind as half his invention.

Thus Rumsey was able to compromise, while Fitch was incapable of doing so. On this occasion Rumsey showed the greater intelligence, but the race between the two men was by no means over.

Perhaps in the end fanaticism would accomplish more than smiling good sense.

The Rumsean Society had decided that the most immediately valuable of Rumsey's inventions was the pipe boiler which, whether steamboats proved practical or not, could be applied to any kind of engine. Hearing a rumor, certainly false, that Fitch was trying to patent the pipe boiler in England, they resolved that the most effective counter-move would be to send Rumsey abroad. They subscribed $1,000 for his expenses and gave him "the best letters [of introduction] that Philadelphia can afford me."

Benjamin Rush, America's most famous physician, wrote Dr. John Coakley Lettsom: "Nothing but a matter deeply concerning the interests of science and justice should have induced me to trouble you with a letter by the packet. A certain Mr. Rumsay [sic] from Virginia (strongly recommended by General Washington) lately produced a plan of a machine in our city for improving the steam engine by reducing the fuel consumed by them to an eighth part of the usual quantity. The plan, it is suspected, has been copied with a few trifling variations, by a person of this city (equally well known for plagiarism in philosophy, and a licentious opposition to the proposed constitution of the United States) and transmitted to Mr. Boulton of London with a view of obtaining a patent for it." Rush asked Lettsom to assure Watt's partner that Fitch was not the true inventor. Rumsey, Rush continued, had recently built a steamboat which went 4 miles an hour upstream, and he expected to increase this to 10 "by the application of the principles of his new steam engine to the discovery. . . . Mr. Rumsay possesses a very uncommon mechanical genius. . . . His modesty is equal to his talents for invention."

Franklin wrote Benjamin Vaughan, an influential businessman in London, famous for his radical, even revolutionary, views. Praising the pipe boiler, the philosopher said that another American mechanic "is endeavoring to deprive him of such advantages by pretending a prior right to the invention." He asked Vaughan to help Rumsey, and before sailing Rumsey wrote Washington that Vaughan and Robert Barclay "are to be two of my confidential friends."[4] Rumsey. was delighted with such powerful connections; he could not know that Franklin's letter to Vaughan was to do much to prevent him from being the acknowledged inventor of the steamboat.

It will perhaps give us some insight into Rumsey's married life that on the eve of sailing he wrote a letter of instruction about his children not to his wife but to his brother-in-law. He asked Charles Morrow to "remember me" to his wife. "Tell her I sincerely wish her all happiness and tell my child to be a good girl, and remind her that it is in part for her that I toil." He asked that his son Edward, who was deaf and dumb, be kept "with the doctor if possible, or some other school. I shall endeavor to have him some clothing got against winter, and if nothing else can be done, send him here to Joseph Barnes. I have laid a train for him to finish his studies, but it will be expensive, and therefore must be the last shift except my circumstances change. . . . Charles, take [care] of my child and all the little business I left with you. I can make no promises, but I think I shall not go to Europe for nothing. If I do not, you shall be remembered. If Mr. Page's and Mr. Fitzhugh's houses can be done by any means, it will save me some character."

Fitch had long yearned for an English engine; Rumsey was now sailing to London with $1,000 in his pocket and letters of introduction to Boulton and Watt. No wonder the Virginian concluded his letter by writing, "This, Charles, is my meridian. If I do not do something now, I am done."

XII. *There's Many a Slip*

IT MAY have been Rumsey's "meridian," but it certainly was not
Fitch's. His friends had withdrawn his bill from Congress, since
Rumsey's pamphlet had killed any chance of favorable action.
"When I received information of that, and reflecting how I had
ruined myself to serve my country, and how many sleepless, restless
nights I had suffered to bring about one of the greatest events, and
such exquisite tortures of the mind, and had placed myself on the
base dependence of my friends, it affected me beyond measure. . . .
At that time I did religiously curse my savage captor, Captain
Buffalo, for withholding his bloody hand, and slacking his nerves
from not forcing his tomahawk into my head, when the blow was
fairly drawn, and left my body on the banks of the Ohio, in a savage
wild, to be devoured by wolves, rather than permit me to return to
so unkind, ungenerous, and unmanly a people as my own nation.
Thus situated, drinking only seemed to be my relief, although I
have never as yet rendered myself unfit for business by said practice,
nor more than gladden my mind and place it above the frowns of
the world."

The new boat, with its pipe boiler that had made possible the removal of 3½ tons of brickwork, was tried out in July 1788. When
the partners had got it "to work pretty well," they invited several
members of their company to make the ambitious 20-mile trip to
Burlington. As they moved easily toward their destination, Fitch
gloried in the long faces of the boatmen they passed, but when they
were 20 or 30 poles from the upper wharf in Burlington, the pipe
boiler sprang a leak, and with a gasp or two the engine died. Determined not to be cheated of their triumph, the members of the company said they had anchored from choice. Fitch, however, grimly
told the truth, and added that if the Devil had really wanted to test
Job he would have set him to steamboat building.

The partners were forced to drift back to Philadelphia with the tide. However, they had made the longest non-stop trip ever yet achieved by a steamboat and were not too discouraged. "Mr. Voight and myself knew that the great laws of nature was equally binding on all the fates as on us; therefore we knew that if we could make our boiler tight, that they could not prevent us from going."

Indeed, they soon made several trips to Burlington and back "under the auspicious guidance of the God of Nature." Sometimes they traveled 4 miles an hour independently of the current. Fitch secured a number of certificates of achievement from political and philosophical leaders, but Franklin remained lukewarm; he wrote on October 24, "We have no philosophical news here at present, except that a boat, moved by a steam engine, rows itself against tide in our river, and it is apprehended that the construction may be so simplified and improved as to be generally useful."

Count Brissot de Warville, the French traveler, examined Fitch's boat. The machinery appeared to him "well executed" and suited to its purpose. He was told by a member of the company that the three broad oars "made 26 strokes per minute, with a promise of 60." A larger boat of 10 or 20 tons, his informant continued, could be built for £3,000 or £4,000, and could be managed by two men. This Brissot regarded as theoretically possible, but he thought that in practical commerce the engine would demand many men to tend it, and many expensive repairs for the breakdowns "which must frequently result from the rapidity and multiplicity of the motions." If the engine could be made stronger and its movements simplified, the boat might have some value for America "where manual labor was dear, and where the rivers were not, as in France, accessible for horses and for men." Even this lukewarm opinion, he noted, cheered Fitch's backer "who, I saw, was assailed with jokes on account of this steamboat" and "annoyed by these pleasantries which appeared to me to be very much out of place." The Frenchman felt the members of the company deserved praise for their altruism, since the steamboat, which might help allay the labor shortage in America, clearly would never make any money. Brissot's not too enthusiastic comments take on added significance when we realize that he was an unusually sympathetic observer who felt he was defending the invention against its detractors.

Fitch's steamboat was still not fast enough to make money on the Delaware, on whose flat banks stagecoaches moved rapidly, and whose broad reaches were well suited to sailboat operation. Indeed, the Delaware was almost the worst river Fitch could have chosen; it is hard to understand why he did not take his steamboat elsewhere. He had a New York monopoly: why did he not try the Hudson, later to be the scene of Fulton's triumph? The trip from New York to Albany was not only longer than any heavily traveled route on the Delaware, but it was much less suited to existing means of loco-motion; flanking mountains created freakish winds and bad, hilly roads. Probably, Fitch regarded Philadelphia as the natural proving ground for his boat because it was the home of his collaborator and his patrons. His eyes were so fixed on the Mississippi as his eventual objective that it did not occur to him to operate temporarily on a more suitable eastern river. This mistake was to cost him very dear.

Although he had made the best steamboat the world had seen, he was closer to failure than ever. When his backers realized that a new boat and engine would have to be built, they were angry: had not Fitch told them two years before that the invention was complete except for the routine application of fool-proof plans; had they not stuck with him through unexpected failure after unexpected failure? This was too much; the steamboat company refused to put up another cent.

Troubles were multiplying. Rumsey's assistant Barnes had pub-lished *Remarks on Mr. John Fitch's Reply to Mr. James Rumsey's Pamphlet*, in which he argued the whole case over again, and pro-duced new evidence concerning the dates of Rumsey's boats, which made Fitch's strictures seem most unconvincing. The tone of his publication is indicated by the following passage: "It may be neces-sary now to add that the heavy charges of perjury, falsehood, want of memory or candor, which are so illiberally brought by Mr. Fitch against the fairest characters, were made by a man, who not only attempted to bribe a gentleman of character to swear to a falsehood, but who actually committed this heinous offense, in order either to avail himself of Mr. Rumsey's invention, or to prevent him from deriving the emoluments due to his ingenuity. How Mr. Fitch can after this instance of flagitious conduct expect the patronage of any honest man, I am at a loss to determine." Two other Rumsey pamphlets rushed from the press, one describing his steamboat in detail, and the other his inventions for raising water and improving mills.

Beginning in October 1788, the Rumsey forces moved on the legislatures of Pennsylvania, Virginia, New York, and New Jersey in a campaign to have them repeal or modify Fitch's laws which gave him the right to all steamboats, whoever invented them. Although committee reports showed that faith in Fitch had been greatly shaken, the legislatures refused to act on the grounds, as Pennsylvania put it, that "however improper so extensive a law may be in its principles," yet since much money and labor had been spent in reliance on the monopolies they should not be changed "unless upon the most pressing necessity." However, time and treasure that should have gone into building Fitch's new steamboat was absorbed in litigation before one assembly after another.

During the New York battle a new element appeared which Fitch, in his absorption with fighting Rumsey, hardly noticed. The wealthy New Jersey landowner, John Stevens, Jr., asked the legislature to protect a steamboat idea of his own. Later Stevens was to explain how he became interested in the subject. Making no mention of his signing in 1786 Fitch's petition for a New Jersey monopoly, Stevens stated that his attention was drawn to steamboats at the end of 1788 by the pamphlet war between Fitch and Rumsey. After reading their publications, he decided that Rumsey had the best claim, and on September 5, 1788, he wrote the Virginian, explaining in the manner of the great addressing the lowly the advantages of the pipe boiler, just as if its inventor had never thought of them. He then gave Rumsey several pieces of advice, the most interesting being that the fire be placed above the boiler and the smoke sucked down through the coals before it passed between the pipes, a device designed to produce more heat.

In a month or two Stevens progressed from advising inventors to inventing on his own. He wrote a member of the New York legislature that as neither Fitch nor Rumsey "have brought their schemes to that degree of perfection as to answer any valuable purpose in practice," neither was entitled to a monopoly of all steamboats. Although he used a pipe boiler and jet propulsion, Stevens insisted that his machine was totally different from his predecessors'. He wished an exclusive privilege for the change in the boiler he had shortly before offered to give Rumsey, and for a steam engine he had invented. The latter device represented a huge step backward, since Stevens intended to pump water from the stern with a modification of Savery's fountain engine, which had been discarded a century before because of its inefficiency. We gather that Stevens' plans were altogether on paper, made without benefit even of an experimental model; this new contestant was a gentleman, and therefore incapable of doing anything with his hands.

Perhaps because of his previous support of Fitch's monopoly, Stevens' petition to the New York legislature was unsuccessful, yet his entry into the lists marked the opening of a new era in the invention of the steamboat. Till then the leading American projectors were simple artisans, men pragmatically trained and without formal education, lacking money and political influence. It is an indication of the future that Stevens did not use his riches and power to back either of the persons of no importance who had already made significant advances; no, he started out again from scratch with a scheme of his own. If he were to have a collaborator, it must be someone of his own class; soon he was to interest his brother-in-law, Robert R. Livingston, who was even richer and more politically powerful than he.

While Fitch's boat languished for lack of funds and litigation sprang up on every side, an even more deadly blow was dealt him from an altogether unexpected direction. Differences over a woman came between him and the invention of his dreams.

During the years since he had fled his disastrous relationship with his wife, Fitch had consciously avoided women, "and have in that time frequently treated the sex unbecoming a man, for which I ask their pardon. I have in this time kept a solemn Lent for more than seven years together, which, sir, I look upon too scrupulously un-reasonable in either sex. . . . I do believe that the greatest torment that a man can have in this world is to be teased with a woman, and have ever been of the opinion since I left New England, and not being a very handsome man, and one of very indifferent address and of no flattery, you might reasonably suppose that I have steered through life upward of twenty years without the worst of ills be-falling me."

Love, however, has a way of creeping into your blood before you know it is there. If any man ever needed a refuge from the world, Fitch needed it now. His former difficulties, he wrote, were incon-siderable compared with "the indignities offered me by my best friends and patrons, who in many instances treated me more like a slave than a freeman, whilst I was in the most excruciating tortures of devising plans of completing my undertaking, which was far beyond my abilities. Not only that, but was obliged to collect moneys from my best friends, who rather esteemed it as moneys levied and collected by me, and extorted from them from a mere point of their honor, which has ever been more severe to my feelings than anything which I ever experienced before. Not only that; I have been continually teased with duns from our workmen, and embarrassed with constables for debts; and continually so bare and mean appearance that every decent man must and ought to despise me from my appearance. Not only that, but dare not scarcely show my face in my lodgings, which occasioned me never to remain in them longer than I could with the greatest expedition swallow down my food, which always in the evening drove me out to a tavern, and though I always kept good hours, at my return drove me to my bed. Not only that: although they were worthy, respectable people, I dare not find fault with anything, which I might with propriety do could I have paid them weekly, but was obliged to suffer just indignities from my landlord and be henpecked by the women. Added to all this there was the most powerful combination against me, who thought they could not serve God or themselves better than saying every ill-natured thing they could of me, which made me heartily curse my barbarous capture for staying the savage blow."

Yet Fitch had one human resource, one refuge from the world. "I once, sir, had two friends, a male and a female. The female was a widow and kept a public house where my male friend met me every evening, and many friendly hour we passed without ever being interrupted by jars or different sentiment, as our sentiments were the most uniform of any two men I ever saw, although our persons and passions were as different as any two." Here in the parlor, with the blinds drawn and the fire going, Fitch was enveloped in a little world where everyone believed in his steamboat.

If he wished to use his mind by enunciating heretical sentiments in religion or politics, no one called him immoral as Benjamin Rush had done; his friend Voight joined in, and the landlady, Mrs. Mary Krafft, listened with soft eyes shining over her embroidery. There at his elbow was a "cheering glass" that was filled just as often as if his elbow were not sticking out from his coat. Beyond the window, he was "crazy Fitch" the steamboat madman, or the plagiarist who had stolen Rumsey's invention; here where the sounds of the street sank to a lulling murmur, he was a man of importance, loved and admired.

Although Fitch had tremendous energy, like many ill-adjusted men he wore it out so fast that he needed a great deal of sleep. "I always kept early hours and was never out much after eight o'clock, and seldom ever failed for being at home and in bed by nine o'clock in the evening, and always left my friend with my other friend, and a long time passed before I suspected their friendship but to be as pure as my own." One day a horrible realization crawled into his Eden like a snake: Voight, although married, was having an affair with the widow.

Convinced that his sense of outrage was based entirely on their breach of morality, Fitch lectured the lovers by the hour on their faults and duties. They listened soberly and were more cautious, but finally "the productions of love appeared. I was much alarmed for them, as both of them had valuable families of children of six or seven each, and to see the destruction of those families who were the only friends I had in the world wracked my tortured soul to the extreme."

After several weeks of agonized brooding, Fitch suggested a way out that delighted Voight; he offered to marry Mrs. Krafft. He assured the widow that his only motive was an altruistic attempt to save the situation. He would pay for his room in her inn like any other boarder, and he pledged "my word of honor never to bed with her. . . . She being a shrewd, sensible woman probably thought that there was some trap laid for her, and treated the offer not only with contempt but with considerable resentment, when heaven knows that there was nothing but the purest and undefiled friendship designed. I did at that time pledge my plighted faith of honor to do everything which lay in my power to save the reputation of my friends and their families. . . . I took lodgings in the house of my female friend and took every opportunity of lecturing them on the impropriety of their conduct."

As the pregnancy advanced, Voight became frightened and kept away; Mrs. Krafft felt he had abandoned her. "The grief and hysterics which it caused and sleepless nights which I experienced made my heart to bleed for the woman's distress." Naturally, Voight found it increasingly difficult to face Fitch, who vibrated with moral fury like a prophet from the Old Testament.

At this moment when the steamboat experiment was already almost overwhelmed by a multitude of difficulties, Voight announced his withdrawal. He had greatly injured his family and trade by his attention to so impractical a scheme, he announced sententiously; he would have nothing more to do with it. Since, as Fitch wrote, "many of the company put more faith in his philosophical and mathematical abilities than mine," Voight's desertion "must have staggered the most sanguine" of them. Fitch was again friendless; and concerning his invention he wrote, "I hardly had an idea that it would be possible to pursue it any further."

XIII. *England Enters the Game*

WHILE difficulties swarmed around Fitch, Rumsey was offered the invention of the steamboat as a gift. On July 3, 1788, he went to Birmingham to see Boulton and Watt, and soon he had so impressed the engine builders that they offered to become his partners. Rumsey was to patent the Watt engine in the United States on a profit-sharing basis; had this effort succeeded, Fitch would at once have been stopped. Furthermore, under certain financial conditions, the firm was to back Rumsey in securing an English steamboat patent, and place their skill as engine makers at his disposal.

The American may have been, as he asserted, taken aback when his hosts put their understanding of the agreement in writing, but it is certain that when he returned to London, Boulton and Watt believed the whole matter was settled. They had filed in the British patent office a caveat or legal warning that they would oppose the efforts of anyone else to patent steamboats; on July 14 they wrote their lawyer to withdraw the caveat since they had "made an agreement" with Rumsey.

The invention of the steamboat seemed on the point of completion. Boulton and Watt, the most skillful steam engineers in the world, knew how to build apparatus admirably suited for navigation; one of their engines was many years later to power the so-called *Clermont*. True, the experienced Watt, like his contemporaries of every shade of ignorance, had been taken in by the fallacious simplicity of achieving jet propulsion with a pump, yet had he set to work on the problem, he would probably have discovered his error. Fitch and Fulton now seem hopelessly out of the running; certainly our story is almost told.

At this juncture, the letter Franklin had given Rumsey to Benjamin Vaughan becomes one of the determining documents of history. When Rumsey showed his adviser the contract offered him, Vaughan, who seems at some previous time to have won the distrust of Boulton, urged Rumsey to ask for better terms. Making the mistake of thinking that Rumsey's steamboat was a completed invention, he assured the American that he could get on very well without the Birmingham engineers. Supposing the firm did have an English patent for their engine; that could be got around by building the boat in Ireland, and certainly Watt, who had no patents in America, had no right to make any demands about that country. Rumsey should force Boulton and Watt to sell him engines at less than the market price, and ask for other concessions. Himself convinced that he was as good a mechanic as anybody and that his steamboat plans were foolproof, Rumsey was delighted, and asked Vaughan to put his opinions in a letter which he enclosed with one of his own.

Rumsey's communication summed up Boulton and Watt's proposals, and then gave his answer to each.*

1. *The firm agreed to give up their claim for steam for driving boats.* Answer: This could only apply to England, "where in your opinion this invention will be of little use, except in particular places." Elsewhere the firm had no claim.

2. *The firm agreed to supply engines at their usual terms.* Answer: This was no favor.

3. *Rumsey was to agree to use only Boulton and Watt engines in all countries: in return the firm would pay one-half the cost of his English patent.* Answer: This was a great deal to ask for a payment of less than £100.

4. *The firm agreed "to take out a partnership patent in America for the engines and all their appliances, you paying two-thirds of the expense and receiving two-thirds of the profits."* Answer: Watt had made the "invention of the double application of the power of steam above and below the piston; but I had myself independent of your invention thought of a separate condensing vessel, and the boiler is

---

* The firm's suggestions are printed here in italics, Rumsey's ideas in regular text type.

clearly my invention. This would therefore be to renounce all my own pretensions and to subject myself to your premiums in return for your paying two-thirds of the expense of the patent."

5. *Rumsey to use no other engines for any purpose.* Answer: "It deprives me of any means of availing myself of future improvements, even my own, except on your terms."

Rumsey summed up: "I came to you as persons who are possessed of the English market, and flatter myself that I can improve your hold upon it, but I did not expect that our agreement should operate to tie my hands in other places."

He then made proposals of his own: (1) "To omit all mention of foreign parts." (2) Rumsey to receive one-half the profits on engines used in Great Britain for navigation. (3) The firm to pay one-half the cost of his English and Scotch patents and his trip to the Continent. (4) Should the firm wish to use his pipe boiler, they should treat with him for compensation. Rumsey ended by stating that "if the above terms are not worthy of your attention," he would proceed to patent his boiler in his own name.

On August 14 Boulton forwarded this letter, with the one from Vaughan, to Watt. "I do not send them for the sake of pleasant reading, but for the purpose of giving you time to cool, to reflect, and to write a guarded answer, as I consider Vaughan a dangerous man."

The next day, Boulton wrote Watt, "I am now sending you my answer to Rumsey whom Vaughan seems to have the total possession of, but he shall never have possession of me." The part of Vaughan's letter in which he intimated that he could evade Watt's patent by having the engine made in Ireland "shows the principles of the man in so clear a point of view that I cannot express how much I detest him, but perhaps you'll say I am in a passion. Perhaps I am, and I hope I shall never be so void of feeling as to be insensible to such rascally principles; there is a sycophantic affectation of respect and threat through his letter." Fearing that Rumsey would apply to Jonathan Wilkinson to build him an engine, Boulton said he intended to write Wilkinson that they would regard any assistance to Rumsey as "a declaration of war against us, and act accordingly."

Boulton's letter to Rumsey said, "It appears to me there is so great a change in your sentiments that I have little hopes of our forming any connection, because you reason as if you expected shadows to counterbalance substance." Boulton admitted it was no concession to sell engines at the usual price, but they had to make their profit and "do not wish to restrain you in your profits upon goods so bought. You say that in America we cannot make you any concessions, not having the claim, but surely our knowledge, our experience, our fair profit, and trouble, etc., in manufacturing we have a natural claim to in all countries. . . .

"As to boilers, you must allow me to observe that Mr. Watt was the first and only discoverer of the precise quantity of water and the exact quantity of steam of a given elasticity, as well as the knowledge of the total quantity of heat procurable by a given measure of such coals as this country produces, and therefore we are enabled to know the utmost limits of our boilers." Vaughan's reasoning on Rumsey's pipe boiler made Boulton smile: "when he hath tried as many boilers as we have hundreds, he will discover some mistakes in it." Boulton and Watt evaporated 10 pounds of water with 1 pound of coal "and in as much as your boiler will do more, so ought its nearer approach to perfection to be estimated. You may easily determine its ratio by experiments which are worth a thousand fancies or theories."

Boulton ended by assuring Rumsey, "You have mistaken your road to the goal in view."

Rumsey thereupon sent further proposals, which were answered on August 29 in a letter signed by both Watt and Boulton: "Though we are in general much averse to partnerships or close connections for carrying on new inventions, yet from the very favorable opinion we formed of your abilities and character we were induced to make your offers which we shall probably not make to any other persons in the same circumstances." On fully considering Rumsey's objections, they felt there was no possibility of making "a connection agreeable to both parties; it is therefore our opinion and *desire* that the negotiations should now terminate. . . .

"In regard to your new boiler, consisting of a narrow tube bent in a spiral or zigzag form, containing the water within it and having the fire or flame applied to the outside of it (the drawing of which you showed us) we shall give no opposition to your obtaining a patent for it, and shall observe the necessary secrecy until the patent is completed, in which we wish you success." They added, however, that Watt and others had made pipe boilers on the opposite principle, in which the flame passed in pipes through the water.

Boulton and Watt stated that they made no claim to Rumsey's mill inventions, but "it is with regret that we find ourselves obliged to say that we cannot resign our claim" to the use of steam engines to propel boats "by the reaction of water confined in tubes and acted upon by pistons and oars; and also in rivers and canals by means of poles acting upon their bottoms; and the same candor you have observed to us obliges us to inform you that we shall immediately take such steps as will render any patent for that purpose of no avail.

"We are extremely sorry to differ so widely in sentiments from you and your friends in England and wish that it would have been otherwise; but as it is we hope that you and they will excuse our following what appears to be our own interest, as we certainly shall excuse you for pursuing yours."

Thus Rumsey lost the best opportunity ever given a steamboat inventor to win the race in a walk. Although his disagreement with Watt seems to have been based on a series of chance incidents—Franklin's letter to Vaughan, Vaughan's oversharpness, Rumsey's own willingness to take advantage of loopholes in the patent law—behind the whole drama was a fundamental difference of point of view that went far to explain not only Rumsey's troubles but Fitch's, and even why the steamboat waited so long before it was successfully invented. Boulton and Watt were experienced engineers; they regarded Rumsey's plans as a general idea that would require a vast amount of working out in minute detail. Rumsey, however, like Fitch, thought that as soon as he had conceived of a steamboat he had invented it.

Neither of the Americans realized that the success of a machine depended on minute calculation. Every part had to be built in exact correlation with every other part; if the condenser were too big for the cylinder, that would not work any more than if the cylinder were too big for the condenser. To evolve the correct proportions by trial and error was a laborious and costly business, as Fitch was discovering, especially when you attempted to do it on a full-scale engine. Some of the difficulty could be overcome by the use of an endless number of experimental models, but even these would hardly serve unless you understood the physical laws involved. Watt, for instance, had spent much labor determining the elasticity of steam at different temperatures, but neither of the Americans had worried about such a consideration.

Fitch and Rumsey were struggling with an industrial invention in the manner of craftsmen building the simple devices of the Middle Ages: a wagon, perhaps, where the size of the wheels need have no exact relation to the size of the body. True, the Middle Ages boasted a few very complicated machines, like the sailboat. But its ramifications had not been worked out by one man in a few years; they were the result of centuries of evolution. And even this accumulated experience was unable to produce as perfect a machine as the application of scientific tables did in one generation; the clipper ship, the acme of sailboat design, was a nineteenth-century invention.

The profession of civil engineering, of which Watt was an outstanding example, was new everywhere in the world. Not a single American could justly claim the title. Our countrymen, it is true, had been driven by frontier conditions into developing great practical ingenuity, but in their struggle with their environment the first answer had usually been more valuable than the best answer. When a settler carried his family into the wilderness, he needed immediate fortifications for protection from the Indians; and if he did not get his crops in at once, he would starve the following winter. There was no leisure to think out difficulties coolly; you went at them slapdash. Indeed, had some dreamer wished a knowledge of general principles, he could not have achieved it, since men who read books were scarce and the books themselves scarcer.

As clearings turned into villages and villages into towns, the bustle went on. Society was passing through centuries of evolution in a year or two. Edinburgh had been settled before the days of Rome and had been growing quietly for two thousand years; within a generation after Penn's arrival, Philadelphia was bigger than Edinburgh, the second largest city in the British Empire. Always there were problems to be solved and solved quickly, or you were behind the procession. Ingenuity took the place of profound thought.

A further check on the development of American mechanics was our lack of industry. Although the restricting English colonial laws had been swept aside by the war, war had brought its aftermath of financial depression, and the English themselves had not given up their ideas as to the agricultural role of the North American continent. They were careful to see that machines or mechanics able to build them did not escape from their borders to the United States. It was no coincidence that Fitch was never able to meet anyone who really knew how to build a Boulton and Watt engine.

In America, nothing that could not be made or repaired by a village blacksmith was capable of general application. This created a paradoxical situation: Americans were given to improvising gadgets, but as soon as a gadget became complicated, it was forced into the position of a freak, a philosophical toy. A brilliant man could build an exquisite machine like Rittenhouse's orrery, but it would be regarded in the way we nowadays regard a fine painting, as something rare and strange, to be admired particularly because only one example existed or was likely to exist. Franklin thought of the steamboat not as something industrial or economic; it fell into the category of "philosophical news." This attitude was easier to hold because it was the point of view of everyone's forefathers. The industrial revolution, which was to change the whole attitude of mankind toward innovation, had not yet dawned in America.

Invention in its more complicated forms was still not the attribute of a man of business, but rather of a showman wishing to titivate the public. In every city there were museums that placed among their waxworks mechanical wonders which people paid admission to see. In 1797, for instance, the Columbian Museum in Boston advertised an automatic "canary bird which sings a variety of beautiful songs, minuets, marches, etc., as natural as life," and a clock that marked the hours by a mechanically motivated tableau showing "King Herod beheading John the Baptist, and his daughter holding a charger to receive the head." Charles Willson Peale, the Philadelphia painter, used his engineering abilities to simulate by the use of complicated devices sea battles on a miniature stage.

Fitch was too far ahead of his times. If instead of setting his steamboat up as a commercial rival of the stages that ran beside the Delaware he had advertised it as a curiosity and charged the populace for rides, he might easily, by barnstorming from city to city, have raised much more money than he did with his sober, practical-minded approach which brought him little but ridicule. Indeed, it was by barnstorming that the balloonists of his generation, and many generations after, supported their experiments.

In England, manufacturing, with all the interest in new techniques it implied, had already begun on a large scale, and, since it had paid dividends, there was much money available for the support of further schemes. Invention was rapidly passing over the line that separated the curious from the valuable. Furthermore, although they were not yet very numerous, skilled mechanics existed who understood the importance to invention of meticulous calculations aimed at ascertaining basic scientific principles. Most important of all from the point of view of the steamboat, England was the home of the Watt engine. And now England was entering the lists.

Undaunted by threats of opposition from Boulton and Watt, Rumsey applied for an English patent; exaggerated rumors of his activity created consternation in Scotland. In September 1788 James Taylor, a gentleman's tutor, and William Symington, still said by English writers to be the inventor of the steamboat, were busy on the banks of an ornamental lake installing machinery on a curiously contrived pleasure boat when a newspaper paragraph stopped their breaths short in their throats. "We were a good deal surprised," Taylor wrote their employer, Patrick Miller, "to see in our last newspapers 'that some person had obtained a patent for driving ships with a steam engine.' If so, certainly somebody claims a thing they have no title to. I don't believe any man in England entertained the idea until you published it. . . . I flatter myself we shall yet be the first in motion, and shall venture to say that, though there were twenty others, the method you will see practiced at Dalswinton will be the most commodious and elegant of any."

Miller, the recipient of this letter, was a self-made man. A former banker and merchant in Edinburgh, a major stockholder in the Carron Iron Works, he was, like Boulton, a representative of the new class of capitalists, growing in England but non-existent in America, who had made their fortunes from the industrial revolution. In 1785, at the age of fifty-four, he had retired from business, bought an estate at Dalswinton, and gone in for scientific farming; however, his mind continued to stray toward practical invention. Why, he asked himself, could not warships be driven into the wind by men turning capstans if hulls were built in twins or triplicates, with paddle wheels placed in the spaces between? To persuade skeptical professional seamen, Miller arranged races between his contraptions and more conventional boats; on one occasion Taylor, the tutor of Miller's two children, took his hand at the capstan. Being a white-collar worker, he found the going hard, and finally, in the heat of the race, he shouted at his employer a sentence to the effect, "You ought to use a steam engine." This was in 1787, when Fitch and Rumsey had already been working for two years. After much argument, Taylor persuaded his employer to add to a treatise on multiple boats he published in that year the words, "I also have reason to believe that the power of the steam engine may be applied to work the wheels, so as to give them a quicker motion and consequently increase that of the ship. In the course of the summer I intend to make the experiment."

Taylor thereupon introduced Miller to Symington, with whom he had gone to school. Born in Leadhills, North Britain, in 1764, Symington was the son of a millwright. He had been educated for the ministry at the Universities of Edinburgh and Glasgow, but the clanking of the mill wheels had entered his brain; he veered into civil engineering,* and found employment at the Wanlockhead Lead Mine, which was kept free of water by one of Watt's engines. In daily association with this newly invented wonder—how Fitch would have loved such an opportunity!—Symington speculated on its possibilities. First he built a model of a "steam carriage," an elegant brougham, complete in his drawing with top-hatted coachman, placed on the same set of wheels as a separate engine which pushed from behind. In September 1786 he wrote that his carriage would use one of Watt's machines, but that he had invented a steam engine of his own particularly adapted to "working boats on canals." This engine, for which he secured a patent on June 5, 1787, contained what he considered an improved method of condensation, and in achieving rotary motion dispensed with "a fly wheel to regulate and equalize the effects of the steam engine" by using "the alternate action of ratchet wheels."

Early in 1788 Symington was in Edinburgh searching for a patron when Taylor appeared with Miller. The capitalist feared at first that a steam engine would set any boat on fire, but after much argument he was persuaded to commission Symington to make an engine for a small but elegant double skiff, complete with paddle wheels, which he kept on a pond in his estate. After brass castings had been secured in Edinburgh, Symington and Taylor spent the summer putting the engine together; it weighed half a ton and filled an area 5 feet long between the paddle wheels. One of their worst problems was a bombardment of impatient letters from Miller, who could not understand why the operation took more than a week or two. Taylor explained that they had been held up by minor defects in the castings; they were doing their best, working from six in the morning till dark, and they had called in the assistance of the local watchmaker.

Finally the engine was completed and carried to Miller's estate. The trial was made on October 20, 1788, Symington tells us, "in

---

* In those days, all types of engineering that were not military were called "civil engineering."

the presence of Mr. Miller and various other respectable persons, and the boat was propelled in a manner that gave such satisfaction it was immediately determined to commence another experiment upon a more extended scale." Taylor was to state that the boat went 5 miles an hour, which was a greater speed than either Fitch or Rumsey had claimed. For several weeks the steamboat continued to ply around the little ornamental lake to the delight of Miller and his visitors; then the engine was unshipped and mounted as a trophy in the capitalist's library.

The relative ease with which Symington put together his steamboat is an indication of the great advantages enjoyed by English inventors. He had been able at his leisure to study a Watt engine in action and even make experiments with it. The boat which he used, with its paddle wheels, was the result of researches made by a rich man over a number of years, and this same rich man had singlehanded put up all the money required. Brass castings were easy to come by, since there were expert workmen in Edinburgh; the imperfections Taylor complained of were small and quickly remedied.

It seemed in the cards that the larger boat which Symington now had the backing to build would solve the problem unless Rumsey, who was also working among the capitalists and expert mechanics of England, reached the answer first.

No sooner had Rumsey's negotiations with Boulton and Watt broken down than he met an elegant Englishman named Whiting who traveled in an aura of great wealth. Whiting listened to Rumsey's enthusiastic outpourings and, smoothing the ruffles on his waistcoat, said that if Rumsey needed money he, Whiting, would supply it. The inventor was to order a boat and send the bills to him. Rumsey tells us that "under the allurement of brilliant prospects" he much expanded his engagements.

Boulton and Watt had for some reason thought better of fighting

Rumsey's steamboat patent; they withdrew their caveat, and on November 6, 1788, the inventor received a patent that covered (a) several variations of his pipe boiler; (b) three slightly different applications of jet propulsion to a boat; (c) a combination of his pole boat with steam, in which the poles were fixed to a carriage pulled backward and forward along the keel of the boat by ropes attached to the engine; and (d) a type of steam engine so wild that we must suppose that it was at least partially inspired by the need of something, anything that would not violate Watt's patents. The piston which went up and down in the cylinder was hollow and doubled as a condenser. Although Rumsey could thus claim that like Watt he used a separate condenser, the basic principle of the Watt engine, that of keeping the cylinder hot and the condenser cold, was impossible of application.

On New Year's day 1789, Rumsey wrote Morrow, "I have the friendship and support of men of influence and money. . . . The perfectness of their mechanism here insures me success; and my intention is to get a vessel (if possible) large enough to go to France and Holland by steam alone." He traveled to Dover where he ordered a boat of 100 tons burthen at the cost of 600 guineas to be paid by Whiting. This was much the largest steamboat yet attempted, about twice the size of Fitch's, which should have been a great advantage, since it was easier for a big boat to carry a suitable engine.

When Rumsey returned to London, Thomas Jefferson, the American envoy to France who was busily trying to get him a French patent, gave him a lift in his carriage. Those were golden days. In March 1789 Rumsey wrote his brother that the boat was on the ways, "the engine is making for her, and I expect to make the trial in May. Much depends on the execution. The eyes of many are upon me; the newspapers have something to say about the matter often; and even the playhouse had its strokes of wit upon the occasion. The following lines begin an epilogue spoken the other evening by the celebrated Mrs. Jordan:

> Cunning projectors may pretend to find
> A scheme for sailing ships against the wind;
> But never poet yet could start a scheme
> For navigating plays against the stream. . . .

"This may be truly called the crisis of my life. Should I succeed, I shall gain more reputation than I ever thought possible to fall to the share of one man. If I fail, I shall be ridiculed and abused in all the public prints in Europe; but I think I need not alarm you, for I assure you I am very sanguine and have all the philosophers on my side."

The next week, Rumsey went to Paris to push his claims there. He described his adventures to his new intimate, William West, a fellow-pupil of Robert Fulton's at Benjamin West's studio. "I have this day had a good ride upon my hobby," Rumsey wrote, referring of course to his steamboat scheme. "It was by the particular request of our American ambassador that I took this ride, and glad I was of the opportunity of mounting, having been so long out of practice, by being in a country where the people could not understand the language in which I explained hobby gaits. Mr. Jefferson's hotel was the place appointed for me to exercise, and had not long been mounted before Mr. Jefferson bore me company, and fine sport we should have had, had time permitted, but dinner time came on and company arrived. . . . The horse was therefore obliged to be stabled; however, Mr. Jefferson was so pleased with hobby that he then borrowed him of me, with the explanation of his gaits."

Jefferson, he continued, had been very attentive to his business, calling on the nobility to gain their support. Indeed, Rumsey was in high fettle; he spent hours on the quai, counting the boats that crowded the Seine, and imagining on each an engine that paid him a royalty. Could West stand there too, Rumsey insisted, he would "no longer blame me for being so fond of riding hobby. I have such a friendship for you, that nothing short of observing how pleasantly your little horse [painting] carries you, would prevent me from giving you an invitation to mount along with me, and after a little practice to go to the Emperor of Germany or the King of Spain to solicit exclusive rights or rewards for the use of hobby. This kind of style perhaps [does] not suit business of importance. So seriously let me hear what you would think of such a tour. The countries I speak of exceed France for advantages, and I think there is no human event not yet come to pass that can be calculated upon with such certainty as the boat plan." Rumsey added, in a passage heretofore overlooked but extremely important, that he had met a Mr. Barlow, a "steady, clever man," whom he might make his agent. We shall hear of Barlow again.

Fitch thought of his steamboat experiments as a battle to the death with the fates and all the gods in heaven; Rumsey was playing a delightful game. He described to Morrow his call on Monsieur Leroy, a leading member of the Academy of Arts and Sciences, who "was very clever, understood the business, and spoke English well, but you will pity me when I tell you the necessary preparation to wait on such characters, or in short on any genteel person (if in the afternoon). I was obliged to be dressed in a black coat-waistcoat, breeches, and stockings, my hair handsomely dressed and powdered, and the hind part in a large black bag; by my side a sword, my hat in my hand, and (hard at my—) a lusty French servant brought up the rear; in this order (to use my sister Mary's expression) I went tacking along. You may perhaps think I am joking when giving this description of what is necessary to pay a French visit, but be assured it is true; and that it is as common for genteel persons to walk the streets with their hat under their arms as it is in our country to have them on our heads. In short, many of their hats are nothing more than a three-square flat thing on purpose to be convenient to carry, and are never put on at all. I had like to have forgot the muffs for the hands, which in truth are often as big as a half barrel; and are generally worn by both men and women; you will naturally conceive the appearance. These are things, Charles, that at first I had no idea was a necessary connection of a steamboat."

Leroy greeted him enthusiastically, since he had received communications praising Rumsey from Jefferson and Franklin; indeed, everyone was enthusiastic. Jefferson wrote Dr. Willard that Rumsey's "principal merit is in the improvement of the boiler, and instead of the complicated machinery of oars and paddles proposed by others, the substitution of so simple a thing as the reaction of a stream of water on his vessel. . . . He has suggested a great number of mechanical improvements in a variety of branches; and upon the whole is the most original and greatest mechanical genius I have ever seen."

There was one blot in the French picture, but Rumsey was sure that with such backing he could erase it easily. On November 10, 1788, one of Jouffroy's former supporters, L'Abbé d'Arnal, had been granted an exclusive privilege for steamboats in France. Jefferson did not consider him a formidable contender, since he had hardly been able to make his steam mill run. And then, as Rumsey wrote Morrow, "Frenchmanlike full of politeness, as soon as I arrived, he took his departure for another world from where no travelers are yet returned." Yet because of d'Arnal's previous claim, Rumsey's advisers decided not to push his scheme in France until the steamboat that was building in England proved a success.

Leaving Jefferson and Barlow in charge of his business, Rumsey returned to England in April; he assured everyone that he would have his boat running in less than a month. When he reached London, he donned his elegant French clothes to call on his elegant backer, Whiting, but that gentleman was not at his lodgings. He was in debtor's prison. The boat had not been paid for, and Rumsey had contracted for it under his own name. A few days before, he had written Morrow in high spirits, "Poor America! I could have lived better in you for a whole year for the money the last twenty days has cost me." Now the inventor was frightened. The prison which had swallowed up Whiting seemed to yawn for him as well.

However, his gambler's luck held. Not only did a timely remittance from the Rumsean Society in Philadelphia pay his immediate debts, but he met a lamb, "a good-natured, honest creature that knew no more of my schemes than an idiot," who obligingly bleated out an offer of £500. Vaughan and Barclay added £200 between them, and Rumsey continued to spend in a regal style. Since as an alien he could not register his boat in his own name, he did it in the lamb's. But soon there was a knocking on his door. The innocent had decided he could invest his funds better in another way; "with as little concern as he would break a child's plaything," he remarked that he must have his money back or he would sell the boat. Rumsey scrambled through his correspondence and found that in one letter the lamb had made himself liable for the vessel. "I prevailed upon the founder to call upon him, and make a demand of the money for it. This frightened him so that he came to terms immediately."

Rumsey demanded more funds from his Philadelphia backers, but they felt they had already advanced him enough to build his boat; as soon as it was proved a success, they notified him, they would pay for machinery to be used in America. "I have written them a spirited letter," Rumsey reported to Morrow, "in which I told them that as this experiment would be at my own risk, that I expected all the profits, should any arise, of that vessel." He then borrowed huge funds in his own name, since he estimated it would cost more than 1,000 additional guineas to finish his steamboat.

"This, you will say, is a great deal of money for me to borrow in in a strange country," he wrote Morrow. He was not unused to debt, he implied, but "the foregoing difficulties at time bear harder on me than you ever knew me to encounter in America." His financial troubles had been the reason "for the delay of the experiment to so late a period." However, the boat was now in London; the engine had been placed on board and was "going slowly together. I am quite sanguine. She is a beautiful vessel. . . . I have called [her] *The Columbian Maid*, but think to change it to *The Rumsean Experiment* as soon as success is ascertained." Here is a nice evaluation of the relative importance of patriotism and personal pride.

Rumsey, who had a passion for secrecy, found it "a great undertaking to attempt such an experiment as mine under the eyes of one million souls." Since "several attempts are making in different parts of the Kingdom to work vessels by steam, though not on my plan," he had been forced to make his efforts public in order to secure the patronage "necessary in a country like this, where almost anything can be accomplished by bribery."

Like the good gambler he was, Rumsey moved with a cheerful, self-confident air through the world of huge assets and huge debts in which he was thrown. Conscious that all England was watching him, he drew a lace handkerchief from his sleeve with so graceful an air you would not guess his hands were more used to running a grist mill on a wilderness stream. Yet there was homesickness in his heart. As he heard the accomplished players of London—Garrick perhaps—speak lines of incisive wit, his eyes misted and he saw instead the little log playhouse in the frontier hamlet of Bath. He wrote Morrow a particular request to tell him how that theatre prospered. "I am always glad to hear the transactions of a people so dear to me as the Americans are; for believe me, Charles! what little freedom and virtue there is in the world is mostly in poor America." But even his thoughts of home were not altogether peaceful. "I am astonished," he wrote, "at Fitch's perseverance and rascality. I wish you had got him taken with a writ."

Jefferson was all eagerness to hear that Rumsey's steamboat had triumphed; periodically the inventor assured him that the delays would last only a few more days. In September he wrote, "I am not under the least apprehension of failing. I have by a weight (hung to a cord made fast to an anchor and drawn over a pulley in the seat of the vessel) tried what power was necessary to hold her against the current of the Thames. The power of the engine being known, it may be (nearly) ascertained how fast she will go." He had little doubt that she would cover 150 miles a day, moving sometimes at a rate of 10 miles an hour.

When Jefferson sailed back to the United States in October 1789 he wrote Rumsey, "As I feel infinitely interested in its success, would you be so good, my dear sir, as to drop me a line as soon as the experiment shall be made?" Once the *Columbian Maid* had triumphed, "Mr. Short will do for you at Paris whatever I could have done toward obtaining you a patent there."

Six months later, on April 27, 1790, Jefferson wrote William Short, "What has become of Rumsey and his steamship? Not a word is known here. I fear therefore he has failed."

Symington in the meanwhile had not been idle, and many facilities that could not help smoothing his path were placed at his disposal. Miller had given him all the money he needed, and supplied a large double boat, complete with paddle wheel, the result of long and expensive experiments in that method of shipbuilding. The engine was made under Symington's and Taylor's supervision at the Carron Iron Works, one of the most advanced metalworking shops in all England. An expert builder, John Heriot, constructed the oak frame on which the engine rested. Work went swiftly according to American standards: on May 19, 1789, Symington wrote that he was setting out for Carron the next day; on June 24 the vessel was delivered to the iron works; and by November the completed steamboat was moored in the Forth and Clyde Canal, ready for its trial.

The two cylinders of the engine were placed upside down, the piston rods connected to the opposite ends of a walking beam suspended below them. A belt of rope leading from the ends of the beam looped over a wheel hung above and between the cylinders, and another belt carried the oscillating motion of the wheel to two paddle wheels, each fixed with a ratchet so that it would turn in only one direction. The cylinders were 18 inches in diameter, the exact width with which Fitch was experimenting, and had a 3-foot stroke.

A trial in November proved unsatisfactory, since it revealed weaknesses both in the engine and the paddle wheels. These matters mended, a second experiment was made early in December. Accounts of the results vary. Miller's grandson says the boat went 7 miles an hour, the figure accepted by most authors, and an Edinburgh newspaper some months later gave the velocity as "no less than 6½ to 7 miles an hour." But Symington himself when an old man wrote that "the boat glided along, propelled at the rate of 5 miles an hour, and all parties interested declared themselves satisfied with the success of my performance."

Whichever of these figures we accept, Symington's boat, although it had not gone as far as Fitch's, was the fastest ever built by man. Yet Miller was disgusted. On December 7, 1789, he wrote Taylor,

"You may easily imagine that my thoughts have been a good deal taken up, since I saw you, with what passed at Carron on Wednesday and Thursday. I am now satisfied that Mr. Symington's steam engine is the most improper of all steam engines for giving motion to a vessel, and that he does not know how to calculate frictions or mechanical powers. . . . Remember the iron bolts or rabbets that drew on two different trials; they will do so again, if they are not made stronger. It was folly in the extreme not to have perceived at first that their strength was not in proportion to the other parts of the engine." Furthermore, there was too much friction in the engine itself. "This is past remedy. . . . The engine cannot be of any use to me now." He instructed Taylor to sell it.

Thus Miller washed his hands of Symington forever, and Symington, making no great effort to secure other backers, turned his attention for the time being to other things. Yet the boats they had built with a comparatively small amount of labor and expense had functioned at least as well as any of the American boats whose inventors were still trying.

The probable explanation is that the more sophisticated British had higher standards than the Americans. No one had criticized Fitch or Rumsey for not understanding "how to calculate frictions or mechanical powers"; yet Symington's lapse in this direction was enough to damn him completely in his patron's eyes.

Symington was a tyro compared to Watt and several other English steam-engine builders; why was not the best mechanical skill available in England applied to the steamboat? Perhaps we shall get an answer from Miller's next move, which was to offer to go into partnership with Boulton and Watt for the building of such vessels. On April 24, 1790, Watt wrote Miller's agent a letter that is among the most important documents in our history. Watt said he had received vague accounts of Miller's experiments, "from which we could gather nothing conclusive except that the vessel did move with considerable velocity. From what we hear of Mr. Symington's engines, we are disposed to consider them as attempts to evade our exclusive privilege; but as we thought them so defective in mechanical contrivance as not to be likely to do us immediate hurt, we thought it best to leave them to be judged by Dame Nature first, before we brought them to an earthly court.

"We are obliged to Mr. Miller for his favorable opinion of us. . . . We are also fully sensible of his kind intentions in offering to associate us in his schemes; but the time of life we have both arrived at, and the multiplicity of business we are at present engaged in, must plead our excuse for [not] entering into any new concern whatsoever as partners, but as engineers and engine makers we are ready to serve him to the best of our abilities at our customary prices for rotative engines, and to assist in anything we can to bring the scheme to perfection.

"We conceive that there may be considerable difficulty in making a steam engine to work regularly in the open sea, on account of the undulating motion of the vessel affecting the *vis inertia* of the matter; however, this we should endeavor to obviate as far as we can.

"It may not be improper to mention that Earl Stanhope has lately taken a patent for moving vessels by steam, but we believe not by wheels. His Lordship has also applied to us for engines; but we believe we are not likely to agree with him, as he lays too much stress upon his own ingenuity."

This letter reveals what a tremendous loss the world sustained when Rumsey's partnership negotiations with Boulton and Watt broke down. The disillusioned engine builders clearly did not intend to offer to anyone else the opportunity that had been so abused. Although for a time charmed into a more sanguine attitude by the notoriously persuasive American, Watt now made it clear that he was skeptical about the possibility of applying steam to navigation. This was to create a major impediment to English development, since Watt's patents were so basic that they kept anyone else from building an engine suitable for a steamboat. Whatever improvements of their own other engine builders evolved, they were forced to use the separate condenser and thus infringe Watt's patents. Jonathan Hornblower, who developed the compound engine, was sent to jail for attempting to apply his important discovery.

However, Watt said he would be glad to serve any steamboat inventor as engine builder. Why was immediate advantage not taken of this offer? Partly, it seems, because Watt placed all the prestige of his great accomplishment behind the statement that steam engines would not work on rough water. This discouraged Miller so completely that he abandoned the project forever.

Watt's comments on Lord Stanhope give us an indication of another difficulty. Flying as they were in the face of the best mechanical opinion, steamboat projectors were likely to be visionary fellows who had ideas of their own they wished to apply, while Boulton and Watt were not willing to work with a man who laid "too much stress upon his own ingenuity."

Stanhope himself was one of the most eccentric of that eccentric body, the British peerage. An earl with a vast landed estate, he was so great a person that whatever he did was condoned, if not admired. He proved to be very able and very uncontrolled: powerful, brilliant, and wild. Sent at the age of eleven to Geneva to be tutored by a leading scientist, four years later he was an acknowledged genius; he painted pictures and invented a mathematical instrument. At eighteen he won a prize from the Academy of Stockholm for his paper on the pendulum.

On his return to England, he married the sister of William Pitt. Although he hung tenaciously to his vast estates and took no back talk from his inferiors, he became a powerful spokesman for democracy. Several times while England was locked in a death battle with Napoleon, he presented resolutions to the House of Lords extolling the hated French ruler. Forming a "minority of one," he was known as "Citizen Stanhope." His secretary was arrested for treason, but no one dared lay a finger on the great peer himself.

He enjoyed associating with mechanics, and during his life made several important inventions; he is regarded as the father of stereotyping. His interest in steam engines was aroused by two of Watt's double-acting rotary engines which ground corn at Blackfriars. Having studied these most up-to-date machines, Stanhope set out to improve them. Soon he had installed an engine in a skiff on one of his private lakes. There is no record that the boat moved under its own power.

On October 23, 1789, he wrote Boulton a letter which must have seemed perfectly natural to him, but reads today like a masterpiece of insolence. He wished Boulton to give him plans of one of Watt's "best fire engines," so that he might modify and improve them, and furthermore wanted the manufacturer to supply him with an experienced workman to put his own ideas into effect. The letter, which was written in the third person as becomes a communication from the great to the lowly, contains such statements as "Lord Stanhope would be glad to be informed whether Mr. Boulton had made any new discovery in respect to his fire engine since his patent, and what is the nature of such discoveries." Clearly he meant to include them in his own contemplated improvement.

In May 1790 Stanhope inquired the price of a Watt engine and then followed up his request with a letter telling Boulton how steam engines should be built. The powerful manufacturer, as we have seen, expressed his irritation with Stanhope to Miller, another commoner; but to the peer himself he was obsequious. The firm, he wrote, did not quite understand his Lordship's desires. "As soon as one of us can come, we shall do ourselves the honor of waiting your Lordship. . . . In the interim we remain with respect, My Lord, your Lordship's most faithful and obedient humble servants. . . ."

The firm next submitted diagrams of their conception of a marine engine; in return they received several large sheets, closely written and headed, "Objections to the plans of Boulton and Watt." Eventually Stanhope had an engine built according to his own design by an independent firm of mechanics. He intended to apply it to the boat he had already patented, a double-ended vessel to be motivated by duck's feet similar to those often suggested and already tried by Jouffroy. However, the peer had a thousand other affairs to attend to, and perhaps his steam-engine ideas were more original than sound. For the time being, his boat experiments came to nothing.

Some time between November 1789 and February 1790, Rumsey put in motion the big, vastly expensive vessel of more than 100 tons that had been built by professionals at Dover and fitted with the engine he had constructed after studying the machines of Watt. The experiment was made in secret at a London wharf and Rumsey communicated the results to no one, until at last he wrote Morrow on February 27, 1790, "The fate of my affairs took so much a turn for the worse that I never after dare communicate them to you. . . . Every possible disappointment attended my experiment." Speaking of his boat, he continued, "When it was all put together, it proved so imperfect that almost the whole of it had to be done over again."

"The great delay and enormous expense attending it made my friends doubtful and uneasy," he complained. People who had once reached cheerfully into their pocketbooks, now refused to lend him money to meet the bills that were piling up on his desk. Then a man from whom he had borrowed £90 went bankrupt, and "his assignees were as inexorable as devils"; they swore out a writ against him. "My friends on hearing of this stood aloof." For a fortnight Rumsey kept away from his lodgings and dodged through the streets, evading "the vigilance of the London bailiffs, or rather devils, which would without the least remorse have taken me to (hell) prison."

While he was thus lying low, he heard that an elegant gentleman, who professed to be a lord, had been calling at the wharf to see his boat. "I thought this was a scheme of the bailiff to take me," but when the man called a third time Rumsey sent William West to take him on board. West reported that the man had proved to be Pitt's brother-in-law, Lord Stanhope, but the eminence of his visitor did not make it any easier when, having had all explained to him, "his Lordship . . . petitioned for a patent for a similar invention. I have stopped him and we are to have a hearing I expect soon before the Lord Chancellor. How it may end I cannot tell."

Then "the machinists took alarm from my not attending vessel as usual, and all came on me at once." In these terrible straits, Rumsey rose to the height of his gambler's skill. Although he had not a cent to pay them, he called his employees together. "Previous thereto having before learned the value thereof, I dressed myself in style. I therefore had on my head [a wig] as large and white as a lord's wig." He marched into the meeting of clamorous mechanics with a haughty air, and surveyed them for a minute while he took a calm pinch of snuff; if he was searching to see if the bailiff were there too, his expression did not show it. In a bored drawl that rose gradually to the pitch of high-born indignation, he told his employees that if he paid them now, as they asked, he would instantly dismiss them; he could find plenty of other workmen who would wait "as usual" until six months after the vessel was completed. "This maneuver, and an air of importance that I forced on (much against my natural inclination) made the mean rascals (for such the most of them are) bow to the ground and tell me with one consent that they would finish the work, if I would let them have the *honor*. . . . This enabled me to go on a while longer, during the time I kept myself concealed."

At last William West and some other friends lent him enough money to satisfy the bailiff; he could walk the streets freely once more, but he had many other debts that the bailiff might hear about at any moment. He considered trying to make up with his Philadelphia backers, but he discovered that as he had not mentioned their share in the invention in applying for his patent, if he acknowledged it now the patent would be broken. And at this moment the growing suspicions of the members of the Rumsean Society induced their treasurer, Wynkoop, to try to get their money back; he drew a note on Rumsey for £1,000. The inventor was unable to pay; this fact, noted at a public office, "was a new drawback upon my reputation."

"My last hopes of relief being thus cut off, it became absolutely necessary for me to delay the experiment, lest an unsuccessful attempt should make my creditors all fall on me at once. This I did by discharging part of the hands, but the disappointments was so frequent in obtaining the different parts of the mechanism from people that had not the best faith respecting their pay, that no deception became necessary to the spinning out the time."

Rumsey considered his invention so valuable that he had consistently refused to sell a share of his patents, although he had borrowed thousands of pounds. Now, since no one would lend him a farthing, he was forced to negotiate with two men who had long wanted to buy part of his rights; they jockeyed for position during three months, "both parties acting like armies of observation." Finally, on March 25, 1790, Rumsey entered into partnership with Daniel Parker, originally of Watertown, Mass., and Samuel Rogers. They were to advance him £2,000, one-half in cash and one-half in goods. This was to be increased to £7,500 when the boat was finished.

Rumsey had money again, but his boat remained recalcitrant. On April 23, he wrote: "My vessel has not yet been tried; you will think it strange, but the truth is I cannot get my machine perfect as yet, though I have proved it principally [in principle], and have made from 20 to 22 strokes in a minute. My vessel was fast moored; therefore, I could not see what effect it would have. It would not do to let her loose, as I could not depend upon the continuance of the engine. I have now a great part newly made new, and expect soon to give it another trial. Of success I have no doubt, but am distressed on account of the delay which takes place. If I had not made the sale [of his patent rights] I must have been in a London jail before this. The danger, however, is over."

Six months later, on October 24, 1790, Rumsey admitted to Morrow that he had staged no public experiment yet, nor would he venture to set a time. "Appearances, however, is in favor of its going soon."

XIV. *Lord High Admirals of the Delaware*

Fitch had been plugging doggedly along in provincial Philadelphia, a scarecrow figure in worn-out clothes, spending pennies where Rumsey spent pounds. Thrift helped him little; he too had financial difficulties. During the winter of 1788-89, a year or so before Rumsey's steamboat had failed at its trial, Fitch's backers refused to put up another cent for his experiments. The indefatigable promoter, however, snatched victory from defeat by organizing a second company, which agreed to take over the old boat and build another, on condition that if this vessel succeeded, the two companies would merge and draw equal profits. Although he had already spent more than £1,600 without return, he succeeded in selling forty additional shares for £10 each. Of the members of the old company only Richard Wells, Richard Stockton, and Dr. Say subscribed; new shareholders included Isaac Morris, brewer; Richard Morris, merchant; Robert Scott, engraver; Sam Wetherill, druggist; Wood Lloyd, tailor; and Francis White, "dealer in public securities." But most important of all was Dr. William Thornton, who bought sixteen shares.

Thornton was the first scientifically educated man to work with Fitch. Born to a wealthy American family, he had attended the famous medical school in Edinburgh and had completed his education in France, becoming intimate with advanced natural philosophers. He had just arrived in provincial Philadelphia, where his foreign manners and familiarity with the European great made him an object of awe and veneration. He bought a fine house, joined the Philosophical Society, and launched with applause into many arts: he was painter and poet, doctor and astronomer; he was an expert on government. As an architect, he designed rich men's houses, and was to draw the plans on which the national capitol was based. And now he was backing Fitch's steamboat.

Thornton showed eagerness to take over active direction of the enterprise, but Fitch, although he wrote, "I am conscious that my abilities are inadequate to the task," did not wish to collaborate with a fine gentleman. To fill Voight's place, he hired John Hall, an English mechanic who had once worked on inventions with Thomas Paine. They ordered a new 18-inch cylinder. While the Atsion Furnace was proceeding with slow puzzlement on this assignment, Fitch continued his warfare with Rumsey's backers; they were still trying to undermine his monopolies by legislative action and court decisions.

Seeking evidence to disprove his rival's claims, Fitch invaded Rumsey's home village of Shepherdstown. He registered at Winkoop's Inn under an assumed name, but he could get no information until he explained his business. Although he did not like the landlord's face, yet "thinking as a tavern keeper it was his interest to keep my secrets for the sake of keeping me," Fitch asked how fast Rumsey's steamboat had gone. Winkoop replied, "nearly as fast as he could walk." When he saw Fitch write the words down, he changed his statement to "faster than he could walk." Fitch commented later that the landlord had such spindling legs that "I will risk a hundred dollars on it that I can find two men who will roll a hogshead of molasses on level ground faster than he can walk, run, or in any way that he will get along with the help of his legs only."

Fitch wandered into the barroom, stood a drink or two to the loungers there, and then under the guise of idle gossip brought up the subject of Rumsey's steamboat. As the intruder's seemingly casual questions elicited unsuspecting replies, the landlord became greatly agitated; he paced back and forth outside the open door, as if waiting for someone to come out. Finally he beckoned to one of the men, and the two of them, after a whispered conference, disappeared down the street.

Fitch then proceeded to another tavern, where he was told that Rumsey's boat had never gone more than 400 yards under steam, and that a man who had bet it would move at the rate of 3 miles an hour had lost his money. Delighted with this gossip, Fitch returned to Winkoop's Inn.

"I discovered from my landlady's looks that there was something extraordinary on foot." A big man, sitting quietly with a glass before him, observed Fitch with sober interest. Then Winkoop bustled in, called Fitch to another room, and warned that should he meet Rumsey's brother-in-law, Charles Morrow, he would certainly be attacked. Returning to the barroom, Fitch paid his reckoning, but as he prepared to leave, the large man rose from his table and asked for a word with him. They went into the other room, where the man asked if he was John Fitch. On receiving the intruder's assent, the man introduced himself as Charles Morrow.

"Mr. Morrow, I have no private discourse to hold with you," said Fitch, skipping back to the barroom. That chamber was now full of drinkers, but Fitch "was not much alarmed on account of its being Sunday, knowing that in a general way the Scots-Irish parsons have made their Scots-Irish hearers nearly one-seventh as civil as Quakers, and although they allow them to give a loose to their passions six days out of seven, for every kind of dissipation and debauchery, yet to atone for these they seem to be obliged to be civil one day in seven."

Morrow, however, "began to abuse me in words exceedingly, and although I believe that I made cool, determined, and many replies, he found that my temper could not be ruffled to excess." Noticing that the drinkers laughed at Morrow's sallies and frowned at his, Fitch decided "had I been a Goliath and he a child, he could have abused me in that place what he pleased"; and "finally concluded that it was best for me to retire. When he saw that I was about leaving the room, he crossed his hands as if prepared for boxing, and run his right hand with his fingers extended into my face, which hit me on the chin. When without saying much more, I turned and went out."

Fitch fled across the river into Maryland, "not knowing but he might have an inclination to follow me." From Sharpsburg, he wrote

Morrow that he was willing to take their difference before a court, and that if they met again, "I hope you will have too much honor to avail yourself of your superior strength or youth."

Nervous but not daunted, Fitch continued to secure affidavits in the Rumsey country. One evening he resolved to stop at "a sort of a whiskey tavern for woodchoppers and forgemen." As he neared the house in the twilight, he heard boisterous singing. A man put his head out the window, shouted, "Here he is!" and the singing instantly ceased. Then a "stout, portly looking man" hurried from the door; he stared at Fitch with such intensity that he missed the step and fell headlong. Stepping over him, Fitch walked into the tap room which was full of men flushed with whiskey. Instantly, Fitch threw himself down on a couch, thinking "the greatest ruffian could not attack a tired man lying on the bed." To conciliate his companions, Fitch ordered a drink all round: most of the topers accepted, though with bad grace, but the portly man, who had followed Fitch in, refused to drink. When a supper of milk-bread and boiled potatoes was served, Fitch, fearing to sit up, said he was too tired to eat. The portly man "went and took a large potato out of the dish. I at once let in an opinion it was intended for me, and turned my-self . . . to watch him, and kept my eyes fixed on him. Some short time after, getting one of his companions between him and me, he threw the potato with all his seeming strength and hit me on my breast near the pit of my stomach, but the hurt was not great." Springing from the bed, Fitch upbraided his assailant for attacking a man who had given him no offense. His words seemed to cow the crowd, who offered him no more injury, although as he left the portly man said with a leer that he would be back the next morning. Taking the hint, Fitch rose with the dawn and, his business done, hurried back to Philadelphia. He had collected a lot of hearsay evidence which did little either to strengthen or weaken his case.

Fitch's new cylinder had been cast and bored in June 1789, but the workmanship was so defective that it had to be lined with copper, a task which took till August. Then at last the engine was set up, with a condenser invented by Hall. At the last moment, Dr. Thornton rushed up with a condenser of his own design; he overrode Fitch's objection that it was too weak and forced them to take the engine apart again so that it could be installed. At the first trial, Fitch's gloomy prophecies proved correct: it crushed like an egg shell. "And when we took them out had the appearance of Pharaoh's lean kine, and looked worse than anything that I ever saw in the land of Egypt." While Thornton had another made of heavier copper, Hall's condenser was tried; the boat moved, but not fast enough.

Fitch, who was still staying at old lodgings, was increasingly maltreated by his landlord because he could not pay his rent; "had it not been for one of the best and most manly generous women on earth, Mrs. Krafft, the excesses of my wretchedness would have been intolerable." Despite her love for Voight and her pregnancy, Fitch wrote, "All I can say in return is, I pray that I may die before her, and be appointed her guardian angel to conduct her to heaven." He attended her during her lying-in, and saw that the baby, which was born in secret on August 10, was placed with a good nurse. Then Voight returned to his lady and his collaborator; both received him joyously, for neither could get on without him. Again the members of this strange triangle sat together contentedly in the snug parlor; Fitch's jealousy was lulled to rest by the promise of the other two that they would have no further relations.

Voight's offer to return to work on the steamboat "was the most acceptable to me of anything I ever experienced, unless it was a dish of sturgeon spawn boiled in fresh water without bread in the time of my savage captivity. The comparison is coarse, but the feelings similar, as both alleviated my distress of mind." What a joy it was when he hurried to the river front to spend another day on the endless task of completing his boat, to see his friend there before him, calmly smoking his pipe as he hammered in a bolt!

But Fitch's encouragement was short-lived; Thornton's strengthened condenser proved as much of a failure as the others. Despite the enlarged cylinder, which Fitch had been certain would almost double the vessel's speed, the steamboat went no faster than it had the year before, "which alarmed me beyond measure when I made a representation to the company which is here too hideous to insert."

Fitch admitted that he could not imagine what was wrong, that he did not know how to complete his engine. At that time, "the horrors of a [debtor's] prison were my most extended and exalted ideas of happiness. . . . Could I once become so happy as my savage captors made me, I should not think of complaining." He was too discouraged even to visit his steamboat any more.

Voight continued with the project alone. He invented a new condenser and a curious forcing pump to throw water into it; neither helped. Then Fitch had an idea which brought him running to the workshop: the air pumps were clearly too small. When larger pumps had been built and installed, a quick trial showed that the condensation was still imperfect.

Trying to keep from falling again into the pit of despair, Fitch nourished the hope that the engine would work better in a more extended test. A day was set, and in the early morning he placed a fire under the boiler. Soon, however, clouds towered in the sky and the wind began to blow a gale; Fitch quenched the fire, or so he thought. That night, as he tossed uneasily in his sleep, he heard shouts under his window. Springing awake, he realized that someone was screaming that his boat was aflame.

Fitch leaped into his clothes and hurried down the street, stopping only to pound on a neighbor's door. Mr. Streby pulled the bolt sleepily, a candle in his hand. But when Fitch had blurted out his need for help, the neighbor came wide awake. Portentous in his nightcap, he leveled an accusing finger and told Fitch that this was clearly a judgment of Heaven to punish him for operating his boat on Sunday. He, Streby, would certainly not interfere with God's justice. The door slammed.

Fitch ran on alone through the empty streets of midnight. As he neared the boat he smelled smoke, saw a glow against the sky. He leaped on board the crackling vessel, and managed to sink it, thus putting the fire out. Looking down at the water under which his beloved contraption lay, he decided that he was really defeated at last.

"But as my mind had become so callous to disappointments, after the first day's shock it did not seem to affect me, and [I] began to conclude within myself that the gods thought it [the steamboat] too valuable to be possessed by mortal man, and meant to dispute it with me inch by inch."

Throwing his challenge upward to the gods, Fitch raised his vessel and mended it. At last the new air pumps were given an extended trial, but they too failed to make the 18-inch cylinder propel the boat faster than the 12-inch cylinder had done.

Now the boat was put up for the winter. A year had passed with much activity and expense, but Fitch was in a worse plight than he had ever been in, since he had tried everything he could think of, and had failed to improve his engine.

Fitch was a hard man to discourage. When the worst of the winter weather was over, a month or so after Rumsey had made his disastrous trial of his English steamboat, Fitch returned to work. He ran at once into a disagreement with the directors of his company. Convinced that when something did not work the answer was to enlarge it, the stockholders had ordered a huge boiler of the old-fashioned type and an even bigger condenser than had yet been tried. Fitch objected to the augmented boiler, but they paid no attention, for they had lost confidence in Fitch. While the inventor squabbled with his patrons in an ecstasy of misery, hating them because they were gentlemen and he of inferior station, the new contraptions were made and installed. On Easter Monday the directors, led by the two elegant physicians, Thornton and Say, flocked to the wharf to try out their improvements. Fitch, who wanted the boat to succeed but liked to be proved right, must have felt mingled sorrow and joy when the craft moved sluggishly, barely stemming the tide.

Suddenly, when all seemed lost, Fitch conceived one of the basic principles of steam-engine building. He remembered that they had used a small condenser, a mere pipe, in 1787, when the boat had worked most efficiently; Voight had often commented that the steam overran the condenser and penetrated into the air pump. Suddenly he realized that since the object was to have as complete a vacuum as possible after the steam had been destroyed, the condenser should be so completely filled with steam that every bit of air was driven out. "The smaller that the condenser is," he wrote, "I believe the more perfect the vacuum can be made, provided the steam can be destroyed in time." To achieve quick condensation, he favored spraying in a jet of water. After years of struggle which had several times carried him to the brink of total defeat, Fitch had reinvented Watt's condenser which had been in common use in England for a decade.

The new apparatus was installed and tried out on April 12. While Fitch and Voight held their breaths, the engine moved with a new power: they seemed to fly into the center of the Delaware; but then, so great was the force exerted, a rope broke and the paddles came to a standstill. The inventors dropped anchor and asked some of the sailboats, which were scudding by them in a strong northwest wind, to tow them ashore. "Every one refused us assistance, and most of them exulted and seemed to feel heartfelt pleasure in seeing us in distress." They were "ignorant watermen who . . . would rather that we should be sunk and drowned than that we should make a boat that should go faster than their own. This made me curse Christians and wish that Heaven had been so kind to me as to have let me have been born in some barbarian or savage country." But despite his fury, Fitch must have realized that he was about to show them.

The damage was repaired, and a new trial made on April 16. "Although the wind blew very fresh at the northeast, we reigned Lord High Admirals of the Delaware, and no boat on the river could hold way with us, but all fell astern, although several sailboats, which were very light, and heavy sails, that brought their gunwales well down to the water, came out to try us. We also passed many boats with oars, which were strong manned, and no loading, who seemed to stand still when we passed them. We also run round a vessel that was beating to windward in about 2 miles, which had about 1½ miles start of us, and came in without any of our works failing. . . .

Thus has been effected by little Johnny Fitch and Harry Voight one of the greatest and most useful arts that was ever introduced into the world."

Soon a formal test was undertaken to determine the exact speed of the boat. A mile was measured on Front Street and a member of the company stationed at each end with a flag. Fitch and Voight got up steam, and when the tide was absolutely motionless, started the vessel in the direction of the first flag. The engine puffed and rocked, while the paddles in the rear, clanking roisterously, pushed the vessel ahead with an uneven motion whose strength and certainty delighted the inventors. They were careful to get up full speed before they passed the first flag. Then they leaned forward, as if by their will they could make the vessel go faster. When steam began to escape from the safety valve, they almost certainly hung a weight on it, as Fitch admits they did on various later occasions. While the city rushed by, as if they were behind a galloping horse, did the minutes seem short as seconds or long as hours; did Fitch's heart contract with anxiety or flush with exaltation? We do not know, for in his autobiography Fitch was concerned only with failures and sorrows; he passed over the successful days of his boat with hardly a mention.

The engine had not faltered, the paddles had not missed a stroke, when the second flag was passed. How eagerly the inventors must have steered for shore to learn the result. Holding watches in their hands, the members of the company greeted them joyously; the steamboat had covered the mile at the rate of 8 miles an hour. Amid universal jubilation it was agreed that this was fast enough to enable them to compete with the stages that ran along the Delaware. Everyone admitted that the long years of experiment had finally been crowned with success, and by mutual agreement, the two companies, the old and the new, were united.

But before commercial trips could be undertaken, a cabin had to be built. As a distinguished architect, Thornton rushed home to make the design, but when he showed the graceful result of his genius to Fitch, the steamboat builder cried out that it was too high and would slow up the boat. Passengers could stoop to reach their seats, he

insisted. "If it must be elegant, make it low and line it with gold."
A dispute arose which "shook the foundations of our scheme," but
again Fitch was overruled; the high cabin was installed.

The members of the united companies agreed to a levy of £10
a share to build the second boat required to fulfill the conditions of
the Virginia monopoly, and took steps to put the existing boat into
commercial operation. For the first time the newspapers noticed
Fitch's project; the following paragraph, published in the *Gazette
of the United States* for May 15, was quite generally reprinted:
"Burlington, May 11, 1790. The friends of science and the liberal
arts will be gratified in hearing that we were favored, on Sunday
last, with a visit from the ingenious Mr. Fitch, accompanied by
several gentlemen of taste and knowledge in mechanics, in a steamboat constructed on an improved plan. From these gentlemen we
learn that they came from Philadelphia in three hours and a quarter,
with a head wind, the tide in their favor. On their return, by accurate
observations, they proceeded down the river at the rate of upward of
7 miles per hour."

In May, Ewing, Rittenhouse, and General James Irvine all swore
they had been carried through the water at 6 miles an hour. On June
5 Lewis Rue and John Shaffer were carried 90 miles in twelve and
one-half hours. This was by far the longest trip ever taken by a
steamboat, but it was only a beginning.

Starting on June 14, the company ran the following advertisement
in the *Federal Gazette* and other papers: "THE STEAMBOAT is now
ready to take passengers and is intended to set off from Arch Street
Ferry, in Philadelphia, every Monday, Wednesday, and Friday for
Burlington, Bristol, Bordentown, and Trenton, to return on Tues-
days, Thursdays, and Saturdays. Price for passengers, 2/6 to Burlington and Bristol, 3/9 to Bordentown, 5s to Trenton."

On June 16 Governor Mifflin and the august council of Pennsylvania trooped on board. After a successful though smoky ride, they
authorized Fitch to buy flags at their expense. The man who longed
for honor above everything was hilarious with delight, but later he
was to be bitter, for the Governor refused to make a formal presenta-
tion, saying the members of the council had subscribed for the

flags as individuals. Yet the flags remained his most cherished possession.

For the first time in history a steamboat was making trips on a regular schedule, covering not a mile or two but, during that one brief summer, 2,000 or 3,000 miles. Breakdowns were rare. By hanging weights on the safety valve, Voight blew out the boiler three times; an axle tree broke twice, and once the grate burned out. No other mishaps occurred, Fitch insists, that took more than two hours to fix; the boat ran 500 miles between accidents. Its velocity seems to have been between a minimum of 6 miles an hour under unfavorable conditions, and a maximum of 7 or 8 when every resource was mustered for speed.

Citing these facts, a steadily increasing number of authorities say that the invention of the steamboat had been completed; Fitch was the true and only inventor. Fulton, they insist, was merely a late follower of Fitch. Let us reserve judgment until we have examined the rest of the story.

Money has a way of determining events, and despite its efficiency Fitch's steamboat did not operate at a profit. On a better than average day, for instance, only seven passengers boarded the boat at Philadelphia—two for Trenton, one for Bordentown, one for Bristol, and three for Burlington—a total take of 20 shillings, while the trip cost the company 30. Although the steamboat went faster than a river sailboat with anything but a following wind, the stagecoaches reached Burlington in an hour and a half less time, and the fact that the steamboat only charged half the coach fare did not seem to overcome the difference. Even when the directors advertised ridiculously cheap trips on Saturday to that amusement center, Gray's Gardens on the Schuylkill, most people used the more expensive regular ferry. An attempt to lure passengers by serving sausages with beer, rum, or porter in Thornton's elegant cabin failed materially to increase business. The citizenry still preferred traditional methods of travel.

Fitch was himself to explain these difficulties as follows: "By unseen and unavoidable events, the City of Philad. have become my enemies. The disgust which new projects gives to many, my despicable appearance, my project being calculated to make the watermen my enemies, the great interest which Rumsey has made against me, and the great numbers who gave their opinions against my scheme who are loath to have their judgments called in question:— it may be supposed that I have scarcely a friend left. The most infamous character or scheme, surrounded with friends, is applauded; the greatest virtues, surrounded with enemies, is treated with contempt."

Probably the basic difficulty that the steamboat had to face was the inherent timidity and conservatism of man. People will pay to see somebody do something novel; they are less eager to do it themselves. And only by imagining yourself back into the eighteenth century can you realize how novel the steamboat was. The inventions that would have entered your life would always have been simple devices that you yourself could understand: an adjustable candleholder, perhaps, or an improved spit that any blacksmith could manufacture. Such had been the pattern of the world not only through all your days but through all the days of all your ancestors; indeed, since history had first been written. It was difficult to conceive that the pattern could be changed by a shabby man who could not even keep himself in decent clothes.

As a citizen of the eighteenth century, you knew that when you wished to move from place to place, you had to make use of the legs of some living organism, or the wind, or perhaps the current of a stream. These means had been supplied by God at the time of creation, and had been used by man ever since. Now there came a crazy fellow who claimed that by joining up some pipes and building a fire beneath them he could make a boat move in a way that no boat had ever moved before.

Admittedly you had with your own eyes seen the boat push against the tide, but somehow this was not a reassuring sight. It is insulting to suggest that your suspicions were due to fears of magic or witchcraft; you were no longer a child; you did not believe in such things any more. No, you were being hardheaded and practical. Take the machine that moved the vessel; you had never seen a machine like it, and it did not look safe to you now. A man can get a nasty burn from steam, and what was to keep that teakettle from exploding? Furthermore, the contraption made an unnatural noise, like the beginning of a catastrophe, an earthquake perhaps. And it vibrated unpleasantly, and it was dirty—ugh! All in all, Fitch's steamboat was a good thing to keep away from.

So much for the point of view of the common man. What of the philosophers? They knew there was a great break between science and practical application; there always had been. Savants made ingenious devices which they demonstrated to the American Philosophical Society, but they realized that these mechanisms were just demonstrations, experiments. They did not try to use them to make over the world. Of course, the philosophers were open-minded. They admitted that it was possible that some day a machine might drive a boat, but certainly not this machine which had been made in their city by a man most of them despised. Rumsey might conceivably have done it, although it was unlikely—he could talk like one of them, and they had elected him to their society—but obviously not this strange wild man who, it was generally admitted, had stolen the idea from Rumsey.

If someone had argued that the boat was actually moving there in the river and had gone several thousand miles, the philosophers would have replied, "Well, yes, perhaps, but don't be gullible. It will break down in a day or two; did last week in fact, we are told, when the boiler blew. And suppose you made many steamboats; who would keep them in order? They're too complicated, too expensive, impractical. Of course, Fitch deserves credit for having achieved a clever stunt; but is it really more?"

XV. A Killing Frost

JOHN BROWN, a member of Congress from the Kentucky region of Virginia, was sitting in his room one morning when a tall, shabby man walked in and introduced himself as John Fitch, inventor of steamboats. Before he was well in a seat, the intruder stated that it was Brown's duty to advance him $400, since the invention would be so beneficial to the western country. The Congressman, who had seen Fitch's boat break down twice, replied that he did not have money to spare. At these words, Fitch sprang up and towered over Brown.

"Well, sir!" he cried. "If you will not advance me the money, I will go to the Secretary of State's office, and cause it to be entered, that it may remain *res perpetua memoria*, that I, John Fitch, inventor of steamboats, having exhausted all my means in carrying my invention into perfection, need $400 to complete my work and give evidence to the world of its value and utility; that I called upon you, John Brown, member of Congress from the Kentucky district, in the state of Virginia, to loan me $400 to complete my machinery and give unanswerable evidence of the utility and importance of my invention, and that you refused it."

"You may do so, Mr. Fitch, if you please."

Slapping a very battered hat on his head, the inventor said with mock politeness, "Good morning, Mr. Brown, member of Congress from Kentucky district."

Brown replied, with equal politeness, "Good morning, Mr. Fitch, inventor of steamboats."

Poor John Fitch was searching for money once more, just as if his steamboat had not been a mechanical success. When the account books had been added up in the fall of 1790, and it was discovered that the boat had lost money, his backers had thought better of the £10 levy they had voted toward a second vessel. They decided to build the craft on credit and pay at some later date. Terrified lest he should be forced to skimp on materials and spend much of his time dodging duns, Fitch was in agony.

The Virginia monopoly, which would expire that November unless he had two boats operating there, was at the heart of his scheme, since Virginia still controlled the Mississippi, the river toward which all his efforts had been aimed. He would never, he wrote, have accepted the time limit in the law if he had had any conception "that it would have employed so great a length of time merely to acquire the art of making a steam engine." Every day that was now lost threatened the entire future of his invention.

Having unsuccessfully asked for loans from many western members of Congress, including Albert Gallatin, Fitch invited General Gibson to become a partner in building at Pittsburgh a boat which, he pledged his reputation, would ascend the Ohio 100 miles a day. "Sir, I am determined that the navigation of the Mississippi and Ohio shall be made easy, whether the western people will have it or no. I really pity men who have worried at the oar these six thousand years past, and [am] determined to relieve them." Gibson was not interested.

In the meanwhile, Fitch and Voight were busy slapping together the new steamboat, quickly, any way, so long as it would by moving satisfy the Virginia law. But when the so-called *Perseverance* was almost completed, a violent northeaster broke it from its moorings, and drove it so far up on Petty's Island that it took ten or twelve days to get it off. Blind, haphazard, meaningless fate had interfered disastrously. The Virginia law lapsed, the two boats were put up for the winter, and the steamboat company, disappointed for the hundredth time, fell completely to pieces.

Fitch, however, refused to give up; he wished "to put it out of the power of future generations to make excuses for the present one. And if I should die in penury, want, wretchedness, and rags, that my country may have no excuse, and that I may have the secret pleasure in the contemplation of receiving real pity from future generations." He sent the members of his company "one proposal more";

which was that he should induce Congress to promise a grant of 50,000 acres of western land as a reward for sending a steamboat from the mouth of the Mississippi to the rapids of the Ohio.

Without waiting for their reply, he suggested to Robert Morris, Philadelphia's leading capitalist, that they unite in setting up a trading house at New Orleans which would build steamboats to operate to Kentucky and Illinois. The Spanish city, he pointed out, should naturally be "the largest city in North America," and would instantly become so if the navigation of the Mississippi was made easy. He himself, he added, intended to become a Spanish subject "and hope to meet with indulgences as such."

Fitch could hardly have made a proposal less likely to please the eastern ruling class; that his proposition had a practical sound only made it more terrifying. Morris and his peers could not be jubilant at the idea of having their eastern docks and warehouses by-passed. When the inventor who had once spurned the Spanish ambassador suggested, in his disillusionment with the treatment he had received at home, that he become a Spanish subject and contribute to the aggrandizement of Spanish New Orleans, he involved himself in an international conflict of which he had no conception. He undoubtedly thought his invention more important than any individual national interest; American statesmen could hardly be expected to agree. The King of Spain, they knew, was still trying to use his control of the Mississippi to wrench the western country away from the United States; perhaps it was not chance that one of Fitch's supporters in Kentucky was General James Wilkinson who, as was discovered many years later, was in the pay of His Most Catholic Majesty. We need not be surprised if Morris and his colleagues decided that Fitch and his invention were both dangerous.

Fitch had intended to go West to promote his schemes there, but he was kept at home by the emergence of national patent legislation. Stevens, still smarting under his New York State defeat, wished a national monopoly for his steamboat ideas. At his urging, Congress on April 10, 1790, set up a patent commission comprising the Attorney General and the Secretaries of War and State. There was no appeal from the decisions of this body, Fitch's request for a clause providing trial by jury having been brushed aside. It is no coincidence that our first patent law was enacted to deal with steamboat claimants, since this was the earliest of our important inventions.

No sooner was the law passed than Fitch, Rumsey, and Stevens appealed for patents. As the "first inventor," Fitch felt himself entitled to all steamboats, however constructed. Could he secure such a patent, he would be in a stronger legal position than he had ever been, since his right would cover the whole nation; if he failed, his defeat would be disastrous. During the discouraging winter of 1790, he flooded the commissioners with written arguments that could have done nothing but prejudice them against him; his petitions were so interminable and so scrambled that they might easily have seemed the work of a deranged mind. The commission set February 1, 1791, as the day to hear all steam inventors, not only the three steamboat men but also Nathan Read and Isaac Briggs who projected steam carriages.

Fitch had more reason to be concerned about the outcome than he realized. As an inventor in his own right, Jefferson, the Secretary of State, was the most influential of the patent commissioners, and he considered Rumsey the greatest mechanical genius he had ever known.

Utter poverty overtook Fitch while he waited to learn his fate. He was evicted from his lodgings, but this was not altogether a sorrow; "the most noble-spirited woman on earth, Mrs. Krafft," took him in, "and never gave me a sour look on account of bad pay, but treated me the same as if I paid her weekly." Living on charity, his company disjointed, his whole steamboat scheme in abeyance and depending on a turn of fate's wheel which was weighted against him, Fitch cast himself in an even more exalted role than the creator of a new earthly dispensation; he cast himself as Messiah.

He and Voight were both Deists, religious radicals who denied the divine inspiration of the Scriptures. "There being great numbers of people coming to see us at the boat, and we frequently getting middling glad in liquor, [we] spoke our sentiments perhaps more freely than was prudent." Many of their visitors, they soon discovered, agreed with them, "although too delicate to confess it." This gave Fitch the idea of establishing a religion in which good works were inspired not by supernatural fears but a sense of honor. He "determined to let the world know, as contemptible as I was and despised by all ranks of people . . . that I could call in all the world into my doctrines, the Jews with the fullness of the Gentile nations, and establish one array throughout the world."

He would found a society which combined what he considered the best of Free Masonry and Quakerism, "excepting only that all questions should be freely discussed, even to the denial of the divinity of Moses, Jesus Christ, or Mahomet." Members of all creeds would be admitted; since worship would consist of debates from which no idea was banned, Fitch was convinced that everyone would soon see the light of atheism. When money was available, a school would be founded to which children of any faith might be sent, but their names would be kept enrolled as long as they lived, and they would be publicly expelled, even if one hundred years old, should they behave dishonorably. Indeed, all the members would be held to the good life by the threat of public disgrace.

When he had thought this all out, Fitch explained the plan to Voight. The two friends gathered together a few choice souls and launched the Universal Society. Its first meetings were held in February 1790, but the steamboat intervened; the organization did not really get going until winter. Then it was decided to establish a new calendar, beginning with the date of their first meeting. Although this was February 29, Fitch tried to have the year begin on January 21, so that he might enjoy "the secret pleasure" of having all future ages base their calendar not on Christ's birthday but his own. He did not dare give his reasons, and the later date was adopted, to Fitch's "secret chagrin."

The members proposed topics for discussion; Fitch's suggestions included: "Is a plurality of wives right or wrong? What are the duties of men and how are they to be known? Is there any religion which can be formed useful to society; if there is, on what principles ought that religion to be founded? Did all mankind proceed from one man and woman? What makes North America colder in winter than other countries in the same degree of north latitude? Which do we derive the greatest benefits from, our friends or enemies, as to useful lessons in life? Do all men enjoy an equal share of happiness in this world? Why is the eastern part of our continent more sandy, rocky, broken, and barren than it is west of the Allegheny Mountains? Is life an element or not? Is there any such thing as conscience, or does not what we call conscience arise altogether from education? Is gratitude due from the young to their parents for their care and protection in raising and nursing them when [they] are not able to protect themselves?" And, most significantly, "Can suicide be a noble act in any case whatever?"

Fitch never cast himself as the popular leader of the sect, but rather as the power behind the throne. "My despicable appearance, my uncouth way of speaking and holding up extravagant ideas, and so bad an address, must ever make me unpopular; but was I a handsome man and a good writer, I could now do more than ever Jesus Christ or George Fox did." He appealed to the Rev. Mr. Irwin to lead his sect. Since Fitch was convinced that at least half the wealthy Philadelphians were Deists in their hearts, he assured Irwin that the standard bearer would not only do good but would make large sums of money and gain much power; he could be elected president of the United States, and his name would be remembered when those of Washington and Christ had been forgotten. Irwin did not listen to this siren song, so Fitch had to accept the Rev. Mr. Palmer, who had been deposed from the Baptist pulpit for heretical teaching. One glorious public meeting was held in a hired hall filled with artisans, who cheered so loudly when Palmer denied the divinity of Christ that the society was emboldened to advertise in the newspapers that on the following Sabbath he would again preach Unitarianism. At this, the forces of religion, led by Bishop White, went into action; they intimidated the owner of the building into refusing to rent his room any longer to the heretics, and frightened Palmer into hasty flight. Fitch's Universal Society tumbled around his ears, having done nothing but make him even more unpopular with the powerful men of America.[1]

Fitch needed popularity, for in his search for an income to enable him to continue his experiments, he was seeking a government appointment. First he applied for the position of sergeant-at-arms to the Pennsylvania legislature, and then asked to be made a surveyor or supervisor of roads. In January 1791 he and Voight petitioned Washington for jobs in the newly established mint: "John Fitch is a goldsmith by trade and flatters himself that he could render essential service to his country as an assay master and superintendent of the workmen in the mint. The other, Henry Voight, is perfectly acquainted with the whole process of coining, and all the machinery for the business, and can make the instruments himself, having worked in a mint in Germany in his younger years, in which he flatters himself that he had introduced some valuable improvements." Voight, whose qualifications were outstanding, was appointed chief coiner, a position he held for many years; Fitch got nothing.[2] He was greatly chagrined, because "I consider myself as a man the most entitled to public favor of any man in the United States." If his autobiographical manuscripts had been finished, he would, he wrote, have killed himself in the speaker's chair of the Pennsylvania Assembly "for the purpose of making my country ashamed of their base treatment of me."

The patent hearings had been postponed, since a bill had been presented to Congress making it a condition for receiving a patent that the applicant relinquish any state monopoly rights he might hold. This would have saved endless legal difficulties in the future, and greatly expedited the introduction of the steamboat, but Fitch objected that it was a provision aimed by his enemies especially at him. He was delighted when the measure died in committee, but enraged when the patent commissioners continued none the less to postpone the steamboat hearings. He called on them day after day. To emphasize his need, he shouted that he was wearing "all the clothes I had in the world, except a few old shirts, and two or three pair of old yarn stockings, all in darns, like those which I had on, that they could see I was then all in rags."

The commissioners were hesitating because they were in a quandary. They were all highly important officers of state, with heavy duties apart from their patent function, and the record was so confused that even a full-time study of the documents available to them would hardly have revealed who deserved what steamboat rights. If there had been a patent law when Fitch and Rumsey began their experiments, the problem would have settled itself automatically, each receiving rights in order of application; but now the commissioners had to work backward. Fitch, of course, claimed that his state laws were in effect patents, and that it was the commissioners' duty to confirm legal rights already granted him. But the federal patent law was merely intended to protect actual discoveries, while state monopolies were also given to encourage infant industries. In which classification did Fitch's laws fall? The Virginia statute, which required that two boats be put in operation within a stated time, was clearly intended as an encouragement.

While Jefferson, Knox, and Randolph wondered what to do, Fitch continued active. He proposed to Morris and another merchant that they take over the *Perseverance*, which he would fit with sails and navigate by sea to the mouth of the Mississippi and then up to the falls of the Ohio. Once the efficacy of the vessel had thus been proved the promoters could not fail to make 1,000 per cent profit on the cost of the boat, which he set at £750. Morris replied that he would consider no proposition until a permit had been received from Spain to navigate through New Orleans.

International matters were concerning Fitch more and more. The steamboat company made a contract with Aaron Vail, the American consul at Lorient, who agreed to build a boat in France at his own expense. There was a strange silence from the Rumsey forces when, after his return to Europe, Vail applied for a patent, which the French government allowed him on November 29, 1791.

Fitch's American patent negotiations were less successful. Having vainly attempted to get the claimants to come to some agreement among themselves, the puzzled commissioners on August 26 gave each inventor a certificate repeating exactly the wording of his application. Since the rights thus granted were in conflict, this merely shifted the responsibility to the courts, who would have to rule on infringement suits. What a mockery was the paper handed to Fitch! As he read the words, it seemed that he had been granted everything he desired, but actually, since Rumsey and Stevens had received similar papers, his claim to be the sole inventor had been denied. Even the state monopolies he had already secured were worthless, since any move would certainly lead to litigation.

At this moment, as if to add insult to injury, he received a permit to take his boat through New Orleans, but only once, and then without carrying any cargo. Spain would let the boat enter the Mississippi, but intended to keep it bottled in the upper waters.

On receiving his patent, Fitch resolved to spend "no more time on such trifling conduct of my country, and never to lift a single finger toward completing the scheme till I could have the matter decided and go upon sure grounds." He believed the commissioners dared treat him so shabbily because they were sure he would continue his steamboat efforts none the less; if he stopped for a year, in their fear of losing the invention they would meet his terms.

However, his temperament would not permit him to remain idle. He told his backers that he was going to Kentucky to raise money; should they refuse to pay his expenses, he would feel free of any further obligation to them. Clearly he was trying to shake himself loose from the situation in which the company kept title to the invention although making only half-hearted efforts to complete it. The investors were determined not to let Fitch worm himself free; they even went so far as to pay his wages, which were long in arrears, and gave him £14 to buy new clothes. They resolved to sell such parts of Fitch's historic successful boat as anyone would buy, and to use the proceeds to complete the larger *Perseverance*.

Reluctantly, Fitch returned to work on the *Perseverance*; he was forced to struggle on alone, since woman trouble had again come between him and Voight. After Mrs. Krafft's child had been born, Fitch had lectured the pair on chastity for six months until he believed that he had prevailed. He did not notice it particularly when, toward the end of 1790, the lady announced she was going on a trip to visit some friends, nor was he uneasy until one day a hurried messenger told him that "his wife" had been brought to bed with child in another part of the city. "Reason," Fitch comments, "must and always will give way to love, especially in the female sex." Mrs. Krafft had been unable to resist Voight, and when "the effects of love promised further increase to their families," the guilty pair had not dared face Fitch. Mrs. Krafft had fled into hiding, but she was recognized by some of her friends, and in her surprise and shame had declared that she was now Mrs. Fitch.

"You may have some conception of the convolutions of my mind though in a very imperfect manner, for to acknowledge one, who had prostituted herself, to be my wife was degrading the man too much, and could not endure the thought, but on the other hand I knew her goodness of heart and that she was led into her errors by the purest love, that her connections with him had much diminished, her friends and he totally refusing to give her any countenance and refusing to go see her in her distress, and to have so valuable a woman without a friend on earth I could not, especially as my reputation would be more injured by neglect than by a compliance. . . . When I consider her situation and probable surprise, I forgive her, and had the child been so much of my complexion as that I could have fathered it with repute, it would have given me a very little uneasiness. . . .

"All I can say of the matter is this: I think this is a damned wicked world, and when I get clear of it never wish to come back to it any more. I have frequently been apt to conclude that it is a place where they transport souls from other planets that is not fit to live in them, the same as Great Britain used to send convicts to Virginia, and if I was sent here as a lunatic to Bedlam or for running into chimerical whims, I am sure my lesson of caution will be sufficient to make me more cautious when I get back to Jupiter again."

Torn between love and his lifelong struggle to prove himself honorable and worthy, better than the men he envied because they were adjusted to their environment, Fitch followed love, and tried to save honor by pretending that Mrs. Krafft was his legal wife and the child really his. Playing the part of husband, he assumed the direction of Mrs. Krafft's family "as her distress carried her to excess in hysterics." He thought that if he helped her in every way, he could wean her affection from the man who had treated her so basely. Although he had a legal wife still living in Connecticut, he intended to marry Mrs. Krafft "as soon as I could be persuaded her affections were so called off from him as that I could feel myself safe." Voight "being sensible of my determination became much enraged, as if I had debarred him from his choicest pleasures." Fitch's partner became his bitter enemy.

The two men had worked together on the steamboat, each making important contributions. "The principal part of the original thoughts of any part of the works proceeded from me," Fitch stated, "but I hardly could propose anything that he would not make some improvement upon it; and after the plan was adapted, [I] left the execution of it to him, which filled him at times with almost too much importance, but always gratified his honor. . . . He was certainly the first mechanical genius I ever met with in the whole course of my life, and I do believe his superior mechanical genius is not to be found. He is the man most ready of mechanical improvements of any on earth, and I am persuaded I never could have completed the steamboat without him."

Convinced that to initiate ideas was much more important than to make them practically effective, Fitch evaluated his contribution as being many times greater than Voight's; undoubtedly his pathological need for self-justification urged him to this conclusion. He refused to give his collaborator any public credit for the invention. Yet he realized that Voight was being somewhat cheated. He tried, so he tells us, to make up to his partner by praising him in private to their backers and also, as we have seen, in his manuscript writings. Just before their final quarrel, he permitted his friend to patent the use of their paddles for a boat driven by horses or oxen. Until sexual jealousy intervened, Voight had been satisfied; but now ominous rumors reached Fitch that he was saying that the inventor had relied so completely upon him that he could not complete the steamboat without his help. To make matters worse, Fitch was not altogether sure this was not true.

He needed a fellow-artisan to share "a cheering glass" as they struggled with temperamental steam and recalcitrant metal; he needed a human companion to modify a little the violence of his terrible moods. But when he asked his backers to employ Peter Lukens, a blacksmith he had known in Bucks County, they replied that six years before he had said he could build a steamboat. Now he wanted help; no, they would save their money. In his depression, Fitch replied that although he had prided himself on the success of his former boat, "it is not sure I can do it again, as our works will be so varied."

Although he still felt he could do better in Kentucky, Fitch, the slave of duty, labored on in Philadelphia, rebelliously, with no friend to aid him. The directors of the company continually intervened, installing innovations of their own, and Fitch was unable to prove them wrong by any figures or facts. It was his intuition and experience against theirs; as they controlled the purse strings, they prevailed. Fitch had great difficulty securing workmen, since the removal of the federal government to Philadelphia had produced a building boom in which all the mechanics were engaged. Lonely week passed after lonely week. He was horrified when the wooden boiler case ordered by one of the directors proved too short; since there was no money to buy a better one, he did his best to piece it out. All the pipes including the steam pipe were made of lead, probably another economy measure. The largest engine he had ever built was taking form, but would it function?

On September 7, 1791, Fitch anxiously made the trial. When the fire was lit, water gushed out of the boiler in streams. He could not generate enough steam to move the engine, and it was too heavy to turn over by hand. The directors thereupon decided the air pump was too small; Fitch was not sure, but argued that they should first fix the boiler and give the existing pump a fair test. As none of the disputants could think of any way of determining the size of the pump except by trial and error, the directors again triumphed, and a larger pump was ordered, although Fitch objected: "Whether the new one can ever be got in its place or not heaven only knows without making the principal part of the works new." The project used up all the funds, so that when Fitch wished to make a slight adjustment in one of the cocks, he could not get the money. His salary was again in arrears, and he did not even have a penny to buy soft soap with which to wash out the pump. Although winter was "crowding on like an army with bayonets," the work came to a standstill.

Fitch skulked through the streets, avoiding the taverns where his artisan friends gathered, for he could not pay for a drink even if he found the courage to step into the circle of conviviality he had once so loved. Through the windows of his old haunts, he may well have seen Voight, who was secure in his position as coiner of the mint, standing in the center of an admiring group with a glass in his hand. And rumor soon brought him news that Voight was saying that he alone knew how to build steamboats; with $100, he could in three days make the *Perseverance* go 9 miles an hour. Since Fitch had no money at all, "it appeared to me as unmanly as an unprovoked assault to a prisoner bound in chains."

The two old friends passed the winter in violent controversy. When his longing for Mrs. Krafft became too great. Voight would get drunk, and then he would stumble over to "The Sign of the Buck" where Fitch and the lady were doing their best to keep up their respectability by pretending they were really married. He would pound on the door, and once, in a drunken frenzy, he shouted out for all the neighbors to hear that the child was not Fitch's but his. Thus he wounded Fitch in his most vulnerable place, his reputation. During December this persecution drove Mrs. Krafft to New York, where she passed as Mrs. Mary Fitch. Now the inventor was all alone, but he preferred that to calumny. When his lady, worried for fear her business would evaporate, wrote that she was coming back, Fitch advised her to sell her assets and go to New Orleans. "Be assured if you return to Philadelphia to live again you lose the patronage and protection of your John."

But Mrs. Krafft returned none the less. Fitch indignantly moved to other lodgings. From this isolation, he wrote the woman he loved, reminding her that she and Voight had promised always to stand by him. But now, he told her, "you have lost the most sincere friend you ever had. . . . I do not want to hurt your feelings, but I wish you to have serious reflections. Farewell."

The fight with Voight went on and on. The former friends wrangled about who deserved credit for the steamboat and the application of their paddles to a horse boat; they wrote each other furious letters; they refused to meet, and then did meet, falling on each other's shoulders with tears of contrition. Sometimes they signed documents in which each gave the other credit for all the other had done, but soon they would be at swords' points again. During his periods of fury Voight told the members of the company that Fitch did not know how to build a steam engine, a statement that strengthened a growing suspicion in their minds. Fitch brought his manuscript history of the steamboat to a close with the statement that Voight's "striving to destroy the confidence which the company had in me no doubt will prove my ruin."

Fitch had guessed correctly. When spring brought round once more the season of flowers and steamboat building, the company refused to put up any more money. Fitch borrowed £40 on his own credit, and raised a little money from his western lands, but the sums did not go very far. The work went more and more slowly, and then one day his pocket was completely empty; Fitch was forced to abandon his attempt to complete his steamboat. Even in the history of this mechanical monster of fire and brass, love for a woman played a determining part.

Fitch's hope to achieve self-justification by the invention of the steamboat was squashed, he feared forever. His own generation despised and laughed at him; he decided to have nothing more to do with the age into which he had been born. But new men were treading on the heels of the old; the grave would soon gather in all the mockers, all the dishonest players. The rich and great who had scorned him because he was poor, who had cheated him for reasons he did not understand, would soon lie silent beside the foul-mouthed boatmen who had refused him a tow and laughed at his misery when his steamboat broke down. The hand of time, moving inexorably, would clean the slate on which were scribbled the caricatures and lies; there would be space then to write down the truth. His own generation was a stiff-necked generation, but the men of the future should realize that "little Johnny Fitch could do something of importance."

For more than a year Fitch had been writing an account of his experiments, laboriously copying out the documents so that nothing would be lost, but when he read the manuscript over he realized the story was incomplete. His invention was so much a part of his own life that they could not be separated; seeking the cause of his failure, he wrote his autobiography. First he asked himself whether his misery stemmed from madness, whether, after all, the steamboat was the hallucination of a lunatic. He tried to lay this fear by remembering that many famous men and the legislatures of several states "gave me their opinions that the scheme was rational." Furthermore, the steamboat was a complicated conception requiring "a long train of ideas, and them all connected," while mania was characterized by "a train of deranged, unconnected ideas." If he was to be accused of madness, it would be only for undertaking so great a project that would have bankrupted a nobleman, when he was poor and unknown.

Having decided that his failure had not been caused by lunacy, he needed some other explanation, and in seeking it he wrote down every event and deed of his life he considered significant. He underlined his faults as well as his virtues, since he demanded not indulgence but justice. When the whole story lay before him, he still could find nothing in his own actions to make rational the treatment he had received. "If mankind had been as good as they ought to be, I do not know one instance of my life but I have acted with the same degree of prudence as it would have been if I had to do it again, and yet I have fell in character much below the meanest citizens. . . . Sir, when I take a view of my past life, as singular as it is, I am sure that if Deity is just, which I have no reason to doubt, I stand in no need of a mediator or of applying to his particular friends to intercede for me. Only let me tell plain, simple truths, and I am sure I shall have the softest cushion in Heaven to sit upon. Therefore mean to appear before Him and plead for myself."

He intended to present the six large notebooks, each crammed with writing, to the Library Company of Philadelphia on condition that the package remain sealed for thirty years, unless Jefferson or some of the other men who he insisted had cheated him should try to run for public office. Then the part dealing with them should be published at once. But before he sent the papers off, he wondered if he was being completely fair. He had called the temporal great before the court of posterity; should they not have a chance to defend themselves? He considered Jefferson, who had refused him an exclusive patent, his worst enemy; now he wrote the Secretary of State, offering to send him the manuscript "in which, sir, your candor is very seriously called into question. I, sir, although an indigent citizen, feel myself upon an equal floor with the first officers of government; therefore trust that your exalted station will not permit you to treat this proposal with contempt." Jefferson could keep the notebooks for six days, so that he might write a reply. "This, sir, is from a poor but an independent citizen of the United States of America."

He was prevented from mailing this letter by some of his friends, "who did not know the manner in which I designed to die." He clearly intended to commit suicide. On July 13, 1792, some six months before he finally deposited his manuscripts with the Library Company, he had made his will:

"O, my Lord God, I beseech thee now to enable me to make

this, my last will, in a rational manner and comfortable to the laws of nature; and that it may not be esteemed in any court of justice as coming from insanity.

"My will and pleasure is that I should be buried under ground or sunk with weights to the bottom of some waters, that I do not become more obnoxious to the living than I am now; but if buried, that I may be laid on some public highway or place of the greatest resort of the living—such as the State House yard, Gray's Gardens or some public house, that I could hear the *Song of the Brown Jug* on the first day of February every year. I request this that my life may be a lesson of caution to the living, but beg that I may not be buried on or near any Christian burying ground. . . .

"But as to my burial, my penury forbids any extravagance. I give $2 for my funeral expense, and $1 I bequeath to the man who wheels me to the place of interment, the other [to the man] who shall dig a hole to lay me and cover me up. I also give an Indian blanket, in the hands of Mrs. Lavering [his landlady] to tie my body up instead of a coffin."

He directed that his debts be paid to his landlady and then to his other creditors "in equal proportion as far as the money goes." Anything he still possessed in New England was to be divided between his children, and he bequeathed his scale and dividers to his son John. "As I have lodged £7 or £8 in the Masons' funds, I trust they will have generosity enough to give everyone present a good drink so as to make them feel glad they are alive."

His lands in Kentucky were to be sold and the proceeds invested, the interest to be "annually paid on the first day of February to the person who shall go to my grave on the said day at four o'clock in the afternoon in the presence of several witnesses and sing the *Song of the Brown Jug* and that 'he is gone like a true-hearted fellow,' what shall be shared by him in equal proportion to all present either in liquor or money as the singer shall direct."

In this strange and pathetic document, one mood outshouts every other, a mood of terrible loneliness. Fitch wished to be buried in a well-frequented place where the feet of the living would echo over his head; he wished men to drink by his grave and sing his favorite song. For years he had tried to achieve union with his fellow-men by winning their respect, by showing that he could hurdle the pitfalls of the world better than they. He had abandoned the struggle now. Always he had found drinking a resource, and in defeat he had turned to it as never before. While the alcohol raced through his veins, relaxing his nerves, deadening his inhibitions, he enjoyed for a little while the sense that he was not unusual, a monstrosity, but made of common clay, one with jolly souls around him. The *Song of the Brown Jug* had become his litany:

> With my jug in one hand and my pipe in the other
> I'll drink to my neighbor and friend.
> All my cares in a whiff of tobacco I'll smother:
> My life I know shortly must end. . . .
>
> So we'll drink, laugh and smoke and leave nothing to care
> And drop like a pear ripe and mellow.
> When cold in my coffin I'll leave them to say,
> "He's gone, what a true-hearted fellow!"

Returning to his old trade of silversmith, Fitch earned a little money; he spent it on liquor. But even as the drams burned his throat, his mind refused to lie still. He meditated on whiskey and worked out a new method of distillation.

"Often have I seen him," a contemporary writes, "stalking about like a troubled spectre, with downcast eye and lowering countenance, his soiled, coarse linen peeping through the elbows of a tattered garment." Although Peter Brown, shipsmith, and John Wilson, boat builder, had lost money on his schemes, they felt for him "the kindest sympathy. . . . He was in the habit of calling almost daily at their workshops, to while away the time, to talk over his misfortunes, and to rail at the ingratitude and cold neglect of an unfeeling, spiritless world." On one occasion, Fitch became particularly eloquent about the advantages of steam; after he had left, Brown turned to Wilson and said in a tone of deep sympathy, "Poor fellow, what a pity he is crazy."

Yet Fitch had not shot his last bolt. Defeated in America, he was turning his eyes across the ocean.

XVI. *Death of a Champion*

WHEN we last saw Rumsey, it was the fall of 1790, and he had just entered into a partnership with Rogers and Parker which he was sure would end all his financial troubles. He believed that his steamboat, despite its unhappy beginning, was on the verge of completion.

A year and a half later, he wrote a friend, "View me thus loaded with debt, in a strange country, connected with broken men, and pursuing projects in the success of which but few believe. . . . I have frequently been in the prisons here, on purpose to make them familiar to me, as I have long expected that one of them must eventually become my abode; I will not describe them to you; they are too horrid for your contemplation. . . . Conceive a man shut up with thousands of hardened and unhappy wretches, without the allowance of even bread and water to subsist on! Believe me this is literally true! and add to the horror, be assured that a man, the moment he is locked up, is no more thought of or sought after than if he was in his grave."

Shortly after Rumsey had united with them, Rogers and Parker went bankrupt; he was forced to borrow elsewhere to keep from failing with them. Then his backers in Philadelphia, instead of sending him more money as he wished, demanded the return of what they had already given him, since he had excluded them from his patent. Savagely, Rumsey turned on his first patrons: "The society in America are mostly leaches and sharks. . . . I expect nothing but a breach with the society who has certainly behaved ridiculous to me in a very great degree."

By April Rumsey was sinking so fast in the rising tide of unpaid bills that "a few days more must have ended my career in Europe." As he sat with his head in his hands, his terrible situation revealed by the fact that his lace was not altogether new and spotless, there came a heavy knocking at the door, the kind of official knocking that would be expected from a bailiff. How Rumsey's heart must have jumped! We can see him, after the first moment of shock, straightening his garments and forcing an aristocratic smile for one more bluff before the end. But on opening the door he saw at the threshold two obsequious footmen "in loud livery"; they bowed and presented him with a note. The Earl of Carhampton wished him to call on a matter of business.

When a canal which the earl was building in co-operation with other Irish noblemen had hit a snag, the peer had come to London to engage an expert, and, so Rumsey wrote, "behold, from among the one hundred thousand that profess to be engineers in this kingdom, he pitched upon me!" Since Rumsey now had a chance to make money, his creditors were glad to wait, and he set out for Dublin on a salary of £10 a day. The lords to whom he had to make his report impressed him much more than American heroes like Washington. "It was not an easy task," he wrote, "for an orator such as I am . . . to explain to the Potomac Company my sentiments upon the navigation they were upon; judge then what was my situation, when ushered in to hold forth, in technical language, to upward of twenty imperious and no doubt learned lords, knights, etc., who had been worked up into the expectation (as some of the facetious told me) that I could create both clay and stone. . . . My diffidence (that I shall never get the better of) exposed me more upon this occasion than I expected." But he gave satisfaction.

Rumsey's canal employment had been useful to him principally because it persuaded his creditors to let him leave London; the money he earned was an anthill compared to the mountain of his debt. His job ended, he went into hiding. His agent negotiated with his creditors, and spiders strung their delicate tracery over his boat and steam engine.

"While lying on my oars at Liverpool, Manchester, Chester, etc., I invented a mill upon principles entirely new, . . . and which it is evident saved me from destruction." He was delighted with this invention because it was such an improvement over the ones he had thought of before that it made everything he had sold to his Philadelphia backers worthless. After he had patented his mill on August

24, 1791, and started to build one for demonstration in Liverpool, he was able to raise enough credit on his new prospects to return to London. His creditors were temporarily quieted, but since he was unable to raise new funds, he was forced to remain "passive on the subject of the steam vessel."

He was jaunty again, able to look a bailiff in the eye, when he received a letter from his brother-in-law criticizing the way his wife was bringing up his daughter. Like every adventurer, he was very chary of the virtue of his own women; he highly disapproved of Susan's appearing in any public place in rural Shepherdstown "without a very particular acquaintance being with her." He wrote his brother-in-law that should he "relinquish your authority or she refuse to obey, I should consider her lost; not from bad example but from indulgence I am well assured she will receive. I therefore beg and trust that you will do everything in your power to have her to conduct herself with propriety; if she should not, America shall never see me more!! For it is for my children that I labor, and therefore was it to happen that they should not deserve my endeavors in their favors, I would never wish to see them again as nothing could hurt me so much as their disgrace."

Rumsey saw no prospect of getting home, he continued, but was eager to do so, since "few of the innocent and substantial comforts of this life exist near kings and courts, . . . where many are literally starving for bread while others cannot move a single yard without a half dozen servants to attend them! dressed in clothing more costly by far than our members of Congress! . . . Many individuals spend their ten thousand a year without being half gratified for want of more. . . . So many of these kind of sentiments have I heard, as to be impressed with the same idea! The sound of a thousand sterling is not to me as large as $1000 used to be; nor do I find it so hard to raise 100 guineas here, without resources too, than I did in America to raise that many Penns. shillings when in the midst of all my friends and acquaintances! . . . All this, however, cannot lessen my attachment for my own country, nor prejudice me in favor of this."

Rumsey was temperamentally well suited to the exciting and hazardous career of an adventurer in a great city. He told Morrow not to worry about his difficulties; "they are but the natural occurrences which all men in my line of life may expect to meet with." The gambler from the backwoods was proud that he had been able to keep his end up at the great gaming tables of the world's capital. "It is soon determined, after a man is brought upon this theatre, whether he is fit for an actor or not; I have so far passed muster. . . . My unhappiness is only at intervals, when my philosophy and fortitude forsakes me which is not oftener now, notwithstanding the turbulence and magnitude of my pursuits, than when my greatest want was a grist of your Indian corn without having the money to pay for it!"

His difficulties he was able to blame on his associates. His steamboat would undoubtedly have been running by now "had not all my connections here as well as my [illegible] patrons in America been leeches instead of liberal, disinterested men, characters, by-the-bye, that have no existence except in idea! Of honest men there may be many; I know there is some!"

Rumsey's affairs rose and fell with those of his partners, Parker and Rogers; at last they hit a lucky streak, and Rumsey got back to work on his steamboat, which had been almost untouched for more than a year. In December 1792 he was ready to try the engine. "It worked with very good success. I think it was internally very perfect. . . . The vessel went forward against the tide, and pulled hard to get from her moorings. Mr. Rogers was on board, and highly delighted."

In their enthusiasm, Rogers and Parker determined to invite the members of the Royal Society to a public trial "and like people inflated with insanity talked of instantly putting engines upon ships of the navy against France (to protect the cause of despots against those of liberty, my friend). They talked of £50 to £60,000 as nothing to what they expected to receive. . . . Mr. Rogers was immediately to take a genteel house near the King's dockyard, where he was to superintend the business. I may add he was to have £300 a year. . . . It was with difficulty that I kept them from putting this wild scheme into execution immediately, and to wait till the experiment is actually made."

Always cautious about public demonstrations, Rumsey now expressed another caution added by bitter experience. He had, so he wrote Morrow, "suffered too long to enter into any new schemes that will run me in debt." Even should his steamboat prove successful, he would not take another step until the £200 owing on it was paid, and more money was in the bank.

Rumsey's letter to Morrow was never finished. He laid it aside to refresh himself with a cup of tea before attending a meeting of the committee on mechanics of the Society of Arts, where he was to defend a device he had invented for equalizing the water on water wheels. A friend who sat down with him tells us that he was "in very great spirits," as he had been ever since he had returned to work on his steamboat.

His tea finished, Rumsey hurried to the committee room where in explaining his model he gave the learned members a lecture on hydrostatics. Everyone was impressed, and the august committee told him to draw up his own resolution praising his invention. Eagerly Rumsey sat down at a table, and his pen scratched with enthusiasm over the paper. After a minute or two he stopped and looked puzzled; then he raised his hand to his temple. When he tried to speak, an inarticulate jumble came from his lips. He was rushed to a doctor, and the next evening, that of December 18, 1792, he died. The famous Dr. John Hunter was to use the incident in his lectures as an example of apoplexy brought on by emotion.

Early in 1793 Rumsey's partners tried out his boat. A London journal reported that "a pump of 2 feet diameter, wrought by a steam engine, forces a quantity of water up through the keel. The valve is then shut by return of the stroke, which at the same time forces the water through a channel or pipe of about 6 inches square, lying above and parallel to the kelson, out of the stern under the rudder, which has a less dip than usual, to permit the exit of the water." According to this account, the vessel sailed 4 knots; no distance is given.

Rumsey's supporters assert this boat was so great a success that it makes their candidate the inventor of the steamboat. Legal arbiters, however, appointed by Rumsey's partners on one hand and his heirs on the other, ruled that the estate owed the partners the penal award of £5,000 specified in the contract to be paid if the vessel should prove a failure. In any case, a steamboat that went 4 knots in an experimental run of undetermined length cannot be considered in the same class as Fitch's boat of 1790 which went almost twice as fast and covered several thousand miles.

Although controversy between their partisans still continued, the evidence leaves no doubt that Fitch was a hands-down winner in his race with Rumsey. But this was only one heat in the vast contest to which he had challenged the gods, and even as Rumsey fell by the wayside a new champion appeared, young, able, ready to take advantage of every discovery that had been made before him. Robert Fulton was about to enter the steamboat lists.

XVII. *The New Champion*

Six years before Rumsey's death, Fulton had arrived in London, a tall, intense yeoman artist from the provinces. The city was crowded with people and carriages; footsteps and hooves beat everywhere. Perhaps like another newly arrived American painter, Chester Harding, he stood in a doorway waiting for the crowd that filled Piccadilly to pass. Then realizing that it would never pass, he plunged into the sea of folk. People jostled by on every side of him, but he did not know a soul in the city. The only contact he had with this great new world was one slim letter of introduction. But the letter was of tremendous value since it was addressed to Benjamin West.

Similar letters had been the open sesame to English art and society for almost every American painter of importance during several generations. West received Fulton graciously, as he received all the others. The man of forty-nine who shook the newcomer so cordially by the hand was one of the most famous artists in the Western world. All the Lancaster clumsiness had worn off him years before; he wore sober clothes suitable to a Puritan with an air that made them outshine silks and satins; he moved with the assurance of a man who was the King's intimate friend. Leigh Hunt, a later frequenter of West's studio, writes that in the picture rooms, where hung scores of the master's huge canvases, "everybody trod about in stillness, as though it were a kind of holy ground. . . . The talk was very quiet, the neighborhood quiet, the servants quiet; I thought the very squirrel in the cage would make a greater noise anywhere else. James, the porter, a fine tall fellow who figured in his master's pictures as an apostle, was as quiet as he was strong; standing for his picture had become a sort of a religion with him. Even the butler, with his little twinkling eyes full of pleasant conceit, vented his notions of himself in half-tones and whispers. . . . My mother and I used to go down the gallery as if we were treading on wool," proceeding to the studio where they found "the mild and quiet artist at work, happy for he thought himself immortal."

When West showed Fulton the pictures in his gallery, the provincial was amazed. Like every other American artist who came to London with a little local reputation, he made a painful discovery. "Painting," so he wrote his mother, "requires more study than I at first imagined, in consequence of which I shall be obliged to stay here some time longer than I expected." But if he was awed by the famous artist and his celebrated pictures, it was the only time in his life that he was awed. He had merely discovered, after all, that the world he intended to conquer was bigger than he realized. In his manner toward West, however, there would have been no aggressive self-confidence to offend, merely an impressive dignity growing from a sense of his own worth. Except in the rare moments when his tremendous passions got out of control, Fulton, like Rumsey, was a master at getting on with the great.

Expert through long usage, West found Fulton lodgings and put him to work at learning the sophisticated modes of English painting. Fulton became one of the many young men who of a morning brought their canvases to the master for criticism, waiting in rows on benches supplied for that purpose. Although he did not live in West's studio, as many of his biographers state, nor become a favorite pupil as Stuart had been, yet the master treated him with great kindness, "in consequence," so a mutual friend reported to Mrs. Fulton, "of your son's ingratiating address and manners." The pupil himself wrote, "Mr. West and me are on a very familiar footing, and when he is in town pays me much attention, which is extremely agreeable, as we live near each other."

West's example as a painter had a smaller influence on Fulton's career than West's example as a man. Here was an American from Fulton's own backwoods who had achieved a world-shaking reputation, much greater, although this Fulton did not realize, than his pictures warranted. The pupil regarded his master as "an ornament to society and a stimulus to young men." Intending also to be a success, he studied West's method of impressing his fellow-men and quickly saw that the artist's secret was to be conspicuously saintly, a shining example of the bourgeois ideal of homely morality. Fulton was to write a friend, "Remember me with the utmost affection to Mr. and Mrs. West, and tell them how much I love them, and wish to imitate their social virtues."

From the moment West had painted birds and flowers as a little boy, the world had poured before him praise, fame, and money; his road to virtue had been a high road. Fulton was to travel a more rocky path, for his natural gifts as a painter were not outstanding. It is easier to be moral in prosperity than when the fates seem to thwart your every desire. When he had been in England about two years, pride led Fulton to deviate from West's high plane of morality; he lied to his mother. "My pictures have been admitted this year into the Royal Academy," he wrote. But the catalogue of this exhibition was innocent of his name.

Since what passed for painting skill in Philadelphia was clumsiness in London, Fulton was unable to get commissions while he studied, and the money he had brought with him was soon gone. "Many, many a silent, solitary hour have I spent in the most unnerved study, anxiously pondering how to make funds to support me till the fruits of my labors should suffice [?] to repay them. Thus I went on near four years—happily beloved by all who knew me, or I had long ere now been crushed by poverty's cold wind and freezing rain." In other words, scorning the more mundane expedient of taking a job, he had borrowed from his friends. He felt justified in this because, as his entire life story shows, he had somehow acquired an overwhelming belief in his own powers, in his ability to triumph over the whole world. Certainly any day now his skill as a painter would be recognized. When it was not, he clenched his jaw and went ahead, doggedly if incredulously, although sometimes he had difficulty even keeping a roof over his head. He wrote his mother, "I am frequently changing my lodgings to suit my convenience."

Naturally the mind of the young man who was unappreciated in London strayed to the green pastures of home where he had had his little triumphs. He was avid for local gossip. "I wish much to know," he wrote typically, "why Pyton left the situation of the sawmill." When Indian raids were reported on the frontier, he expressed continual anxiety for his family; and in quieter times he dreamed of agreeable scenes in Pennsylvania. He wrote his mother, "I conceive your garden to be the best in Washington; gardening was ever your delight, besides you have a taste for that kind of cultivation which perhaps the people of your western country are strangers to. Be assured my ideas often hover around the little spot. I think I see it improved by your industrious hand whilst the flowers of spring lend their aid to beautify the scene; but chief of all, I think I see you on a Sunday evening contemplatively walking the grounds and with silent pleasure viewing the labors of the week. And thus each evening reflect with pleasure on the past day. So shall time pass on and pleasure crown the evening of life."

In 1790, the year of Fitch's successful boat, Fulton made a short trip to France to improve "my taste and eye" by studying the pictures there, and during the following year he at last achieved public exhibition in London. He showed two portraits and two subject pictures at the Society of Artists, and had another pair of portraits accepted by the more exacting Royal Academy. This achievement, however, was so small compared to his dreams that he felt forced to exaggerate it to his mother. In a letter home, the two pictures at the Royal Academy were increased to eight, and although a diligent search of the contemporary newspapers fails to show that his offerings attracted any attention, Fulton said they received "every possible mark of approbation that the Society could give. But," he continued, "these exertions are all for honor; there is no profit arising out of it. It only tends to create a name that may hereafter produce business."

Several writers have given us detailed and impressive analyses of Fulton's English portraits; such art criticism is unfortunately as usual as it is amusing. We may well wonder how the professors came to be so wise, since not a single portrait exists that can be shown to have been painted by Fulton at this time. We have nothing but three engravings made in 1793 after the artist's historical paintings. Two, engraved by Ward, depict *Mary Queen of Scots under confinement* and *Lady Jane Grey the night before her execution.* We can only hope that the engraver libeled the painter, for the prints, although they have a certain archaic charm, are completely without the distinction we would expect to find in pictures produced during the great period of English art. The drawing is poor, particularly in the hands. The compositions depend primarily on chiaroscuro, the central figures being picked out as if under a spotlight; the result is neat but not impressive. Despite their heart-rending subject matter, the pictures reveal little of the melodrama, the excitement so typical of the school of West. The artist, who seems to have been afraid to let himself go, preferred a melancholy restraint that was pretty rather than powerful. Gone is the sincerity, the aching search for truth which had characterized the crude miniatures we have attributed to Fulton's Philadelphia period. In its place we find a superficial sophistication, a somewhat hesitant use of technical expedients which the artist has learned by rote, without feeling them at all. Fulton's style could now express no emotion deeper than sentimentality.

Yet two years before the engravings were made, Fulton had found a patron. Inviting him to his country seat in Devonshire, Lord William Courtenay commissioned a portrait of himself and introduced the painter "to all his friends." In the provinces, Fulton was able to find business; he wrote his mother, "I am beginning to get a little money and pay some debt which I was obliged to contract, so that I hope in six months to be clear with the world . . . and then start fair to make all I can."

Although Fulton was earning his living from painting at last, we find a strange lack in his letters home. Most of the American artists who realized their ambition of visiting the fabled art galleries of Europe were overwhelmed with excitement. In cascades of prose, they described in letters home the pictures they had seen, compared Correggio and Raphael, Rubens and the divine Guido. Of such passages, Fulton's writings are entirely innocent. When he spoke of art, it was only as a trade; esthetic considerations always gave way to the monetary. He studied great paintings not so much to improve his technique as to improve his earning power.

We find in Fulton no symptoms of a dedication to the fine arts that would make him stick to his easel through continuing adversity. If he discovered a better way to make money, he might easily grasp it.

Fulton and Rumsey had been friends in London, and some evidence indicates that they were quite intimate; Fulton was probably also acquainted with Rumsey's partner Parker, with whom he later had business dealings.[1] Among the younger man's papers we find a detailed analysis of "Messrs. Parker and Rumsey's experiment for moving boats." The sophistication of this statement suggests, however, that it may have been drawn up some years afterwards, when Fulton had become an experienced engineer. He blamed Rumsey's failure on the fact that "the engine was not loaded to its full power, that the water was lifted four times too high, and that the tube by which the water escaped was more than five times too small." He felt that the method of jet propulsion was worth further experimentation, although, when he considered that the engine had to waste power in lifting the water and that the water loaded down the boat, he suspected that "the power of the engine cannot be applied to advantage by this means."

Fulton's appearance in the steamboat lists during June 1793 follows by a few months the final failure of Rumsey's boat; perhaps he decided that since both Fitch and Rumsey had now been defeated, a new principle was wanting. Why should he himself not discover it? He meditated for a while, and suddenly he struck on a principle that seemed obviously the right one. The most efficient sea animals were fish; fish propelled themselves by a springing motion of their tails; a steamboat's paddle should imitate the tail of a salmon. What was more simple than to have the engine wind up the cord of a large bow, and then, when the tension was great enough, to allow the bow to unwind, moving a stern paddle with a fish-like motion!

Despite its logic, this idea was far from practical; it did not indicate that Fulton would be a dangerous contender. But then the young man did something that should have made cold shivers run down the spines of his rivals: he built a little model boat and began painstaking experiments. Finding that the return motion of his scull impeded the boat, he attached the bow to paddle wheels. Soon he was attempting to determine the most efficient design for such wheels.

Fulton was at the point of abandoning art for engineering. Various high-flown and patriotic reasons have been given for this change, but the most authentic statement is that of Benjamin West, who said that his pupil "came to England with an intention to study painting, but doubting his success turned his attention to mechanics." In September 1796 Fulton himself wrote home, "I have laid aside my panels, and have not painted a picture for more than two years, as I have little doubt but canals will answer my purpose much better." What this purpose is he does not state, but since he regarded art and engineering as alternate routes to achieve it, it must clearly have been the winning of fame and fortune.

Why did it take him so long, until he was about thirty years old, to find his true profession, especially when the seeds of his interest in invention had been sown during his boyhood in mechanically minded Lancaster? Perhaps his apprenticeship to a jeweler had cast the die. Although this trade involved metalwork as well as the creating of ornament, miniature painting fitted more easily into a jeweler's shop; if he had wished to make rifles, he would have had to break his apprenticeship, by no means an easy matter. And once he had set up as a painter, that pursuit seemed to promise him a livelihood; he did not abandon it till he had failed.

His failure became plain to him in a place and time that seemed to promise a fortune to engineers. England had gone canal mad. When the first canals were built there in the 1760's and 1770's, their projectors had been scorned as lunatics, but soon some ventures were making profits as high as 1,000 per cent; doubt gave way to the wildest financial speculation. Artificial waterways were projected everywhere, and Devonshire, where Fulton was struggling to get portrait commissions, contained some of the most successful.

Once Fulton turned to engineering, his mind seethed with ideas. He invented a mill for cutting marble, which was built and for which he received a gold medal. Next he wrote Lord Stanhope, who was planning a canal to connect Bristol with the Channel, suggesting that the nobleman discard the use of locks, pulling boats instead to higher levels on inclined planes. He added that he had some steamboat ideas which he would be glad to communicate if his Lordship was interested. Stanhope replied that inclined planes were an old idea, but that he would be glad to learn Fulton's steamboat thoughts as "it is a subject on which I have made important discoveries."

In his next letter, Fulton described the experiments on propelling boats we have just discussed, and stated a principle he was to apply many years later. Mechanical vessels, he wrote, "should be long, narrow, and flat at bottom, with a broad keel, as a flat vessel will not occupy so much space in the water." Although Stanhope's reply is lost, we may be sure that he did not express much enthusiasm for having a steam engine apply its power by winding up a bow.

During this correspondence, Fulton had dealt with both steamboats and canals, but canals interested him the more; trying to improve them became his major occupation for the next six years. He made only an occasional abortive gesture in the direction of steam navigation, as when he wrote Boulton and Watt on November 4, 1794, requesting the price of a rotary engine of 3 or 4 horsepower "which is designed to be placed in a boat." He asked other questions which showed that he wanted Watt to design the engine for him, and perhaps the boat as well; naturally they were not interested.

His method of approaching his canal work is highly significant. Although so poor that he had to borrow in order to eat, he did not seek employment in any of the many construction projects; he spent three years visiting canal after canal as an independent inventor. The former self-styled "yeoman" now wrote himself down as "gentleman," and gentlemen did not in those days serve as subordinates. Furthermore, his temperament was not suited to receiving commands. The instant he set himself up, with no particular training, as an engineer, he felt his ideas were too valuable to be shared with anyone else, or carried out except under the most grandiose auspices.[2]

The most interesting feature of Fulton's conceptions at this time is their tremendous scope. His *Treatise on Canal Navigation*, published in 1796, attempted to outline a complete system that would by itself solve the inland transportation problems of the whole world. He wished to build canals much smaller than those then used, which, being cheaper, could penetrate into regions where there was not much trade. When the amount of business increased, this would be met by increasing the number of boats until at last the canal would be "full of boats from one extremity to the other." Here we find a similarity to modern railroad practice, in which many small cars are used instead of an occasional large carrier. Indeed, Fulton intended to use his boats in trains, attaching a string of ten to a single horse.

The more we study his ideas, the more clear becomes the analogy with modern railroading. Rather than following easy geographical conformations as the existing canals did, Fulton wished his waterways to go directly to major cities, even if they had to climb hills or be carried by bridges across deep valleys. The canals should be uniform and the boats everywhere of the same size, so that once goods had been transhipped into a barge, they could be carried anywhere the system penetrated. He designed various kinds of boats for various purposes: fast cutters for passengers, somewhat slower but yet quick market boats for perishable produce, and lumbering freighters for heavy goods. The system was to be operated as a whole with uniform rates and perhaps a single managership. In some other particulars he was not quite so up-to-date: the shippers were to supply their own boats; the actual haulage was to be done by independent boatmen who, however, would be under the supervision of centrally employed traffic managers.

A large part of the book is given over to the description of mechanical devices: inclined planes, boats, aqueducts to cross valleys, etc. Since speed of movement was necessary to make the trains of small boats practical, Fulton was concerned with increasing the efficiency of the laborers operating his devices; like a modern efficiency expert, he analyzed the movements necessary to work a machine and tried to cut them to a minimum. And in a manner most significant for his subsequent inventions, he tried to improve the speed of his boats by mathematical calculations of water resistance.

However, and this also is of greatest interest in relation to his subsequent career, he does not insist on the originality of the mechanical devices he uses. Advances in mechanics should be considered improvements rather than inventions, he wrote, "as the component parts of all new machines may be said to be old; but it is that nice discriminating judgment, which discovers that a particular arrangement will produce a new and desired effect, that stamps the merit. . . . The mechanic should sit down among levers, screws, wedges, wheels, etc., like a poet among the letters of the alphabet, considering them as the exhibition of his thought, in which a new arrangement transmits a new idea to the world." He claimed as his own not the appliances he used but their combination into a useful whole.

As is so often the case with an immature worker, Fulton's large conceptions were more impressive than his detailed solutions. He considered his most important mechanical contribution his method of dragging boats uphill on inclined planes through the motive power supplied by vast buckets of water dropped down vertical shafts; when the buckets reached the bottom, the water was let out, so they could easily be pulled up again. Concerning this device, and others he patented in 1794, Dickinson, an engineer usually sympathetic to Fulton's projects, writes, "It is difficult even for a trained mind to see in this specification anything more than a crude idea, ill digested; better methods, worked out in a more practical manner, were already in use."

While writing his book on canals, Fulton lived in Manchester. Through his friendship with the socialist reformer, Robert Owen, he became a member of a group of learned idealists including Dr. John Dalton, the father of the atomic theory, and the much younger poet, Coleridge. From the long talks that occupied the long evenings, Fulton became conversant with the most advanced economic and political ideas of the time. Again, as in the studio of Benjamin

West, he found himself surrounded with successful people who spoke less of self than of the improvement of the whole world. Fulton referred to himself and his friends as volunteers "in the *corps of benevolence and unanimity*," and added, "That all men may be *drilled* to this glorious exercise, *God in his infinite mercy grant*." Under the influence of his new friends Fulton wrote some political and economic tracts which, however, were not published.

Like his associates, Fulton was an enthusiastic democrat who supported revolutionary France in its war with England, where he lived. "It is almost incredible," he wrote home, "with what vigor the French meet their enemies, while *Live the Republic is the constant song, and liberty or death their motto*." Within the very nations trying to stamp out the democratic ideal, "the people contemplate the nature of a republic, and the more they think the more they admire it. When a revolution once takes place in the mind, it will soon make its appearance externally. And I assure you that there are numbers who do not hesitate to say that monarchial garments are going out of fashion." France would certainly win and all Europe go republican. However, he did not wish America to join the battle for freedom. Since his native country had no troublesome neighbors, no foreign possessions or alliances, "the art of peace should be the study of every young American."

Idealism and advanced economic theory found their way into his *Treatise on Canals*. The better internal transportation his inventions offered would, he argued, make society richer and happier, spread knowledge, remove local prejudices, raise the living standards of the poor by creating prosperity, and abolish war by enabling each nation to be self-sufficient.

In his book he included a letter to General Mifflin, the governor of Pennsylvania, urging that his canal system be applied in his native commonwealth. Probably following the ideas of his socialist friend Owen, he argued that the project should not be permitted to contribute to the aggrandizement of the rich, but should be undertaken by the state.[3] A legislative appropriation would build a section of canal, from Philadelphia to Lancaster let us say, and the earnings from the tolls would then be used to extend the system. Since with each extension the earnings would increase, the project would snow-ball until at last there was no inch of the state which did not enjoy the advantages of cheap transportation owned and operated by the government. Thus Fulton wrote and thought unselfishly, but, as had been the case in Benjamin West's studio, he was separated from his fellow high thinkers by the fact that he had no money.

Fulton's teeming brain threw out idea after idea for possibly valu-able inventions: a machine for cutting canals, a new method of tanning, devices for spinning flax or twisting hemp rope. He bor-rowed on these inventions when he could, or sold rights when he had to. Becoming his principal backer, Owen lent him large sums; part, he later insisted, Fulton never bothered to return. The inventor always gave the most enthusiastic reports on his prospects, but somehow nothing seemed to jell.

Fulton had already proved himself much more clever financially than his deceased friend, Rumsey. Both tried to put over inventions in England on borrowed money, but while the older man had lived in the perpetual shadow of debtor's prison, Fulton proceeded on an even keel, exuding respectability, idealism, and probity. Probably part of the explanation is that he borrowed hundreds of pounds where Rumsey borrowed thousands, and found better creditors, men like Owen who were not likely either to fail themselves or to call in the bailiff. We can only add that the young inventor seemed to have mastered the art Thackeray describes as "living on nothing a year."

Yet Fulton had moments of grinding poverty, and certainly the perpetual dashing of his hopes was unpleasant. Although thirty-two, he had succeeded at nothing. His failure in painting was a blow to him; it was several years after the event before he could bring him-self to mention in his letters home his change of profession. And his major object, his canal system, was gaining no backers. Searching for an explanation of his difficulties, Fulton began to suspect that he had been too idealistic. Perhaps he should appeal not to the virtues but to the cupidity of man. As a beginning, he tried to lure Lord Stanhope with the promise of huge profits into financing privately canals that would facilitate navigation between New York, Philadelphia, and Baltimore. The rich nobleman, however, only expressed dismay at the poor inventor's descent from the ideal of state-constructed canals.

On December 28, 1796, Fulton wrote Stanhope, "Your Lordship's good will toward men and your public spirit I see extend 'itself even to America, for Your Lordship appears to have taken in the idea that I am about to sacrifice public good to private gain; and in doing this I am deviating from my first principles of small and creative canals." On the contrary, Fulton insisted, "it shall be one of my principal exertions to get it introduced. . . . They will move onward, stretch into distant regions, and bending their branches round each hill, millions of intellectual beings will glide on their smooth surface and draw comfort from the system—when Fulton shall be long lost to the memory of man. No, My Lord, the system is sacred; by me it shall not be violated.

"Still there are a few situations which I formerly alluded to which do not come within the creative system." The proposed canals would be very short, and, as they connected arms of the sea, not capable of extension. "I see also that those points will ere long be laid hold of by some of our enterprising Americans who perhaps would not give the public such good terms as I propose." His company could easily pay a profit of 40 per cent; he was being very altruistic in limiting it to 20 per cent. "Now, My Lord, am I not right to endeavor to obtain these advantages which would otherwise fall into the hands of other individuals? . . . In contemplating Your Lordship's great talents for such works, I wished union with Your Lordship." He hoped Stanhope would reconsider.

He needed money, he explained, to live on till he could put over his idealistic ideas. "Penury frequently presses hard on the projector; and this, My Lord, is so much my case at this moment that I am now sitting reduced to half a crown, without knowing where to obtain a shilling for some months. This, My Lord, is an awkward situation to a feeling mind, which would devote every moment to increase the comforts of mankind, and who on looking round sees thousands nursed in the lap of fortune, grown to maturity, and now spending their time in the endless maze of idle dissipation. Thus circumstanced, My Lord, would it be an intrusion on your goodness and philanthropy to request the loan of 20 guineas?" The request "really gives me pain, but, My Lord, men of fortune can have no idea of the cries of necessity."

The idealist was becoming bitter, not at injustice in general, but at injustice against himself, a dangerous sign. And indeed, less than two months after he wrote Stanhope that his idea of government control was "sacred" and "shall not be violated," he tried to violate it. He had long wanted to interest George Washington, and had at first tried to appeal to the President on a high altruistic plane. Sending him a copy of his *Treatise*, Fulton wrote, "The discovery of the mariner's compass gave commerce to the world. The invention of printing is dissipating darkness and giving a polish to the mass of men. And the introduction of the creative system of canals, as certain in their effects, will give an agricultural polish to every acre of America." Washington was not impressed; he sent Fulton nothing but a courteous acknowledgment that he had received the book.

Remembering perhaps that the Potomac Company, Washington's own canal enterprise, had been organized as a stock company, Fulton tried a year later to appeal to the hero's interest in profits. In February 1797 he wrote Washington that he had at first conceived of his canals as national works, but now he thought it might be better to have an incorporated company which would be required to spend half its earnings on further construction; the stockholders could keep the other half. When the whole country had finally been honeycombed with ditches, the farseeing capitalists would pocket two million pounds a year, since canals would be so much more effective than turnpike roads.

Although Washington showed no interest, Fulton's appeal to the profit motive finally paid. On April 28 he wrote Owen that he had sold a quarter of his canal prospects for £1,500 "to a gentleman of large fortune and considerable enterprise who has gone to reside at New York." This transaction, as Dickinson has pointed out, was an amazing achievement, since Fulton had nothing tangible to sell except his patent, and that was worth very little. According to the agreement, Fulton was to proceed immediately to France and patent his system there. He hoped to be back in England by Christmas "and about this time next year I expect to sail to America, where I have the most flattering field of action before me, having already converted the first characters in that country to my small system of canals." Since there is no evidence that Fulton had interested any important American, this statement seems extreme; perhaps it was on the basis of similar ones that he had hooked his backer.

Although his principal attention was given to canals, Fulton was not permitted to forget the steamboat. His correspondent, Lord Stanhope, was still experimenting with such a vessel, called the *Ambi-Navigator*, designed to go backward or forward with equal facility. It was to be a warship of 200 tons, and he had induced the British government to pay for it, provided that he reimburse them if it failed. Although the passing years brought no tangible results, the earl remained confident that he was making great discoveries. He wrote Boulton and Watt, "Your steam engines in their present [state] are not fit to be sent to sea." Their boilers were too heavy, and their cylinders would not work if thrown out of plumb in a boisterous swell. He had obviated these objections "by means both of new principles and new contrivances discovered by me, which are really admirable." He wished to consolidate his inventions with those of Watt "though I do not doubt but that I can, without any man's co-operation, perform what is highly useful to mankind. Your exclusive privileges are about to expire; but if you act as you ought to in this business, I mean to stand your friend. For I bear you good will both as brother mechanics and (as I understand) as worthy citizens." Whatever the inventor of the modern steam engine thought of this insolent high-bred threat, we may be sure he sent the powerful peer a polite reply.

In 1796 Fulton wrote Stanhope, "Has Your Lordship heard of a gentleman at Mr. Roundtree's factory, Blackfriars Road, who has constructed an engine acting by the expansion of air or inflammable air created by spirits of tar? The *Ambi-Navigator* has just put me in mind of it."

Fulton must have been referring to the alcohol engine patented the year before by Edmund Cartwright, the inventor of the power loom. Soon Fulton was to meet Cartwright, and "his vivacity of character and original way of thinking" made him a favorite in the English inventor's house. According to Cartwright's daughter, they discussed navigating by steam hour after hour, since Cartwright believed that his alcohol engine was particularly adapted to that purpose.

Taking advantage of a temporary cessation of the Napoleonic wars, Fulton sailed for France in the spring of 1797. Success seemed at last almost within his grasp; the revolutionary government, he was convinced, would bring wealth to the masses by undertaking internal improvements. The abolition of the regional divisions which had flourished under the monarchy seemed to have prepared the way for a national transportation system, and Fulton had a system in his pocket which he was sure was the best the world offered. Thus canals were in the front of his mind, but the idea of steamboats still moved within him. And he was soon to come again on the trail of Fitch, who had preceded him to France four years before.

XVIII. *A Stormy Sunset*

I
N 1793 Fitch stood on the deck of a sailing ship that was taking
him to a new world and a new future. He watched Philadelphia
vanish like an unpleasant dream. America had always been his
home, but there was nothing in America to hold him now. The half-
completed *Perseverance* was rotting at her wharf, untouched and
uncared for. Of close human connections he had none. His wife still
lived, it is true, but to him she was dead. Voight and Mrs. Krafft
moved somewhere in these diminishing houses; they also were ghosts
that should be forgotten. He was traveling to new companions who
would be more constant than the old. Only one pang assailed him,
and that was for his children: the son who had been a baby when he
said farewell, the daughter he had never seen. He would bring them
back a fortune to show that their father was a great man.

Fitch was on his way to France to build a steamboat for Aaron
Vail, the man who had bought the European rights from his company. Vail had promised to supply all the necessary funds, and Fitch
did not for one moment doubt that the French river banks would
soon reverberate to the even chugging of a smooth-running steam
engine, the sweetest sound in all the world. He knew, of course,
that France was in the throes of civil upheaval, but like his contemporaries in Philadelphia he believed that the struggle was a repeti-
tion of the American Revolution. Since the Girondists, liberal bourgeois like the American leaders, were now in control, it was clear that
the battle was over. And two influential Girondists, Brissot de Warville and Thomas Paine, were old acquaintances who could be
counted on to help him. Furthermore, the simple fact of being an
American was said to open any door in the new France that was
imitating the institutions of the United States. Fitch had brought
along a miniature Stars and Stripes to wear in his hat so that everyone would recognize him at once as an honored friend.

Long days of rolling ocean gave way at last to the grassy banks of the Seine, and then Paris opened up before him, his first view of the Old World. With his American flag in his hatband, he walked down the gangplank into the shouting streets, a prophet come from the wilderness, confident that he was bringing with him the dawn of a new day. How long did it take Fitch to realize that something was amiss? Instead of smiling at his American colors, the passers-by frowned and muttered unintelligibly. Finally, someone who spoke English advised him to hide the dangerous symbol. The United States, he was told, was no longer popular. Puzzled, he sought de Warville, only to learn that his friend was in prison. And Paine, although alive and free, was hidden away in a suburb, under perpetual danger of arrest. Fitch visited him; he was cordial, but powerless to help. The Girondists had been overthrown. The revolution was moving toward the left and into the long nightmare of the terror.

Yet Fitch managed somehow to be presented to the Convention. This was an honor he had hoped for, and he had prepared a dramatic gesture for the occasion. His dearest possession was the flags of the State of Pennsylvania that had been presented to his steamboat by Governor Mifflin and the executive council. Unknown to his company, who considered the flags their property, Fitch had smuggled them to France; he now presented them to the Convention as a gesture of international amity. Whether they were gladly received, the record does not say.

Back in the streets, Fitch stood before the guillotine in silent horror; he was "disgusted to see the executioner dressed in the national uniform." However, so he wrote Thornton, "the nation of France most certainly know their own policy better than I can point it out, and I now mean to turn my attention to my little boat." Uninterested, while he battled the fates, in the human wars around him, Fitch tried to ignore the French Revolution.

He traveled to Nantes, where his castings were to be made. Full of his important mission, he called at the furnace, but to his extreme annoyance, no one paid any attention to him. The founders seemed to have other things on their minds, as if anything was more interesting than a steamboat. Oblivious that Nantes had become a center of counter-revolution, Fitch had been caught all unawares in the bloody civil war of La Vendée. "Soon after my arrival," he complained to Thornton, "the furnace became a frontier from the insurrection in that part of the country, and shortly after the town was besieged, when I made my escape out of it."

As the guest of Vail, Fitch waited at the city of Lorient for the storm to blow over. Vail had a little daughter, and sometimes, as the infant sat on the inventor's knee, he forgot his steamboat hunger, forgot the terrible inner compulsion that had driven him like a fury through the world. He imagined that this child was his own, that he was an ordinary man, the possessor of home and friends and the simple joys of ordinary living. But in a month or two the fates beckoned and he set out again on his endless pilgrimage. When it became clear that years would pass before there would be a chance to build an engine in France, Vail sent him to England to buy one there.

On the sailing ship that carried him to London, Fitch kept his mind busy by following the course of the ship, and soon he had worked out a chart by which it was possible to determine a vessel's traverse without the use of geometry or logarithms. This, he was sure, was a very important invention, since it would "reduce the art of navigation to the smallest capacity." The instant he arrived in London, he bought a piece of copper, smoothed it out, and engraved upon it his chart, which he published in connection with a little explanatory pamphlet. Then he hurried down to the waterfront, climbed on board the anchored ships, and offered his invention, *The Columbian Ready Reckoner*, to the masters of craft. Instead of being delighted and grateful, they were indignant. If Fitch's device really worked, it would enable any common seaman to know as much as his officers, even to become an officer himself with a little study. This was revolution; it smacked of those horrible goings-on across the Channel. In vain Fitch argued that his invention would abolish mutinies, since mutinies were caused by ambitious men who saw no other way to rise; give them an opportunity to be officers, and they would behave as they would want their own men to behave to them when they took command. This very profound piece of social reasoning was laughed at by the sailboat captains, who knew that the best cure for dissatisfaction was the whip and the gallows. Fitch found himself hustled off ship after ship. He thereupon wrote Catherine the Great of Russia for an exclusive right to sell the *Ready Reckoner* in her lands.

Vail had given Fitch letters to a Mr. Johnson, who was to handle the steamboat business in London; Fitch went to see him in high hopes. But Johnson told him what he and his partner should have realized: the English laws forbade the exportation of machinery, and it would be madness to suggest to the government at this time that a special permit be granted to send a steam engine to France, with which England was at war. Fitch then asked Johnson to honor a draft Vail had given him, so that he might pay his fare back to France. It was high treason to negotiate French bills of exchange, Johnson replied; the best he could do was pay Fitch's way to America. With an exaggerated sense of honor, Fitch refused money for this purpose, since it would not advance the French steamboat.

His steamboat mission thwarted, unable to sell his *Reckoner*, Fitch stayed in London in a state of extreme poverty, hoping for some chance to get back to Lorient. But the British blockade around France tightened instead of lifting; Fitch could not even send a letter to Vail explaining what had happened. Finally, in despair he took a steerage passage to Boston, agreeing to work out the cost after he had landed there. It was a melancholy trip home; he was fed abominably and kept below decks most of the time. Whenever he got up into the air, he spent his time searching the horizon, hoping to see a French boat that would carry him to the nation where Vail waited with the money to build a steamboat. But the British had cleared the ocean of French boats. Impoverished, in debt for his passage, he landed in Boston some time in 1794.

Now, in his deep discouragement, Fitch surrendered to his environment. He told no one who he was or what he had attempted to do; like any other journeyman, he secured employment on the waterfront. "The happiest days of my life," he wrote, "is since I came to Boston. My labor is an amusement and affords me a moderate sustenance and my accommodations are modest and agreeable, and I live retired and unknown, and go every day in the fore and after-noon with the greatest freedom and pleasure to [the] water. I have no cumber of business on my hands, no villainous acts to disturb my repose at night. . . . The whole burden which I have on my mind is to discharge the debt of my passage, which I am as yet by no means teased for."

Yet he was still tormented by projects. His *Reckoner* still bothered him; he set up an agency for its sale. Furthermore, he had invented a method of applying his cranks and paddles to mills; and as soon as he had called it to the attention of prominent mechanics, he suffered from the fear it would be stolen. At last his nervous drive got the best of his repose; he seems to have lost his job, perhaps because he resented too violently some real or imagined wrong. He tried to borrow money that would carry him to Philadelphia, but in vain.

Now, after all his years in the horizonless reaches of tremendous deeds and overweening dreams, he remembered the little Connecti-cut town where he had spent his childhood. Twenty-five years before, he had left behind him all the ties of blood; now they were the only ties that remained. He returned to Windsor to stay with his favorite sister, Sarah, and her husband Timothy King. But here too there was no rest. He could not force himself to become friendly with the woman who was still his wife; they passed on the street as if they did not see each other. Although his daughter and son-in-law were polite, his son cut him when they met. Love, companion-ship, a home that is a refuge from the world, all these still eluded John Fitch. For him there was no harbor this side of the grave. The first man to drive a boat consistently against wind and tide was a symbol now of the buffetings of fate.

While Fitch floundered, the idea he had fostered moved across the North American continent; a skeptical contemporary complained

that the United States was afflicted with "steamboat mania." All over
the nation, in brick buildings in the gardens of great estates, in
dilapidated sheds behind crumbling farmhouses, there was a sound
of hammering. The tinder-dry imagination of dreamers in every
state took fire with the vision of mechanical power, of vehicles that
would move with no man or horse to move them. Anything seemed
possible; probably fewer steam engines were being constructed
than perpetual motion machines.

Rivers and bays surrounded with houses or unbroken forests,
cattle ponds in pastures and mill ponds in mountain streams, suddenly
bore skiffs or rowboats or rafts on which home-made machinery
steamed and sweated and sprang leaks with derisive bursts of steam.
But occasionally the leaks were repaired and the tinkering continued
until tiny boats moved through the most improbable waters, while
farmers looked up from their plows to shake their heads over grown
men who bothered with such toys. It would be a thankless task to
follow this activity in detail; we will let a few projectors stand for
the rest.

Early in the 1790's Elijah Ormsbee, a carpenter and millwright,
disappeared from his usual haunts in the village of Cranston, Rhode
Island. His friends were not worried. One of them remarked, "Oh,
'Lige is gittin' up sumthin' some'eres; he'll come round when he gits
it done"; Ormsbee was famous for his crack-brained ideas. This time
he had an unusually large chimera by the tail. Working in an ore
bed at Cranston, he had become fascinated by a pumping engine
there. Then a stranger had appeared from Pawtucket; David Wilkinson was nominally a blacksmith, but he had invented a press for
making nails from cold iron, and his associates had learned by
experience to keep all machines out of his reach, so that he would
not try to improve them. When Ormsbee remarked that it would be
fun to put a steam engine on a boat, Wilkinson had agreed, and
rushed back to Pawtucket to cast and bore a cylinder.

Borrowing a copper still from a friend, Ormsbee retired to a local
cave where he was sure of not being bothered. The still, plus Wilkinson's cylinder, stirred together with a heavy dose of native ingenuity, ended up as a steam engine of sorts. Ormsbee first tried to place

it in a canoe he had dug out of a log; then he borrowed a long boat from the captain of an Indiaman. At Wilkinson's suggestion, he attached his single-acting engine to mechanical ducks' feet. On a pleasant autumn evening he stepped into the craft, started the engine, and glided out into the bay, proceeding, so the story goes, at about 3 miles an hour to Long Wharf in Providence. The next day he steamed up the river to Pawtucket to show Wilkinson. Everyone was given rides, the local urchins were allowed to steer, and then the time came for returning the long boat. The contraption was taken apart and the various pieces restored to their owners. As Wilkinson put it, "Our frolic was over."

A more serious-minded contender was Samuel Morey, an artisan who lived on the upper Connecticut River at Orford, New Hampshire. In 1790, or a year or two later—he could not himself remember the exact date—he profaned the Sabbath. For some time he had been secretly building a steamboat in a shed behind his house; he wanted to try it on the river when no one was looking. The obvious time was while every villager was in church. Legend does not report whether the pounding of his engine drowned out the cadences of the minister, but it does say that the little craft, so full of machinery that it was almost impossible to insert a steersman, breasted the current. A few days later he made a public trial, and the schoolmistress, softened perhaps by her own curiosity, allowed her pupils to rush out into the yard to see the contraption pass.

Although self-educated, Morey corresponded with the great Professor Silliman of Yale; at this savant's urging he came to New York where, so he tells us, he "built a boat and during three successive summers tried many experiments in modifying the engine and in propelling. Sickness in my family calling me home, I had the boat brought to Hartford as a more convenient place, and there ran her in presence of many persons." Trying to use a single paddle wheel and yet not interfere with the rudder, he placed his machinery, engine and all, in the bow, so that the wheel pulled the craft along.

In the meanwhile, John Stevens had not been idle. He continued to draw the most marvelous designs on paper, but he was too incompetent with his hands to construct even a model. About 1793 he employed John Hall, the English mechanic who had once worked with Fitch. He allowed his assistant to do nothing for himself, interfering by letter at every stage of the construction of what he hoped would be a steamboat; the impracticalness of his ideas is shown by his using a piston of cork, and wheels and gears of wood. Perhaps to get himself more into key with Stevens' wild commands, Hall picked up his tools less often than his bottle. When Stevens finally dismissed the mechanic for drunkenness, he was, so he tells us, "compelled to give up for want of a competent workman."

In 1795, however, a shabby figure called at Stevens' palatial estate; the butler brought in the name of John Fitch. Fitch explained to Stevens that he was promoting a scheme to drive a boat by having horses motivate the cranks and paddles he had invented for his steamboat. He had sold most of his rights to John Nicholson, a Philadelphian who had already built a craft that had gone to Trenton and back in ten hours. Perhaps Stevens would like to invest some money and use the invention for the ferry he owned between Hoboken and New York.

Face to face at last with the greatest steamboat inventor of his time, Stevens seems to have asked him no questions about steam, to have made him no offers. He merely said he would consider Fitch's proposition. The butler gladly showed the ragamuffin out. Then Stevens wrote to Philadelphia for details of the horse-boat scheme.

Although Fitch, wishing to throw some sop in his assistant's direction, had sold Voight the rights to the horse boat for a glass of ale, he felt that this discovery, like all those made by the two collaborators, was really his own. Naturally, Voight did not agree. He told Stevens' correspondent that he owned the patent. Fitch's statement that the horse boat had gone to Trenton was a lie, he added; it was the steamboat that had made the trip, and that not under Fitch's but Voight's own direction. The breach between the two friends had clearly not been healed.

In 1813 Stevens was to build a horse ferry somewhat like that Fitch recommended, but now he washed his hands of the scheme. Among Stevens' papers are three pitiful letters in which Fitch insists his invention is foolproof, and excoriates his partner for applying ideas other than his own. Stranded at Sharon, New York, Fitch needed money to go to Philadelphia, but this his partner, who wanted no interference, refused to send. Like a dog for many years a mighty fighter, but now old, blind, and toothless, Fitch was chained to an alien doorstep. While lesser men pranced by him unmolested, he could do nothing but growl.

The many books which tell us that in 1796 or '97 Fitch operated a steamboat with a screw propeller on Collect Pond in Manhattan Island all base the statement on a broadside not published until 1846. In this document John Hutchins claims that as a boy he rode with Fitch, and that Fulton and Livingston were also on board. Fulton's presence was of course impossible, since he was in Europe. The affidavits of two other individuals quoted by Hutchins speak of seeing the boat, but do not use Fitch's name. Hutchins' description of the vessel is very voluminous, complete with an illustration of the boat and a diagram of the engine.

Modern scholars, however, have noticed that not a shred of independent evidence exists to back up Hutchins' statement. The few Fitch letters of the period that have come down to us make no mention of such a boat, nor is it discussed, as we would expect it to be, in the papers of Livingston or Stevens. Probably Fitch never ran a boat on Collect Pond.

The steamboat Hutchins described could possibly have been a blurred memory of one belonging to Morey. That inventor tells us that in 1796, "having made sundry improvements in the engine, I went again to New York and applied the power to a wheel in the stern, by which the boat was impelled at the rate of about 5 miles an hour. I invited the attention of Chancellor Livingston, and he, with Judge Livingston, Mr. Edward Livingston, Mr. Stevens and others went with me in the boat from the ferry as far as Greenwich and back, and they expressed very great satisfaction at her performance and with the engine."

Chancellor Livingston, no doubt envying the pleasure his brother-in-law Stevens got from steamboat projecting, decided to take a hand in the game. Morey tells us that Livingston urged him "to devise a better mode of propelling; and I continued my experiments through that summer, encouraged by his promises, which were to give me a considerable sum, provided I succeeded in making a boat run 8 miles an hour. He offered me at that time, for what I had done, $7,000 for the patent right on the North River and to Amboy. But I did not deem that sufficient and no bargain was made."

When Morey returned to New Hampshire for the winter, Livingston, so he insisted, visited him there, "and at his request and expense I went once to see him at Clermont." But Livingston soon lost interest in Morey, probably because he thought it would be more fun to invent a mechanical boat himself; he was so used to praise and power that he did not doubt his ability to do so. In 1797 he hired a craftsman named Nisbet to build a horse-propelled vessel according to his own design.

Morey persevered. "I went to Bordentown on the Delaware in June 1797, and there constructed a steamboat, and there devised the plan of propelling by means of two wheels, one on each side. The shaft ran across the boat with a crank in the middle, worked from the beam of the engine with a shackle bar. . . . I found that my two wheels answered the purpose very well, and better than any other mode that I had tried, and the boat was openly exhibited at Philadelphia. From that time I considered every obstacle removed."

If we accept Morey's own description, written in 1818, of his 1797 boat, we must credit him with a great advance in design. The use of twin paddle wheels motivated by a crank was simple and efficient, vastly superior to the complicated contraption of his predecessors. Yet nothing came of his efforts. When the backers he had secured ran into financial difficulties, Morey deserted the steamboat for other inventions.

He was undoubtedly a man of great mechanical genius. He took out twenty-one patents covering, among other things, methods for generating illuminating gas, several types of steam engines, and an internal combustion engine, complete with carburetor, which the automobile pioneer, Charles F. Duryea, insists was the father of all modern gasoline motors.

After steamboats had become common and lucrative, Morey

mourned that he had turned his attention elsewhere. Pointing out that Fulton had used devices very like his own, he shouted in the quiet streets of Orford, "Damn their stomachs, those cusses stole my invention!" In 1820 he launched in a landlocked pond a small mechanical boat, the *Aunt Sally*; it has been conjectured that he applied to it his internal-combustion engine, thus creating the world's first motor boat. Yet his novel craft gave him little satisfaction, since others were getting all the credit for improvements in navigation. One angry day, tradition tells us, he filled the *Aunt Sally* with rocks and watched her sink. According to old inhabitants, on quiet summer nights, when the surface of the pond is dim and strange with mist, a chugging is audible, more regular, more metallic than the voice of the bullfrog. Visionaries who were born in the dark of the moon can see a little ghost boat hurrying nervously through the fog, steering again and again for the shore and then veering away, as if the hand at the tiller was seeking a passage that would carry the boat out of the landlocked lake where it is imprisoned, out into the great world of prosperity and fame.

Late in 1796 or early in 1797 Fitch attempted to return to the savage paradise of which he had dreamed so long; he set out again for the bottom lands on which he had laid out his land warrants fifteen years before. But where were the long aisles of trees, the solitary paths that had been grateful to his feet? He had been looking for land that would be good for settling, and his foresight had been vindicated. His 1,300 acres had been taken over by squatters who had changed them into six flourishing plantations. As usual, Fitch's fellow-men had spoiled his dream. He started lawsuits, and expected soon to be worth $13,000. But what use was money, when all he wanted was forgetfulness?

Alexander McCowan, a tavernkeeper in Bardstown, Kentucky, always remembered the arrival at his door of a tall shabby old man with a twitching face. He had no cash, the stranger stated frankly, but he owned some of the best farms in the neighborhood. He was sick and would die soon. If McCowan would board him for the rest of his life and give him a pint of whiskey a day to help hurry him out of the world, he would leave McCowan 150 acres. This strange deal was closed, with a legal bond.

Fitch was remembered in the Kentucky village as a "striking figure, 6 feet 2 inches in height, erect and full; his head slightly bald but not gray; his manner dignified, distant, and imposing. He appeared on the streets of Bardstown in a black coat, beaver hat, and black vest, with light-colored short breeches, stockings, large shoe buckles and coarse shoes: the representative of another age and school of life. Among the hunting shirts of Kentucky, such a style of dress and intercourse attracted observation."

Fitch's pint of whiskey a day gave him a few hours of release, but of necessity he was sometimes sober, and then he talked of steamboats, declaring over and over "that he should descend to the grave poor and penniless, but should leave in his discoveries a legacy to his country that would make her rich." He mumbled the strange name of Rumsey, or sneered impiously at the sacred Jefferson. Before the second or third drink had quieted his mind, he fought in the barroom of McCowan's tavern the old fights that meant nothing to his listeners. Some thought him a bore, some thought him mad. When the local urchins, hooting in the streets, revived the cry of "Crazy Fitch," his screaming fury was so terrible that it frightened even the bravest of them.

Yet he made some friends. The attorney William Rowan, who was handling his lawsuits, had a little daughter, Eliza. Fitch played her games with a serious face, gently cradling her dolls in his arms, and while she smiled up at him he forgot the past. But suddenly, in the middle of a romp, he would remember his own son who had cut him dead on Windsor's streets. All the old bitterness of his marriage came back, all the old bitterness of Mrs. Krafft and Voight. Then he would rise and unceremoniously leave the house. His acquaintance knew that some domestic affliction preyed on his mind, but he did not speak of it, even to his "trusty friend" William Rowan. It seemed a final blow when Eliza, who led him for a few hours into the paths of innocence, died as all his hopes had died.

Yet in this desolation, his gnarled craftsman's hands refused to be altogether still. He secured the right to a bench in a blacksmith shop, and made silver spoons and other "trifling keepsakes" for his friends. Occasionally some gleam of ambition must have come back to haunt him, for he built a model boat about 3 feet in length, with a brass steam engine. Running it on a local creek, he experimented with paddle wheels. As he launched his toy boat on the little stream, setting the rudder so that it would return to him, and then waited for it on the shore, what thoughts passed through the brain of the inventor who had hoped to remake the world? Was he planning one large experiment more? Or did the creek expand in imagination to the Mississippi; did he for a glorious moment believe that this was the vessel that would fulfill all his dreams? His mind, his friends were convinced, was giving way.

His lawsuits dragged on eternally, and this last piece of injustice preyed on his nerves. Often he told his friends that he meant to kill himself. He had hoped that whiskey would do it, but whiskey was failing him. Perhaps he was taking too little. One day he approached McCowan. "I am not getting off fast enough," he said. "You must add another pint, and here is your bond for another 150 acres of land."

He trusted for a while in his two pints a day, but tenacious life still pulsed through his veins bringing memories to his mind that even alcohol could not still. Now his vision of being accepted as "a jolly good fellow" fled after his other hopes. He could no longer bear people around him; he retired to his room, having even his meals served there. Slumber deserted him, and the doctor prescribed opium pills, giving them to him one by one. In a final act of courage, he hoarded them, going through sleepless night after sleepless night in his hopes of a sleep that would never end. One evening he gulped all the pills, washing them down with whiskey.

The door of his room remained closed while Fitch lay in a stupor that carried him gently toward the final release of death. And for once the fates were kind. No hand beat on the door, no busybody broke in to call the doctor before it was too late. Fitch's body surrendered at last to the will that had been frustrated by the world so long.

His landlord piously laid the corpse in a corner of the local graveyard. No stone was raised to mark the spot, and it seemed for a time that the inventor's dust might return to the earth, untroubled by the bickerings and ambitions of men. But even over this half-forgotten spot the winds of controversy still raged. In 1828 a bill was introduced into the Kentucky Senate providing that the state raise a suitable stone. "While the resolution was pending," its sponsor tells us, "I heard that a young man of some talent, and a grandson of James Rumsey, was a member of the lower house, and had expressed a determination to resist the passage of the resolution, on the ground that his grandfather, not Fitch, was the discoverer of the steamboat. I thought it best not to press the matter further." Another attempt, made in 1844, was also unsuccessful.

Gradually the rubble of time, decaying pieces of surrounding monuments, gathered on Fitch's grave, which was marked by a little depression in the neglected sod. A path went over the middle of it, and here in the cool evenings of summer the feet of lovers sometimes passed over the remains of Fitch, who had wanted to be "laid on some public highway or place of the greatest resort of the living."

In 1908 the ladies of Bardstown organized the John Fitch Chapter of the Daughters of the American Revolution, and two years later they raised over the grave the simple marker given by the United States government for every revolutionary soldier. Fitch would have been pleased, for he always recognized in himself the potentialities of a great warrior. And perhaps he would not have been offended that the song raised over his remains was not, as he had once wished, the drunken jubilation of Mississippi boatmen, but the clear piping of school children. Fitch the wanderer, homeless and alone through all his long days, had become part of the life of a small village at last.

XIX. *The Birth of the Submarine*

ULTON was on his way to France to add to the blessings of the Revolution the blessings of his small canal system which he was convinced would bring universal prosperity. Yet traveling across the Channel on a French boat, the young man who usually expressed himself as so confident of his future may well have been bewildered and depressed. On the narrow decks, crowds were jabbering in a language he did not know, and beyond, stretching in every direction, rolled untamed water. The boat, as it moved onward, seemed to get nowhere in the unchanging expanse of emptiness. Was this an allegory of his life: motion without result, and always loneliness? In moments of depression, Fulton hated his unanchored, nomadic life, where hopes always had to take the place of substance. He wanted to get married, but had nothing to offer a woman except debts. "My sisters," he had written home, "have been extremely active in making me uncle to many, as they find my bachelor ideas still possess me. However, I am not old enough to grow musty, and possibly I may one day try how I may like it. But at present there is not the most distant prospect."

Perhaps such thoughts occupied Fulton as the deck careened queasily under his feet. Suddenly a dark man began shouting at him in French; the message was imperative, but he could not understand. His bewilderment increased. Then a very handsome young girl separated herself from the crowd. Her neck was long and her shoulders slanted in the exact fashion of the day; her eyes were big and tipped in at the centers to give her a mischievous look; her beautifully shaped mouth was large, generous the eulogists of the day would have called it. Although herself French, she spoke perfect English. She interpreted for Fulton, and later, after they had landed, she assisted the helpless foreigner in his struggles with the passport officials.

As a result of some slight irregularity in his papers, Fulton was detained at Calais for three weeks. While he was waiting to get off to Paris, he heard that his beautiful translator was under arrest and in serious trouble. Although she stated that she was Mme. François, a shopkeeper's wife on her way home to her plebeian husband, she was suspected of being an aristocrat. Forgetting in a sudden rush of blood to the head all the careful planning of his career, Fulton hurried to the hotel room where she was under guard. The lady herself described the interview.

" 'Madame François,' he said, 'listen to me. You are in a very bad situation and I have come to rescue you.'

" 'A thousand thanks; but be so kind as to explain.'

" 'They are going to take you to Paris and put you in prison there, and once there, you are lost. Now listen to what I have to say. Nothing could be easier than to save you from this danger; nothing could be more simple; marry me; *do marry me!*'

" 'Oh, thank you; but I am married already.'

" 'Oh, what a pity, what a pity! I would make you rich. I am going to make my fortune in Paris.' Then he spoke of his inventions. 'And it will be quite easy to save you; only say the word and I will go and claim you. I will marry you, and that will be the end of it.' "

The lady smiled. She was, as the officials suspected, a member of the high nobility, and to her the self-made American was merely an object of amusement. "I thanked him as seriously as I could," she wrote. "His little plan seemed to him *so simple*, and he proposed it so kindly and heartily, that while I laughed I could not help feeling grateful to him. I begged him not to trouble himself any more about me, assuring him that providence and my own good cause would be the means of saving me. He sighed and departed." Fulton was not to learn her real identity until much later.

Shortly after his arrival in Paris, Fulton finally made a domestic connection, but it was with an older couple who regarded him as a son. For some time, he had been moving in certain psychological directions. The character of his new patron, Joel Barlow, who was eleven years his senior, represented the end of that evolution. Like Fulton, Barlow had been born to poverty in America; during his youth, he too had lived uncertainly by his wits. The idealistic phrases, which Fulton so loved to employ, also rolled easily off Barlow's tongue, but the older man had learned how to talk morality without impeding his advancement in the world. Perhaps he had been perturbed twenty years before by having to pretend religious zeal he did not possess in order to get a job as chaplain in the American Revolutionary Army; probably such things worried him less now.

Barlow had done what Fulton wished to do. He had made himself an intellectual reputation; he was universally regarded as a good man; and in addition he was rich. When he had been younger, he had been publicly involved in a financial scandal. As European agent of the Scioto Association, he had sold worthless deeds to gullible foreigners, and even sent a group of Frenchmen to their deaths in the American wilderness. He emerged, however, from the subsequent investigation with his reputation unimpaired, and from then on he kept his financial activities underground. Even Congress was unable to discover the source of his wealth. Modern scholars have done little better, although their researches imply that he was engaged in running goods across boundaries closed by war.

With $120,000 in safe investments, Barlow became a statesman and philosopher; he was considered the most cosmopolitan American of his age. As a poet, he enjoyed an immense reputation in the United States, although it is impossible to read his verses now; as a political thinker, he impressed the revolutionary French government into making him an honorary citizen of France; as a savant he published letters on mechanics, education, scientific agriculture, etc. He was later to become American minister to Algiers; and on a special mission from President Jefferson to Napoleon, he met his death during the retreat from Moscow.

Fulton went to live in Barlow's house. The older man expressed his affection for the younger in terms extreme for those days when reticence was usual. To his wife, Barlow wrote, "Always repeat to him how much I love him; you cannot tell him too much of it." Before the inventor started on a dangerous mission, her husband asked Mrs. Barlow to remind him that his body was more valuable than any machine he could make, "and that unless he could create me one in the image of himself, he had better preserve his own automaton. Read this lecture to him, or a better one on the preservation of his health and vigor, every morning at breakfast."

Once settled in Paris, Fulton set to work with his customary energy to find backing for his canal scheme. Although he wrote Stanhope that he had created "a revolution in the minds of all the French engineers I have met with," and that his inventions "now are contemplated on an immense scale of extension," the months passed without any concrete results.[1] Fulton's vitality spilled over into other projects. Unlike Fitch, to whom the idea of the steamboat had become self and the world and god—the whole universe— Fulton was a professional engineer seeking an idea, an inventor in search of an invention. He wrote Cartwright asking how his steamboat plans were coming and offering to act as agent for any of his friend's discoveries.

Then Fulton happened on a conception which he always considered more important than his steamboats. He had written some tracts arguing that free trade would abolish wars and bring the millennium; he sent them to the rulers of France, but they paid no attention. This refusal of the Directory to accept the truth from his lips convinced him, so he tells us, that "society must pass through ages of progressive improvement before the freedom of the seas could be established by an agreement of nations that it was for the true interest of the whole." Convinced that navies were the cause of all the world's troubles, "I turned my whole attention to find out means of destroying such engines of oppression by some method which would put it out of the power of any nation to maintain such a system, and would compel every government to adopt the simple principles of education, industry, and free circulation of its produce." Only two things, he decided, were needed to achieve this end: "First, to navigate under water, which I soon discovered was within the limits of physics; second, to find an easy mode of destroying a ship, which after some time I discovered might be done by the explosion of some pounds of powder under her bottom."

Fulton claimed these two principles as his own discovery, as indeed he claimed the entire method of submarine attack. Yet there can be no doubt that he borrowed most of his basic ideas from another American inventor, David Bushnell. The similarity between the two men's work is so great that it cannot be explained by coincidence. Yet it is conventional to accord Bushnell only passing mention as a precursor of the great advances made by Fulton.

Since Bushnell's story is one of the most fascinating in the history of American invention, it requires the greatest self-control not to tell it in all the detail it deserves. There is space here only to summarize the adventures of the obscure and forgotten man who was undoubtedly one of the greatest mechanical geniuses this country has ever produced. A more full account must wait for another time.*

Bushnell was born near Saybrook, Connecticut, about 1742; he was an exact contemporary of Fitch's, and the two boys grew up within 30 miles of each other. Bushnell too lived on an isolated farm, where he worked from dawn to dusk in his father's fields, and like Fitch he had a passionate desire for learning. However, rebellion did not run so strongly in his blood. He stuck to plow and harrow until his father died when he was about twenty-seven. Then he sold his inheritance, moved to the village of Saybrook, and prepared for college.

In 1771 he entered Yale, and during his freshman year he established the first of the two basic submarine principles Fulton claimed as his own. Doubting an instructor who said gunpowder would not explode under water, Bushnell proved his point in a manner most unconventional for undergraduates of those days: by actual experiment. And he discovered that a small amount of gunpowder will do

---

* Should any reader know the whereabouts of any original letters or documents dealing with Bushnell, the author would be much obliged if he would communicate with him, in care of his publishers.

tremendous damage if submerged, since the force of the detonation does not dissipate itself as it would in easily compressible air, but is concentrated on the hull of the ship.

As the Revolutionary War rushed closer, Bushnell began to wonder how he could attach bombs to the keels of warships; clearly he needed a boat that would row under water. He was not the first who had dreamed of submarine navigation; for centuries the idea of imitating fishes had fascinated leading minds in Europe, but no one had ever succeeded in building a boat that could actually move when submerged. At one step, the young American solved profound problems that had tripped up his betters. Although the boat he constructed with great secrecy on the Connecticut River in 1775 lacked a periscope and electric power, it contained many of the basic principles of the modern submarine. In addition to this, Bushnell made a major contribution to surface craft, for he was the first, as far as can be ascertained, to make actual use of a screw propeller.

The *American Turtle*, as Bushnell named his submarine, was 6 feet high and designed to hold only one man. Thin and tall, it looked like a gigantic pocket flask stood on end, or to use Bushnell's own metaphor, like the shells of two tortoises pressed together, a little conning tower rising where the heads would be. When the vessel floated, only the conning tower, which resembled a large brass hat, was visible; and if the operator opened a valve that let water into a tank on the bottom, the additional weight pulled the craft completely below the surface. Pumps operated by foot power forced the water out again when the operator wished to rise. Also at his feet was a treadle like that on a sewing machine with which he motivated a propeller extending behind. Other propellers were supplied to draw the boat sideways or up and down.

Details were perfected with a logical brilliancy amazing in the dawn of mechanical science. Ventilators that rose from the conning tower—one to carry away bad air from the top of the boat, the other to suck good air into the bottom—were fitted with valves that shut automatically when the *Turtle* submerged. Should the windows in the conning tower break, the apertures were closed immediately by other automatic valves. And in each case a second set of valves was supplied to be actuated by hand if the automatic ones stuck. A perforated plate over every valve strained the water so that no moving part would become clogged. All the holes through which apparatus extended were made of brass pipes into which iron rods fitted exactly, no mean feat in those days of inexact iron work. The joints were kept full of oil to prevent rust or leaking. To show the operator his depth under the surface, Bushnell invented a barometer, a sealed tube open at one end to the water, on which the pressure was recorded by a floating indicator.

We can see him climbing into the half-finished submarine, closing his eyes, and imagining he was submerged. How would he find the many complicated pieces of apparatus without groping? "Particular attention," he wrote, "was given to bring every part, . . . both within and [extending] without the vessel before the operator, and as conveniently as could be devised; so that everything might be found in the dark, except the water gauge and compass, which were visible by the light of the phosphorus, and nothing required the operator to turn to the right hand or to the left, to perform anything necessary."

The more we study Bushnell's submarine, the more amazing it seems in relation to its period; it was perfected a decade before Fitch even conceived of the steamboat, when Fulton was only ten years old. In those days, the mechanical arts were in so primitive a state that any apparatus that would work somehow was satisfactory to its inventor. Refinements were made after long years of experimentation, and often by a second or third discoverer. Yet Bushnell's submarine seems to have sprung out of his imagination in one burst, complete and actual. And who was Bushnell? A farmer lad who had been to a college concerned with giving future ministers knowledge of the classics and the true Congregational faith.

A bomb was attached to the rear of the *American Turtle*, and a rope stretched from it to a spike which rose through the conning tower. According to Bushnell's plan, his vessel would operate at night, approaching an enemy frigate awash, with only the small conning tower above the surface. When the frigate was reached, the *Turtle* would submerge and slip under the enemy's keel. Hammering from the inside, the operator would drive the spike into the wood of the ship. Then he would release the bomb, which would float against the enemy's side and remain there, held by the rope leading to the spike. A clock, which had been set in motion automatically the instant the bomb was released, ticked away ominously while the operator pedaled off as fast as his legs could turn the propeller, so as not to be caught in the holocaust. This conception was crude and not very practical, but as we shall see, Fulton adopted it with the rest.

Bushnell convinced the leaders of the American revolutionary effort that his invention might be the answer to England's overwhelming sea power. Franklin, Washington, Jefferson, Governor Trumbull, members of the Continental Congress, and many other patriots placed money, munitions, and troops at his disposal. Too weak to propel the boat himself, Bushnell laboriously trained several operators in the functioning of his very complicated machine.

Although Bushnell's attacks on the British fleet form an Homeric saga, we can only summarize them here. The first attempt, which was also the first military submarine action in the history of the world, was carried out in 1776 in New York harbor against the British fleet that held Washington besieged. The *Turtle* actually succeeded in getting under the keel of the British flagship, but the operator was unable to drive the spike into the hull; he assumed he had hit a part sheathed with copper. Some time later, in the Hudson River, the submarine again reached a British vessel, but this time after the operator had submerged, he was unable to find the keel of the boat. In October 1776, while the *Turtle* was being ferried across the river on a surface craft, it was sunk; although Bushnell recovered it, his supporters lacked the confidence to have it put back in condition.

Bushnell then tried other methods of applying his torpedoes to enemy shipping; we shall discuss these expeditions when we come to where Fulton imitated them one by one. Failing during 1779 to secure further support for his projects, Bushnell accepted a commission in the Revolutionary Army. After the peace, his trail became obscure.

In 1785 an attempt in Paris to use a screw propeller made Jefferson wonder whether Bushnell did not deserve credit for this device. He wrote President Ezra Stiles of Yale to ask if the inventor would not entrust him with an account of his submarine. "I would engage never to disclose it, unless I could find an opportunity of doing so for his benefit." In October 1787 Bushnell sent to Jefferson in France a detailed description of his experiments, his apparatus, and his attempts against the British fleet. The narrative ends in 1778; it may well be the thesis that he submitted to Yale in that year for his M.A. degree.

Since Bushnell's essay was not published until several years after Fulton started on his own submarine work, we may well wonder how Fulton learned of his predecessor's experiments. A persistent rumor places Bushnell in Paris at the same time as Fulton, also trying to interest the Directory in submarines. This seems extremely unlikely since, had Bushnell's work been known to the French officials, Fulton could never have convinced them that he alone possessed this terrible secret weapon.

Although he clearly had a general knowledge of Bushnell's work, Fulton was forced to invent some of the details over again, and of others he remained ignorant until Bushnell's account had been published. Thus we may assume that he secured his knowledge of the *American Turtle* not directly from Bushnell or his writings, but from some other man who was quite familiar with the invention. That during the Revolution the submarine was an open secret among officers of the American Army is shown by a full description contained in the diary of Dr. James Thatcher under the date February 10, 1788. Plans and models of the boat were demonstrated to the Connecticut legislature and the Continental Congress.

Fulton's companion Barlow had been in a particularly happy position to learn all about Bushnell's discovery. His freshman year at Yale overlapped Bushnell's senior year, when the inventor was hard at work on his experiments; Barlow was still at Yale when Bushnell received his M.A.; Barlow was intimate with David Humphreys, one of Bushnell's closest collaborators in the Continental Army. Probably we need look no further for Fulton's source of information than to the man who habitually sat on the other side of his parlor fire.

On December 13, 1797, Fulton presented a proposition to the Directory. He was capable, he wrote, of building a "mechanical *Nautilus*" which he hoped would annihilate the British fleet; and a stock company he had organized was willing to construct such boats at their own expense if the government agreed to pay them 400 livres per gun for each British warship over forty guns that they sank, allowed them to keep all prizes they captured, and gave them an exclusive right to such boats, unless the government decided to build them themselves, in which case the government would pay the company 100,000 livres for each they built. Had this proposition been accepted, and the submarine proved effective as Fulton hoped, he would have received a large fortune. But the inventor insisted his purpose was the idealistic one of bringing freedom to the seas.

The boats should be built at once, he continued, so that they could facilitate the projected invasion of England. "As a citizen of the United States, I hope that it may be stipulated that this invention or any other similar invention be not employed by the government of France against the United States, unless the American government first use it against France." Since submarine attack, like the use of fire ships, would probably be considered against the rules of war, he added a stipulation that the Directory give his company's sailors commissions stating that if they were executed or treated otherwise than as ordinary prisoners, the French would retaliate on British captives in their hands.

That the government seriously considered Fulton's proposals shows that they must have known more about the nature of the *Nautilus* than he stated in his petition. However, on February 5, 1788, after several months of negotiations about terms of payment, Fulton was notified that the Directory had turned down his proposal. The stumbling block had been his demand that his sailors be given commissions. "The government," the Minister of Marine wrote, "cannot publicly avow men who undertake this type of operations." The English would soon follow suit, "and this would be in some sort to scratch out from the code of war the just punishments inflicted on those who are naturally inclined to fight in an atrocious manner." The Minister was clearly shocked by the proposal, and the revolutionary government of France agreed with him.

New weapons have always been thus received. The crossbow was declared a diabolic machine by the Lateran Conference, and Bayard, who was usually good to prisoners, put all crossbowmen to death as "villains and cowards." Greek fire, red-hot cannon balls, and incendiary bullets had, during the previous generation, been turned down by the French as unsuited to national honor. The submarine remained in disgrace for more than one hundred years. When the Germans used it in the First World War, this was *schrecklichkeit*, but in the Second World War all combatants are using submarines without criticism. We have seen aerial bombing of cities move from the realm of atrocity into ordinary warfare. Perhaps the normal development is that a weapon is disapproved of while it is in the experimental stage and thus seldom employed. As soon as the deadliness which its detractors feared is proved, the advantages of resorting to it become so great that some major nation is unable to resist doing so. Then the opposing side has to do the same. Limited warfare is an impossible conception. The only way to abolish atrocities is to abolish war itself.

Disappointed in his submarine scheme, Fulton called his small canal system to the attention of Napoleon, who was rocketing up into political power. Although so far a complete failure in life, the obscure inventor saw nothing incongruous in giving advice to the most powerful leader in France. He enclosed a tract on freedom of trade. His political reasoning, which stemmed from Adam Smith, was the conventional liberal reasoning of the time, but he preached to Napoleon as to a complete tyro. Since labor was the source of all wealth, he pontificated, the more numerous the workmen, the richer the country. Governments must encourage industry and eliminate war.

In a personal letter to the general whose whole career had been based on armies, Fulton stated: "Among all the causes of wars, Citizen General, it is true that we see every day disappear those that relate to kings, priests, and the things which accompany them. But, nevertheless, republics themselves are not exempt from melancholy quarrels, inasmuch as they do not separate themselves from the erroneous system of exclusive commerce and distant possessions. All who love their fellow-men should attempt and seek to destroy these errors. Ambition itself should not ask for glory further than to show to men the way of truth and to set aside the obstacles which hinder nations from arriving at a lasting peace—for what glory can survive that does not receive the sanction of philosophy?

"To liberate the nations, Citizen General, you have embarked on great enterprises, and the glory with which you have covered yourself, should be durable as time."

He hoped that Napoleon would use his prestige to "favor projects the execution of which would render happy millions of men. Could virtuous genius find a more delightful satisfaction! . . . If success crowns the efforts of France against England, it will only remain for her to terminate this long war gloriously by granting freedom to trade and by compelling other powers to adopt this system. Political liberty would thus acquire that degree of perfection and of scope of which it is susceptible, and philosophy see with joy the olive branch of eternal peace sheltering science and industry."

If Napoleon read this epistle through, he must have laid it aside with a smile; he did not know that he would hear a great deal more from its author.

A new Minister of Marine having been appointed, Fulton submitted his submarine proposals once more, and this time the government set up a commission of distinguished savants to examine the invention. Fulton showed them a model, and their report, dated September 5, 1798, gives us our first description of his machine. In essence it was the *American Turtle* enlarged to serve the needs of the Napoleonic wars: while Bushnell had merely to operate in his home harbors, since these were infested by the enemy fleet, Fulton would have to seek the enemy in the open channel.

Keeping Bushnell's conning tower, Fulton lengthened the body beneath it to make the hull approach the cigar shape of a modern submarine; his boat was designed to hold three men and a lighted candle. Like Bushnell, Fulton placed near the keel tanks that could be filled with water to make the vessel submerge, and from which the water could be ejected by forcing pumps. Like Bushnell, Fulton used a screw propeller motivated by the crew, but so that more than one man could get purchase, he attached the shaft not to a foot pedal but to a group of hand cranks. In his desire for a greater range, he added an anchor and also a sail that could be used on the surface and folded against the top of the boat before it submerged. For the vertical propeller with which Bushnell tried to regulate his depth under water, Fulton substituted a pair of horizontal rudders more like the fins of a modern submarine. His apparatus for attaching a torpedo to the hull of a warship was exactly the same as Bushnell's and his torpedoes themselves were identical in principle. However, Fulton did not in this case, as he had done with his canal scheme, admit that he had based his ideas on those of others. He claimed that every aspect of submarine warfare was altogether original with him.

Ironically enough, most of the objections made by the examining commission applied to particulars in which Fulton's plan differed from Bushnell's. Thus, they pointed out that the boat would not move fast enough to make the horizontal rudders effective in regulating depth; they agreed, however, that Fulton had solved the problem when he suggested a vertical propeller. Fulton had intended to renew the air by merely raising the conning tower above water; when the commission stated that this would not serve, he added the system of ventilating pipes Bushnell had used. Fulton met the commission's objection that the crew would not know how far they were submerged by suggesting Bushnell's barometer.

In several other respects the commission condemned Fulton's independent inventions. His sail, they reported, could not work, since the boat, being almost exactly the same density as the water, would capsize. Bushnell's practice had been to approach the enemy at night with the conning tower above water, relying on the darkness and the smallness of the protruding part to escape the vigilance of lookouts. Fulton intended to approach the enemy under water. The commission pointed out that since the submarine would be completely blind, it would be almost impossible for it to establish contact with the foe.

Yet the famous scientists were deeply impressed with the submarine Fulton showed them. France, having a weaker navy than England, would be benefited by the annihilation of both, they pointed out. "The weapon conceived by Citizen Fulton is a terrible method of destruction, since it acts in silence and in a manner almost inevitable. . . . The weapon is undoubtedly imperfect; it is the first conception of a man of genius. It would be very imprudent to try to take it from his workshop across the sea to attack the English ships in their roads. It will be necessary for the inventor, who intends to maneuver it himself, to find the required companions and to practice with them so that he acquire confidence by experience and perfect his method of managing the boat; and that he make experiments that will lead him to a better method of piercing or breaking the sides of ships. This will not be the affair of a day." However, the commission felt confident that the man who had already accomplished so much would not fail in perfecting his scheme. They recommended that Fulton be given funds to build a full-sized submarine.

But the Directory did not act. In October, Fulton tried to speed matters up by sending Barras a verbal attack on the "monstrous government" of England. The terror created by his invention, he insisted, would render the British fleet null after only a few warships had been sunk. Then "the republicans in England will rise to help the French invasion, or to change their government themselves, without shedding much blood and without any expense to France. With England made republican, the seas will be free." His scheme, he continued, only seemed revolting because it was extraordinary.

"It is certainly the gentlest and least bloody method that the philosopher can imagine to overturn this system of brigandage and perpetual war."

Although Fulton professed to the French inviolable hatred for the British government, he allowed his friend Josiah Gilpin to carry tidings of his secret weapon to London, where he told Pitt's brother-in-law Stanhope and others. Soon Fulton was assuring Gilpin that he was not a partisan of the French cause; his only desire was "to promote the interests of mankind. . . . I cannot unite with any party or polity, nor will I aid them unless I clearly see that an obstacle between society and a lasting peace or improvement can be removed."*

Such sentiments were noble, but they did not keep a roof over Fulton's head; he needed cash. A year before he had written Cartwright, who had invented a rope-making machine, that he had built one too, although "I still conceive you have superior ideas on the management of such an engine, particularly the means of giving equal tension to all the strands." Now Fulton took out a French patent of his own version and sold the right to Nathaniel Cutting.

Years later, when Fulton was famous because of his steamboats, Cutting insisted that the inventor had cheated him by selling the machine as his own invention, without mentioning that Cartwright had patented an almost identical device in England. Fulton thereupon threatened to sue Cutting for libel; he insisted that the patent right he had sold was not for an original invention but for an idea imported into France. However, imported inventions could be patented for only ten years; Fulton's right, as Cutting pointed out, ran for fifteen, which meant he must have sworn the machine was his own discovery. Fulton's libel suit never materialized.

In 1799 Fulton remembered that when he had been in London a projector had made a fortune by showing tremendous pictures on the inside of a dome; the American now took out a ten-year im-

---

* At about this time Fulton sent drawings of his small canals to France's enemy, Russia, with whose political ideas he was avowedly in intense disagreement. The drawings were acquired many years later by an American who was told, on how good authority it is impossible to determine, that they had been accompanied by detailed plans of Fulton's submarine and torpedoes.

ported patent for the panorama. A building having been erected for the purpose near the Boulevard Montmartre, he depicted melodramatically a fire that had destroyed Moscow some years before. The irony of this subject was lost on every person then alive. In the crowds that gawked up from below with pleasurable excitement, there must have been hundreds who were to die of hunger and cold because in 1812 Moscow burned again. Probably Napoleon himself saw the prophetic painting.

Turning from mechanics to showmanship, Fulton hit the jackpot; at last he was connected with a venture that actually made money. His exhibition was so successful that the street was named after it— *Passage des Panoramas*—and a popular ballad ran:

> Paris pas plus grand que cela
> Jouit de succès légitimes.
> Un savant vous le montrera
> Pour un franc cinquante centimes.
> Et tout le monde donne ou donnera
> Dans le pano, pano, panorama.

Fulton sent some of his earnings to his mother. He had been so busy, he wrote her, "that I have not had time even to fall in love. And now having arrived at the age of thirty-two years, the ladies of my acquaintance, who, good creatures, are much concerned for my future happiness and honor, begin to fear that I shall die an old bachelor; hence with eyes full of regard and the sweetest arguments they persuade me to avoid so miserable an end." He intended to marry, but he was holding his affections "for some amiable American whose customs and manners I prefer to anything I have yet seen in Europe."

One day, however, Fulton's equanimity was disturbed by a face in the street; it was the beautiful lady he had tried to marry at Calais. Rushing up, he addressed her by the name she had used then. "Dear me, dear me! Madame François!"

The lady herself describes the interview: "He seized both my hands, even the one that was resting on my brother's arm, shook them, and pressed them in his rough, frank, American style. 'Dear me, Madame François, how glad I am to see you!'

"My brother-in-law thought this very extraordinary, and said to him, 'Monsieur, the person to whom you have the honor of speaking is Mademoiselle de Montaut.'

" 'No, no, it is Madame François. She is married; she told me so at Calais. But what did you say? Mademoiselle what? Mademoiselle de Montaut.' He took out his tablets and wrote down Mademoiselle de Montaut, and put them back in his pocket. Then he immediately began on the subject with which his mind was filled. 'Monsieur, I have come to Paris for a sublime thing—to blow vessels up in the air, to run boats under the rivers and by steam.' Upon this announcement, my brother thought he was absolutely mad; and, cutting short the conversation, he bowed to him, and we did not see him again."

Tenacity was one of Fulton's outstanding qualities. Having failed to interest France in his submarine scheme, he tried to sell it to the Batavian Republic; although he did not succeed, a rich Hollander, Mr. Vanstappoist, is said to have put up enough money to enable him to build his boat.

Now he threatened the French government. "I sincerely hope for the honor of France," he wrote, "that I will not meet the objections of narrow spirits or little intrigues which will put me to the necessity of publishing the principles of the *Nautilus* and their happy consequences, or to seek in Holland or in America the encouragement which I hoped to find in France and which liberty and philosophy demand." Then, perhaps afraid he had gone too far, he added that he was "a sincere friend of France and the cause which she sustains so gloriously." Perhaps to prove his ardor, he enclosed an essay in which the British navy was made responsible for "all the incalculable horrors that are committed daily," and the intrigues of the British government for "two-thirds of the crimes that have marked the course of the Revolution." His *Nautilus*, he argued again, would force England to become a republic, and, by destroying Britain's commercial domination, make France the most powerful country in the world. In addition, his invention would bring the millennium. Since all surface warships would be sunk and two under-water fleets could not fight each other, no nation could ever again invade another by water.

At the very moment Fulton was using as a threat the possibility that he would publish his invention for all to use, Bushnell's complete and exact account of his own submarine was brought out in the *Transactions of the American Philosophical Society*. Since this journal had some currency among French savants, Fulton could not rely on Bushnell's article not being seen. Yet this indomitable man abated not a whit his threats or his claims of complete originality. Perhaps he thought it would be time enough to face the issue when someone called Bushnell's work to the attention of the French government. Then he could insist he had made improvements so great that they constituted a new invention; he may even have believed this to be true, since he never underestimated the importance of his contributions. His audacity was soon rewarded.

XX. *Aristocrats Take a Hand*

ARLY in 1798, when Fitch was trying to hurry himself into forgetfulness by the continual application of whiskey, a man as different from him as it was possible to be reached out to appropriate what assets remained to the broken artisan. This man was Chancellor Robert R. Livingston. Patrician, epicure, statesman, and self-appointed mechanical philosopher, Livingston had inherited vast estates set up on the Hudson by Dutch feudalism. Through his personal energy and his family connections he possessed such tremendous political power in New York State that he had no difficulty pushing through the legislature a bill stating that he was "possessor of a mode of applying a steam engine to a boat on new and advantageous principles," but that he was deterred from using it by the monopoly which had been given Fitch. Since "the said John Fitch is either dead or has withdrawn himself from the state," the legislature resolved that Fitch's act be repealed and similar privileges be given Livingston for twenty years provided that he build within twelve months a boat of at least 20 tons capacity which would move against the ordinary current of the Hudson at least 4 miles an hour.

Livingston's "new and advantageous plan" was one he had developed with horse boats in mind; he had never attempted to couple it with steam. He had planned to build under the stern of the boat a little box which would be full of water. In this "well," a miniature paddle wheel was to turn with such velocity that it drove out of a narrow aperture a stream of liquid that would push the boat along. Thus Livingston "hoped to escape the encumbrance of external wheels of paddles, and the irregularities that the action of the waves might occasion." He was not enough of an engineer to see that most of the energy would be lost in raising the water and driving it against the closed sides of the box.

Incapable of constructing anything himself, he looked around for a mechanic and fixed on Nicholas J. Roosevelt, who had in 1794 established at Belleville, New Jersey, America's first engine-building plant.[1] Livingston was too smart a business man to offer to buy what perhaps he might get paid for; on December 8, 1797, he wrote Roosevelt, "Mr. Stevens mentioned to me your desire to apply a steam machine to a boat. Every attempt of this kind having failed, I have contrived a boat on perfectly new principles which both in the model and one on a large scale have exceeded my expectations." He tried to frighten the mechanic by stating that he was about to write to England for an engine, and that a gentleman was clamoring to buy his invention; then he graciously offered to sell the discovery to Roosevelt.

When Roosevelt proved unwilling to buy, Livingston asked him how much he would charge to build an engine "large enough for a sawmill." After further negotiations, the mechanic considered entering into a partnership, and showed Livingston's drawings to his assistant, Charles Stoudinger, who had once been employed by Boulton and Watt. The expert warned against the scheme, and seems to have tried to show the patrician his errors. "That the Chancellor cannot be convinced that his plan is not the best I told you before," he wrote Roosevelt. "Everyone has a certain proportion of philauty, and rich people particularly. They are not used to hear the truth, and their idea is exalted by flatterers."

In those days the Roosevelts were simple people; Nicholas could not bear to refuse association with so great a man. He agreed to build the boat and accepted a 12 per cent share of the enterprise, in which Stevens, who was still looking for a mechanical ferry boat, also had a share. Stoudinger thereupon wrote that he and another English-trained engineer, Smallman, "will make the drawing of the Chancellor's vessel according to his description, but if it should not succeed and have not the expected effect, do not blame us for it."

Roosevelt soon had cause to regret his bargain. Livingston, whenever he could spare a moment from his multitudinous affairs, would get a new inspiration and hurry off a letter dictating some change of plan in which "you will find every defect of the original plan removed." And he would take no back talk from the engineers on the job; he treated them like servants commanded to lay a table. He even curtly pushed aside the suggestions of his brother-in-law Stevens. When he happened belatedly on a book on water resistance, he decided he had under-calculated this factor, and told Roosevelt to build the boat out of the lightest possible boards so that it would draw only one foot. The unhappy engine builder had to content himself with scribbling on the back of the letter, "How can an engine be kept in order when every part of the boat gives?" Livingston would order an alteration that required complete rebuilding, and on the following day ask indignantly why the boat was not completed. "Had I had the least conception of these delays, I should have written at once to Watt and Boulton for the machinery." Complaining bitterly of every new expense, Livingston forced his engineers to build with the cheapest materials.

That the boat was ever completed seems a miracle, yet in August 1798 it lay in the water ready to be tried. Roosevelt got up steam. When he attempted to start the engine, he found that it could not turn Livingston's wheel, which was so geared for speed that three-quarters of the power was lost. Hearing of this failure, Livingston flew into a mighty fury. It was impossible that the fault had been in his wheel—the insolence of the suggestion astounded him. Obviously the engine was faulty. He wrote Roosevelt that it was now up to him to pay for the entire experiment since he and his English engineers were too incompetent to build a steam engine.

Having lost confidence in his employees, Livingston sent on an outside expert, a Mr. Mouchette, but that gentleman found the engine more powerful than the specifications called for. And the guilt of the wheel was proved by pulling the boat out of the water. The engine went 40 to 45 strokes a minute, but when water was allowed into the well its resistance on the wheel instantly brought the machinery to a standstill. Livingston's comment on this was to ask why they had not done the experiment before; he could not be expected to guide their every move from a distance of 150 miles.

Roosevelt now had the temerity to suggest that until a stronger engine be built that could move Livingston's wheel, they try paddle wheels over the sides; Stevens, chiming in, suggested one wheel at the stern. But Livingston would have none of either suggestion, as he was "perfectly convinced from a variety of experiments" of the superiority of his own plan. He did, however, allow Roosevelt to alter his wheel so that it would offer less resistance, and at last the mechanics were able to make the boat move.

On October 21 Roosevelt wrote Livingston, "The Spanish minister was on board the day we made the last experiment, and was perfectly pleased with the operation of the engine. . . . During our sail he, at the time the wind and tide favored us, supposed we went at the rate of 6 miles an hour, but I think the delight he felt expressed by the novelty of the voyage caused his mistake. My report to you was 3 miles in still water which I have reason to believe was accurate." Livingston's first reaction was to argue that the Spanish minister must have been right, but soon the business man in him got the best of the inventor, and he began deluging Roosevelt with orders to make an exact test of speed. Four miles an hour was needed if the monopoly law was not to lapse.

Roosevelt continued to tinker, and then one day wrote that he would take the boat up the Hudson to the Chancellor's estate, Clermont. The patrician put off a family picnic so that he could watch the arrival. But his straining eyes failed to discern among the many sailboats on the river any craft that moved by steam. Angry because his day had been spoiled, he sent Roosevelt a sizzling letter. The mechanic's reply is lost, but the upshot makes it clear what had happened. The boat had proved such a failure that even Livingston was forced to consent to trying something else. The alternatives were the paddle wheels Roosevelt had suggested, and a new device just developed by Stevens. When the choice lay between the ideas of a mechanic and the ideas of a gentleman, who could hesitate? Livingston gave the preference to Stevens. But he never really discarded his conception of driving water from the stern with a high-speed wheel. In 1812 he stated that "when boats are designed for very rough water, it may be eligible to adopt it in preference to external wheels."

No sooner had Livingston's boat ideas failed than he invented a steam engine which he considered a great improvement on Watt's. He tried to interest Roosevelt, who was building pumping machinery for the Philadelphia water works; but the artisan endorsed his letter: "His new-invented steam engine which he wishes tried at my expense." Nothing came of Livingston's epoch-making contribution.

John Stevens now stepped into the forefront of American steamboat investigation, a position he was to hold until Fulton's sudden appearance on the scene. Like Livingston he had received the education of a gentleman of the day, who used his hands for such matters as eating and drinking, while servants executed any more complicated tasks. However, bitter experience had taught him that this was a crippling handicap. When his son Robert Livingston Stevens was still a baby, the rich landowner determined that the boy should be handy with tools; a screw driver vied with the conventional rattle for the child's attention.

But the father's busy imagination could not wait for his son to grow up. As he walked through his elaborate greenhouses or beside the furrows on his model farm, marvelous mechanical conceptions flashed into his brain. Quickly, inexpertly, he sketched a plan on paper and crammed the sheet into his coat-tail pocket. When the tail bulged so that his wife objected, he would repair to a little brick workshop he had built on his lawn and there try to put his hazy ideas into some coherent form. One morning he awoke in bed, his mind glittering with a new mechanical idea; having no paper handy, he sketched the vision with his finger between his wife's shoulder blades. She awoke at the pressure, and he asked her, "Do you know what figure I am making?" "Yes, Mr. Stevens," she replied. "The figure of a fool."

When in 1799 Livingston finally allowed him to apply his ideas to their common boat, Stevens employed Fitch's idea of pushing from behind with paddles motivated by cranks; but he increased the number from three or four to a multitude arranged in rows. Unlike Livingston, he respected the practical skill of Roosevelt and his assistants, asking them to "lay your heads together on this subject" and communicate with him "as soon as you have fixed upon the plan you conceive will be most eligible." But when the device was finally installed, Livingston's error in having built the boat of laths became manifest; under the wracking of the machinery, the vessel fell to pieces and became useless.

This mishap convinced Stevens that "no strength of timber in a boat" could withstand the vibration caused by the changes in pressure in the cylinder of an ordinary steam engine. Resolving to abolish pistons altogether, he designed a high-pressure engine on the principle of a modern turbine. In 1802, with the assistance of his son who was now in his teens, Stevens built a vessel that has been the admiration of engineers ever since.

His machinery was marvelously simple. He laid on the bottom of the boat a brass cylinder, 8 inches in diameter and 4 inches long, which contained two blades like those of a propeller, on which the pressure of the steam was exerted alternately. This turned an axle which actuated a screw propeller. Since he dispensed with condensation, using only the elasticity of high-pressure steam, he needed no piston, condenser, air pump, or valves. To secure the necessary high temperatures, he employed a pipe boiler, which was a more refined application of the principle Rumsey had established.

This machinery he applied to a boat 25 feet long and 5 or 6 feet wide. "She was occasionally kept going till cold weather stopped us," he wrote. "When the engine was in the best order, her velocity was about 4 miles an hour. I found it, however, impractical on so contracted a scale, to preserve due tightness in the packing of the wings of the cylinder of any length of time. This defect determined me to resort again to the reciprocating [Watt type] engine."

Stevens had not been alone in the high-pressure field. His rival was the brilliant Philadelphia mechanic, Oliver Evans. When a young man he had invented a flour mill that operated without the intervention of human hands, and he became one of the world's outstanding pioneers in high-pressure engines. As early as 1785 or 1786, he began talking of hitching such light and powerful motors to paddle wheels. But he was a poor artisan able to build only what he was paid for; he had to content himself with applying his engines to mills.

After many years, the opportunity he had been awaiting came. New Orleans having passed into the hands of the United States through the Louisiana purchase, some capitalists decided to build a steamboat there, and commissioned Evans to make the engine. Early in 1803 the vessel was assembled near the mouth of the Mississippi. But the jealous gods that had frustrated Fitch had not abandoned their vigilance; a spring flood picked up the vessel and deposited it half a mile inland. The 80-foot hull was surrounded not by the rustle of water but the hum of bees. Unable to carry the boat back to the river, its owners sentenced the engine to driving a mill.

Evans could only mark time until given another opportunity. Commissioned in 1805 to build a steam dredge to clean out the docks in Philadelphia harbor, he determined to demonstrate the possibility both of steam carriages and steamboats. When he built his mud scow in his workshop a mile and a half from the water, and there, in the city street, erected on it tons of brickwork and a heavy engine, his neighbors asked him if like Noah he was expecting a flood. Laughter gave way to wonder when he hitched his engine to huge iron wheels and set the dredge waddling like some prehistoric monster into the heart of Philadelphia. For several days the ponderously named *Orukter Amphibolos* (amphibious digger) inched thunderously round and round the waterworks in Center Square, while the impoverished inventor passed the hat. Then the monster dragged its vast bulk to the Schuylkill and wallowed into the water. Hooking up a temporary stern wheel and steering with an oar, Evans navigated the river for a few hours before he anchored his barge and set it to its plebeian task of pulling up mud in buckets. For the whole city to see, he had demonstrated that his high-pressure engine could move a vehicle on both land and water; he waited for capitalists to come running. None came. He approached Stevens, but that gentleman was more interested in following his own ideas than in using the brilliant contributions of others.

Livingston had left the country several years before to become American minister to France. Up to the moment of sailing he had continued experimenting with steamboats, but all his ideas had failed. He had been disillusioned about his own abilities as an inventor, but was still convinced that an efficient steamboat would make money when, during October 1801, he had departed for Paris, the stamping ground of Robert Fulton.

XXI. *Undersea Adventures*

O N JUNE 13, 1800, the Périers' steam pump was chugging away
on the banks of the Seine, unnoticed now, for it had become
commonplace. The crowd in front of it were staring into
the river. It was no ordinary crowd; leading scientists were there,
and at least one cabinet minister. With increasing frequency they
lifted their eyes from the water to look at their watches; then they
would frown and consult in grave tones. Finally one of the usual
ripples expanded until it became unusual, a white eddy appeared, and
up from below the surface rose a metallic hump. Some of the spectators rowed to the spot. The top of the hump opened and out of
it stepped Robert Fulton and two sailors. Scanning them excitedly,
Forfait, the Minister of Marine, was pleased to see that "their faces
showed no alteration."

Fulton's submarine, which had been built at Périers' workshop,
was undergoing its first trial. In a report sent directly to Napoleon,
Forfait wrote that shallow water and rapid current had prevented
any attempt to move below the surface, but the *Nautilus* had plunged
and risen with great facility, and stayed submerged for forty-five
minutes. Somehow the boat had been balanced so that it had traveled
on the surface under sail. Delightedly, Forfait stated that the vessel
would be ready in a month to brave the open sea and destroy the
British fleet. But the inventor, who had received nothing from the
government and spent 28,000 francs, wished a loan of 6,000 francs.

Exactly what had persuaded Fulton at long last to build the *Nautilus* at his own expense is not altogether clear. That the Minister of
Marine was present at the trial and reported directly to his master
suggests that Napoleon, who had become First Consul five months
before, had given the inventor encouragement. Indeed, Fulton must
have been promised the tremendous rewards he wanted for sinking
British ships, since his petitions to the government were now limited
to a single request: that his sailors be protected from execution by

threats of reprisal. On June 15 he wrote a letter which he asked Napoleon to sign:

"Bonaparte, First Consul of the French Republic to His Majesty, the King of England, and the officers of his navy:

"Citizen Robert Fulton, author of a method of submarine navigation for the destruction of navies and the assurance of free trade for all nations, having demanded my protection for the execution of his enterprise, and seeing the immense advantages that might result in the state of Europe, the cause of all wars destroyed and good feeling established between nations, I accord him this protection, and I declare to you that if the said Fulton or his companions fall into your hands and are not treated as prisoners of war, I will use the right of retaliation on the English officers and sailors that the fortune of war places at my disposal. And as I regard the machine which he makes use of as an instrument of liberty and humanity, I declare that I will not suffer that it be used to oppress the British people but to protect the commerce and industry that is the interest of all nations and should be the object of all government."

Fulton had his submarine towed to Rouen and then to Le Havre. In each place he made trials. At first he experienced great difficulty moving under water with his hand-driven propeller, but, as he wrote Forfait, "Patience and perseverance are the friends of science." When he modified his propeller, which had resembled a section of a complete screw, into wings like those of a windmill, he felt he had solved the problem. But still he did not attack the British fleet.

To brave the open sea in his little cockleshell; to move under water where a jammnig of the machinery or the slightest leak would mean certain death; to drive spikes into the keels of the most powerful warships in the world from a tiny skiff that any blow or shot would sink; to scuttle off quickly before the explosion would destroy the *Nautilus* as well: all these things he was willing to do. He had designed the ship himself; he was confident that it would not fail. Among all the dangers he would face, only one haunted his imagination. He could not forget that if he were captured he would be ignominiously executed as a violator of the rules of war. Execution seemed to him infinitely more horrible than death by drowning or by slow suffocation on the ocean's bottom. He refused to proceed until Napoleon gave him a safe conduct.

In Paris, Barlow was acting as Fulton's agent. Not only did he collect the money from the panorama with which Fulton was clearly financing the submarine, but he importuned the government to avow the invention officially. He fought his way in to see the Minister of Marine, but that officer merely shrugged his shoulders and said, "*Je ne puis pas. Je ne puis pas.*" Although the bureaucrats were willing to make use of Fulton's new method of fighting, which they considered unfair and horrible, they were unwilling to give it official sanction. Barlow wrote Fulton, "Your old idea that these fellows are to be considered parts of the machine, and that you must have as much patience with them as with a piece of wood or brass is an excellent maxim. . . . I have told it to several persons, who say it is a maxim to be quoted as the mark of a great mind. I will take care that it shall not be forgotten by the writer of your life."

Faced with Fulton's stubborn refusal to proceed on any other terms, the government at last gave him papers sanctioning his new method of warfare. Instantly, the inventor sprang into action.

On September 12, 1800, Fulton set out in his 20-foot shallop to destroy the greatest navy afloat and to remake the political economy of the world. Certainly Don Quixote never undertook a more grandiloquent adventure, but there was nothing in the American's manner to remind you of the mad knight of the Mancha. He spoke not the language of chivalry but of science; formulas not sonnets fell from his lips. He was young and strong and handsome; he had skillful hands, a nimble brain, and a persuasive tongue. When he talked, anything seemed possible. Yet he suffered from more than a touch of megalomania. Although confident that he could sink all the navies of the world, he was not sure that the *Nautilus* would stay upright in the open sea. He was delighted, so he wrote later, to discover that she rode the waves like any other ship. There seemed nothing incongruous to Fulton in the contrast between his great aims and his imperfect means.

Moving under sail through smiling weather, the *Nautilus* traveled without mishap to a little harbor 7½ miles from the Marcou Islands, where two blockading British brigs rode habitually at anchor. Then came a succession of frustrating storms. At last Fulton took advantage of a comparative calm to set out on the attack. Having proceeded on the surface as far as he dared, with the help of his two assistants he furled the sails and collapsed the mast while the little boat rocked in the darkness of midnight. All then clambered below, and after the porthole had been closed and checked, Fulton stepped on a pedal. Water rushed into the tank in the keel; the *Nautilus* went straight down under the ocean.

The three men were now crouching in a small tubular room, like the inside of a boiler, whose rounded iron roof was about 4 feet high. Grasping the handles that turned the propeller, the sailors sweated mightily, while Fulton steered, his eyes glued to barometer and compass. He had chosen a time when the tide was running toward their objective, but the *Nautilus* moved with such difficulty that before it reached their foes, the tide changed. Then the most heroic cranking was useless. Fulton cast anchor and ordered that the ventilator pipes be raised. The tide would run for six hours and Fulton intended to spend this period beneath the ocean.

Although the men in the submerged boiler sat as still as they could, since each gesture would increase their use of oxygen, the most dangerous motion of all continued involuntarily: the swelling and contracting of their diaphragms. After they had looked blankly in each other's faces for a minute or two, Fulton probably blew out the candle. Now each man was locked alone in his little universe of darkness and silence and such thoughts as visited his brain. Probably each was very conscious of his breathing, searching for the choking sensation that meant the oxygen was gone. Toward the end of their wait Fulton may well have struck a light so that he might look at his watch. Then the whole scene was dazzlingly clear: the iron roof sweating moisture; the tense still bodies and strained faces of his companions. Probably he was glad to blow out the light and return to a darkness that might be the darkness of anywhere.

After six hours the tide turned. Motion was grateful to the still figures; eagerly they pulled up the anchor and resumed their cranking. However, all their strain and activity came to nothing. Before Fulton reached his quarry, the British brigs raised their sails and beat out to sea.[1]

On another occasion, the inventor hunted the same two brigs, but again the vessels departed from their anchorage before he could reach them. They vanished over the horizon, never to return. The British secret service had been playing its invisible part, as is shown by an Admiralty order warning the Havre squadron of "Mr. Fulton's plan for destroying ships." The captain of H.M.S. *L'Oiseau* had replied, "I shall be very much on my guard."

Fulton now laid up his submarine for the winter. He had sunk nothing, not even a rowboat, but he insisted that his experiments had been a great success, since he had proved the possibility of navigation under water. He besieged the French government to take over the financing of his project. He was granted an audience with Napoleon. Concerning this interview, many writers have composed moving passages. Only the British fleet, they point out, stood between the First Consul and his ambitions. "Fulton," Parsons states, "offered Bonaparte world dominion. Bonaparte listened and took the offer under consideration." French naval historians are equally critical of Napoleon's lack of enthusiasm. Such statements involve taking Fulton's submarine at his own estimate; its efficacy in warfare had not been proved, and Napoleon probably suspected that it never would be.

After much negotiation—arguments and threats on Fulton's part; hesitation and delay on the government's—Napoleon's ministers decided to go along with Fulton. They gave him 10,000 francs to pay for improvements and promised a liberal bounty for any British boats he sank; a single frigate of more than 30 tons would pay 400,-000 francs. The next spring, Fulton had his *Nautilus* carried overland to Brest, where he made a few experiments with it, but soon he laid it aside.

A quarter of a century before, Bushnell had faced the same problem that Fulton now faced; he had discovered that although his submarine would submerge and even move under water, it was ineffectual in bringing a torpedo into actual contact with an enemy ship. Seeking another method of applying his mines, Bushnell had rowed out into New London harbor in a whale boat and tried, by manipulating one at the end of a long line, to make it smash against the hull of a British frigate. The sailors on a small schooner moored behind the frigate saw Bushnell's line and pulled on it out of curiosity. Finding a cask tied on the end, they lifted it on board; there was a tremendous explosion and the schooner disappeared.

Now Fulton followed again in Bushnell's footsteps; he resolved to apply his torpedoes by fishing for frigates from a surface vessel. For this purpose, he fitted a pinnace with a screw propeller that was driven by hand cranks similar to those with which Patrick Miller had motivated the paddle wheels of his multiple boats. Miller, when he found hand power inadequate, had hired Symington and undertaken England's first practical steamboat experiments. Fulton too was greatly disappointed by the speed of his manually driven boat, but instead of turning at once to steam, he undertook careful experiments to determine the best dimension and angles of his screw propeller.

With fifteen sailors sweating at the cranks, Fulton's pinnace never made more than 4 miles an hour, yet he was determined to use it for attacks on the British fleet. He asked for six armed cutters to guard his escape. The local admiral, who did not approve of new-fangled modes of warfare, turned down his request. Bravely, Fulton resolved to proceed without protection, but he was completely frustrated by the precautions taken by the British, who must again have been forewarned. Lookouts scanned the sea with glasses, while small boats rowed perpetually round frigates anchored near to shore.

Although the summer of 1801 passed with even less success than the previous summer, Fulton returned to Paris in September with new petitions for Napoleon. His attempts to bring torpedoes to bear from surface craft having failed, he revived the idea of a submarine. He would not, as formerly, try to attach bombs directly to enemy keels; his undersea vessel would carry the bombs into English waters and release them there, either floating awash or anchored 5 or 6 feet beneath the surface at the entrances of harbors. Again Fulton was following Bushnell, who, when he gave up angling for the enemy at the end of a line, had floated his torpedoes into the British anchorage at Philadelphia harbor. However, Fulton's new plan contained several refinements Bushnell had not thought of. The earlier inventor had never anchored his mines or used his submarine to lay them.

Realizing at once that Fulton's submarine would have to cross the channel under water if it were to block the Thames with mines, Napoleon wished to examine it so that he might judge of its capacity. To his request, Fulton replied that since she leaked and was "an imperfect engine," he had destroyed the *Nautilus*. His new plans, he insisted, were far superior; however, he refused to show them to any representatives of the government. In giving his reasons, he dismounted from the high idealistic horse he liked to ride in public. Not mentioning his unselfish desire to create peace and the freedom of the seas, he stated, "I consider this invention as my private property, the perfectionment of which will give to France incalculable advantage over her most powerful and active enemy, and which invention, I conceive, ought to secure me an ample independence. . . . Consequently the government should stipulate certain terms with me before I proceed to further explanation. . . . You therefore will be so good as to beg the First Consul to permit you to treat with me on business." When shown this letter, Napoleon remarked that Fulton was "a charlatan, a swindler who wished solely to make money."

Fulton tried to stir up interest by inspiring the publication of an account of his new *Nautilus* "in the construction of which he is now employed." It was to be much larger than the old, to hold eight men, to dive 100 feet below the surface, to contain enough air to stay submerged for eight hours, and to move under sail just like a common boat. The government paid no attention.

But fate was moving obscurely to bring Fulton fame in a direction he did not foresee. When Robert R. Livingston reached Paris in November 1801, he heard at once of Fulton's reputation as an inventor. Early in 1802, so Fulton tells us, the two men "accidentally met." Livingston expatiated to his compatriot, as he had to Morey and others, on the large sums he would pay for a practical steamboat, and Fulton left the interview with a frown of deep thought.

All logic, however, indicated that Livingston and Fulton had met too late, for in that same year of 1802 a steamboat was being built in Scotland on a most advanced plan and with important financial support. Thomas, Lord Dundas of Kerse, a governor of the Forth and Clyde Canal, had never forgotten the experiments Symington had conducted with Miller a dozen years before. In 1801 he employed Symington to build at the expense of £7,000 a steam tugboat for his canal. The lagging inventor, who had dropped his steamboat ideas when he had lost his first patron, was glad to pick them up again now that a new capitalist offered support. He drew plans, patented them, and set to work. The cylinder of his condensing engine was inclined at an angle of 45 degrees, and without the interposition of any other machinery, drove by a crank the paddle wheels dropped over the sides. Morey, if we accept his claims, had already used a crank and wheels, but Symington undoubtedly arrived at his solutions independently, and they were excellent solutions that promised excellent results.

In March 1803 the steam tug *Charlotte Dundas* was tried on the Forth and Clyde Canal. Lord Dundas was on board, accompanied by an archbishop, when the squat craft was hitched to two barges, each loaded to about 70 tons. Symington himself tells us that "with great ease they were carried, without the assistance of any horses, through the summit level of this canal to Port Dundas, a distance of 19½ miles in six hours, although it blew so strong a breeze right ahead during the whole course of the day that no other vessel in the canal attempted to move to windward, and this experiment not only satisfied me, but every person who witnessed it, of the utility of steam navigation."

Delighted with the trial, Dundas interested that great canal pioneer, the Duke of Bridgewater, who called the inventor to his London mansion. Pointing to the dark old masters that hung on his walls, the Duke said they were worth £100,000, but steam navigation might be worth even more than that. He ordered eight boats like the *Charlotte Dundas* for his canal, "and pressingly requested me to devote my whole time to executing this order with as little delay as possible."

Never before had steam navigation come so close to being an established fact, but fate combined with the conservatism of an old nation to change the situation overnight. Bridgewater died and his heirs had no interest in the scheme, while the governors of the Forth and Clyde Canal, afraid lest the action of the paddle wheels wash away the banks, forbade further use of the *Charlotte Dundas* on their property.

"This so affected me," Symington continues, "that I probably did not use the energy that I otherwise might have done to introduce my invention to the public notice, and perhaps it was from this circumstance that the introduction of steam navigation was postponed in the United Kingdom of Great Britain till after the Americans had taken advantage of it and carried the invention into general practice." He then went on to claim that his experiments with Miller, which, of course, antedated the early experiments of Fitch and Rumsey, made him "the first individual who effectively applied the power of the steam engine to the propelling of vessels." He further told a long and substantial story of how Fulton had called on him when the *Charlotte Dundas* was in operation, had asked innumerable questions and taken innumerable notes, and had at his pleading been taken for a trial run on the canal. This story has been accepted by many writers who should know better. Fulton did not arrive in England from France until almost exactly a year after the directors of the canal had forbidden Symington to use his boat there. Since the vessel had been laid up for many months, Fulton could not have taken a ride on the *Charlotte Dundas*.

English historians continue to claim that this vessel was so advanced in design that its construction made Symington the inventor of the steamboat. How far they are justified, the rest of our story may help us to judge.

XXII. *Fulton's First Steamboat*

FULTON had been playing with the idea of steamboats for many years, returning to it half-heartedly between his enthusiasms for other inventions, but not till early in 1802, when Livingston opened to him the possibility of immediate financial profit, did he become a serious contender He was a new kind of champion, different from all who went before him. An experienced inventor, he had cut his teeth on many mechanical problems, both theoretical and practical. Although the principles of his submarine had not been original with him, and although it had not produced concrete results in warfare, the machine he had evolved was the most advanced under-water boat the world had seen, exceeding Bushnell's in size and scope of action. He had made the drawings from which it had been built, and he had operated it with his own hands.

Indeed, Fulton combined qualities hitherto separate. Like Fitch, Rumsey, and Symington, he had come from the artisan class; his hands knew the feel of tools, and practical considerations were of great importance to him. Like Stevens, Livingston, and Stanhope, he read books and was conversant with theory. One group of his predecessors had been characterized by action without thought, the other by thought without action. Bringing together the two traditions, Fulton was the first engineer in the modern sense to work on steamboats.

Various national attitudes toward inventing also met in his character. He had lived in the centers of American ingenuity: first in Lancaster, where new problems were solved by the native wits of humble craftsmen; then in Philadelphia, the metropolis that represented the finest flowering of Colonial genius. During his ten years in England, he had associated with artists like West and Coleridge, political economists like Owen, aristocrats like Stanhope, mechanics like Cartwright. In Paris too he was friendly with artists, scientists, and engineers: Houdon, Montgolfier, Périer, and many others. He had profited from the best influences in the three nations that were leading the scientific and industrial procession.

Add to this the fact that he was less interested in originality than results. Fitch and Rumsey had cut each other's throats arguing who had conceived of steamboats first, a question irrelevant to practical application. Fascinated by their own inspirations, Livingston and Stevens had discarded the experience of their predecessors; Stanhope had been so completely bemused by his self-awarded superiority to Watt that he had been unable to profit by Watt's technical skill. But in his first attempt at fame, his canal treatise, Fulton had written that advances in mechanics should be considered improvements rather than inventions, "as the component parts of all machines may be said to be old; but it is that nice, discriminating judgment which discovers that a particular arrangement will produce a new and desired effect that stamps the merit." We may question his ethics when, as in the case of the submarine, he claimed complete originality for ideas not his own, but it is impossible to overestimate the practical advantage of a point of view that enabled him to use a device no matter where he found it.

Fulton's steamboat predecessors were the products of the age of enlightenment that preceded the age of science; Fulton represented a more modern point of view. He realized that making a machine that would work was only one part of invention; it was more important to understand why it worked, for only then could you repeat your triumph. In 1802, the year when he began his serious steamboat efforts, he wrote, "For this invention to be rendered useful does not consist in putting oars, paddles, wheels, or resisting chains in motion by a steam engine," but in determining what must be the size of cylinder, chains, and other parts to achieve a specific speed. "All these things being governed by the laws of nature, the real invention is to find them. Till the artist knows the necessary proportions . . . he must work in the dark and to great uncertainty, and cannot be said to have made any clear and distinct discovery or useful invention."

Consciously, Fulton set out to combine existing discoveries into an effective steamboat. On March 10, 1802, he wrote Cartwright asking him how his steam engine was progressing, and defining exactly the amount of power he wanted. If his boat was 40 feet long and 5 feet wide and weighed, including engines and passengers, 6 tons, he had figured that 720 pounds purchase would be required to drive it 10 miles an hour. "From this calculation," he told Cartwright, "you will be able to judge what can be done by your invention."

To determine water resistance, Fulton had used the results of Colonel Mark Beaufroy's recently published experiments. Since Beaufroy's tables applied to solids of various shapes pulled not on the surface but altogether under water, they were not directly relevant to ships and had been ignored by naval architects. No one before Fulton seems to have attempted to employ them in actual boat construction; indeed, according to his biographer Dickinson, "it is hardly too much to say that he was the first to apply theoretical investigations to practical boat design, so entirely was the latter at that time a question of 'rule of thumb.'"

When Cartwright sent Fulton an account of his alcohol engine as vague as it was glowing, Fulton wrote him, "Although attachment to you makes me believe everything you say, yet such belief is merely a work of faith, for I cannot see the reason why you have 13½ pounds purchase to the square inch." Fulton soon discarded the idea of using Cartwright's engine, but he made no attempt to invent one himself; he was sure he could buy a suitable power plant somewhere. Only one aspect of his problem had not been worked out to his satisfaction by others; he determined to experiment himself on how to apply power to the surface of the water.

During the summer of 1802 he accompanied Mrs. Barlow to the fashionable spa of Plombières. Soon a model boat which had been built by the celebrated instrument maker Étienne Calla, was delivered to him; 4 feet long and 2 feet wide, it was driven by two strong clockwork springs. Having dammed up a rivulet to make a stagnant pond 66 feet long, Fulton tested the speed made by the model when the force of the clockwork was applied to the water by various means: paddles, a screw propeller, sculls, wheels, etc. The most effective method of driving a boat, he decided, was to attach flat, board-like paddles to an endless chain that ran over pulleys at bow and stern. The chain would drive the paddles through the water for the work stroke, and then carry them back through the air. This conception was similar to the first that Fitch had tried.

Fulton was preening himself on having solved the steamboat problem when Barlow wrote from Paris that he had gone to the National Depot of Machines, an adjunct of the patent office, "and there I saw a strange thing: it was no less than your very steamboat, in all its parts and principles, in a very elegant model. It contains your wheel oars precisely as you have placed them, except that it has four wheels on each side to guide round the endless chains instead of two." This model, the work of Desblancs, had been patented by a company in Lyons which, according to Montgolfier, had raised two million francs for the navigation of the Rhône. Barlow added significantly, "I shall say nothing to Livingston of this model."

When Fulton examined Desblancs' work, he decided his rival had invented nothing since he had made no attempt to determine exact proportions. This judgment proved correct; the Frenchman never succeeded in making his steamboat go. Yet his claims had an important result; fearful of infringing Desblancs' patent, Fulton changed his own plans to include paddle wheels.

Although Fulton's steamboat experiments had been inspired by Livingston, neither of the men trusted the other. Barlow wrote Fulton that Livingston was afraid the beating up and down of the piston would smash the boat. "I see his mind is not settled. . . . He thinks the scale you talk of going on is much too large, and especially that part which respects money." For his part, Fulton was afraid that Livingston would steal his ideas. "I did not leave your memoir with Livingston above three or four days," Barlow assured him "I brought it home for the same reason which you suggest, and locked it up, and here it is. I talked with him yesterday again. He seems desirous of bringing the thing forward. There is no danger of his trying to do the thing without you; . . . he sees too many difficulties in the way."

Barlow and Fulton, however, had many thoughts of doing the thing without Livingston. They were negotiating with another capitalist, the same Daniel Parker who had backed Rumsey. Barlow wrote Fulton that although Parker "is highly gratified with your experiments," he feared that the wheels might not act as effectively on the water in a large scale as they did in the little model. This suggestion Fulton very unwisely pooh-poohed, becoming so sanguine that he even left Barlow behind him. "I see without consulting Parker," the poet commented, "that you are mad. Sixteen miles an hour for a steamboat, *le pauvre homme!*"

However, Barlow became so fascinated by the vision of large profits that he urged Fulton to cut Livingston out altogether. He suggested that his friend take advantage of a lull in the war to go secretly to England, buy a boat and contract with William Chapman for a steam engine with a 12-inch cylinder, "and make experiments on that scale, all quiet and quick." If the attempt succeeded, Fulton should hurry to New York, get an American patent, and begin operations. "I think I will find you the fund without any noise for the first operation in England, and if it promises well you will get as many funds and friends in America as you want." The two friends did not act on this suggestion.

The steamboat was still secondary in Fulton's mind to the submarine, and he had not given up the hope of selling that device to Napoleon. However cold and calculating he was sometimes, he was a wild enthusiast when his imagination was stirred; he determined to construct a new "plunging boat" at his own expense. Barlow complained to his wife, "Toot is calling for funds. Besides the 3,000 which I must pay him tomorrow, and 3,000 more at the end of the month, he wants 3,000 more still to build a new boat at Brest. I see no end to it; he is plunging deeper all the time, and if he don't succeed, I don't know what will become of him. I will do all I can for him, but the best way I can serve him is to keep a sheet anchor for him here at home that he might be sure to ride out a gale there if he can't keep the sea or get into port."

Barlow clearly refused to lend Fulton the money to build a new submarine, but proof soon appeared of Fulton's astuteness in sending reports of his secret weapon to the enemy from whom he was pretending to keep it secret.[1] On May 13 Barlow reported that

Stanhope had risen in the House of Lords to demand that the galleries be cleared, as "he had a matter of such importance to communicate to the House in secret as would admit of no delay." When Lord Moira objected, Stanhope replied, "If his noble friend was possessed of the secret he was going to communicate, he would surely not oppose the galleries being cleared." Barlow then quoted the account in the *Morning Chronicle*: "We understand that his Lordship's communication was relative to submarine navigation, which to his certain knowledge was being brought to that perfection by a person in France as to render the destruction of ships absolutely sure, and that that person could at any time blow up a first rate man-of-war with 15 pounds of powder, and that there was no way of preventing it." Barlow continued to Fulton that their mutual friend Harry Grant "is all in the high ropes about it, and thinks it was a plan concerted between Stanhope and St. Vincent [the first Lord of the Admiralty] that the former should give the facts to the house as preparatory to the latter's taking some measures with the author of the invention."

Waiting for some concerete submarine development, Fulton continued his steamboat efforts. On October 10, 1802, he signed a momentous contract with Livingston. In the first clause Livingston insisted that he as well as Fulton had "tried various mechanical combinations" and that the invention stemmed from them both; the rest of the document makes it clear that the principles to be applied were Fulton's. A patent "for a new mechanical combination of a boat" was to be taken out in Fulton's name. Fulton was to go immediately to England, and there construct a trial boat for which he was to borrow a steam engine, Livingston putting up £500. If the experiment was unsuccessful, Fulton was to pay half of this in two years; if successful a passage boat was to be built at New York under Fulton's supervision to navigate to Albany. Afraid of Fulton's grandiose ideas, Livingston specified that the vessel should not be more than 120 feet long, 8 wide, and 15 deep. "Such boat shall be calculated on the experiments already made with the view to run 8 miles an hour in stagnant water and carry at least 60 passengers allowing 200 pounds weight to each passenger." A hundred shares were to be divided evenly between the two projectors; the partnership was to run for the length of the United States patent and its extensions, providing only that Livingston might withdraw if he wished after £500 had been expended.

The fact that Livingston had dabbled in steamboats as an independent inventor for more than a decade might have been expected to cause trouble for Fulton, but it had the opposite effect. If the wealthy patrician, habituated to a lifetime of adulation, had been dealing with steam for the first time, he would undoubtedly have insisted on injecting his own impractical ideas, as he had done in his collaboration with Roosevelt. But he had been so schooled by failure and frustration that for the time being he allowed his expert to go ahead unimpeded. Thus he did not force his weaknesses on the partnership but contented himself with contributing his strengths: money and political power. Some years later Fulton wrote, speaking of himself in the third person, "To produce the first useful steamboat, it required the fortunate circumstances of adequate genius and capital in the same person or persons; he and Mr. Livingston had both."

The partners set to work with energy. Livingston, whose New York State monopoly had expired for the second time, wrote to the subservient legislature in Albany, who obediently granted him and Fulton an exclusive right for twenty years provided that within two years they run a boat of 20 tons 4 miles an hour on the Hudson. Fulton, in the meanwhile, made his first public steamboat claim. On January 24, 1803, he sent to the demonstrators of the *Conservatoire des Arts et Métiers* a description of a scheme for towing linked barges with a steamboat. This he intended "to put in practice upon the long rivers of America," where there were few roads and labor was expensive. In France, since good roads abounded and haulage was cheap, "I doubt very much if a steamboat, however perfect it might be, can gain anything over horses for merchandise. But for passengers it is possible to gain something on the score of speed."

"In these plans you will find nothing new," he stated; paddle wheels similar to the ones he used had been often tried but then abandoned on the theory that they gave a disadvantageous purchase on the water. "After the experiments I have already made, I am convinced that the fault has not been in the wheel but in the ignorance of proportions, speeds, powers, and probably mechanical combinations. . . . Consequently, although the wheels are not a new application, yet if I combine them in such a way that a large proportion of the power of the engine acts to propel the boat in the same way as if the purchase was upon the ground, the combination will be better than anything that has been done up to the present, and it is in fact a new discovery."

He intended to invite the demonstrators to see his experiments. "If they succeed I reserve to myself the right of making a present of my labors to the Republic, or to reap from them the advantage which the law allows."

Fulton and Livingston had decided to make their first large-scale trial not in England but in France. They ordered a boat 70 feet long, 8 wide, and 3 deep, with paddle wheels 12 feet in diameter, and leased from Périer an 8 horsepower steam engine. That Fulton was not entirely past mechanical naïveté is shown by his plan to use a pressure of 32 atmospheres. For this purpose he designed a very advanced modification of the pipe boiler; just enough water was injected into a red-hot chamber to make the steam required. As was to be expected, this early example of the "flash boiler" did not stand up under the high temperatures involved; Fulton reverted to low pressure and an ordinary boiler.

At about this time, Desblancs complained in the journals that Fulton was infringing his patent. Replying that his invention differed materially since he used paddle wheels, not endless chains, Fulton lectured his rival on the advantages of his system, and offered to pool the rights to their inventions in France, where Fulton had never intended to use his boat, if Desblancs would share the cost of his experiments. To this the Frenchman did not agree. In defending himself, Fulton wrote that if anyone could claim priority to steamboats in France, which he doubted, it would be the author of the experiments done at Lyons twenty years before. Jouffroy, who had returned from his exile, was excited by these words; he hurried to Paris and entered into a debate with Desblancs, but seems to have paid little attention to Fulton.

Naturally the supporters of both these Frenchmen claim that Fulton stole their heroes' ideas, and the same charge is made by the partisans of every steamboat inventor who preceded the triumphant American. Evidence abounds that Fulton was familiar with the work of most of his predecessors. He studied Desblancs' model, as we have seen, and he had easy access to Jouffroy's plans, since these had been sent to Périer, who was building Fulton's boat. He had discussed steamboats both in person and by mail with Stanhope; Rumsey had been his friend, as was Rumsey's backer, Parker. Livingston had been able to give him first-hand information not only about his own work but about the efforts of Stevens, Roosevelt, and Morey. Nathaniel Cutting was to testify that Aaron Vail, Fitch's backer in France, had stated that "he had lent to Mr. Fulton at Paris all the specifications and drawings of Mr. Fitch, and they had remained in his possession several months." Although Fulton objected publicly to other accusations made by Cutting, he never denied that he had studied Fitch's plans. Certain it is that in Fulton's patent specifications we find a drawing of stern paddles strangely similar to Fitch's.

The only important steamboat inventor from whom we cannot draw a direct line to Fulton is Symington, whose charges concerning Fulton disprove themselves, but the chances are that the American found some way of studying the Englishman's work; maybe Symington remembered inaccurately a meeting that actually took place several years after the date he specifies. Like a careful student, Fulton was appraising the efforts of all who went before him, so that he could build his invention not as an isolated phenomenon but as a part of the accumulated knowledge of mankind.

Eager to secure assistance wherever he could find it, he turned to Boulton and Watt. He ordered, provided they could secure a permit to export it to America, a 24 horsepower double-acting engine with a 4-foot stroke, complete with air pump and condenser. However, he carefully hid the fact that he was building a steamboat. "The situation for which the engine is designed and the machinery which is to be combined with it will not allow the placing of the condenser under the cylinder as usual," he wrote guardedly. Enclosing sketches of how he wished the parts situated, he requested the engine builders to use their "better judgment," and keep to his plans only when they could do so "without diminishing the power of the machine." Then he launched into a long series of questions: What should be the size of the boiler? How should it be placed and how designed? If he burned wood not coal, what changes would he have to make? What would be the dimensions of the cylinder and how fast would the piston travel? Since "in the place where the engine is to work the water is a little brackish," he wished to know what would be the consequence of a little salt in the condensing water.

How pleasant it was to be able to profit by the errors of many predecessors, and to have engineers in whom he had complete confidence work out his problems for him! What a contrast this was to his other schemes! His plan to substitute centrally unified waterways for the roads to which every government was committed had been so vast in scope that it was in itself a social revolution. In promoting submarine warfare, he not only smashed against the prejudice of ages, but he was working in the mechanical unknown, trying to solve problems for which perhaps no solutions existed. On the other hand, many pioneers had prepared the public mind for steamboats, while mechanically the invention required nothing but the combination of already established principles. The political and financial aspects were being taken care of by Livingston. It all seemed so easy, and yet the project promised the personal goods for which he had striven vainly during thirty-eight years. If his steamboat succeeded —and who could doubt of its success?—it could not fail to bring him fame and fortune. As the vessel went together on the Seine in front of the Périer workshop, Fulton's spirits soared higher and higher.

On July 24 he wrote his friend Fulmer Skipwith, "You have experienced all the anxiety of a fond father on a child's coming into the world. So have I. The little cherub, now plump as a partridge, advances to the perfection of her nature and each day presents some new charm. I wish mine may do the same. Some weeks hence, when you will be sitting in one corner of the room and Mrs. Skipwith in the other, learning the little creature to walk, the first unsteady steps will scarcely balance the tottering frame; but you will have the pleasing perspective of seeing it grow to a steady walk and then to dancing. I wish mine may do the same. My boy, who is all bones and corners just like his daddy, and whose birth has given me much uneasiness or rather anxiety—is just learning to walk, and I hope in time he will be an active runner. I therefore have the honor to invite you and the ladies to see his first moves on Monday next from 6 till 9 in the evening between the *Barrière des Bons Hommes* and the steam engine. May our children, my friend, be an honor to their country and a comfort to the gray hairs of their doting parents."

Napoleon found Fulton's steamboat plans impressive enough to make him overcome his aversion to the inventor. The newly crowned emperor had often stated that if he could control the English Channel for a few hours, he would control the world. Now he saw that the answer might easily be steam tugs towing invasion barges when the British fleet was immobilized by a calm. On July 21, 1803, he wrote M. de Champagny, Chancellor of State in the Marine Department, "I have just read Citizen Fulton's proposition, which you have sent me too late to permit it to change the face of the world. However, I wish you immediately to refer it for examination to a commission composed of members selected from the different classes of the Institute. It is there that the wisdom of Europe should seek judges to solve the problem in question. Be sure that this does not take more than eight days."

Fulton went to sleep those nights with a smile on his lips, but one midnight he was awakened by a precipitous knocking on the door. As he brushed sleep from his eyes, a voice cried out, "Oh sir, the boat has broken to pieces and gone to the bottom." Outside he heard the screams and poundings of violent storm. Jumping into his clothes, but without bothering to put on his coat, he rushed through the rain-drenched streets to the Quai Chaillot. As he stared at the agitated strip of water beneath which his boat lay, all the failures of thirty-eight years rose in his blood to overwhelm him. He felt, so he tells us, such despondency as he had never known.

For all his mechanical experience, Fulton had stepped into the booby trap into which so many of his predecessors had fallen; he had not built his boat strong enough to withstand the tremendous weight of the engine. With the energy of despair, he set to work to raise his boat. He worked for twenty-four hours under the whiplash of his nerves, without stopping to eat in all that time. When finally the vessel was raised and all the apparatus saved, he staggered home, feeling deathly ill. His physician, Dr. Hosack, attributed to these "laborious exertions" when he was "very much agitated" a "debilitation of the stomach" which brought on "chronic dyspepsia." In more modern terms, his nerves went back on him, and the resulting mental hypertension manifested itself physically in disorders of the stomach.

Fulton rebuilt his steamboat as it had been before. The *Journal des Débats* reported that on August 9 "a trial was made of a new invention, the complete and brilliant success of which should have important consequences for the commerce and internal navigation of France. During the past two or three months there has been seen at the end of the Quai Chaillot a boat of strange appearance, equipped with two large wheels mounted on an axle like a cart, while behind these wheels was a kind of large stove with a pipe as if there some sort of a small fire engine was intended to operate the wheels of the boat. Several weeks ago some evil-minded persons threw the structure down. [Was this Fulton's public explanation of the catastrophe that was really due to his own miscalculation of stresses?] The builder, having repaired the damage, received the day before yesterday a most flattering reward for his labors and talent.

"At six o'clock in the evening, helped by only three persons, he put the boat in motion with two other boats in tow behind it, and for an hour and a half he afforded the strange spectacle of a boat moved by wheels like a cart, these wheels being provided with paddles or flat plates, and being moved by a fire engine.

"As we followed it along the quay, the speed against the current of the Seine seemed to be about that of a rapid pedestrian, that is, about 2,400 toises [2.9 miles] an hour; while going down stream it was more rapid. It ascended and descended four times from *Les Bons Hommes* as far as the Chaillot engine; it was maneuvered with facility, turned to the right and left, came to anchor, started again, and passed by the swimming school.

"One of the boats took to the quay a number of savants and representatives of the Institute, among whom were Citizens Bossut, Carnot, Prony, Périer, Volney, etc. Doubtless they will make a report that will give this discovery all the celebrity it deserves; for this mechanism applied to our rivers, the Seine, the Loire, and the Rhône, would bring the most advantageous consequences to our internal navigation. The tows of barges which now require four months to come from Nantes to Paris would arrive promptly in from ten to fifteen days. The author of this brilliant invention is M. Fulton, an American and a celebrated engineer."

As Fulton received the congratulations of the spectators, did he succeed in keeping a smile on his face? They might be pleased, but he was disappointed; his ship, which he had expected to go about 16 miles an hour, had moved at 3 or 4. How he must have hated the people who did not have to hurry, as they strolled on the quay, in order to keep up with his invention! Parker, he was forced to admit, had been right: the purchase of the wheels on the water was not the same in proportion to the weight of the boat in a full-scale experiment as it had been in his little model. So deep was his discouragement that it was to color his thinking forever after; although Fitch's vessel had moved at 8 miles an hour, Fulton was always to insist that 6 miles an hour was the maximum speed for a practical steamboat.

An experienced engineer, Fulton made use of his failure to correct his figuring; on the basis of the evidence presented by the experiment, he calculated anew the relation between boat resistance and power applied at the paddle wheels. To make the New York monopoly effective, he needed to go only 4 miles an hour, and this speed, his formulas revealed, it was quite possible to obtain.

French historians, remembering the great future triumphs of the steamboat, have criticized Bonaparte for not using Fulton's invention to descend on England and thus win dominion of the world. As old men, some Napoleonic statesmen have described in their memoirs how with rare vision they urged the steamboat on their master. The Emperor is reported to have replied, "There are in all the capitals of Europe a crowd of adventurers and men with projects who circle the globe, offering to all the rulers pretended discoveries that exist only in their imaginations. They are so many charlatans or impostors who have no other end but to make money. That American is one of them. Don't speak to me about him any further."

It is easy to see why Napoleon took this attitude. In his submarine negotiations, Fulton had claimed much and achieved nothing practical; he seemed to be following the same pattern with his steamboat. Undoubtedly the inventor, who was never conservative in describing his future triumphs, had in his appeal to the government stated that his boat would go 16 miles an hour, the speed he had hoped it would achieve. Not only had he failed in this promise, but his vessel, anchored in the sheltered waters of the Seine, had foundered in a storm. Napoleon was not interested in future developments but in present possibilities; he was sure the steamboat could not cross the channel. Before we say he was wrong, let us remember that in all his career Fulton never sent a steamboat into the open sea.

Shortly after his steamboat trial, new happenings drove that invention into the back of his mind. Behind locked doors, he was conferring with a mysterious gentleman who, in the manner of a comic opera secret agent, called himself "Mr. Smith." But there was nothing comic in the proposals he brought.

XXIII. *Death for Sale*

As A result of the exaggerated reports of his submarine scheme which Fulton had spread in England, Lord Stanhope had formed a committee of gentlemen to consider what action the British government should take. Shortly thereafter one of Fulton's friends arrived in London from Paris and got in touch with Lord Sidmouth, the First Lord of the Admiralty. When he returned across the Channel, this friend traveled under the alias of "Mr. Smith."

In Paris, he told Fulton that the British wished to use the submarine against the French fleet. When the inventor replied that it could not possibly be to the interest of England to introduce into practice a vessel which would destroy all surface navies, Mr. Smith said that "on consideration that might be true; but ministers wished to be fully acquainted with the properties of my invention, and wished me out of France and in England. That would I go over and explain to them my engines I should be rewarded in proportion to their value." Since "it was too dangerous to carry letters on such a subject," the emissary had brought no written proposition, but as proof of the liberality of the British government he had been allowed "£800 to pay his expenses and mine in bringing me over."

Insisting that "Mr. Smith" bring back a written agreement, Fulton gave him a series of demands to carry to London. He wished £10,000 "for leaving France and the pursuits which at present occupy me, and for going to England." Within three weeks of his arrival there, a commission should be appointed to consider the following claims: That a submarine 35 feet long, 10 wide, and 8 deep could with a crew of six persons stay at sea twenty days, remain under water three hours without renewing air, and renew air in three or four minutes with two small tubes. That it could rise and sink. That in a current of not more than 4 miles an hour and at a depth of not more than 60 feet, the vessel could cast anchor and remain stationary at any depth, being thus enabled to operate at night and lie hidden beneath the surface during the day. That while submerged, the submarine could move at pleasure in still water and drift in moving water. That she could carry 30 bombs, each containing 100 pounds of powder and capable of destroying a frigate. The commission was either to agree to these claims from a study of his drawings, or else the government was to grant him £10,000 to prove his contentions by building an actual plunging boat.

"It will be seen," he wrote, "that England may draw many advantages from these inventions, or that they may be turned to the total destruction of the British marine. In either case, it is of importance to the British government to have the entire command of such engines to do with them as they think proper. But as these inventions are the produce of my labors for some years, I now consider them as rich gems drawn from the mines of science and which I and my friends have a right to convert to our own advantage, and which I now offer for sale to the British government." For showing how to build the submarines and bombs, and for explaining his method of attack, "I require the sum of £100,000."

Having carefully memorized Fulton's proposals, Mr. Smith departed. Since he was to bring back a written proposition, it was agreed that Fulton should await his return in neutral Holland.

Much has been written to defend Fulton from the charge of being a traitor in offering to switch from the side of France to that of England. The banner of Anglo-Saxon solidarity has been waved and waved. It is further said that the inventor had been disillusioned by Napoleon's unsympathetic treatment of him. As a true republican, the defense continues, he was horrified when Bonaparte became emperor; he came to realize that England, whose "monstrous government" he had denounced a few years before, was really a democracy at heart. To these arguments of his backers, Fulton added one of his own. He wrote some years later that as his method of submarine attack would inevitably destroy all navies, it made little difference to his ultimate aim of bringing peace and free trade to the world which country introduced it.

This discussion overlooks the most interesting point of all. As his own writings make extremely clear, Fulton never believed that the

English would put his method of attack into operation, since any cheap way of undermining the power of warships was manifestly to their disadvantage. In a letter he sent Pitt in 1805, summarizing all his negotiations with the British, Fulton spoke of the proposals he had made from France, "the purport of which on my part were, that on my arrival here [London], I would exhibit the principles of my engines to the government, and should they conceive that the introduction of them into practice in France, America, or elsewhere to be injurious to the interests of Great Britain, I proposed to take the value of one ship of the line of £100,000 to let the discovery lie dormant."

We have no way of knowing how sincere Fulton may himself have felt were his perpetual statements that he had invented submarine attack in order to bring a millennium to the world; we cannot tell how convinced he was at heart that this millennium would result; but it is impossible to deny that he was now offering to sell the millennium—idealism, freedom of trade, world peace, and all—for £100,000.

The British government had a hold on Fulton which they did not intend to relax; they refused Boulton and Watt a permit to export the steam engine he had ordered. Fulton thereupon wrote the American Minister, James Monroe, telling him that it was his patriotic duty to secure the necessary paper, since steamboats would be advantageous to the United States, and "the fact is I cannot establish the boat without the engine"; he had no intention of fashioning his own steam engine as all other American inventors had done. He continued to Monroe, "It will be well to ask this permission for yourself without mentioning my name, as I have reason to believe government will not be much disposed to favor any wish of mine." When Monroe did not answer, he besieged him with a barrage of letters. And to Boulton and Watt he wrote, asking them to go ahead with his machine despite the lack of the permit as "I have not confidence in any other engines."

For three months Fulton waited in Amsterdam for the British secret agent. His nerves tightened every time an ocean-going vessel tacked into the harbor and he hurried home to wait for the knock

on his door that never came. The contrast between what he expected
of destiny and the real acts of that fickle maid must again have been
unpleasantly clear in his mind; all his schemes were at a standstill. He
was more unsuccessful now than he had ever been. He tried to calm
his apprehensions by returning to the love of his childhood, by making comic drawings of the Dutch peasantry, but at last his patience
snapped. He returned to Paris without having heard from the
British.

Then, when he least expected it, the long expected knock on his
door came. Mr. Smith was there, looking insignificant and bourgeois
as always; only after the door had been carefully locked and the
shades drawn did he extract from a hiding place on his person a letter
in cipher but bearing the signature of Lord Hawksbury, the Home
Secretary. Decoded, it read: "The responsibility attached to His
Majesty's ministers in their official capacity renders it impossible for
them to advance the sums which you have required, in the form
pointed out by you, without exciting such public attention as must
be equally unpleasant to you and His Majesty's ministers; if, however,
you have sufficient confidence in His Majesty's government to offer
them your invention, you may rely on being treated with the utmost
liberality and generosity. . . . A negotiation personally conducted
would smooth many difficulties, and every facility and protection
shall be granted to you. And should you be disposed to accept active
employment from the British government, you may rely on the most
liberal treatment, proportioned to your efficient service."

This was much less than Fulton had hoped for, but he had come to
the end of a road where there was no other turning; the only possible future for his submarine and his steamboat lay in England. If
he co-operated with the government there, perhaps they would give
him a permit to export a steam engine; perhaps they would pay him
£100,000. He crossed the Channel, traveling under the alias of "Mr.
Francis."

When "Mr. Francis" arrived in London in the spring of 1802, the
government with which he had negotiated was out of office; Pitt
was now Prime Minister, and Lord Melville First Lord of the Admiralty. Secretly, the inventor was put in touch with a gentleman

who called himself "Mr. Hammond," perhaps Lord Hawksbury. The English officials had no desire to admit any connection with Robert Fulton, the notorious inventor of an immoral means of war; unlike their French colleagues, they kept all the submarine documents out of the public records, hiding them in their own personal files.

Fulton hoped to clear up his business in England in a few weeks: having been paid a large sum for suppressing his invention, having received a permit to export a Watt engine, he would hurry to the United States to build his steamboat. When a fortnight had passed and he had received no reply to his proposals, impatience got the best of his good sense; he went over "Mr. Hammond's" head by writing the Prime Minister, demanding an interview in far from courteous terms.

We gather that Fulton, who was well known in London, was being kept incommunicado until the government made its secret decision. His nerves, already undermined by long years of discouragement and disappointment, could not stand the strain of enforced idleness. His stomach refused to function. He could not get to sleep, and when at last he dozed off toward dawn, frustration welled up in his mind in a long procession of nightmares. He wrote "Mr. Hammond," on June 22, "The first day I had the pleasure of seeing you, I promised you candor, and should time make me more known to your government, they will find frankness one of the leading lines of my character. Now I candidly declare that having been here five weeks in some degree like a prisoner, and at present as much in the dark as on the day of my arrival, such a state of suspense begins to grow extremely unpleasant." He had been brought to England by "flattering and I believe candid promises, . . . and as yet I do not repent it. . . . I came here to acquire wealth by communicating a new system to the government." He demanded that he receive a reply by the following Tuesday.

The enormity of this letter becomes clear when we remember that those were very aristocratic days in England; the rich masters of the nation could hardly see far enough to recognize a common man. That they put up with the impudence of the American upstart shows that they were taking his invention very seriously.

Actually the government had moved with amazing speed. Fulton's written specifications had been submitted to a very distinguished commission: Sir Joseph Banks, president of the Royal Society; Henry Cavendish, the great chemist; Major William Congreve, artillery officer and inventor; Sir Home Popham, naval commander; and John Rennie, perhaps the most famous civil engineer in England. The plan they were examining was similar to the one Fulton had refused to show Napoleon without emolument two years before. An uncompressible copper cylinder, 6 feet in diameter and 18 or 24 feet long, fitted with a dome to be used in getting in and out, was imbedded in an ordinary sailboat measuring 30 feet by 10. The extra space in the enveloping ship contained the water tanks used for submerging, as well as racks holding thirty bombs, which were to be anchored in channels or permitted to drift into enemy harbors. This was Fulton's old *Nautilus* enlarged and redesigned to carry more torpedoes, to move really effectively under sail, and to range much farther, crossing the Channel if necessary.

The commission reported that the under-water boat was mechanically possible, but not likely to achieve much in practice. However, they endorsed an alternate scheme Fulton had suggested, agreeing that fleets anchored in enemy harbors could be blown up with submarine bombs manipulated from partially submerged rafts which had been carried close to the shore defenses by ordinary naval vessels. As Pitt's agile brain at once perceived, if the bombs had to be applied by surface vessels rather than submarines, they could only be used by the power that controlled the seas. The invention then would work to the advantage of England, not France.

Fulton was furious at the commission's lack of interest in his underwater boat; he threatened the government, assuring them that they could not suppress his invention without paying him, and that if their decision "should necessitate me to seek fortune elsewhere," it would be just too bad for the British Empire. When it became clear that Pitt was considering making use of his under-water bombs, Fulton was hardly more pleased. Instead of receiving the immediate payment for quashing the invention on which he had relied, he would have to wait for his money until results were achieved. He would have to stay in England, postponing indefinitely his American steamboat plans.

Invited to breakfast with Pitt on July 20, Fulton made a brave attempt to convince the Prime Minister to suppress submarine warfare. The American tells us that when Pitt "remarked that this is an extraordinary invention which seemed to go to the destruction of all fleets, I replied that it was invented with that in view, and as I had no design to deceive him or the government, I did not hesitate to give it as my opinion that this invention would lead to the total annihilation of the existing system of maritime war."

Pitt smiled and said, "But in its present state of perfectionment those who command the seas will be benefited by it, while the minor maritime powers can draw no advantage from what is now known." To Fulton's insistence that Pitt was ignoring the deadliness of the plunging boat, the Prime Minister answered "that it would probably be some years before any nation could bring into perfection such a vessel; that it was not to the interest of the Briitsh government to use such vessels; that consequently there was not at present much danger to be apprehended from that part of my system; at all events there would be time to fit future politics to future circumstances. If at present the French preparations could be destroyed by submarine attack, it will convince Bonaparte and the whole world that Frenchmen can never make a descent on England, for any future fleet prepared by them may be burned in the same manner."

Deciding to take what he could get, Fulton signed the very liberal contract offered him by the government. He was to be given £7,000 for expenses, and a retainer of £200 a month. Should the government decide to suppress his invention, he was to receive £40,000 provided a committee of arbiters agreed that the weapon was effective; but if the government applied the invention, he was to superintend operations and get one-half the value of the ships destroyed. If he retired from active participation, his share was to be cut to one-fourth. Fulton was not to divulge any part of his principles during the fourteen years of the contract, and was to withdraw an account of his method which he had confided to a friend for delivery to the American government in case of his death. Fulton signed this last stipulation with the others, but he considered it wiser to leave the account in the hands of his friend.

In pursuit of the fortune which this contract promised him, the inventor, whose motto was "The freedom of the seas will be the happiness of the world," prepared to strengthen the blockading power of the British fleet by directing an attack on the French flotilla bottled up in Boulogne harbor.

Fulton had not forgotten his steamboat. Almost his first act on reaching British soil was to ask for a permit to export an engine. The canny British, who wished neither to offend him nor to relax their hold on his interests, gave him a certificate that would enable Boulton and Watt to make the motor, but added that Fulton would have to get another permit when the boat on which the machinery was to sail had been determined.

As soon as Pitt had decided to make use of Fulton's undersea mines, the strict control on the inventor's movements seems to have been relaxed; he hurried to Birmingham for a personal interview with the engine makers. Watt, whose ill health had forced his retirement, was not there, but Fulton met Boulton. Walking into the clanging factory and sending up his name, he expected to be received with enthusiasm as a fellow-inventor and benefactor of mankind; however, the dour Scotch business man, who controlled the greatest practical invention of the age, had seen too many promoters and steamboat enthusiasts to be impressed by any of them. That Fulton was rebuffed, a passage in a letter he wrote Boulton after his return to London makes clear: "I hope at some future date to acquire sufficient merit to be admitted among the [circle] of your friends when solicitations to promote useful improvements will give more pleasure than pain." We gather that Fulton, after his usual high-sounding, idealistic preamble, had suggested some association between them to put over their mutual ideas. Boulton seems to have replied, as he had to so many others, that he would enter into no partnerships, but was glad to serve as engine maker to any man who had the money to pay him.

After Fulton had sent a guarantee for £380 signed both by George W. Erving and the firm of Lees, Satterthwaite, and Brassey, Boulton consented to go ahead with the engine. During July, letters went back and forth, Fulton suggesting changes in the position of various parts, and Boulton modifying his client's ideas according to his own practical knowledge. One of Fulton's drawings showed the cylinder connected with the paddle wheels by a bell crank; according to Dickinson, this demonstrates that Fulton was the originator of the bell-crank engine, which is usually attributed to William Murdoch.

During midsummer, Fulton went to the Portsmouth dockyards to superintend the preparations for an attack on the French fleet; he was impeded by bad health. "His stomach," his physician tells us, "became so deranged that he was in a great degree restricted to the exclusive use of animal food, and a glass of weak brandy and water as the principal drink at his meals." His liver also functioned badly. Forced to decline all invitations and to observe the strictest regularity at his meals, he "abstained from suppers and retired to rest at an early hour." Yet he could not sleep. If his physician's diagnosis of nervous dyspepsia was correct, it is clear that he was mentally very uneasy.

As a young man seeing before him a glorious future, Fulton may well have been sincere in his desire to imitate his rich and successful friends—West, Owen, Stanhope—by benevolently turning his talents to the advantage of mankind. When his submarine scheme 'had first occurred to him, it had presented delightful possibilities of combining high-mindedness with financial profit. However, to achieve the freedom of the seas he would have had to sell his invention to the French government. After Napoleon had spurned his schemes, there seemed little possibility of putting submarine warfare over; he may well have argued to himself that, since the invention was bound to die in any case, he might as well achieve wealth by killing it at the request of the British. So he had crossed the Channel. But then fate had played an unexpected trick on him; Pitt had seen a way to turn the invention against the freedom of the seas, against all the idealistic considerations Fulton had preached for so long. And apart from astronomical rewards should the scheme succeed, Pitt offered him £200 a month, an income many times greater than Fulton had ever earned before. As a boy he had known the squalor of poverty; later he had seen his fellow-American and steamboat inventor Rumsey totter and fall because of debt; he had lived for years on the charity of his friends, which must have brought bitter moments to his proud soul. How could he refuse the pieces of silver that Pitt showered into his hand?

Up to this time he had always been able to justify his desires to himself and to the world on idealistic grounds; now he was forced to change his style. He could not bring himself, when writing importuning letters to the British ministers, to ape the high-flown arguments with which they justified their war on France. He stated his claims baldly in terms of money.

Perhaps during the long wakeful nights he met in the mazes of his mind the young man he himself had once been, a proud, intolerant, self-confident youngster who was going to conquer the world with the sword of rectitude. Then the middle-aged Fulton would argue with his younger counterpart. "Don't be childish," he would say. "Ideals are of the intangible texture of dream; they pass over the world but do not touch it. Nothing touches the world but hard facts. You must be a realist, my boy!" But the young Fulton sneered as in those glorious days of confidence he had sneered at all middle-aged realists. And as for the older Fulton, his arguments must have sounded a little tawdry even to himself there in the sleepless silence of his midnight room.

With the coming of morning, Fulton hurried out to spend some of his new-found wealth as unselfishly as possible. Generosity had always been one of his virtues. In Paris, for instance, he had sent a rival steamboat inventor a description of his own experiments on methods of propulsion that might have enabled his correspondent to anticipate him in important discoveries. Now he paid $500 for sumptuous illustrations to embellish *The Columbiad*, a forthcoming poem by his friend Barlow. The man who had failed as a painter became a patron of the arts on a large scale. He bought canvases by West and other famous artists, intending to use them as the nucleus of a public art gallery in Philadelphia.

The raid against the French fleet at Boulogne, for which he had been preparing all summer, was made on October 2, 1804; that the British were taking the experiment very seriously is shown by the presence of Admiral Keith and Lord Melville. Dropped from larger vessels near the enemy coast, sailors tried to sneak unnoticed into the heavily fortified harbor on catamarans, submerged rafts that permitted only the faces of the operators, camouflaged with black masks, to show above the surface. The attackers towed submarine bombs which they hoped to attach to the anchor cables of the moored French frigates in such a manner that the tide would float the torpedoes under the bottoms of the ships. William Cobbett thus described the expedition in his anti-administration *Political Register:*

> Dundas is gone to Boulogne;
> He has a *pawky* plan
> To burn the French flotilla:
> 'Tis call'd *Catamaran.*
>
> Like ladies in romances
> Their knight's exploits to spy
> Aloft in Walmer Castle
> Stand Pitt and Harrowby. . . .
>
> Dundas our tars haranguing
> Now shows his new-made wares.

As at some peddler prating,
Jack [Tar] turns his quid and swears. . . .

"See here my casks and coffers
With triggers pulled by cocks."
But to the Frenchman's riggings
Who first will lash these blocks?

"Catamarans are ready"
(Jack turns his quid and grins)
"Where snugly you may paddle
In water to your chins.

"Then who my blocks will fasten
My casks and coffers lay?
My pendulums set ticking
And bring the pins away?"

"Your project new?" Jack utters;
"Avast! 'Tis very stale;
'Tis catching birds, landlubbers!
By salt upon the tail!"

So fireships, casks, and coffers
Are left to wind and tide;
Some this, some that way wander,
Now stern before, now side.

Ships, casks, and coffers blazing
Now brings Vauxhall to mind;
As if ten thousand galas
Were in one gala joined.

Aloft in Walmer Castle
Stand Pitt and Harrowby,
"The fireworks are beginning!"
With eager joy they cry.

"There in that blaze go 50!
And there go 50 more!
A hundred in disorder
There run upon the shore!"

From them the joyful tidings
Soon flew to London town:
By hundred and by thousands
They burn, sink, kill and drown.

How longs Dundas for morning
His triumphs to survey, —
But lo! the French are laying
Just where before they lay. . . .

But now to them who never
Did England's hopes deceive,
Our soldiers and our sailors,
Their business let us leave.

May Pitt from colonelling
Retire upon half pay
And Admiral Lord Melville
The yellow flag display!

The French ships had avoided the torpedoes which exploded harmlessly on the shore. Fulton, however, persuaded Pitt that the expedition had failed because the officers in charge had not carried out his ideas. The Prime Minister put up another £3,000 to build more bombs, and gave Fulton, who now in his sudden prosperity had become a spendthrift, £10,000 "to relieve me of some pecuniary embarrassments."

There, however, the matter rested; no one seemed inclined to make another attack on the French fleet. Perhaps deciding that the trouble might be that he had not pulled out his idealistic stop for so long, in January 1805 Fulton finally brought himself to writing a high-sounding political essay on the British side. The cause of humanity depended on the destruction of Napoleon, "a man who has set himself above all law, 'a' wild beast, unrestrained by any rule, 'who' should be hunted down as the enemy of mankind." He sent his effusion to Lord Melville, who must have smiled sardonically at such words from a man who had less than two years before been doing everything to help Bonaparte. And Fulton, finding that his cause had not been helped, dismounted from his righteous high horse and went back to his ungarnished demands for money.

In July and again in August he tried to induce Pitt to pay him—either for communicating or quashing the invention—and let him go; he wished to return early in September to America, where he had "previous engagements of such magnitude which call for my attention and do not warrant my losing time." His steam engine had been delivered in London, accompanied by the drawings for which he had asked showing how it should be put together. A copper boiler, weighing 4,399 pounds, was also completed. All his machinery was in readiness, and his New York State monopoly would expire in April 1807 if he had not by that date operated a steamboat on the Hudson.

Pitt, however, had no intention of permitting Fulton to leave England as long as the threat of French invasion remained. Having fortified Boulogne harbor, Napoleon had collected there eighteen hundred invasion barges and two hundred thousand soldiers; he himself had taken up residence in the town. Several attempts had been made by the British navy, one under Nelson himself, to destroy the invasion fleet at its moorings, but the attackers had failed to penetrate the shore defenses. In despair, Pitt turned again to the inventors, planning to try both Major Congreve's scheme to fire enemy ships by striking them with rockets and Fulton's torpedoes.

On the night of September 30, 1805, fast galleys each containing a commanding officer, eight oarsmen, and a coxswain slipped into Boulogne harbor and succeeded twice in attaching a yoke of two torpedoes to the anchor cables of French gun brigs. Rowing away under musket fire, the excited crews were delighted to hear tremendous explosions behind them. For a moment the warships were obscured by cascading water, but when the spray descended they were seen riding at anchor as calmly as before.[1] When the commanding officer reported to Fulton the next morning, "I was much at a loss to account for the brig not being blown up," but a half hour's deep thought finally convinced him that the torpedoes had been so much heavier than the water that they were not washed under the keel, but had hung perpendicularly from the sides of the boat.

Having remedied this error, Fulton felt the need to restore confidence in his invention; he secured permission to try to blow up a captured Danish brig lying in Deal Harbor. Admiral Keith and the major officers of his fleet were present when Fulton set out in a rowboat dragging a yoke of torpedoes behind him. As the attackers in their puny craft approached the anchored vessel that towered above them, Captain Kingston remarked that if torpedoes were placed under the cabin while he was having dinner, he would continue his repast without concern. A moment later the brig vanished in a tremendous explosion.

Fulton's success only made the conventional navy men even more opposed to his invention; Earl St. Vincent said, "Pitt is the greatest fool that ever existed to encourage a mode of war which they who command the seas do not want, and which if successful would deprive them of it." The members of government, however, were delighted. On October 27 Viscount Castlereagh wrote Nelson of the success of "Mr. Francis's" weapon, which he hoped the Admiral would use in his battles with the French fleet. Nelson never received this letter. Six days before, although the news had not reached England, the battle of Trafalgar had been fought and Nelson had died on the deck of his flagship. With him Fulton's hopes had died, for Britain's supremacy of the sea was now so complete that no inventions were necessary to help enforce it.

The government played along with Fulton for a while, but with continually abating interest. Sir Sidney Smith, the officer in direct command of the torpedo operations, expressed the general opinion when he wrote, "Mr. Francis's coffers, we know, will blow brigs up and many larger ships, but placing them is a perilous business; his boats are too ticklish for these seas."

However, Fulton was no man to take failure lying down. He explained to Pitt that his scheme had misfired only for lack of a separate naval unit specially trained to apply it, not in a series of isolated attempts but as " a system." He had a right to expect, he added to Castlereagh, that systematic application would be attempted, since without it "there is little hope of my acquiring the emolument from my invention" to which he was entitled. If submarine warfare had been "prosecuted according to the terms of my contract, I should acquire an immense fortune. The destruction of thirty ships of the enemy's line would entitle me to half their value or more than a million sterling"; hence, whether his invention was used or not, justice dictated that this should be his reward. "But," he added magnanimously, "I have no such ambitious views; tranquillity and a much less sum will content me. . . .

"Although I feel a high sense of my independence, of the immense and incalculable consequences of my discovery, of the right which I have to dispose of it as I think proper and to convert it to my own emolument and ambition, in doing which I might change the whole politics of this country and even Europe, yet on a fair and honorable agreement with this government there is nothing to be feared from me." He pointed out that the only way to keep him from using his invention against England "is to put it in my power and make it to my interest to remain tranquil. . . . For this purpose I propose to receive £60,000 and my present salary of £2,400 per annum, the annuity to be forfeited if I break the treaty. . . .

"And I assure you that great as this demand may appear to be, I am not much interested in its success, for by agreeing to let my invention lie dormant, I feel that I abandon a subject in which there is the most philosophic and honorable fame, and perhaps the interests of my country, which is dearer to me than all considerations of wealth. However, I hope America and England will so well understand their mutual interest that it will not be necessary for me to introduce my invention into practice for our own defense, and I have no desire to use it for the advantage of any other nation."

In his original negotiations with England, Fulton had specifically stated that he would deprive his native land of his invention for a sum of money; now he was hedging on this, but in sentences whose meaning was not entirely clear. Was he being smitten with pangs of patriotism, or was he using patriotism as a threat to get action from the English government? When he had been working for Napoleon he had approached the British so as to have a second string to his bow; now that he was working for Pitt, he had sent two letters to President Jefferson "on the progress I had made and on the final happy consequences of such a system."[2]

At a later date Fulton attempted to justify selling to a foreign nation a military invention that might have been useful to his own country. Jefferson, he noted, did not even answer his letters; until America agreed to compensate him for his experiments, he felt he was correct in doing "everything in my power" to guard his own interests and those of his backers. "Will any American or liberal-minded man call such actions sordid and wish me to abandon years of industry to the public good, while neither he nor the government have offered one shilling to promote so glorious an enterprise?" In any case, America had no immediate need for submarine warfare; therefore the prosecution of the invention could be considered "on the broad scale of general good. It is no abandonment of my plan to take some years to reflect on it and give it to the world with every demonstration of possible success."

His steamboat invention, he continued, promised to be more immediately valuable to the United States than any submarine. The annuity he had hoped England would grant him for suppressing under-water warfare would have enabled him to carry his part of the steamboat expenses; and he could have given up the annuity if America ever needed the submarine.

Having argued thus, Fulton arrived triumphantly at an idealistic peroration: He intended to make his submarine plan public "as soon as consistent with strict justice to all with whom I am concerned. For myself, I have ever considered the interest of America, free commerce, the interest of mankind, the magnitude of the objective view, and the rational reputation connected with it superior to all calculations of a pecuniary mind."

Yet there remained the necessity of getting money out of England. On January 6, 1806, he wrote Pitt that he had complete confidence in his ability "*should I think proper*," to sink all navies and give the weaker powers advantages over the stronger. Although he had agreed in his original contract to withdraw his plans from his friends, he now revealed that he had not done so. He had come to England not so much to do that nation good "as to show that I had the power and might, in the exercise of my plan to acquire fortune, to do you an infinite injury." This, he implied, he would proceed to do unless he was paid at once.

What Pitt thought of such words from a commoner whose invention had never succeeded in destroying a single enemy ship, we do not know, for the Prime Minister died on January 23. Fulton now had a new administration to deal with; Grenville was Prime Minister and Lord Howick First Lord of the Admiralty. The inventor did not delay in deluging these officials with rude letters demanding that, as provided in his contract should the ministers abandon his invention, a commission of arbiters be appointed to determine how much he should be paid. But governments never move quickly; months passed without any action being taken.

One evening as Fulton lounged at the opera, he was pulled upright by a vision: Was it possible; could it be his French charmer who was sitting, in fine clothes and bedizened with jewels, in the Duke of Portland's box beside Lord Clarendon? He stared so hard that the lady noticed him. She turned to her companions and whispered to them; then she leaned over the rim of the box and gave Fulton a deep bow. He sprang from his seat and hurried to her. Grasping her hand without ceremony or embarrassment, he cried, "What a pleasure, Mme. Montaut, to find you again here! I could hardly believe my eyes."

A French gentleman intervened. "Monsieur," he said, "is in error, for Madame is the Viscountess of Gontaut." At this remark, everyone in the box laughed.

"Oh, dear me!" the charmer remembers that Fulton exclaimed. "This is too much! Always changing her name. It is enough to drive one mad. But I see that these gentlemen are in on the mystery. If it is a joke, let us laugh together."

The lady wrote, "His good and simple manner touched me, and I told him that since we were in a friendly country, I could explain the mystery." Fulton learned that she was the daughter of Count Montaut Navailles, one of the most powerful noblemen in Louis XVI's court, and the wife of Viscount Gontaut-Biron. She had fled to England with her family from the revolution. When it had become necessary for someone to return to France to look after important affairs, she had volunteered to make the dangerous journey under an assumed name; it was on this voyage that she had met Fulton. In Paris, she had been forced to take a second alias.

"Now I understand," said the inventor. "I wish to compliment your husband on having a wife who was on the point of sending me to the devil."

Fulton probably was just as glad that the charmer was married and out of reach, for he believed himself on the point of marrying a rich widow. All we know of this amorous interlude is contained in a letter which Barlow, who was now living in America, sent his friend. "I write you with a heavy heart. Your letter of the 12th of January [1806] came upon us like a shipwreck. We see in it at least the wreck of our most brilliant prospects of domestic happiness if not of public usefulness." Although he wished Fulton to do what he thought best, he felt it his duty to point out that the widow would never be contented away from London, while Fulton could only be happy in the United States. "Your mind is American, your services are wanted here. Your patriotism, your philanthropy, your ideas of public improvement, your wishes to be a comfort to me and my wife in our declining years (if we should unluckily have many of them) would tend to make you uneasy at such a distance from the theatre of so much good. . . .

"Oh my estimable friend, my younger self, my expansion and prolongation of existence! You cannot conceive the pain it gives me to communicate these ideas." He was looking forward to finishing a poem on canals for which Fulton was to supply the data. "Is that mighty fabric vanished? It seems gone forever. You have a more substantial happiness in view, at least you think so, and who shall say the contrary? I cannot in friendship and conscience advise you to give it up. As to fortune: I would rather take you with only what you have now, than with the largest in the world. Great expenses are great vexations. My taste is so decidedly for simplicity and moderation that it would spoil me, whatever it did to you, to be the slave of a splendid income."

Although Fulton's affair with the widow fell through, he intended, if he could possibly manage it, to be the slave of a splendid income. He tried all the old arguments on the new Prime Minister, but even the most passionately sketched picture of the British fleet all beneath the waves failed to turn ministerial blood to ice. Then he remembered how anxious the government had been to keep their negotiations with him secret; he threatened to make the entire correspondence public. But this, as he must have realized, was a double-edged threat; his own letters had been less idealistic, more mercenary than the picture he liked to draw of himself before the world. Before he published, he would have to mend his own publicity fences. How to do this without relaxing his financial demands was a problem which he solved by suddenly bringing into his correspondence a pair of partners.

He wrote, "I am not a man much governed by money; an honorable fame is to me a much more noble feeling." He was only insisting on a payment of £40,000 "to gratify two friends who have been kind to me and are more governed by the hope of gain than I am. . . . Gentlemen, should your award not meet their views of wealth, I shall feel free to act as I think proper."

Now that he was writing for possible publication, he took a long step in the direction of patriotism: "At all events, whatever may be your award, I shall never consent to let these inventions lie dormant should my country at any time have need of them. Were you to grant me an annuity of £20,000 a year, I would sacrifice all to the safety and independence of my country. But I hope England and America will understand their mutual interest too well to war with each other, and I have no desire to introduce my engines in practice for the benefit of any other nation."

Even this statement, which has been much quoted by Fulton's biographers to show that he was motivated by nothing but idealism, marks a considerable retirement from his original claim that he intended not only to benefit the United States but bring happiness to all mankind by abolishing war. Now he used as a threat the power he believed he had to create a millennium; should the English refuse to pay his £40,000, "I shall hope to succeed in my first object of annihilating all military marines and giving liberty to the seas." He would not only publish all his negotiations with the British government, but such exact drawings and descriptions of his invention that any nation might put it in operation.

At last the arbiters met, but they did not decide as Fulton had hoped. They ruled that since the invention was impractical, England would not be harmed if other nations attempted to apply it. Thus Fulton was not entitled to payment for its suppression. Although the commission showed liberality in awarding the inventor £15,000, he had already received all of this except £1,608.3.2. Naturally Fulton, to use Fitch's phrase to describe indignation, "rose up on end." Insisting that he was doing so merely to satisfy his partners, he bombarded the government with arguments and threats.

Finally, on September 23, 1806, he published some of the correspondence in a small booklet which he sent to individuals closely associated with the negotiations, stating that if they did not come round to his point of view, he would make the pamphlet public. He added as a P.S.: "As His Majesty, and His Royal Highness the Prince of Wales are most highly interested in this subject, I shall cause these letters to be submitted to their perusal."

From this publication we learn that the ghost of Bushnell's *American Turtle* had at long last risen to haunt Fulton. The arbiters had stated that the submarine was not an original invention. Thus smoked out, he for the first time in all his writings mentioned his predecessor: "That which approaches the nearest to my inventions and combinations is a machine made by Mr. Bushnal [sic] in America, during the war, which was called the *American Tortoise;* in which I believe he once or twice went under water; there were also some kegs of powder floated down a river with common gunlocks on them, and a string tied to the trigger, in hope that some of the British ships would take the kegs on board, and while working about them, the men might pull the string and blow themselves up.

"In what Mr. Bushnal did there was much ingenuity, and no one respects his talents more than I do; had he prosecuted his studies, he probably might have perfected thought after thought to the annihilation of all ships of war. But whether his mind only viewed the subject as limited to little operations, or whether he thought too many difficulties attended it, he certainly did not compose his machines so as to make them of any use, nor did he organize anything like a system; and perhaps it is for these reasons that he had abandoned the subject for more than twenty-five years, and it is now dormant in him.

"But imperfect and scattered ideas are so very unlike perfect engines and efficient arrangement, that the latter may with justice be called novel invention."

Thus Fulton apportioned the credit between himself and his predecessor.[3] It is hard for the historian to agree, since the basic principles applied by both men were Bushnell's, and Fulton's devices, although improved in some respects, were no more effective against the enemy than Bushnell's had been.

In his pamphlet, Fulton challenged the arbiters, who had declared his invention useless, to spend eight nights in the dark of the moon on a brig he would buy for that purpose and anchor in Walmer Roadstead. They should be at liberty to defend themselves in any manner made possible by the usual armaments of a brig from attack by an agent of Fulton's supplied with three galleys of six oars each, armed only with submarine mines. "If he does not blow you up in eight nights, I will give you a thousand guineas and pay all expenses. . . . If you shrink from this fair experiment, which brings the subject home to your feelings, it is a proof that you fear the engines."

This challenge was, of course, ignored, and there Fulton allowed the matter to rest while he made final plans for his return to America. To Barlow he wrote, "My arbitration is finished, and I have been allowed the £10,000 which I had received, with £5,000 salary, total £15,000, though the £1,600 which I received on settling accounts will just square old debts and expenses in London, and leave me about £200. My situation now is, my hands are free to burn, sink, and destroy whom I please, and I shall now seriously set about giving liberty to the seas by publishing my system of attack. I have, or will have when Mr. Parker sends my £2,000, 500 sterling a year with a steam engine and pictures worth £2,000. Therefore I am not in a state to be pitied."

It is significant that in describing his financial state to his most intimate friend, the man who shared all his confidences, Fulton makes no mention of the tough partners who, according to his public statements, had forced him, against his idealistic desires, to demand a fortune. He speaks of "old debts and expenses in London"; we should have to torture these words to make them apply to partners, especially as Fulton had previously stated that his associates were in America. Are we to infer that Fulton's backers were altogether a pretense, a screen behind which he could hide motives of which he was ashamed? Certainly there is not a shred of independent evidence that they existed. Only two men, Barlow and the Dutchman Vanstappoist, can be shown to have advanced Fulton money to prosecute under-water warfare. Barlow is eliminated as a tough partner by his letters to Fulton in which, instead of urging his friend to hold up the British for large sums, he advised the opposite. Vanstappoist is eliminated by not being in America.[4] We may add that Daniel Parker, another capitalist with whom we know Fulton had close business connections, owed the inventor money, rather than it being the other way.

Of course we cannot specifically scratch out every individual who could conceivably have been one of Fulton's submarine partners; there is, for instance, no evidence on Livingston. Yet the fact remains that Fulton made it clear in his letter to Barlow that he regarded his submarine earnings as altogether his own. Probably Fulton's tough partners were nothing but window-dressing. And good window-dressing it was, since their existence has never been questioned until this moment.

In October 1806 Fulton became involved in a controversy over the application of Stanhope's invention of stereotyping; he wrote the Noble Lord, "If stereotype printing can ever succeed in this country, it must be placed on the liberal footing of other manufactures. If thrown open on a broad basis to all who choose to employ it, free from restrictions and the spirit of monopoly, it will succeed, and those who have embarked their property in it will reimburse themselves with profit." A few days after he wrote these words, Fulton sailed home to America, eager to build a steamboat that would assure to him and Livingston a monopoly on the waters of New York.

XXIV. *"The Most Fearful Wild Fowl Living"*

IN DECEMBER 1806 Fulton arrived at "our Athenian Garden in America," as he called Barlow's palatial manor near Washington; he was soon at work embellishing the estate, designing a summer house for "the grounds of our mansion." He had been abroad a few months less than twenty years. During that period great changes had come over the obscure miniature painter, the self-admitted "yeoman" who had been sent to Europe through the charity of leading citizens. Now one of his workmen wrote, "With his rattan cane in his hand, he always appeared to me the counterpart of an English nobleman." It had taken him a long time, but at last, in contrast to every other inventor we have discussed, Fulton had succeeded in making money from his mechanical innovations. And he was just on the threshold of his successful steamboat work.

But before he turned to this avowed object of his trip home, he made another attempt to put over his greater love; he interested the United States government in his torpedoes. During July 1807 he succeeded after several false starts in blowing up a brig anchored for that purpose in New York harbor. His object now was to fight the British whom he had served a few months before; war seemed imminent because of the *Chesapeake* incident. When the crisis blew over, Fulton was forced reluctantly to lay his torpedoes aside and to put his major energies on building the steamboat that came to be known as the *Clermont*.

The hull had been taking shape for some time at the yards of Charles Brownne at Corlear's Hook; when completed it was towed to Paulus Hook ferry on the Hudson, where Fulton had rented a workshop. Since the New York State monopoly was on the point of expiring, Livingston busied himself in the legislative halls, and in April a new statute was passed, extending the time limit for two more years. On April 23 Fulton took possession of the engine which had been lying unclaimed at the custom-house for six months; on July 4 he wrote Livingston, "I have all the wheels up; they move admirably." The contraption, which as it lay at its wharf was visible to the open river, began to look so formidable that the boatmen whose livelihood was endangered were frightened. As usual, fear led to violence. On June 7 Fulton noted in his expense book, "$4.00 to the men for guarding the boat two nights and a day after the vessel ran against her." And again, on June 13: "$20.00 to pay to the men who guard the boat."

Expenses were running over calculations. Having put as much of their own money in the speculation as they thought it warranted, the partners tried to borrow. Livingston naturally turned to Stevens, with whom he had a contract that provided they should share their steamboat experiments. However, the rival inventor supplied not capital but criticism: paddle wheels, he stated, were inferior to a screw propeller, and in any case Fulton's vessel was so long and thin it would certainly founder. The partners then tried to interest other friends, but they were received everywhere with incredulous smiles. "Never did a single word of encouragement or bright hope or a warm wish cross my path," Fulton wrote. "Silence itself was but politeness, veiling doubts or hiding reproaches." When he finally persuaded several men to lend him $1,000 apiece, they insisted on remaining anonymous, as they did not wish to be publicly connected with anything so crack-brained.

On August 9, four years to a day after he had demonstrated a steamboat on the Seine, Fulton took his new craft into the river. Although the paddle wheels were not completed, she went 3 miles an hour, which proved, so he wrote Livingston, that "she will, when in complete order, run up to my full calculations. . . . I beat all the sloops that were endeavoring to stem the tide with the slight breeze which they had; had I hoisted my sails, I consequently should have had all their means added to my own. Whatever may be the fate of steamboats on the Hudson, everything is completely proved for the Mississippi, and the object is immense."

Like Fitch before him, Fulton had turned his eyes on the West.

What made him, despite his legislative monopoly, doubtful of the possibilities on the Hudson, we do not know. It has been clear from the first, however, that Fulton underestimated the usefulness of the invention he was about to complete.

The elementary school textbook has become, through universal education, the common denominator of our culture. If you wish to go down through time as one of the heroes of our civilization, do not aim for the histories written by college professors; try to squeeze into the pages of a fourth-grade reader. Then your name, like that of Nathan Hale or Betsy Ross, will be indestructibly engraved on the minds of everyone, from office boy to president.

Similarly the great moments of history are those that custom has hallowed by placing them in every primer in the land. Fulton's first steamboat voyage to Albany falls into this category, and down to the last syllable of recorded time his vessel will be known as the *Clermont*, because the textbooks have given it that name. Fulton rarely, if ever, called it that himself. While the boat was building, he referred to it simply as *The Steamboat*, and it was thus known at the time of its historic first trip. When commercial voyages were undertaken some months later, Fulton advertised *The North River Steamboat*.* After the boat had been so completely rebuilt in the winter of 1807-08 that he had to register it again in the custom-house as a new vessel, he named it in his application *The North River Steamboat of Clermont*. In all documents, Fulton continued to call it *The North River Steamboat* or more briefly *The North River*. That the traditional name, however, made its appearance at an early date is shown by this statement published in the *Hudson Bee* for May 13, 1810: "*The North River Steamboat* is believed to be the first one built on the river and has lately been known by the name *Clermont*, that is in books."

---

* North River is an alternate name for the lower Hudson River.

Rising as it does from the textbook page like an isolated mountain peak, with no account of what went before and little of what went after, Fulton's first trip to Albany appears as synonymous with the invention of the steamboat. Before this great event, so folk culture tells us, such vessels did not exist; afterward, they were universally accepted. Let us see what really happened.

We shall be handicapped by the fact that Fulton's contemporaries did not take the voyage seriously enough to write about it at the time. The recollections of eye-witnesses were put on paper many years later, sometimes at second hand by persons to whom they had spoken. Only one newspaper announced the experiment. On August 17, 1807, the *American Citizen* published a short paragraph: "Mr. Fulton's ingenious steamboat, invented with a view to the navigation of the Mississippi from New Orleans upward, sails today from North River, near State's Prison, to Albany. The velocity of the steamboat is calculated at 4 miles an hour. It is said it will make a progress of 2 against the current of the Mississippi, and if so it will certainly be a very valuable acquisition to the commerce of the western states."

This brief notice, plus the unusual bustle at the wharf, collected a little crowd around the strange-looking craft as the time for the sailing approached. To the spectators the ship looked more like a section of a raft than the high-pooped vessels with which they were familiar. It was narrow and long—150 feet by 13—its flat deck rising but a few feet from the water. His experiments had made Fulton completely discard curves; the bow and the stern were cut off at an angle of 60 degrees to form a point. A small mast that rose at the stern was dwarfed by a fat and alien chimney in the center. The greatest whispering of course was caused by the steam engine which was in plain view in the middle of the boat, since it had not been decked over. Two cumbersome paddle wheels, unobscured by guards of any sort, hung over the sides, their bottoms immersed in the tide. When Fulton began to get up steam, when fire glowed redly from the boiler and black smoke issued from the stack, *The Steamboat* resembled, as a spectator pointed out, a backwoods sawmill mounted on a raft and set afire.

From time to time, the crowd separated to let through one of the accredited passengers. If Fitch was looking down from the clouds, he must have smiled grimly at the little group that gathered on the deck. They were not the work-stained artisans with whom he had associated, the mechanics and tradesmen touched with a visionary faith. It might have been a fashionable picnic that was gathering there. Each man was elegant in spotless ruffles and professionally arranged hair; each lady dimpled charmingly from under a correct bonnet, from over a stylish dress. The Livingston clan, the most mighty political and social force in New York State, were gathering with their friends and hangers-on to countenance the adventure of their patriarchal leader, the Chancellor. But unlike Fitch's common and slightly drunken friends, they had no vision, they did not believe. Although every word was gently modulated, although every smile was carefully controlled, they gave off an air of sophisticated disdain.

Among them moved Fulton, looking more like an English lord than ever, striding on his long legs for a final inspection of everything, his handsome face grave, almost sad in its intensity. He had pulled himself up into this world by his own bootstraps, and now his mettle was being put to the test before the sneering eyes of those he wished would consider him their peer. More hung in the balance than his steamboat invention. Among the prettily dressed ladies was his patron's young cousin, Harriet Livingston. She was handsome, she was accomplished, she was elegant, she was rich. When he had been apprenticed to a jeweler, such visions had swept sometimes into his shop, but the narrow counter that separated clerk and patron had been as wide as the whole world. Now while he hurried back and forth among her slightly amused relations, his stock becoming disarranged, his hands blackening with grease, she gave special little smiles of encouragement.

Some weeks before, so we are told, Fulton had approached his patron, the dynastic leader of the Livingstons. "Is it presumptuous in me," he asked, "to aspire to the hand of Miss Harriet Livingston?"

The great patrician frowned in thought for a moment, and then replied, "By no means. Her father may object because you are a humble and poor inventor, and the family may object, but if Harriet does not object—and she seems to have a world of sense—go ahead and may my best wishes and blessing go with you."

Harriet had accepted his proposal and an understanding existed, but Fulton knew that Livingstons were not permitted to marry failures. If he disgraced himself before the well-dressed people who were smiling a little wanly now as soot from the smokestack began to envelop them—well, love might fly with fame and financial hope.

Finally the test could be put off no longer: he commanded that the engine be started. The boat strained at its mooring, and when the line was cast off it began to inch out into the river. As he scanned the faces of his guests, did Fulton even notice the anonymous populace, the people of the city who lined the shore? It is said they cheered and clapped; did Fulton hear the sound? Writing of the event later, he only mentioned the passengers:

"The moment arrived in which the word was to be given for the boat to move. My friends were in groups on the deck. There was anxiety mixed with fear among them. They were silent, sad and weary. I read in their looks nothing but disaster, and almost repented of my efforts. The signal was given, and the boat moved a short distance, and then stopped and became immovable. To the silence of the preceding moment, now succeeded murmurs of discontent and agitations, whispers and shrugs. I could distinctly hear repeated, 'I told you it was so. It is a foolish scheme. I wish we were well out of it.'

"I elevated myself upon a platform and addressed the assembly. I stated that I knew not what was the matter, but if they would be quiet and indulge me for half an hour, I would either go on or abandon the voyage for that time. This short respite was conceded without objection. I went below, and examined the machinery, and discovered that the cause was a slight maladjustment of some of the work.[1] In a short time it was obviated. The boat was again put in motion. She continued to move on. All were still incredulous. None seemed willing to trust the evidence of their senses. We left the fair city of New York; we passed through the romantic and ever varying scenery of the highlands. . . ."

The uncovered paddle wheels creaked and splashed, the engine rocked the deck, smoke bellied and sparks fell, but the steamboat kept on moving. Little by little the strained face of the passengers relaxed. Relieved, slightly hysterical laughter swept from lip to lip. And then a throng of gaily dressed gentlemen and ladies gathered in the stern to sing. Soon the wooded flanks of the highlands rocked to the music of *Ye Banks and Braes o' Bonny Doon:*

> Ye banks and braes o' bonny Doon
> How can ye bloom sae fresh and fair;
> How can ye chant, ye little birds,
> And I sae weary fu' of care?

While the sad song rang back gleefully from the hills, Fulton's heart quieted down, began to beat with the even rhythm of the engine. All was well: the boat continued to move; his guests were happy, relaxed as if they were attending a picnic on the even lawns of Clermont.

He now had the peace of mind to observe the spectators on the river banks. Crowds had been attracted by the strange mechanical noises that were for the first time breaking the agricultural stillness of the middle Hudson. Having reached the river, they were pulled up stock still by the strange sight of a ship that smoked as if it were on fire and moved against the current without sails. The more sophisticated cheered, but the farmers watched in terrified silence. After a single look, an occasional countryman would take to the woods, like the yokel who is supposed to have startled his wife by pounding down the road as if a bear was after him, leaping into the house, locking the door, smashing closed the shutters, and then, at long last, shouting that the devil was going up river to Albany in a sawmill.

As darkness fell, the steamboat became increasingly terrifying. Bursts of sparks from the pine logs flew upward in a flaming cloud when the furnace was stirred. Amid terrible sounds, a fire was consuming the water in the center of the river. An eye-witness tells us that a group of spectators on a height near Poughkeepsie gave way to hysterical argument. To the contention of the ungodly that the boat was a sea monster, the churchgoing element replied that such an opinion was blasphemy since the phenomenon was clearly a sign of the approaching judgment.

The boatmen actually navigating on the river were in the most exposed place of all as the monster rocked upstream. Some, recognizing a business rival, shook their fists and hoped for a breakdown, but the more simple-minded either stared in dumb amazement or beached their craft and lay hidden in the woods until the steamboat had passed. Occasionally a local aristocrat, who knew that this was an experiment of the great patroon, stepped into his private yacht and sailed into mid-river to offer courtly congratulations; then there was a terrible bustle to keep him, as he drew alongside, from smashing into the paddle wheels.

Now upon the boat itself candles burned and the nervous excitements of the day gave way to exhaustion. The ladies were bedded down on improvised cots in one of the cabins; the men stretched out in the other cabin or on the vibrating deck. Standing alone in the bow, Fulton may well have looked upward at the stars that seemed so far from the earthly strivings of men. Then the stars were obscured by a burst of smoke, and he heard again the chugging of the engine which, if only its motion did not cease, would carry him to money and fame and social position and love, all the prizes for which he had struggled so painfully and long. Was this his last trip as a homeless wanderer, or would it have all to be done again?

Dawn arose behind the hills, a spreading universe of cold, clear light; virginal, pure, the beginning of a new world. Did he think then of his young manhood when he had believed that he could both follow his ideals and make his fortune? Now he was accomplishing something at last, but what, what was the meaning of it all, to what distant bourne had his feet wandered? Were his speculations bitter or joyous; was he sorry or glad when a stirring among his guests called up again the courtly manners of the new life to which he aspired?

The breaking day revealed a different type of activity on the river banks. Word of the steamboat had traveled faster than its laborious 5 miles an hour. Terror before the unknown had given way to joyous excitement. Now a thin line of people waited on both shores, waving handkerchiefs; now there were organized demonstrations on the quays below the river cities. More and more private yachts put out to meet them with banners flying.

A minor Livingston who was on board remembers that as the ship approached the Chancellor's estate, Clermont, Robert R. Livingston strode up on a high portion of the deck and asked for silence. In a graceful speech he announced Fulton's engagement to his cousin Harriet. The name of the inventor, he prophesied, would "descend to posterity as that of a benefactor of the world"; before the close of the nineteenth century boats might even travel to Europe under steam. Livingston's words were accorded polite applause, although there was a noticeable restraint when the aristocrats welcomed Fulton to New York's greatest social and financial clan. John R. Livingston was heard to remark to his cousin John Swift Livingston, "Bob has had many a bee in his bonnet before now, but this steam folly will prove the worst yet."

Twenty-four hours after it had started, *The Steamboat* cast anchor before Clermont, 110 miles up the river. The party spent the night there, and leaving at nine the next morning, arrived at Albany, a distance of 40 miles, in eight hours. These are Fulton's own figures, and from the round numbers employed, we must assume they are an approximation. His vessel, he stated, had gone 150 miles in thirty-two hours, a speed "equal near 5 miles an hour." Not only had the requirements for the New York State monopoly been more than fulfilled, but *The Steamboat* had gone quickly enough to compete with the river sloops which, although an occasional passage was made in sixteen hours, took on an average four days to travel from New York to Albany.

However, Fulton's elegant guests did not throw their hats in the air as he had hoped they would. "We descried the clustered houses of Albany," he wrote a friend years later; "we reached its shores, and then, even then, when all seemed achieved, I was the victim of disappointment. Imagination superseded the influence of fact. It was then doubted if it could be done again, or if done, it was doubted if it could be made of any great value."

The conventional statement of the history books that Fulton's first trip to Albany was equivalent to the invention of the steamboat is easily disproved. We need merely point out that his vessel had traveled more slowly and much less far than Fitch's boat of seventeen years before. Using such arguments, writers have attempted to deprive Fulton of all claims to an important contribution. There would be justice in their strictures if Fulton's work were now complete. Actually he had just crossed the threshold of his steamboat career.

In a letter to Barlow, Fulton described his own reactions to his triumph. "My steamboat voyage to Albany has turned out rather more favorably than I calculated. . . . The power of propelling boats by steam is now fully proved. . . . Having employed much time, money, and zeal in accomplishing this work, it gave me, as it will you, great pleasure to see it fully answer my expectations. It will give a cheap and quick conveyance to merchants on the Mississippi, the Missouri, and other great rivers, . . . and although the prospect of personal emolument has been some inducement to me, yet I feel infinitely more pleasure in reflecting on the numerous advantages my country will derive from the invention.

"However, I will not admit that it is half so important as the torpedo system of defense and attack; for out of this will grow the liberty of the seas, an object of infinite importance to the welfare of America and every civilized country. But thousands of people have seen my steamboat in rapid movement and they believe; they have not seen a ship of war destroyed by a torpedo and they do not believe."

Despite its success, Fulton's voyage to Albany did not create much stir; it was hardly mentioned in the contemporary newspapers. There had been so many flashes in the steamboat pan that it was impossible at the moment to distinguish this voyage from the others. Like each of his predecessors after a successful trial, Fulton faced the task of winning enough customers to pay financial dividends. But he had an overwhelming advantage over such men as Fitch and Rumsey, for he had a partner who possessed social eminence, political power, and a great deal of money.

When it had made its historic journey, his steamboat had not been completed, probably because Fulton wanted it to be as light as possible for its test journey. Now he boarded all the sides, decked over the engine, installed twelve berths in each of the cabins, and strengthened the ironwork. Advertisements began to appear stating that *The North River Steamboat* would make one and a half round trips to Albany a week. On September 4, with fourteen paying passengers, she started on her first commercial voyage.

After that, Fulton's steamboat carried passengers up and down the Hudson as Fitch had carried them up and down the Delaware many years before; like Fitch's vessel, Fulton's broke down frequently. Many weaknesses developed which the inventor, for all his experience and calculations, had not foreseen, but he mended his boat quickly, and from every difficulty he learned a lesson. The one obstacle he faced which had not bothered his predecessor was a symptom of success: rival boatmen, instead of laughing at his vessel, tried to destroy it. Several times sloops ran into *The North River* as if by inadvertence, but there was a suspicious smile on the faces of the sailboat crews when they succeeded in carrying away a paddle wheel.

Fitch had operated at a loss, clamoring vainly for passengers, but despite all his breakdowns and delays, Fulton got passengers in ever-increasing numbers. On October 2 *The Evening Post* reported that *The North River* had come in the night before with sixty passengers and had sailed again with ninety. Some people still feared the new-fangled contraption; a Quaker remembers that an acquaintance asked him, "John, will thee risk thy life in such a concern? I tell thee she is the most fearful wild fowl living, and thy father ought to restrain thee." But John took the trip none the less, and so did many, many others.

In mid-November, after about six weeks of operation, *The North River* was laid up for the season. If she had plied steadily and without any breakdowns, which we know was not the case, she would have covered about 1,600 miles; probably she went between 1,200 and 1,400. This was a considerably shorter distance than Fitch's successful boat had gone during her initial and only season. Yet, in contrast to her predecessor, *The North River* paid a profit.

"After all accidents and delays," Fulton wrote Livingston, "our boat cleared 5 per cent on the capital expended, and as the people are not discouraged, but continue to go in her at all risks and even increase in numbers, I think with you that one [a steamboat] which should be complete would produce us from $8,000 to $10,000 a year or perhaps more; and that another boat which will cost $15,000 will also produce us $10,000 a year. Therefore, as this is the only method which I know of gaining 50 or 75 per cent I am determined on my part not to dispose of any portion of my interest in *The North River*." He was now willing to sell some of his other investments to plunge further into steamboat speculation.

However, experience showed that the existing boat, the mythical *Clermont* of the textbooks, would have to be entirely rebuilt. She was "so weak that she must have additional knees and timbers; new side timbers, deck beams, and deck; new windows and cabins altered; that perhaps she must be sheathed, have her boiler taken out and a new one put in, axles forged and ironwork strengthened." Indeed, it would be best to build another hull, larger and of heavier materials.

When completed the following spring, the rebuilt vessel was for all practical purposes a new boat. Weighing over 182 tons, she drew 7 feet and measured 149 feet by 17 feet 11 inches. She had been considerably widened without any addition in length, a modification whose necessity is shown by the fact that when modern engineers built a replica of the boat of 1807 for the Hudson-Fulton celebration, they were afraid to follow Fulton's proportions lest they drown the celebrants; they arbitrarily added 3 feet to the width. Many other weaknesses of the earlier boat were removed.

An elevated platform behind the main cabin covered the boiler. Next toward the stern came the air pump, and after it the cylinder standing on its condenser. Overhead, some 12 feet above the deck, rose an iron frame containing the cross-head to which the piston rod was attached. From each side of the cross-head hung rods connected by bell cranks with the axles, which turned not only paddle but also fly wheels, since Fulton had not yet realized that paddle wheels would themselves regulate the motion of the engine.

While Fitch had cursed his backers for installing cabins that offered even a minimum of comfort, Fulton paid such great attention to the pleasure of his passengers that even his friends thought he was wasting money. Always glad to expend every cent he owned on his enthusiasms, Fulton made the new *North River* "into a floating palace, gay with ornamental paintings, gilding, and polished woods," thus starting at once the tradition of sumptuous steamboats which flowered mightily on the Mississippi, and continues in the present day transatlantic liner.

There were three cabins containing fifty-four berths, a kitchen, larder, pantry, bar, and steward's room. Since the public was not familiar with such luxuries as Fulton gave them, he was forced to post regulations: "It is not permitted for any persons to lie down in a berth with their boots or shoes on, under a penalty of a dollar and a half, and half a dollar for every half hour they may offend against this rule. A shelf has been added to each berth on which gentlemen will please to put their boots, shoes, and clothes that the cabins may not be encumbered. . . . As the steamboat has been fitted up in an elegant style, order is necessary to keep it so; gentlemen will therefore please to observe cleanliness, and a reasonable attention not to injure the furniture; for this purpose no one must sit on a table under the penalty of half a dollar each time, and every breakage of tables, chairs, sofas, or windows, tearing of curtains, or injury of any kind must be paid for before leaving the boat." The fines were used to buy wine for the company.

In June the boat was ready to move. Livingston, whose self-confidence as an inventor had been restored by Fulton's success of the previous summer, insisted on installing a wooden boiler.[2] This leaked so badly on the first trip that the ship was unable to get back to New York, but when an ordinary metal boiler had been substituted, the rebuilt *North River* was more mechanically proficient than the boat of the previous summer. Unlike Fitch, who had shuttled back and forth between success and failure in an almost random manner, Fulton, by accurately evaluating the data supplied by experience, was able to move in the direction of increased efficiency.

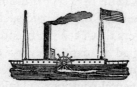

While the new *North River* was building, Fulton had stepped at last into those upper social realms which had once seemed to him a different order of creation. On January 7, 1808, he married Harriet Livingston. Her father, son of the Lord of the Manor, had inherited a part of his vast estate: 28,000 acres of the best land in New York. On a height overlooking the Hudson, he had built a stupendous mansion; this now became Fulton's summer home. He walked through the many chambers with the easy stride of a proprietor, and the liveried servants bowed as he passed.

Fulton was an important citizen; his steamboat represented only one facet of his reputation. Although for the moment the matter was dormant, the government had not lost interest in his torpedoes. The canal fever, which had started in America with Washington's Potomac project, was rising to ever greater heights and was soon to produce the great Erie Canal. Of course, Fulton was consulted by the government; his words, in which he still argued for small canals, were published and read with awe. He was offered at least one canal-building job which he refused because of the pressure of his other interests.

Scientific and cultural societies fell over themselves to make him a member. To the artists of America, still practicing their craft against great economic handicaps, the former miniature painter now took on the guise of a powerful patron. Although English noblemen had for several generations been collecting old and new masters, few such collections existed in the United States; when Fulton lent the canvases he had acquired in London to the Pennsylvania Academy of Fine Arts, entrance fees totaled $100 a month; the inventor graciously allowed the funds to be used to establish a school of drawing from the living figure. The naïveté of the artists and connoisseurs of the period is shown by Charles Willson Peale's queries to Fulton on receiving the pictures: "Who painted Abel? Titian or Poussin? Who painted Adam and Eve? Rubens?"

The Columbiad, with the illustrations for which Fulton had paid $5,000, appeared in 1807 and was a seven days' wonder; Barlow dedicated the poem to his friend as testimony of "an attachment which certainly comprises all the good affections that the virtues and talents of one man can inspire in the breast of another."

Fulton gained additional celebrity by dramatically exposing a famous mechanical wonder. A showman named Redheffer, who had exhibited a perpetual-motion machine of his invention to ever-increasing crowds in Philadelphia, had moved to New York, where he received equal acclaim. One afternoon, many people were gathered in his house, wondering to see wheels spin for no reason. Fulton entered; instantly his practiced ear detected that the wheels were turning unevenly. "Why, this is crank motion!" he exclaimed. While the crowd held back the screaming Redheffer, Fulton knocked away some insignificant pieces of lath, and exposed a cat-gut string running from a pulley through a hole in the wall. With the excited populace at his heels, he traced the string to "a back cockloft" where he burst in upon "a poor wretch with an immense beard and all the appearance of having suffered a long imprisonment," who was gnawing a crust of bread held in one hand, and with the other turning a crank. Redheffer took to his heels; the crowd demolished his machine. Watching with a superior smile, Fulton took over the showman's mantle as a miracle worker.

Here was a successful man, prominent and well connected; a man one could trust. That he was also a good man was clear from his own insistence that he was always motivated solely by his concern for the welfare of humanity. What a contrast there was between this patrician who looked like an English lord and the gaunt scarecrow who had once operated a steamboat on the Delaware! Fitch had seemed a typical mad promoter, impractical and wild, drunken, threadbare, and dangerous. Fulton, on the other hand, was clearly successful, a man of business and a moral gentleman. If he endorsed an invention, it was certainly safe to try it. Before the summer of 1808 had run out, the rebuilt *North River* could not accommodate all the passengers who wished to ride.

Busily, Fulton projected new boats. He sent Nicholas J. Roosevelt to the Mississippi to look over possibilities there, and sold to his wife's kinsman, John R. Livingston, the right under the monopoly to run a steamboat to New Brunswick on the way to Philadelphia. And that mightier Livingston who was his partner had pushed through the New York legislature an act adding to their monopoly five years for every additional steamboat they operated up to a maximum of thirty years.

In March 1809 Fulton wrote Benjamin West that *The North River* had paid a clear profit of $16,000, and that he was building two additional steamboats. Yet clouds were appearing on the horizon. Rival entrepreneurs were preparing to contest the New York State monopoly, and John Stevens was actually building a steamboat with the avowed purpose of operating it on the Hudson River in the very teeth of Fulton's law.

XXV. *Cars of Neptune*

AFTER he had refused to enter into a partnership with Fulton
and Livingston, because he was convinced that Fulton's plans
could not succeed, Stevens had continued to follow his
own star of high-pressure engines. He made one more try on a
29-foot boat in 1807, but he was not able to raise enough steam to
supply his propellers. He was forced to admit the failure of his high-
pressure plans at the very moment when Fulton's steamboat was
ready for its trial trip.

Certainly he knew in advance of Fulton's public demonstration.
We can imagine him pacing up and down in front of his mansion,
walking the broad lawn that overlooked the Hudson as he waited for
The North River to start, and to come to grief as he knew it would.
What were his reactions when the long, thin, animated ship appeared
in his view, moved successfully across it, and disappeared in the distance? How much did this sight, and the subsequent views he must
have had of the steamboat passing below his estate on schedule, influence his decision to abandon high pressure and build a boat similar
to Fulton's?

History has a way of being warped to please the preconceptions
of historians. Thus we read in many learned treatises that Stevens'
first really successful steamboat, the *Phoenix*, was almost completed
when Fulton's steamboat made its historic trip, and that it was
launched a month later. Actually, construction was not begun until
January 1808, five months after Fulton had given his demonstration.

In the *Phoenix* Stevens made use of a low-pressure engine similar
to that Watt had built for Fulton, and he swung paddle wheels over
the sides as his rival had done. However, he did not follow the very
narrow design to which he had objected and which Fulton had
already abandoned. Stevens made various changes in detail of which
he was very proud: his engine rested on braces especially designed

to reduce strain on the hull; he had altered the air pump, the valves, etc.

As soon as his plans were on paper, he tried to browbeat the monopolists into taking him into the partnership he had previously spurned. If they pooled their inventions, they could set competitors at defiance, he argued, but should they squabble, they would open the doors to all contenders. He was sure the boat he had not yet built would be much faster than Fulton's, and this, he pointed out, would make it easy for him to break the monopoly, which was in itself unconstitutional. Stevens contended, as did every successive group which opposed Fulton, that since the federal government granted patents, the states could not legally interfere with the exercise of such patents by enacting local exclusive rights. Livingston replied, "Suppose a man to patent a new musical instrument. Would this give him the right to play in your garden and set your children a-dancing when you wished them to study? No, your garden is your own." Stevens thereupon wrote, "Very sprightly and ingenious but by no means analogous. My garden is my exclusive property. . . . I can prevent any other man from entering it. . . . This is by no means the case with the states. The people have thought fit to form a general government to which they have delegated certain powers which they have declared shall be the supreme law of the land. . . . Among them is the very power in question."

Finally Livingston offered his brother-in-law a fifth share in the partnership provided that if he used low-pressure steam, paddle wheels, or proportions similar to Fulton's he would acknowledge indebtedness. Since Stevens was interested above all in receiving credit, he refused.

During April 1808 the *Phoenix* was launched. Stevens claimed that she went the 30 miles from Perth Amboy to Paulus Hook at more than 5 miles an hour, somewhat faster than *The North River*. We need not describe in detail the continuing quarrel between the two brothers-in-law, nor how Stevens' wife, who was Livingston's sister, tried to interfere in the family squabble and was told to stick to her tatting. Stevens defied the monopoly for a while by running his boat from Perth Amboy to New Brunswick; then he decided to move the *Phoenix* to the Delaware. This was a daring decision since the vessel would have to travel some 150 miles through the open ocean, although even in the Hudson River she had fled rough weather to an anchorage. What sail men considered a mere working breeze was dreaded by steam men because it disturbed the purchase of their paddles.

In June 1809 the *Phoenix* lay tied at Stevens' wharf, every inch filled with firewood, while a schooner stood off from shore, ready to act as escort. On the bluff above, her owner had placed a telescope in the center of his carefully clipped lawn; he strained through it at every cloud, only turning to read the barometer. Finally on June 10 the *Phoenix* nudged out for the first sea voyage ever undertaken by a steamboat, into a complete calm obscured by a little fog. Having got as far as Quarantine, she dropped anchor for several days. On the 13th the weather seemed propitious again, and the *Phoenix* attempted to scuttle across the bay, but in her eagerness she lost a "revolution wheel," and had to pull up in a cove. The next day the calm was so complete that the escorting schooner could not move, but the mended steamboat set out once more. For three and a half hours she braved Neptune, giving him his first taste of the many steamers that were to crawl like fleas across his heaving breast; then a paddle wheel gave way. She was anchored in Cranberry Inlet.

The paddle wheel was quickly repaired, but now the wind blew. Wednesday and Thursday the boat rode at anchor; since on Friday the air was calm again, the captain, Stevens' son Robert, "rose the steam at 8 o'clock A.M., but concluded it rash to encounter the great swell abroad." By the next morning the swell had abated, so they moved once more, but when clouds appeared on the horizon, they fled into Barnegat Bay. Here they remained for three full days while breezes blew. On Wednesday they proceeded to Cape May, and anchored for the night, on Thursday to Newcastle, and finally, on Friday, thirteen days after they had started, they reached Philadelphia. A steamboat had traveled through the open ocean, but hardly with a freedom that promised much for the future.

In contrast to his predecessors, who had taken out patents first and built afterward if at all, Fulton remained content with his New York monopoly and did not apply for a federal patent till his *North River* had been in successful operation for two seasons. He probably realized that he would have difficulty establishing his right to his improvements, since no part of his machine was in itself original. When he finally made a claim on January 1, 1809, he wrote:

"That any determined power of steam engine shall drive a given boat with the greatest speed which such engine can effect will depend on certain exact proportions . . . between the shape of the bow and stern of the boat; her length, draft of water, velocity and total resistance; and the diameter of her wheels, the velocity of their periphery, and the square feet of their propelling boards which continually act against the water. A boat may be moved by the power of a steam engine although exact proportions are not observed, but to drive her with the greatest speed, with a given power, the proportions must be adhered to. It consequently follows that they who attempt to construct steamboats without knowing the proportions and velocities proceed without any certain guide, and cannot give rules to secure success in building and navigating steamboats of various dimensions and velocities so as to apply the power of the engine to the greatest advantage. . . . It is owing to a want of an accurate knowledge of these principles that the essays on steamboats which have been made in different countries for thirty years past have hitherto failed."

His patent covered: "First, the method of ascertaining the total resistance of the boat when running from 1 to 6 miles an hour. Second, the demonstrations on the superior advantage of a propelling wheel or wheels for taking purchase on the water. Third, the demonstrations on the proportions which the propelling boards should bear to the total resistance of the boat, and the velocity which they should run compared with the intended velocity of the boat. Fourth, the method of calculating the power of the engine to supply the loss of power on the propellers [methods of propulsion] and overcome the total resistance of the boat when running from 1 to 6 miles an hour."

More impressive than Fulton's claims were his deeds; he continued to build steamboats and they continued to turn out as planned. In 1810 he had three vessels in operation: *The North River* and the *Car of Neptune* on the Hudson, and the *Raritan* running to New Brunswick. This was the first time any inventor had more than one ship under steam at the same moment.

Fulton soon constructed a new kind of steamboat, and it functioned as satisfactorily as his river craft had done. He designed ferries to cross first the Hudson and then the East River; a grateful public named the road joining them through Manhattan Island "Fulton Street." Admittedly based on Patrick Miller's double boats, with the paddle wheel placed between the twin hulls, the vessels were fat and double-ended like modern ferry boats. To get them easily into their slips, Fulton guided the vessels with a semicircle of pontoons, similar in theory to the piles used today.

The success of Fulton's steamboats inspired other promoters to build vessels of their own, and these rivals precipitated the battle over the New York State monopoly law which has become famous in American legal history. Fulton and Livingston had an initial advantage: their statutes were on the books and their boats were in actual operation. Furthermore, they had two patents, Fulton having taken out a second, for some details of steamboat design, in 1810. That he had the temerity to ask for and receive an exclusive right for paddle wheels, the use of which went back to deepest antiquity, gave him a possible advantage, but also pointed up the fundamental shakiness of his claims. Each item of the machinery he used had been patented individually by some other man. His contribution was their combination and the establishment of proportions, but proportions had specifically been excluded from the patent law. Furthermore, his own lawyer, Thomas Addis Emmet, warned that the state monopoly would not stand up in a federal court since it conflicted with the patent and interstate commerce provisions in the constitution. Clearly, the best policy was to avoid test cases at any cost.

Livingston cracked his whip over the New York legislature and on April 19, 1811, they passed an act which provided that the monopolists might take over any rival boats in the same manner as if the boats had been stolen from them; this meant that they could take full possession of their rivals' assets before the rivals had a chance to test the constitutionality of the monopoly act.

Such heroic measures had become necessary, since Fulton was being accused of having copied his steamboat plans from each and every one of the inventors who went before him. His most persistent enemy was Fitch's backer, Dr. Thornton, who used his position as clerk of the patent office as a sounding-board from which to shout that Fulton's patents were worthless since he was merely an imitator. Fixing on Fulton's statement that boats could not be built to carry a useful cargo at a speed greater than 6 miles an hour, Thornton broadcast everywhere that Fitch's boat had gone 8 miles an hour, and no one remembered that Fitch's boat had been so full of engine that it could hardly be said to have carried a useful cargo. Finally Fulton wrote Monroe, the Secretary of State, "The case of Dr. Thornton is very simple. If he is an inventor, a genius who can live by his talents, let him do so, but while he is a clerk in the office of the Secretary of State and paid by the public for his services, he should be forbidden to deal in patents, and thereby torment patentees, involving them in vexatious suits. He should have his choice to quit the office or his pernicious practices." Thornton went on unchecked.

Doubt as to the originality of Fulton's invention gave a legal and moral rallying ground to opponents of every sort. Whatever inconveniences the passengers on his boats suffered were blamed on the "vicious monopoly," and there were many inconveniences. At first the steamboats had not been crowded and had carried only respectable passengers, but as the months passed they began to overflow with persons of every description. The sleeping rooms teemed and steamed with people confined in offensive air; the decks were strewn with cots; the meals were inadequate and scrambled for. Gleefully the sailboat captains pointed to these conditions, while the merchants of Albany were glad to repeat the charges, since they felt the steamboats were taking the customers to the better stores in New York. Thousands of voices insisted that the illegal monopoly was allowing Fulton to provide bad service and to charge outrageous fares. When the price of wood went up in Albany, it was darkly rumored that this was because the steamboats used so much fuel.

A company had already been formed in that city to run mechanical boats in opposition to the monopolists. Not seeing clearly the difference between steam and perpetual motion, the backers planned to use as motive power the swing of a pendulum; when they found the pendulum would not turn wheels against water resistance, they added a steam engine, and then the pendulum was not necessary. Hiring workmen whom Fulton had trained, and using many of Fulton's and Stevens' ideas, they built two steamboats, the *Hope*, launched May 19, 1811, and the *Perseverance*, which followed shortly after. It is highly significant to our story that both of these vessels functioned satisfactorily.

On June 18 Fulton wrote Barlow, "My whole time is now occupied in building *North River* and steam ferry boats, and in an interesting lawsuit to crush twenty-two pirates who have clubbed their purses and copied my boats and have actually started my own invention in opposition to me by running one trip to Albany; her machinery, however, gave way in the first voyage, and she is repairing, which will, I presume, detain her until we obtain an injunction to stop her. A more infamous and outrageous attack on mental property has not disgraced America. Thornton has been one of the great causes of it." The ghost of Fitch was haunting Fulton continually, just as he would have wished.

After the *Hope* was mended, her captain challenged *The North River* to a race from Albany to New York. On July 27 the two boats lay side by side in their slips getting up steam for the first steamboat race in American history. The *Hope* got off to a better start, and kept the center of the channel, blocking every attempt of *The North River* to pass. Stern so close to bow that they seemed almost one craft, traveling together under a single cloud of smoke, the steamboats pounded down the river at about 5 miles an hour, while spectators crowded the banks to cheer the opponent of "the pernicious monopoly." Two miles above the town of Hudson, *The North River* tried to make use of its lighter draught to pass the *Hope* in shallow water; gradually it pulled abreast of its rival and then there was a resounding crash. The vessels had collided. Although investigation revealed that neither was seriously damaged, the captains called off their race, thus showing less mettle than their descendants on the Mississippi, who were quite willing to take the lives of their passengers if that was necessary to prove their vessels the fastest.

All through the summer of 1811, the *Hope* and the *Perseverance* continued to run in opposition to Fulton's craft through a shower of court actions, pleas, injunctions, and billingsgate. At last the monopolists won their case; gleefully they broke up their rivals' vessels into scrap metal, but the fact remained that during the season they had earned nothing but even more widespread enmity; their books showed a financial loss.

The partners were trying to hold back a popular movement with the rickety dike of a dubious statute; no sooner did they plug one leak than another appeared. Claiming jurisdiction over the Hudson, not to the center of the river as seemed logical, but all the way to the Jersey shore, New York State tried to prevent Jersey steamboat builders from operating out of their own harbors. The result was revolt. Jersey-owned ships operated in defiance of Fulton's law, and the state legislature passed retaliatory statutes which forced Fulton to take his own steamboat off the New Brunswick run.

There is no point in following the tortuous path of the political and judicial battle that followed: suffice it to say that the monopolists were continually pelted with summonses, injunctions, and lawyers' bills, while they balanced with spectacular virtuosity on a legal tightrope which even they knew was not firmly fastened to its supports, the constitution of the land. At any minute it might fall, if they did not compromise with this man, and buy off that man, and whisper in the ears of those legislators, and never, never sue except when some special legal quirk made victory absolutely certain.

Far from being discouraged by their difficulties with their New York State statute, the partners appealed for similar monopoly acts in other states. The ghost of John Fitch rose to oppose them in some assemblies, speaking through the mouth of Dr. Thornton, and usually the petitioners were defeated. Yet they succeeded in securing the most valuable right of all; in April 1811 a law for their benefit was passed by the New Orleans Territory. As Minister to France, Livingston had negotiated the Louisiana purchase; now he had closed the mouth of the Mississippi to all steamboat men except himself.

Already the monopolists had set up a factory in Pittsburgh, which they placed under the direction of Livingston's old associate, Roosevelt. Following plans supplied by Fulton and using workmen imported from New York, Roosevelt built the *New Orleans* at the cost of $38,000. She was similar in design to Fulton's Hudson River boats, and about the same size, being 116 feet by 20. After a short trial trip on the Monongahela, the vessel set out for New Orleans in September 1811. An attempt was made to secure passengers, but no one would take the risk.

When the boat approached Louisville during the night of October 1, and the head of steam was allowed to escape through the valves, the mighty hissing produced an answering creak of bedsprings in the frontier city; lights sprang up in every window. The citizens were convinced that a baleful comet which had been trailing through the sky had fallen into the river.

The next evening Roosevelt gave a dinner on the *New Orleans*. "Well, you have been as good as your word," his friends said as they drank toasts somewhat nervously in the cabin. "You have visited us in a steamboat, but we see you for the last time. Your boat may go down the river, but as to coming up it, the idea is an absurd one." No sooner were these words spoken than a rumbling broke out, and the floor began to rock suspiciously. Convinced that the vessel had broken loose and was drifting toward the falls, everyone dropped their forks and rushed on deck. What was their amazement to see the city disappearing, not upstream, but down; the boat was mounting the current. As the engine warmed to its work, the nervousness of the crowd finally abated. Yet when Roosevelt took his involuntary passengers back to the wharf, they did not waste much time in leave-takings.

For days the *New Orleans* remained at Louisville. Her draught was more suitable for the stolid Hudson than the mercurial western rivers, and the Ohio was low; there was not enough water to carry her through the rapids below the city. Soundings were taken hourly, and everyone prayed for rain. Finally, bad weather somewhere to the north produced a little rise, but when the channel was only 5 inches deeper than the boat, the rise ceased. Since before the days of the telegraph there was no way of telling whether there was any more rain up river, Roosevelt decided to take the risk. Anxious to get as much steerageway as possible, he stoked the furnace high. The safety valve shrieked, and the vessel flew away from the crowd collected to see her off. But if the speed seemed breathless to the crew then, how much more so was it when they entered the rapids! The water whirled and eddied, throwing spray high on deck; black rocks loomed, and before you were sure you had missed them they had passed. For a few minutes the crew felt as if they were dropping down Niagara; then they were anchored in smooth water. But no sooner had they breathed deep with relief than a strange thing happened: the motionless boat shuddered as if it had run aground. They had experienced the first shock of an earthquake.

As they neared the Mississippi, the current of the Ohio began to run backward; clearly the larger river was in flood. Soon they entered a vast plateau of muddy water which spread far out into the forest. Between the boles of trees, Indians paddled in their canoes. Once a war party of Chickasaws darted from the flooded forest and paddled for the *New Orleans* with wild yells. If ever Roosevelt hung a weight on the safety valve, he did it then. For a few minutes the contest was even, and then steam proved its superior endurance. When the frustrated savages returned with a final shout to the forest, did they realize what a shattering defeat not only they but all the tribes on the continent had suffered that day?

Periodically, the steamboat tied up to the bank to refuel. The crew went on shore to cut dead timber, and sometimes as an axe was raised, the ground would tremble. Then the axe remained motionless in the air while the men stared at each other wordlessly. When the *New Orleans* reached New Madrid, they found that a large part of the settlement had gone down the river. Half the inhabitants rushed to the shifting waterfront begging to be taken on board, while the other half fled into the back country, convinced that the steamboat was more dangerous than flood and earthquake, the cause of all their misfortunes.

The farther downstream the *New Orleans* penetrated, the more strange and confusing everything became. It was impossible to tell river from field; all landmarks were obliterated. They no longer dared to tie up by the bank at night, for trees kept toppling into the water. One evening they anchored at the lower end of an island. All that night driftwood banged against the hull, keeping everyone awake, and when dawn restored vision they could not see the island. At first they thought the ship must have broken loose, but the anchor was still fast. The island had disintegrated and moved down the river.

Now the pilot was completely lost. Wandering in a featureless sea of muddy water, he thought it safest to keep to the greatest current; the steamboat went shooting down through strangeness. The relief was tremendous when Natchez loomed below them, putting an end to the difficult part of the voyage.

The earthquake that accompanied the *New Orleans* on her first trip had very little to do with hazards she faced; had the ground remained motionless, the journey would have been almost as terrifying to the eastern mechanics who manned the boat. Low water and high, almost irresistible currents, shifting banks, landmarks that walked away in the night: all these were not freaks occurring once a millennium, but rather the routine of Mississippi navigation. The father of waters would be much more difficult to conquer than the Hudson.

Fulton made no attempt to send the *New Orleans* back to the Ohio, for he knew she lacked the power; she plied between the Gulf and Natchez. His second Mississippi boat, the *Vesuvius*, which was launched in December 1813, was announced for the Louisville run, but she too did not go farther upstream than Natchez. Even on the lower river troubles multiplied: the *Vesuvius* spent a summer on a sandbank; the *New Orleans* struck a snag and sank. The two other western boats Fulton built, the *Etna* and the *Buffalo*, were also often in trouble.

Although Fulton succeeded in keeping steamships in motion on some parts of the western waterways, and thus gave great encouragement to other projectors, he never managed to send a vessel all the way from New Orleans to the mouth of the Ohio or to Pittsburgh; conquest of those greater currents was to remain for other men. Nor was Fulton's western venture financially rewarding; a year before his death he wrote that he was "tired of distant operations" and that his Ohio company was "alarmed and disgusted with the expenses and the state of their affairs."

Fulton was an Easterner who had constructed his boats primarily for eastern rivers; the Mississippi-Ohio system could only be mastered by specially designed vessels with more powerful motors. The first Westerner to attempt to solve the problem followed in Fulton's footsteps. Daniel French of Pittsburgh built the second boat on the Mississippi, the *Comet*, and a year later, in 1814, the larger *Enterprise*, a stern wheeler, 80 feet by 29. During May 1815 the *Enterprise* steamed from New Orleans to Louisville, the first successful voyage up the Mississippi and Ohio. Westerners were still unconvinced, however, since French had been able to take advantage of a flood to steam through fields where there was little current.

Really successful navigation of America's central waterways dates from after Fulton's death. Henry M. Shreve, an experienced keelboat skipper who was intimately acquainted with every sandbar and current in the river, had been captain of the *Enterprise;* becoming convinced that eastern-type boats would never defeat the Mississippi, he resolved to mount a steam engine on a hull as shallow as a keel boat or barge. This involved many changes of design since there would be no space in the hold for the engines. Recognizing that the western currents required motors both lighter and more powerful than any yet applied to steamboats, Shreve daringly essayed high pressure. Building a double-acting machine with two cylinders and four boilers, he placed it on deck; and then, to make up for the loss of space, he added a second deck above the first. His vessel, which penetrated hardly at all below the water and yet rose so high above, was the subject of much ridicule, yet it was to be the progenitor of all Mississippi River steamboats.

In 1817 Shreve's *Washington* churned under normal river conditions from New Orleans to Louisville in twenty-one days, less than a quarter of the time taken by barges or keel boats. Steam had finally been proved stronger than the great middle-western river currents: the celebration on the banks rivaled the rejoicing that had followed Jackson's victory at New Orleans. The inheritors of the Fulton monopoly, however, did not rejoice. Edward Livingston is reported to have said to Shreve, "You deserve well of your country, young man, but we shall be compelled to beat you in the courts if we can." He is further reputed to have offered the young river captain 50 per cent of the western monopoly if he would "instruct his counsel to arrange the business so that a verdict might be found against him." This Shreve indignantly refused to do. The Fulton interests were thus forced either to fight or give up their claims to the Mississippi. After a sharp legal skirmish, the District Court of Louisiana declared the monopoly illegal during 1819. From then on, western steamboating increased so rapidly that the Mississippi fleet became one of the wonders of the world.

Always optimistic, Fulton had written Benjamin West on July 12, 1813, "My success is extending great benefits over the United States. In one year I shall have steamboats running from Pittsburgh to New Orleans, distance 2,300 miles. Also from the Canada frontier on Lake Champlain to Charleston, South Carolina, distance 1,500 miles.

Taking in all the rivers and bays on the route, fourteen steamboats, or I should say ships for some are 300 tons, have been built in five years. And I am now building thirteen for various waters."

On the route stretching from Canada to the southern states Fulton already had a few boats in operation. From Albany passengers could proceed by steam to New York City, and on to New Brunswick, N. J., whence a short stage ride would take them to Trenton, where they would board Stevens' *Phoenix* for Philadelphia; Stevens had finally become an ally of Fulton's company. Beyond Philadelphia, Fulton's plans were all on paper. A coach was to go to the Chesapeake, where a steamboat was to connect with Baltimore and with another stage that rolled to the Potomac on which a vessel was to ply to Norfolk. Using post chaises to cover territory where there was no possibility of protection from the open ocean, Fulton planned four successive steamboat voyages behind islands to carry passengers to Atlanta, Georgia: (1) Norfolk to New Bern, N. C.; (2) Newport Inlet to Little River Inlet, N. C.; (3) the North Carolina boundary to Charleston; (4) Charleston to Savannah. Other boats were to go inland on four rivers: the James, the Appomattox, the Cape Fear, and the Peedee. A vessel was to ply between Charleston and Sullivan's Island.

To secure backers for these boats, Fulton published advertisements in the cities to be served. Claiming that his patents prevented anyone else from legally building an effective steamboat, he offered to license companies on condition that he receive half of all profits over 10 per cent. If the projectors wished to make use of his skill as boat designer, or have him build their vessels, that would be extra, at his usual rates. Since the validity of his patents was dubious to say the least, and since he had won much enmity because of his insistence on state monopolies which most lawyers considered unconstitutional, few capitalists entered with him on these terms. Only one southern boat seems to have actually been put in operation: the *Washington* on the Potomac. In addition, Fulton built the *Richmond* for a James River company but, perhaps because the War of 1812 made its transport down the coast impossible, he used it himself on the Hudson. He was very haughty with such backers as came to him. "I shall always hope," he wrote, "that gentlemen contracting with me for steamboats . . . will not think or deal with me as a common ship carpenter or boat builders. Any gentleman who is disposed to do so, shall have their money with interest and I shall keep my boat."

Although daring projectors in many cities braved Fulton's threats and built steamboats in opposition to him, undoubtedly Fulton's patents and state monopolies impeded the spread of steamboating in America. They did not, however, give him a stranglehold on the invention as history books usually state; on the contrary, they greatly reduced his influence. His rights rested on such shaky legal grounds that his attempt to enforce them was more expensive than it was worth. Endless litigation impoverished his company and discouraged his backers. Livingston wrote that the controversy had kept him from making a cent from steamboats despite large expenditures; he was unwilling to finance any more vessels. "Something must be done," the Chancellor concluded gloomily, "because the public is complaining we will neither exert ourselves or let others do it."

Fulton had forgotten his own advice to Stanhope that to make an invention lucrative you should place it "on the liberal footing of other manufactures. If thrown open on a broad basis to all who choose to employ it, free from restrictions and the spirit of monopoly, it will succeed, and those who have embarked their property in it will reimburse themselves with profit." Fulton's attempt to control steamboating was principally fruitful in making him enemies. Had he, instead of trying to levy tribute, offered to serve as engine builder to the nation, charging only for services actually rendered, his great fame and skill would probably have brought to his workshop almost all the capitalists who wished to enter this lucrative new field. Instead of building twenty-one steamboats, he might easily have built a hundred.

XXVI. *Steamboat Fever*

FROM the moment *The North River* churned successfully to Albany, the chain of successful steamboats in America never stopped or faltered. The banks of river after river reverberated to the harsh screaming of steam, while a pillar of fire moving against the current became to river dwellers a sight creating not fear but jubilation. When the ringing of church bells ushered in the year 1815, steam, although application was still limited to the most favorable waterways, had been generally accepted in the United States as the solution for problems of inland navigation.

The rest of the world, however, remained quiescent. Since Symington's *Charlotte Dundas* had been laid up in 1804, no steamboat of any importance had raised its cloud of smoke on any English or European water. In 1811 J. C. Dyer, having secured descriptions and drawings from Fulton, tried to interest English capitalists in steamboat building, but each in turn replied that although such vessels might succeed in America, "they will never answer in our small rivers and crowded harbors." England's skillful civil engineers also laughed at Dyer, John Rennie in particular assuring him that his scheme was useless.

Triumphant in his own country, Fulton made several attempts to introduce his invention abroad. During 1811 he began negotiations to secure an exclusive right in Russia, provided that within three years he run a vessel between St. Petersburg (Leningrad) and Kronstadt, through a sheltered arm of the Gulf of Finland. For this purpose, he started to build the *Empress of Russia*, but he died before the boat was completed, and the scheme fell through.

Fulton wrote in 1812 to Thomas Law, a former official of the East India Company, "I agree to make the Ganges enterprise a joint concern. You will please to send to me a plan how you mean to proceed to procure a grant for twenty years and find funds to establish the first boat. The work is so honorable and important—

it is so grand an idea that Americans should establish steam vessels to work in India—that it requires vigor, activity, exertion, industry, attention, and that no time should be lost. My *Paragon* beats everything on the globe, for made as you and I are we cannot tell what is in the moon; this day she came in from Albany, 160 miles in twenty-six hours, wind ahead." However, the invention was not introduced into India for another eight years.

The year 1812 witnessed the reappearance of steam on Scottish waters. Henry Bell, like Rumsey a house builder who had become innkeeper at a watering resort, fixed on a mechanical boat as a spectacular way to bring clients to his hotel. After corresponding with Fulton, he launched the *Comet*, a small ship 40 feet by 10½, its somewhat quixotic engine moving somewhat quixotic wheels. Afraid that the smokestack would frighten prospective customers, he tried to camouflage it by combining it with the mast from which he hung his sails. The little boat moved at 5 miles an hour "by the power of wind, air, and steam," and was soon carrying excursionists up the Clyde from Glasgow to Helensburgh.

Not convinced of the superiority of steam over sail and horse-power, the canny Bell had made his venture part of an amusement center; people rode on the *Comet* not for superior convenience but to get a thrill. And his speculation succeeded well enough to be imitated; in 1813 an improved vessel, the *Elizabeth*, was launched on the same waters. In their advertisements, the proprietors of this ship made no pretense that she was faster than the coaches which ran beside the river; instead they dwelt on her beautiful fittings: "A sofa, clothed with maroon, is placed at one end of the cabin, and gives the whole a warm and cheerful appearance. There are twelve small windows, each finished with maroon curtains with tassels, fringes, and velvet, cornices ornamented with gilt ornaments, having altogether a rich effect. Above the sofa is a large mirror suspended, and on each side bookshelves are placed containing a collection of the best authors for the amusement and edification of those who may avail themselves of them during the passage; other amusements are likewise to be had on board." During that year and the following, several more steamboats appeared on this amusement route. Not till hundreds of excursionists had ridden easily and without mishap was steam applied to ordinary commercial purposes in Britain. And many years were to pass before that great maritime nation could compete with the United States in number and quality of steamboats.

Even when England began to dabble in steam, France, the country that had given the world its first steamboat, remained apathetic. Then at last the old master, Jouffroy, came out of retirement. He took out a patent, and in 1816 launched the *Charles-Philippe*. But the former pioneer had not kept up with mechanical progress; his boat was a failure, as was a rival vessel launched at about the same time. After that sporadic attempts came to so little that the government commissioned an engineer to make a study of American steamboats. His report, published in 1824, finally put the Frenchmen on the right track.

Steam continued to move around the world, but with amazing slowness. In 1815 Russia and Java each boasted a boat; in 1816 one moved in Germany, although regular service was not inaugurated on the Rhine till 1825; in 1818 the Danube saw its first effective steamer, while the Ganges followed a year later; in 1822 the Swiss lakes finally experienced the new invention.*

The steamboats of the period were not really suited to European needs. Their inefficient engines, heavy and bulky and using a vast quantity of fuel, left little room for a paying cargo even on a slow river ship that stopped every few miles to replenish its supply of wood. Any attempt to increase the speed, or the length of run possible without refueling, involved such an increase in the weight of the machinery and the space it occupied that it was impractical. Furthermore, the vessels were so frail that they were restricted to

---

* The dates here given must not be taken too literally; they are merely an indication. In every region the same chain of events was likely to take place. First there would be suggestions on paper. When boats were actually built, the earliest were often only experiments that moved for tiny distances. To determine exactly when steam succeeded in any region is a ticklish matter, depending often on the historian's interpretation of what can be considered success.

inland waterways. We have seen the extraordinary precautions
Stevens took to get his *Phoenix* by sea from New York to Philadelphia; he would have proceeded more confidently in a 20-foot
catboat.

The inland waterways of England and western Europe were
almost without exception short and flanked by good roads on
which stagecoaches could gallop faster than any Fulton type steamboat. Since the Old World had been denuded of its forests and only
small quantities of coal were mined, the numerous caches of fuel
needed by a steamboat were almost impossible to secure. And the
one great saving the invention had to offer, the saving of manpower,
meant little in countries where labor was superabundant and cheap.

In the New World, however, the natural arteries of travel were
its many long rivers, some with mountainous banks, almost all devoid
of good flanking roads. Indeed, the very existence of the steamboat
discouraged the building of an expensive turnpike system in the
Mississippi Valley. The invention had arrived there early enough
to create its own monopoly, which was not to be broken until the
advent of the railroad, a generation or two later.*

The forests of America offered a seemingly endless supply of
fuel that did not even have to be transported; you cut down trees
on the river bank, a few feet from where the boats called. And the
saving of manpower which the steamboat offered was a great advantage in the partially settled land where any worker could leave
the labor market by securing his own farm.

Of course, there were long rivers not flanked with good roads in
other parts of the world besides the United States: the Danube, the
Ganges, the Yangtze, the Amazon. On some of these steam was introduced from the outside but the invention could not be expected

---

* It is an interesting characteristic of social progress that innovations are
often introduced more slowly in the centers of culture than on the periphery,
where there is less competition from existing installations and traditional thinking. Thus the best examples of medieval town design are to be found in the
cities built by Spain in South America; Palestine is filled with modern archi-
tecture. Airplane transport is most complete in backward regions lacking
good rail and road communication.

to become indigenous for many years. Where the industrial revolution had not yet taken root, steamboats could not be built, nor could they be serviced except by imported workmen at a few centers.

The Old World needed vessels that could go to sea, not simply a steamboat that could stay afloat in a storm, but one that could compete with fast sailboats for passengers and heavy schooners for freight. We are told that the first ocean crossing under steam was made by the *Savannah* in 1817; actually this was a first crossing by a sailboat that carried an auxiliary steam engine. Mechanically inefficient even for its own period, the *Savannah* used its motor only during calms. Successful spanning of the ocean had to wait until a long period of evolution made engines sturdier, lighter per horsepower, and more powerful. The steam crossing which signalized this great advance was made by the English *Great Western* in 1838. Then the British people sat up and took notice; steam had invaded their domain at last. They took the leadership of steam navigation which they have held ever since.

The first flowering of the steamboat, then, took place in America, and during his lifetime Fulton was clearly the leader in this development. Other builders turned out a few ships each—the Stevens family had launched only three commercial ones by 1815—but Fulton designed twenty-one successful steamboats. On the Hudson there were *The North River*, the *Car of Neptune*, the *Paragon*, the *Richmond*, and the *Chancellor Livingston*; on the Mississippi River system the *New Orleans*, the *Etna*, the *Natchez*, and the *Buffalo*; as ferries plying from Manhattan, the *Firefly*, the *Jersey*, the *York*, the *Nassau*, and the *Camden*; on Long Island Sound, the *Fulton* and the *Connecticut;* on the New Brunswick run, the *Raritan* and the *Olive Branch*; and on the Potomac, the *Washington*. In addition he built the *Empress of Russia*, designed to clinch his monopoly in that nation, and the first steam warship in the world, the *Demologos*.

As was to be expected, the ships tended to become larger: the original *North River* weighed 100 tons; its rebuilt form, 182.5; the *Car of Neptune*, 295; the *Paragon*, 331, and the *Chancellor Livingston*, 526. Increased size involved increased power in the motor. Having studied the engine he bought from Boulton and Watt, Fulton constructed most of his subsequent ones himself, although he purchased at least one more from the English firm. As time went on, he simplified his mechanism, removing such unnecessary parts as the fly wheels whose function was carried out by the paddle wheels themselves. He substituted for the confused bell-crank engine he is said to have invented, the more efficient steeple engine which he admitted borrowing from Stevens.

Experience made him give up the long and thin construction he had originally considered so valuable. The ratio of length to breadth in the original *North River* was about 10:1; in the rebuilt *North River*, 8:1; the *Paragon*, 6:1; the *Richmond*, 5:1; the *Chancellor Livingston*, 4.7:1. For a long time he adhered to the peculiar flat-bottomed, straight-sided, and angular-pointed shape of *The North River*, but when he designed the *Fulton* to battle the wild waters of Long Island Sound, he was forced to substitute the stronger curves of a conventional ship. Discovering that despite his theoretical conclusions this did not increase the water resistance, he employed the usual shape in all his subsequent boats.

The *Fulton* was the first steamboat in the world to ply regularly on an arm of the sea. Although launched in 1814, because of the British blockade then in force she did not attempt until March 1815 the New York to New Haven run for which she had been designed. Most people were convinced she would never reach New Haven. Even if she escaped destruction in the rapids of Hell Gate, she would founder in the waves of Long Island Sound. And certainly she would get lost at night since the iron with which she had been strengthened would make her compass useless. But behind the figurehead of her inventor which stood out from her prow, the *Fulton* moved safely and efficiently through her appointed orbit.

Launched after Fulton's death, the *Chancellor Livingston* embodied his final steamboat ideas. She was the only one of his boats to burn coal, not wood. Her engine, as we have seen, was greatly improved, but since the inventor was always more interested in carrying capacity than speed, he made this vessel only a mile and a half an hour faster than *The North River.* He managed to combine the utilization of every inch of space with large chambers and long vistas that gave a grand effect. Thus the dining saloon, which occupied the whole stern, was given a second function by being flanked with upper and lower berths covered with curtains. This arrangement of sleeping quarters became standard in American steamboats and was taken over from them by the railroads.

How far steamboating, under Fulton's leadership, ran into big money in only eight years is shown by the fact that the *Chancellor Livingston* cost more than $125,000. In 1823 the five ships Fulton had built to ply on the Hudson were estimated to be worth, with the value of the monopoly itself, $660,000, and they were paying 8 per cent on this valuation.

With the approach of the War of 1812, Fulton returned gladly to his military dreams; although his steamboats had been so successful that they took most of his time, his heart was still with his torpedoes. Now that the American government, to whom he was offering his schemes, was on the verge of an alliance with France against England, he felt it safe to return to public admiration of the emperor whom he had denounced so eloquently when he had been trying to sell to Pitt. In *Torpedo War,* a publicity pamphlet he published in 1810, he spoke of Napoleon's "magnanimity of soul" and his "great actions." The British rulers, on the other hand, he now stated had "usurped the domination of the ocean, and laid all nations under contribution." They had "loaded the virtuous people with taxes to pay for ruinous wars, the conquest of America, the establishment of the Bourbons, and the balance of Europe."

From the first Fulton's submarine warfare had been rendered ineffectual by his failure to find a practical method of bringing his bombs into contact with enemy vessels. Now he resolved to attach the torpedoes to harpoons fired from a gun; although they would carry only a few feet, he was convinced this was the answer. In March 1810 Congress appropriated $5,000 to finance experiments, and by that fall he was ready to blow up a sloop anchored off Brooklyn Navy Yard. He believed himself approaching a climax in his life when, his habitual self-confidence heightened by years of success and fame, he set out in an eight-oared boat to prove that at last he had made all navies obsolete. How jocundly his finger rested on the trigger of the harpoon gun while the boat sped over the water toward the anchored sloop! Suddenly, however, his oarsmen backwatered. After he had craned his neck over the bow for a few moments, Fulton ordered them to row for shore. The harpoon gun had not been fired.

In his writings, Fulton had challenged "nautical men and experienced commanders" to show how ships anchored in a calm could escape "total destruction in a few hours"; Captain Lawrence, who was in charge of the sloop, had accepted the dare. He had surrounded his boat with nets fastened to the bottom and with a pen of floating logs. Heavy iron weights hung from the rigging waiting to be plunged down on Fulton's skiff, while great scythes on the ends of spars swept back and forth out of portholes at just the right height to decapitate the inventor. Fulton was so completely baffled that an examining commission appointed by the government was forced to report against his invention.

This failure did not keep Fulton from writing Stanhope, who had patented a type of vessel designed to be immune from torpedoes, that "the ship is very ingenious, but the torpedoes are now so far improved that any plan I have yet seen cannot defend a ship against vigorous attack with them."

Faced with a galling inability to perfect his invention, Fulton was experimenting with a mélange of ideas, some wild, some possibly practical. He designed a curved knife stuck in the barrel of a gun which was supposed to drift against the cable of a boat in such a manner that the knife would catch; then the gun would be automatically discharged, cutting the cable. The ship would drift aground before the sails could be raised, or so Fulton hoped. In 1813 he patented his *Columbiads*, guns intended to be fired below the surface in such a manner that they would strike enemy vessels below the waterline. Although the balls would not carry with any force farther than a few yards, they might be useful in boarding operations. Next he projected one torpedo boat more, and in this last effort he returned to Bushnell's conception of having the craft approach the enemy, not submerged, but awash. The so-called *Mute* was to have its top deck covered with iron heavy enough to repel the enemy balls which, because of its lowness in the water, would have to strike obliquely. Propelled by an armored paddle wheel actuated by the crew of one hundred men, the *Mute* was to creep up on the enemy at night. For more than a century historians have accepted Colden's statement that Fulton's death prevented him from completing any boat of this type.

Recently discovered documents show, however, that Fulton did build a small version of the *Mute*, designed to hold twelve men under its armor-clad deck. Captain Richard Burdett, of HMS *Maidstone*, reported to his government that on June 25, 1814, he was notified that "the wonderful turtle boat which has been so long constructing at New York by the celebrated Mr. Fulton" had set out a few days before to join the American fleet, but had been driven by a gale onto the Long Island shore. One man had been drowned. Captain Burdett sailed to the attack with two warships. "Upon rounding a point of land," he wrote, "I discovered this newly invented machine lying in a small sandy bay, in a wash of the beach, with a vast concourse of people around it, a considerable part of whom were armed militia, who took their stations behind the banks, to the right and left of the turtle boat, which lay on the beach ressembling a great whale." The British ships raked the beach with cannon fire, and then sent marines ashore in small boats. After a brisk engagement, the militia fled, and the marines blew up Fulton's invention.

Turning to his stepchild, steam, Fulton created a warship which promised immediate usefulness. After the War of 1812 had become a horrible reality, the citizens of New York, realizing that they could not defend their city against the British fleet, formed the Coast and Harbor Defense Association. At Fulton's insistence, they contracted to build the world's first steam battleship at an estimated cost of $320,000, if Congress would agree to reimburse them should the boat succeed. In March 1814 Congress promised.

Fulton's design was a completely new departure in warship construction. Anticipating by many years the basic principle of the iron-clad, he built the sides and deck of 5-foot lumber, which also protected a paddle wheel placed between twin hulls, as in his ferry boats. A hundred sixty-seven feet long, 56 wide, and 13 deep, the vessel carried thirty 32-pounders shooting red-hot shot, as well as two *Columbiads* slung over the bow. A huge hose attached to a steam pump was to play on enemy decks, washing off sailors and drenching the guns so they would not fire. To move this tremendously heavy and bulky craft, Fulton planned an engine of 120 horsepower. The *Demologos*, also known as the *Fulton the First*, was to be a floating fort, not capable of going to sea but extremely valuable for harbor defense.

Exaggerated rumors about this monster swept across the ocean. The *Edinburgh Evening Courant* reported that she was 300 feet long, 200 wide, with sides 13 feet thick; she carried forty-four guns, including four 100-pounders. "And farther, to annoy an enemy attempting to board, can discharge 100 gallons of boiling water a minute and, by mechanism, brandishes 300 cutlasses with the utmost regularity over her gunwales, works an equal number of heavy iron pikes of great length, darting them from her sides with prodigious force and withdrawing the same every quarter of a minute." The British secret service paid Fulton the compliment of setting spies on his trail, and one night enemy naval forces patrolling Long Island Sound staged a commando raid on a house where he had intended to sleep. They found his bed empty; he had been delayed by a fortunate accident.

Fulton had the devil's own time getting the vessel built. Because of the British blockade, all goods had to be brought overland, and many a wagon bearing heavy materials went through the surface of roads not designed for a machine age. However, on October 29, 1814, the engineless hull was launched. An eye-witness tells us that it was a bright autumnal day. A multitude of spectators crowded the shores and were seen on the hills, while the river and bay were filled with warships fluttering bright pennants. As the enormous mass, whose bulk seemed to make her incapable of motion, slid down the ways, edged for a moment into the water as if to dive, and then floated serenely, several steamboats moved as if by magic between the anchored frigates with bands of music and cheering spectators.

This was Fulton's last triumph; he died before the engines were installed. It is highly significant to our story that his passing did not stop construction on his ships; he had trained others to carry on his work of invention. In September the *Demologos*, with guns, ammunition, and stores aboard, steamed at 5½ miles an hour, and when her cannon were fired, the repercussions did not impede the even turning of her engine.

Although the War of 1812 ended before the vessel could be tried in action, the possibility of a mobile floating fort for harbor defense had been proved. The American admirals, however, tied the *Demologos* up in the Brooklyn Navy Yard, where she was used as a receiving ship. For more than a score of years steam was hardly employed at all in the navies of the world. Why? Part of the answer undoubtedly lies in the fact that in any boat less heavily armored than Fulton's, the engines and wheels would be extremely vulnerable to cannon shot. The steam apparatus tended to clutter the fighting decks and, if used as a source of auxiliary power, interfered with the sailing qualities of the vessel. Furthermore, until steamships were able to navigate the open sea, they were of little use to a major power whose strategy was based on attack. Yet defense such as Fulton's mobile fortress offered could sometimes be of great national importance. Perhaps we must blame the long quiescence of steam warships on the traditionalism typical of navies, which can only be broken by the bitterest type of experience suffered in actual battle.

Lord Napier undoubtedly expressed the opinion of naval commanders everywhere when he told the British Parliament: "Mr.

Speaker, when we enter His Majesty's naval service and face the chances of war, we go prepared to be hacked to pieces by cutlasses, to be riddled with bullets, or to be blown to bits by shell and shot; but, Mr. Speaker, we do not go prepared to be boiled alive."

Fulton had for some years now been the great gentleman he had always wanted to be. With his rich and aristocratic wife, he lived in an elegant house on the waterfront, and when he wished to go abroad, he had only to ring for one of his coachmen to bring out one of his carriages. He must have been a mature man before he ate off plate; now his servants set it before him every day.

Having earned riches and fame from mechanics, Fulton returned at the end of his life to painting, but altogether as an amateur. Many early nineteenth-century pictures have been attributed to him; only a few can be shown to be by his hand. Over these, traditionalism hangs like a pall. Seeking less for brilliant brush work than to avoid mistakes, he only escaped from self-consciousness when he copied the paintings of men in whose taste and skill he had faith. Thus a self-portrait in miniature, based on a canvas by Benjamin West, is delightful; the colors, which are West's colors, glow, and in reproducing the forms created by the master he allowed himself some fluency in execution. An altogether original miniature of his wife is so different it is difficult to believe it is by the same hand. The colors are pale and unattractive; the forms stand out cramped and harsh, the result of aching care and lack of sureness. He tried in some of his miniatures to achieve a dashing air by adding dashing accessories: wind-blown hair, pearls large as field stones, costumes so elaborate they seem like fancy dress. But the result, although sometimes pretty, is hard, dull, and studied.

His portrait of John Walter Livingston, a typical example of his large oils, is effective from a distance because it is so completely in the mode of the sophisticated painting of the period; the canvas seems quiet, grave, and decorative. However, the closer you come the less impressive it appears, for the technical expedients have been applied by rote, and stilted brush work has made the surface flat and dull. The drawing too is faulty; he was incapable of depicting the far cheek of a three-quarter face.

These timid and conventional pictures seem out of character with the swashbuckler who had set out in a tiny boat to sink the British fleet. We suspect that Fulton was still suffering from a sense of inferiority because he had failed as an artist. His grim attempt to prove to himself and the world that he could have been a great painter tightened the muscles of his hand, atrophied the originality of his brain. He himself expressed delight with the correct appearance of his pictures, telling his friends that their superiority to his previous work was due to his study of the old masters at the Louvre.[1]

Fulton hung his canvases on his walls with the old masters he had collected, and always he was generous to young artists who wanted to study his treasures. Like many another who became rich late in life, Fulton could see no point in having money unless he spent it. He never begrudged throwing vast sums into his schemes, be they submarines or steamboats, and his superflux he gladly handed to men less fortunate. It must have given the adventurer who had lived on borrowed funds for so long great pleasure to turn the tables by lending to others. His brother and sisters had not risen with him; they were poor farmers in western Pennsylvania and on them he showered new barns and blooded cattle. Naturally a little moralizing went with his largess. Expressing regret that his relations had "in general been unfortunate," he stated that he wished to aid them "according to their several necessities and merits. . . . If there is any intemperance in any one of them, I have only to say I cannot be that person's friend, for I feel a kind of contempt for the being who is so imprudent as to extinguish the little sense that falls to the lot of man in the poisonous fumes of ardent liquors—such a person has not sense to be their own friend and does not merit the friendship of others."

Skillful with people when his nerves allowed him to use his

talents, Fulton got on well with his workmen, although, in a manner typical of his time, he played the role of patron, not companion. Paul Sabbaton, his chief engineer, remembered that he was always gentle and never used an ill word: "His habit was, cane in hand, to walk up and down for hours. I see him now, in my mind's eye, with his white, loosely tied cravat, his waistcoat unbuttoned, his ruffles waving from side to side, as his movements caused their movements; he all the while in deep thought, scarcely noticing anything passing." Another witness states that he rarely laughed among his workmen; he was taciturn and grave, giving orders in a laconic manner.

The lung trouble he had suffered with as a young man came back to plague him in 1812, when he was forty-seven. His attacks yielded to treatment, but he remained frail. However, he would not spare himself; always he was building more steamboats, promoting more torpedo and submarine schemes. After the death of Livingston in 1813, the legal battles to uphold the monopoly rested largely on his shoulders. At the advice of his lawyers propping up weak points or abandoning claims that were about to fall, he kept the tottering legal structure upright during his lifetime. So clever were his attorneys that they managed to keep the issue from the Supreme Court until 1823; then, with the oratory of Daniel Webster still ringing in their ears, the Justices ruled the New York State monopoly unconstitutional.

In January 1815 Fulton's lawyer's were working for the repeal of a retaliatory New Jersey statute that gave a monopoly to Fulton's rivals. Although the weather was very cold, the inventor crossed the Hudson to testify at Trenton. Elegant and handsome on the stand, downright in his testimony, he was a powerful witness, and his lawyers made good use of him, as is shown by Emmet's summation at a previous trial. Turning from the jury, he reproached Fulton for being too high minded. In his reliance on the justice of his cause, this good man had spent all his earnings to help mankind. "I admire and applaud you for your readiness to devote to the service of the public the opulence you derive from its grateful remuneration. Let me remind you, however, that you have other and closer ties. I know the pain I am about to give and I see the tears I make you shed! By that love I speak, by that love which, like the light of Heaven is refracted in rays of different strength upon your wife and children; which when collected and combined forms the sunshine of your soul; by that love I do abjure you, provide in time for those dearest objects of your care." Emmet warned that selfish men might succeed by raising the cry of monopoly to get some legislature to "give your property to the winds and your person to your creditors. . . . Yes, my friend!—my heart bleeds when I utter it, but I have fearful forebodings that you may hereafter find public faith a broken staff for your support, and receive from public gratitude a broken heart for your reward."

While his lawyer soared in the empyrean, Fulton had been shivering with cold. The hearing over, he set out with his counsel for New York, but finding the Hudson partly closed with ice, he visited his workshop which was on the Jersey shore. For three frigid hours he inspected the boats that were being built and refitted there. When at last a whistle announced that the ferry had battered its way into the slip, he led his companions on a short cut across the ice. Emmet fell through. "In this moment of great peril," Fulton's physician writes, "Mr. Fulton was exceedingly agitated, at the same time that his exertions to save his friend left him much exhausted." By the time he reached home, he was so hoarse that he could hardly speak.

He took to his bed, but three days later some hitch developed in the building of the *Demologos*. Spurning the advice of his doctor, he ordered out his carriage. Although he did not leave the vehicle between his home and his workshop at Paulus Hook, severe symptoms developed. On February 23, 1815, Robert Fulton died.

His death was an occasion for public lamentation such as is rarely accorded a private citizen. The New York legislature resolved that the members of both houses should wear mourning, and many associations and learned societies followed suit. When his funeral procession started the next day from his mansion on State Street, all New York seemed to be there. The mourners were separated into two crowds. Elegantly attired government and business and social leaders marched behind the bier, while tradesmen and laborers lined the street and watched in silent awe. Many a shop was left closed that day in homage to the inventor of steamboats. As the black plumed hearse moved down the streets, rhythmical booming filled the air; the cannon on the *Demologos* and in the West Battery fired minute guns until the procession reached Trinity Church. After the Church of England burial service had been read, Fulton was placed in the Livingston vault, where the dust of the tailor's son was to mingle till the last judgment with some of America's most aristocratic dust.

If from an unnoticed cloud in the sky a thin, ragged ghost could have peered down, the ghost of John Fitch risen from an unmarked grave in the Kentucky village where he had drunk himself into oblivion, his scarred, intense face would have been contorted with the helpless fury he had known so often during life. Here was the final injustice of a universe which he had always hoped against hope to find just. When his own generation had willfully misunderstood, he had pinned his faith on generations to come, but even these were going back on him now. Would no one ever believe that "poor John Fitch can do anything worthy of attention"? At least he had the grim pleasure of having been a good prophet; "the day will come," he had written, "when some more powerful man will get fame and riches from my invention."

But was the ghost of John Fitch, gesticulating unseen and unheard in the broad expanses of eternity—was this troubled spirit right? Had Fulton stolen his invention? Should we, the living representatives of the future generations to whom Fitch had turned for justice, amend an old wrong? What is the truth of the invention of the steamboat?

XXVII. *Who Invented the Steamboat?*

A<small>N</small> <small>ATTEMPT</small> to define the forces that advanced and retarded the invention of the steamboat raises questions basic to our understanding of history, for the acceptance of this discovery involved a major change in the thinking of mankind. The steamboat was the first result of the industrial revolution to modify in an important manner a common human attribute. Before such vessels could succeed, plain citizens had to be convinced that something which had been impossible through all the aeons of history was now an established fact. When mankind accepted this invention, they accepted an idea so revolutionary that it brought with it a new era in the development of the human race. People had been convinced that by the sober application of scientific principles man could remake his environment. What had during all the millenniums of time been the exclusive domain of the imagination, had become a dray horse to assist ordinary people in their ordinary tasks.

From darkest antiquity, vessels that sailed against wind and tide had figured in human imaginations: these long centuries of dreaming might be called the era of *magical prophecy*. Since no natural means existed to make mechanical boats possible, visionaries turned to the supernatural. A wizard comes out of the east and builds for the Sultan of Bagdad a ship scrawled over with cabalistic signs that moves alone and dreadfully. Along with the jubilation of possessing such a boat comes fear, the fear of the unknown. And this fear lingers on after the invention has been achieved by scientifically explained means. That even today many men retain a suspicion that science is black magic is shown by the recurrence in popular literature—the comic strips and the pulp magazines—of the mad doctor who, syringe in hand, is just going to turn the heroine into an ape when the hero thunders in.

The period of *magical prophecy* merges gradually into the period of *scientific prophecy*, the change being less in the minds of the prophets than in their environment. Moving like a kaleidoscope from one combination to another, mankind evolves mechanisms or principles which might in a century or two solve the problem. But the imagination cannot wait; it springs like a homing pigeon to the eventual end. Thus we find in old books vague descriptions of mechanisms that will some day become realities.

In our steamboat story, Worcester's and Savery's pumping engines inaugurated the era of scientific prophecy. Now a mechanism existed which translated, however inefficiently, heat into motion, although it was only the motion of a flowing liquid. Eagerly dreamers imagined this machine moving a boat. They were still postulating the impractical, yet the advance of science would make their visions come true.

We must be careful not to confuse *prophecy* with *practical invention*. It is silly to say that Icarus or Leonardo invented the airplane, or that the steamboat was invented by Homer or Hulls. They merely pointed out the possibility of such things, as a writer who had never walked up a hill might point out the possibility of climbing Mount Everest.

Only after generations of evolution do we enter the era of practical invention. The change does not take place in the mind of a single brilliant individual; that is impossible. The movement of society as a whole creates the change. To explain fully the invention of the steamboat we would have to deal with almost every aspect of the history of the Western world. Very apposite is the breakdown of feudalism and authoritarian thought; the rise of the bourgeoisie cannot be ignored; the use of applied science to create the industrial revolution is at the heart of our problem. Thousands of experimenters who never even conceived of steamboats made important contributions: they studied the properties of gases and metals; they measured heat and the weight of the atmosphere. Through centuries men had to modify their commercial environment, creating needs more exploitable than the longings of visionary men. Thus not until cities became so large that wells no longer solved their water problem, not until mines became exhausted to such a depth that horse-drawn pumps no longer served, was even the rudimentary fountain engine a practical possibility.

Speaking in terms of centuries rather than years, it is possible to ignore the contributions of individual inventors and deal solely with the mass evolution of the human race. Seen as from an airplane, the stream of history flows irresistibly in its appointed direction, as the Mississippi flows irresistibly to the sea. But should we ground our plane and walk along the river banks, our much more detailed view will reveal that the direction of history can be deflected for a decade or two, even as the great Mississippi breaks around an island. Although an individual cannot stem for long the current which is sweeping mankind toward some invisible bourne, he can make minor changes within his own generation. Had Watt, Fitch, and Fulton never lived, the age of steam would have dawned, and in the year 1900 its sun would have shone just as brightly, but it would have dawned very differently during the period of practical invention, that single generation that intervened between scientific prophecy and improved application.

The exact moment when scientific prophecy gave way to practical invention is not difficult to define in the steamboat story, since the development of the Watt engine was the turning point. Yet the fact that Jouffroy powered with a Newcomen-type engine the first steamboat that actually moved shows that Watt's discovery was only part of a long train of evolution that made the invention possible. How shall we classify Jouffroy? Was he the final scientific prophet or the first practical inventor? He seems to be poised between the two groups.

The straight line of development that ended with the solution of the problem began with the work of Rumsey and Fitch. They conceived the idea independently of each other and without any knowledge of Jouffroy, a phenomenon common in the history of discovery. When social change has prepared the ground for an advance, similar environmental conditions are likely to call independent discoverers into being in many places at about the same time. Symington was another steamboat man who seems to have begun on his own.

A milestone has been passed when a problem becomes so well publicized that new inventors know of the work done before them, and are thus enabled to accept or reject the contributions of their predecessors. Indeed, some historians regard this as the moment of actual invention. That such a point of view is difficult to maintain is shown by our steamboat story. In 1788 the controversy between Fitch and Rumsey called their work to the attention of every interested American, yet the invention was far from complete. Rumsey had built a vessel that moved slowly and for a short distance during two trial runs, and Fitch's little skiff had rowed itself along at less than 3 miles an hour. The inventors themselves did not regard these steamboats as anything more than promising demonstrations, not large or fast enough to be of any real use. Both scrapped their existing vessels and tried again.

If we were to follow the writers who say the steamboat had been invented by 1788, there would be little choice between the contributions of Fitch and Rumsey. Although in his mania for publicity Fitch had yelled earlier and louder, although his method of propulsion was closer to modern practice than Rumsey's, the actual vessels built by the rivals had been about equally successful. And Rumsey had secured the more promising backing.

However, the race did not stop in 1788, and in the next heat Rumsey fell hopelessly behind. His subsequent attempts were a devastating failure, while Fitch built in 1790 a remarkably effective boat. Not only did it cover several thousand miles on schedule, but it went 6 to 8 miles an hour, almost twice as fast as the so-called *Clermont*. Many writers have stated that with this vessel Fitch invented the steamboat.

But we must not forget that Fitch flashed like a meteor through the sky of invention rather than illuminating it with the steady radiance of the rising sun. The year following his triumph, no steamboat moved anywhere; for another sixteen years, steamboats failed universally and without exception. This is a fact of history that cannot be modified by any explanations or argument; or even by our sympathy with this wild genius and his tragic end.

Fitch failed because of a fundamental error in method. Working altogether by trial and error, he never completely understood what he was doing; basic principles eluded him. When a device functioned, he was delighted; when it failed, he was depressed but tried again. And at last he hit on an amazingly successful combination.

Fitch's boat was very like a crew famous in Harvard's athletic lore. It was made up of leftovers from the varsity crews, put together in one shell so the boys would get their exercise. Yet when this combination of ragtag and bobtail raced the varsity, they won with ease. Each oarsman had his serious faults, but by some strange chance their faults cancelled out. The man who rowed a little too short made effective the stroke of his neighbor who rowed too long; if number three had not pulled out of balance on the left, number four would have made trouble by pulling out of balance on the right. As it was—no one knew quite how or why—they swept the river.

The puzzled coach felt that so fast a crew must have some good oarsmen in it. He took the team apart, and tried to find berths for the individual members in the conventional shells. But they were all incapable of rowing efficiently. And when the weird oarsmen were put back together again, even that did not work; something had happened to the mystical combination, no one could ascertain what. They were just a group of duds now, clawing and splashing at the water.

Since Fitch did not understand what he had done, he was incapable of repeating his success or showing anyone else how to succeed. Even if his company had continued to support him, there is no assurance that he could have made his new ship, the *Perseverance*, half as efficient as his old. And had he somehow succeeded in arriving again at an effective combination, steamboat building would hardly have been advanced at all. As long as the method remained trial and error, each individual vessel had to be created through months or years of expensive and heart-rending tinkering. The process of practical invention cannot be said to have ceased with Fitch.

His failure makes it clear that all the elements whose combination will create an invention must not only be known at a single moment of history; they must exist in a single place; indeed, in the consciousness of a single individual. To achieve this is by no means a simple matter of communication, for very often the environmental conditions that foster one element are inimical to another. The rigors of the American frontier had molded Fitch into a man original in conception, daring in execution, and very skillful with his hands; but they had impeded the study of theoretical principles. Improvisation had been encouraged rather than invention.

Ignorance was Fitch's armor and also his Achilles heel. That lack of conventional knowledge can be a great asset is a basic lesson taught by the study of any creative activity. A man of wide learning, faced with the unknown, knows the reasons why others have hesitated to take the step he is contemplating. Although some of these reasons are likely to be intelligent, based on sound understanding of the many complex factors to be solved, others are pure mythology, traditional fears reflecting the inherent inertia of the human mind. Being unconscious of the existence of steam engines when he began his dreaming, Fitch foresaw no difficulties, either imaginary or real. While James Watt, the most experienced engine builder the world had ever known, hesitated to put one of his machines on a boat, Fitch never doubted that a steam engine would work as well on rolling water as attached to the masonry of a mine.

With inferior materials and no fixed plan, Fitch set out to build a steamboat, even as he would have built a shelter in the wilderness, with whatever came to hand. Again and again he ran into difficulties whose seriousness might have frightened him to a standstill had he understood what they were. But he did not understand, and proceeded resolutely onward. And he was able to find backers as innocent as he. It is by no means chance that Franklin, the one American capable of visualizing the steamboat problem in its entirety, regarded Fitch as a grotesque fool. Had Philadelphia been populated with Franklins, Fitch would never have got to first base; indeed, he would not have been allowed to play.

However, the very ignorance that encouraged Fitch to proceed against odds prevented him from achieving a complete victory in the end. Not only did his innocence of the scientific method keep him from placing his feet on the only path that led to total success, but he was forced to invent over again devices already well known in more sophisticated parts of the world. Most of his energies were wasted in developing a type of engine which he could have bought entire had he lived in England.

But if Fitch had been born an Englishman, he would have had other troubles, for the mechanical sophistication of that environment created not only advantages but also difficulties. So much was asked of the British pioneer, Symington, that achievements which would have created jubilation in America were considered failures. Although they went together easily and functioned well, Symington's steamboats merely strengthened the established British opinion that such vessels were a practical impossibility. And, indeed, there was some reason for this higher standard. The very wilderness that had kept America ignorant, also made that nation much more dependent on inland transportation. An inferior boat, which would not pay dividends in England, might pay them in America.

Seemingly all that was needed was to combine American vision, opportunity, and ingenuity with British scientific and mechanical skill. That it was not a matter of chance that this marriage was not consummated at once, Rumsey's partnership negotiations with Watt reveal. Both men were eager to get together, but their points of view were so different that neither could really appreciate what the other had to offer. The pragmatic and the scientific approaches to steamboating were still too far apart to mingle.

Of course we must not forget that although the steamboat epic was the expression of society as a whole, every individual verse was conceived in the mind of a single man and modified by the structure of his brain cells.* Had Symington been comparable with Fitch in perseverance and ability, he might have overcome his lesser difficulties and risen to greater heights. Indeed, the more we reflect, the more we are impressed by the sheer native genius of Fitch. Cutting a precarious, pragmatic path through the forest of ignorance, he penetrated farther into the unknown than even the best educated engineer of his generation. His steamboat that ran on schedule for several thousand miles at 6 to 8 miles an hour will always stand as one of the great monuments to human ingenuity.

Yet the very strengths of his character brought with them compensating weaknesses. Many writers have mourned that he was born too soon; had he come along a few years later, when the times were riper, he would, so they say, have been so clearly the inventor of the steamboat that controversy would be impossible. However, we may well wonder whether such an individual as he could ever be the final figure in the evolution of a great idea. Always Fitch had been unable to stay within the corral of conventional existence; from the first he was a fence jumper, seeking surcease in the lonely and the strange. His habitat was the wilderness, not the plowed field. Could such a man, like the designer of a city, build a new environment in which his fellow-men might live peacefully? Could he be a nice combiner of already established mechanisms, a propagandist who persuaded his contemporaries that the odd was really ordinary? Or was he predestined to be a lone scout on the frontier of progress, following a half-mad idea through derision to defeat? Had the steamboat evolved far enough in his lifetime to be at the point of success, he would probably have turned to some weirder, wilder dream.

After Fitch, steamboat achievement slumped for more than fifteen years, probably because the only new element that entered the

---

* We might note in passing that not a single professional sailor was active in the invention of the steamboat. From Jouffroy to Fulton, the projectors were all landlubbers; Fitch, indeed, was afraid of the water.

picture was unfruitful. American artisans like Morey worked by trial and error just as Fitch had done, while Symington picked up and dropped his project as waves of sophisticated British interest dictated. The one change was the appearance of rich aristocrats who, scorning to back the work of simpler men, set themselves up as inventors in their spare time. Being themselves incapable of working with their hands, they dreamed up theoretical schemes and employed menials to carry them out. At first their theories were thoroughly unscientific, based on uninhibited inspiration; then Stevens, at least, became interested in natural laws. With the assistance of his son Robert, whom he had trained to do as well as to think, he might have solved the problem before Fulton had he not turned his attention to high pressure. The principles on which he experimented were to become very useful, but at the time he struggled with them, they were mechanically impossible. Thus, this aspect of the Stevenses' work is not so much part of the practical invention of the steamboat as of the scientific prophecy of the high-pressure turbine engine.

Fulton has been criticized by a host of writers because he used other people's ideas; actually this was one of his great contributions. What steamboat evolution needed was not another self-appointed genius to go off at another inspired tangent, but someone to combine already existing knowledge into a mechanism that would work every time. Perhaps Fulton, who had more than his share of egotism, could not have been so self-abnegating if the steamboat had been the invention nearest his heart. All his belief in his own unique originality and power was concentrated on his submarine; the steamboat was merely a practical speculation from which he hoped to make money. Seeking short cuts that would enable him to get back as quickly as possible to his schemes for destroying navies, he took the logical course of studying the work of his predecessors. At last someone had appeared willing and able to bring to fruition the partial accomplishments of many brilliant men. That the individual details which made up his invention were all borrowed from others is a fact that qualifies but does not belittle his achievement.

Steamboat literature is full of the following argument: Fulton stole an important aspect of his machine—paddle wheels, proportions, what you will—from my candidate; therefore my candidate, not Fulton, was the inventor of the steamboat. This point of view is specious. Most of the details of Fulton's boat go back in a crude form for many generations. The paddle wheel, for instance, which is claimed for Jouffroy, Thornton, Roosevelt, Morey, Symington and others, was used by the Egyptians who probably borrowed it from even older cultures. Yet no individual who preceded Fulton was able to accomplish what he accomplished.

Having lived in America, England, and France, Fulton was able to combine the mechanical virtues of the Old World and the New. Thus while building for the commercial needs of the United States, and being as pragmatic and practical as his compatriots, he was wise enough to study basic principles. It is a remarkable tribute to the scientific method that it did not desert him although his initial conclusions were almost entirely wrong. The French boat that he had calculated would go more than 16 miles an hour went about 3 miles an hour. His addiction to formulas made this disappointment not a crushing blow but a discovery; he revised his figures according to the newly ascertained facts, and was further ahead than he had been before.

His first American boat was a crazy craft according to modern standards; inferior mechanically to Symington's *Charlotte Dundas* and slower than Fitch's steamboat of 1790. Mistakes in his abstract calculations had induced him to make it so long and thin that it was actually unsafe; his engine was cluttered up with needlessly complicated details. Yet, since he knew exactly what he had done and why he had done it, when a weakness showed up, he was able at once to put his finger on the trouble. Each failure was an experiment that carried him farther on the road to success. His last ship, the *Chancellor Livingston*, was immeasurably superior to the vessel which under the misnomer of the *Clermont* is popularly supposed to have all by itself represented the invention of the steamboat. Fulton's great contribution lay not in this early craft or in its successful trip to Albany, but in his ability to improve his design as he went along and to build effective steamboats at will. The principles upon which he moved were made so clear, both by his own efforts and by the general advance in engineering knowledge, that other designers were able to follow in his footsteps and do what he had done. Now at last the steamboat ceased to be a freak, a philosophical experiment; it became a practical method of transportation on which mankind could rely.

The face Fulton put up before the world undoubtedly contributed to his success; people were predisposed to take anything he did seriously, while they had been predisposed to despise Fitch. The earlier inventor had been regarded as a wicked blasphemer, while Fulton was thought of as almost a saint. This is a cynical commentary on man's reaction to man, for of the two Fitch was overwhelmingly more moral; his life was one long torture because he could not accept the contrast between the Puritan ideals he had been taught in his childhood and the world as he found it. He asked Providence for justice: good returned for good and evil for evil. When his better emotions paid off with pain and his worst sometimes with pleasure, he did not, like most of us, shrug his shoulders and say, "That is the way of the world; it is useless to fight against the way of the world." He refused to give up even a fragment of his high preconceptions; the result was bitterness and defeat. He became a member of several churches, and when all these failed him, tried in desperation to start a religion of his own. And the unslaked agony of his spirit drove him to the usual expedients of pain: he was cantankerous and vicious sometimes; sometimes he sought forgetfulness in drink. A man who is fighting destiny step by step for the establishment of abstract rights cannot expect to be a success in the easygoing world of compromisers, the world of ordinary men. At ease like Roman senators watching earlier Christian martyrs fighting more tangible lions, his contemporaries smiled disdainfully at the pauper whose elbows stuck out from his sleeves and whose toes showed through the front of his shoes. Fitch, they insisted, was an atheist, a drunkard, a lecher, and a madman. Many an argument has been written to show that he could not have invented the steamboat because he was too immoral.

Fulton went through no such public struggles. He too had started out as an idealist, but when he found that virtue did not pay adequate dividends, he discarded the substance of his idealism, preserving merely the façade. Following his worldly interest wherever it led him, even into exact contradiction of his professed principles, he stated over and over that everything he did was for the good of mankind. And because his conscience was more easily quieted than Fitch's, he was able to preserve before the world a grave and benevolent air. Clearly he was a virtuous man. And if further proof was needed, there was the fact of his success. Standards have reversed since the days of early Christianity: then poverty, rags, and a cave were visible proofs of piety. Now the good life is revealed by riches, fine clothes, and the possession of a mansion. Coming from humble beginnings, Fulton was wealthy and socially prominent.

When publicity men make up a roster of their heroes, they should give Fulton a prominent place, for he was a shining monument to the effectiveness of their craft. That he was an effective promoter, both of himself and his inventions, contributed greatly to the success of his steamboats.

His triumph, however, was by no means altogether his own doing; Fulton profited by the whole advance of the industrial revolution during the quarter century since Fitch. Mechanical principles were much more widely understood in his day than they had been before; he was able to make use of recently published scientific experiments, like those of Beaufroy, which Fitch could not have consulted even if he had wished to. Furthermore, the number of artisans skilled in dealing with machinery had tremendously increased. Where Fitch had had to rely on watchmakers and on tinsmiths more used to turning out kettles than boilers, Fulton had little difficulty, even in America, collecting workmen with mechanical experience. The materials he needed were much more prevalent than they had been in Fitch's day, for they were more in use.

Perhaps Fulton's greatest asset was the fact that a multitude of tiny changes, millions of untraceable influences acting on millions of anonymous minds, had finally prepared the public to accept the gifts brought by the industrial revolution. Invention and improvement had been progressively invading the world of the common man. The cotton gin, a simple device capable of being built by any blacksmith, was manifestly remaking the economy of the South. Smoke from tall chimneys darkened many landscapes as factories multiplied. Strange cheap fabrics were appearing on the counters of the smallest country stores. The time had come when ordinary citizens were ready to trust even their persons to the stentorian efficiency of machines.

Faced with a new idea, mankind behaves like a flock of chickens when offered a new food. The silly birds run to the far end of the cage as soon as the strange mixture is placed before them. There in the corner they huddle and cluck. Then curiosity begins to appear. Long necks are craned, still from the far corner. Finally a hardy bird makes a step toward the pail, while the others watch disapprovingly; the pail remains motionless, but the hardy bird suddenly shies violently and jumps backward, starting panic in the flock. "He got closer than anybody," you can hear the fowls clucking; "he is an expert, and even he says that pail is dangerous!"

Now come a long series of sorties and retreats, seemingly random motion, but at the end of this period of confusion the birds stand in a circle around the rim of the pail. A proud note mixes with the excited terror of their squawking. "We are very modern," you hear them say, "very open minded. Look at us; here we stand at the rim of this strange pail." But when a daring individual inclines his head as if to eat, his neighbor pecks him violently, and they all return in self-righteousness to their corner. So it goes until one actually gets a mouthful; he spits it out, while the others nod wisely, clucking, "We always knew it was poison." From time to time one or another reaches in and spits out, until at last a hardy individual swallows. Others gradually follow his example; we have entered the great cultural period of cautious swallowing. This continues until suddenly there is a riot, everyone trying to eat at once; they trample one another and snatch from each other's beaks. The invention is now complete.

Fitch was a first swallower, and as such was justly punished by society for his immorality. After him others swallowed too: Livingston and Stevens and Morey and Ormsbee and Stanhope and Symington. When Fulton put his beak in the pail and pulled out a morsel very like those of his predecessors, the riot of acceptance was almost ready to begin. Although it still took a hardy individual to ride on his steamboats, he did not have to be half as hardy as the ones who had ridden in Fitch's. Thus Fulton's vessel paid a profit.

And, of course, it was the paying of a profit that made the invention complete. In fact, it could be argued that in a capitalist society dividends are the most effective gauge of the development of any idea whose success rests on public support. Scan the ledgers of the promoters, and when red ink at last gives way to black, you will know that history has taken a step forward.

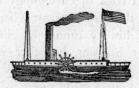

Now that the whole story has been told, we still face the question of who was the inventor of the steamboat. The answer, of course, depends on what you mean by "inventor." Since applied science has triumphed so completely that it has become the core of our culture, the word has taken on a mystical significance: inventors are the saints of our materialistic philosophy. They are conceived in popular legend as great geniuses creating something out of nothing; semi-divine individuals who, like Prometheus bringing fire down from heaven, give the world a boon altogether new. There is no such inventor in the history of the steamboat; indeed it is safe to say that there has not been a single one in the history of the world.

As we have seen, the steamboat evolved out of the consciousnesses of many men, out of a great shift in the whole status of mankind. Not one of the many historical influences that shape changes in civilization failed to have its impact on this development. Like a herd of buffalo stampeding across a prairie, mankind moves through time in a body, and all that can be said of any one individual is that he was half a step ahead.

The term inventor then has a meaning only if taken in the sense of a man who was slightly in advance of the procession at the crucial moment when his civilization was already on the verge of the discovery he was about to make. Like the winner of a race, he is the first individual to step over the line that separates practical invention from improved application. Before him, the discovery was still a partially realized aspiration; after him, it is a reality so well established that its use is continual, without any break.

The inventor is not necessarily the most original or the most able or the most admirable man entered in the race; he is more likely to be a follower than a leader, since leaders usually beat their brains out against a stone wall of inertia and prejudice. The inventor's eminence may be more a trick of chronology than anything else, due to his being active at the very moment when fruition became possible. Yet the facts of history cannot be changed. The poor devils before him, however brilliant, however worthy, went down as martyrs, because the times were not ready to receive and perfect their gift. Running a course made easier by the agony of his predecessors, the inventor crosses the finish line, triumphant and smiling.

According to this definition, popular history is correct: Robert Fulton was the inventor of the steamboat. Whether this means he was the most creative and the most useful man connected with the invention, the reader may decide for himself.

Appendix A

BIBLIOGRAPHY
OF PRINCIPAL SOURCES

This annotated bibliography, which lists only the most important sources consulted, serves a double purpose. The general reader may find here volumes and collections that will give him further insight into the invention of the steamboat. Furthermore, each item is preceded by the key word, set in capitals and small capitals, and enclosed in brackets, with which it will be designated in the more complete reference notes contained in Appendix B.

JOHN FITCH

Fitch's autobiographical papers, written during the winter of 1790-91 and deposited with the Library Company of Philadelphia, have served as the backbone of all subsequent accounts of his career. I was enabled to consult these documents through the kindness of C. Newbold Taylor, president of the Library Company, and Austin K. Gray, its librarian, who exhumed them from the vault where they were hidden for protection against air raids, and sent them to the Yale Library for my convenience. The papers consist of:

[AUTOBIOGRAPHY] Fitch's account of the more personal aspects of his life, occupying a notebook and a half.

[HISTORY] Fitch's account of his steamboat experiments, occupying three and a half notebooks. The Fitch papers also include another notebook, separately paged, in which he made a clean copy of his formal appeal to the patent commissioners.

The other major sources of information about Fitch are as follows:

[THORNTON PAPERS] The files of Fitch's patron, Dr. William Thornton, which are in the Library of Congress, contain documents dealing with the inventor's later years. Since this material has been withdraw from circulation as a wartime precaution, I have been unable to consult the originals. I have picked up what I could from secondary sources.

[ORIGINAL] Fitch, John, *The Original Steamboat Supported, or a Reply to Mr. James Rumsey's pamphlet*, Phila., 1788. As the first edition of this important publication is rare, I have given in the reference notes the paging of the reprint in *The Documentary History of the State of New York*, Albany, 1849.

[WHITTLESEY] Whittlesey, Charles, "John Fitch": in Sparks, Jared, *The Library of American Biography*, 2 ser., VI, Boston, 1847. This, the earliest life of Fitch, is based on a cursory study of the Library Company papers. Its principal interest today lies in the extracts from letters and few bits of personal information which the author seems to have secured from Fitch's children. In addition to this book, Whittlesey published several other accounts of Fitch, but they add nothing material to the record.

[WESTCOTT] Westcott, Thompson, *The Life of John Fitch*, Phila., 1857. This meticulous scholar paraphrased voluminously from the Library Company papers, and added much material gleaned from other sources. An indispensable work.

[BOYD] Boyd, Thomas, *Poor John Fitch*, Putnam's, N.Y., 1935. Boyd paints Fitch as a man of the people martyred by the upper classes. He is interesting about his hero's character and quotes voluminously from the autobiographical writings. Through the courtesy of Ruth Fitch Boyd and G. P. Putnam's Sons, I have repeated some of the Thornton documents from Boyd's pages.

JAMES RUMSEY

Most of the important manuscript material dealing with Rumsey has been reprinted in various scholarly publications.

[MARYLAND] Rumsey documents in the Library of Congress, including items from the Washington and Jefferson papers and the Rumsey collection, are reprinted in *Maryland Historical Magazine*, XXXII, Balt., 1937, pp. 10-28, 136-55, 271-85. The notes by James A. Padgett are unreliable.

[W. & M.] A reprinting of documents included in the record of a suit brought by Dr. James McMechen against Rumsey's executor, Edward Rumsey, for settlement of alleged indebtedness, before High Court of Chancery, Staunton, Virginia, March 1800. In *William and Mary Quarterly*, 1 ser., XXIV, 1915-16, Williamstown, Va., pp. 154-74, 239-51; and XXV, 1916-17, pp. 21-34.

[TURNER] Turner, Maria, *James Rumsey, Pioneer in Steam Navigation*, Mennonite Publishing House, Scottsdale, Penn., 1930. An excellent scholarly life, which brings together under one cover the important source material on Rumsey.

[TREATISE] Rumsey, James, *A Short Treatise on the Application of Steam, Whereby is Clearly Shown by Actual Experiment that Steam may be Applied to Propel Boats or Vessels Against the Current with Great Velocity . . .* , Phila., 1788. This is the Philadelphia edition of Rumsey's pamphlet attacking Fitch. Since copies are extremely hard to find, in my reference notes I have given the paging of the reprint in *The Documentary History of the State of New York*, Albany, 1849.

[REMARKS] Barnes, Joseph, *Remarks on Mr. John Fitch's Reply to Mr. James Rumsey's Pamphlet*, Phila., 1788. The paging in my reference notes refers to the reprint in *The Magazine of History with Notes and Queries*, extra number 39, XXXIX, Tarrytown, N.Y., 1928.

ROBERT R. LIVINGSTON

Despite his important contribution to many aspects of American history, no good life exists of Robert R. Livingston. The most important sources concerning his steamboat experiments are:

[LIVINGSTON] Anonymous (generally admitted to be the work of Livingston, Robert R.), "An historical account of the application of steam to the propelling of boats," in *American Medical and Philosophical Register*, II, N.Y., 1812.

[ROOSEVELT PAPERS] The manuscripts of Livingston's correspondence about steamboats with Nicholas J. Roosevelt are deposited in the New-York Historical Society. That organization has kindly permitted me to quote from these documents and many others in their collection.

JOHN STEVENS, JR.

[STEVENS PAPERS] A marvelously full collection of documents dealing with many members of the Stevens family is deposited in the Stevens Institute, Hoboken, N. J. The W.P.A. Historical Records Survey started out to publish a register of these papers. Their detailed study never got as far as John Stevens' steamboat experiments, and as they worked they scrambled the documents so grievously that it is now almost impossible to find a specific paper. The Records Survey did bring out a list of the highlights of the collection that skimmed through the steamboat years: U.S.W.P.A., *Calendar of the Stevens Family Papers*, mimeographed, Hoboken, 1940. This volume is so inaccurate that no reliance may be placed upon it.

[TURNBULL] Turnbull, Archibald Douglas, *John Stevens, an American Record*, Century, N.Y., 1928. Based on the Stevens Papers, this volume deals with the careers of many members of the famous family. Unfortunately the author has often quoted important documents without giving the dates and other necessary information.

[STEVENS LETTER] Stevens, John, Jr., "A Letter Relative to Steamboats," in

American Medical and Philosophical Register, II, N.Y., 1812. This answer to Livingston's article in the same periodical contains Stevens' own account of his steamboat experiments.

ROBERT FULTON

Since Fulton's papers have been widely scattered among members of his family, institutions, and private buyers, I shall not attempt to list here the collections I have consulted. Exact references for each passage quoted will be found in Appendix B. The most important published sources for Robert Fulton are as follows:

[DICKINSON] Dickinson, Henry Winram, *Robert Fulton, Engineer and Artist, His Life and Works*, John Lane, London, 1913. This scholarly life, the work of a distinguished British historian of engineering, reveals less interest in Fulton's character than in his mechanical achievements. It is, however, basic and of great importance.

[SUTCLIFFE I] Sutcliffe, Alice Crary, *Robert Fulton and the "Clermont,"* Century, N.Y., 1909. Written by a descendant of Fulton's, this biography is weighted just the other way from Dickinson's. The author is less concerned with mechanical problems than with depicting her hero as a charming and moral man. Her valuable book contains many important documents which are or have been in the possession of the Fulton family. I have quoted from this volume, and the one listed below, by kind permission of the author.

[SUTCLIFFE II] Sutcliffe, Alice Crary, *Robert Fulton*, Macmillan, N.Y., 1915. Although designed primarily for children, this biography contains some material, particularly Fulton's letters to his mother, which Mrs. Sutcliffe did not include in her other volume.

[COLDEN] Colden, Cadwallader David, *The Life of Robert Fulton*, N.Y., 1817. This early life of Fulton was written by a close friend who had invested all his savings in the steamboat company. Thus we need not be surprised that Colden cites no uncomplimentary facts which might be useful to the enemies of the monopoly. Yet his book contains much contemporary material of interest.

[DELAPLAINE] Delaplaine, Joseph, "Life of Robert Fulton," in *Delaplaine's Repository of Lives and Portraits of Distinguished American Characters*, I, Phila., 1815-16 [?]. Although bearing a date earlier than Colden's book, this account appears to be largely a rewrite of Colden. It contains a few additions of great interest.

[REIGERT] Reigert, J. Franklin, *The Life of Robert Fulton*, Phila., 1856. This biography, by a highly imaginative author, is the source of most of the legends about Fulton's early years which, despite their complete lack of foundation, seem to have an indestructible vitality.

A score or more other lives of Fulton exist on every scale from brief sketches to heavy-looking tomes. They are rewrite jobs, of little importance. Where I have gleaned material from their pages, that fact is noted in the source references.

Concerning Fulton's submarines there are two basic sources:

[PESCE] Pesce, G. L., *La Navigation Sous-Marine*, Paris, 1906. Pesce gives an excellent account of Fulton's experiments and negotiations in France, quoting in full most of the relevant documents.

[PARSONS] The William Barclay Parsons Collection in the New York Public Library contains an important group of original Fulton manuscripts, as well as photostats and transcripts of manuscripts in other collections. The bulk of this material deals with Fulton's submarine efforts in England, taking up the story where Pesce leaves off. Mr. Parsons published most of the material in his book *Robert Fulton and the Submarine*, N.Y., Columbia University Press, 1922. For the convenience of readers who do not have access to the New York Public Library, I have in my source references cited the paging of Parson's reprints.

Appendix B

NOTES TO THE TEXT

Those notes which contain further material than simple source references have been indicated by numbers in the text; they will be found here arranged according to chapters. The notes are followed, under each chapter heading, by the source references, which are located by page and paragraph number, the numbers referring to the place where the paragraph ends. Books or collections of papers quoted many times are indicated by key words, the complete reference for which will be found in Appendix A. (See, for example, the key word reference in Appendix A: [AUTOBIOGRAPHY] Fitch's account of the more personal aspects of his life, . . .) Not hesitating to sacrifice consistency to usefulness, I have sometimes substituted brief bibliographies for source references, correlated exactly with the text.

Although it has meant the omission of many publications and documents where I found stray bits of information, I have limited myself to giving the sources of material actually quoted. This compromise, which has cut the length of this appendix by more than half, was made desirable by the wartime shortage of paper.

PROLOGUE

p. 2, ¶3. *Westcott,* p. 366.

CHAPTER I   BIBLIOGRAPHY

Many lists have been made of early suggestions that steam engines be floated on boats. None are complete, and it is not likely that a complete list will ever be made. From the time of the fountain engine, the idea sprang into a myriad minds. Indeed, a little digging into the history of any region will turn up new names and new proposals.

The discussions of the beginnings of the steam engine and the steamboat which I have found most useful are:

Chatterton, Edward Kemble, *Steamships and their Story,* Lond. & N.Y., 1910.
Figuier, Louis, *Les Merveilles de la Science,* I, Paris, 1867.
Gilfillan, S. C., *Inventing the Ship,* Follette Pub. Co., Chicago, 1935.
Preble, George Henry, *A Chronological History of the Origin and Development of Steam Navigation,* Phila., 1895.
Thurston, Robert H., *A History of the Growth of the Steam Engine,* N.Y., 1878.
Usher, Abbott Payson, *A History of Mechanical Inventions,* McGraw-Hill, N.Y., 1929.

CHAPTER II   TEXT NOTE

1. That Fitch was a skillful silversmith is indicated by the pieces signed with his mark that have come down to us, but not enough such examples have survived to account for the extensive business he claims to have had. This, plus the fact that some of his journeymen were expert artisans in their own right, raises the question whether his place in the workshop was not less that of a master craftsman than of capitalist and salesman. It was correct silversmithing practice for journeymen to use their own marks, even when

employed by another. If Fitch's role was really that of business man and promoter, he was pioneering in a type of craft organization that did not become common until later in American history.

CHAPTER II   SOURCE REFERENCES

Quotations not otherwise referred to come from AUTOBIOGRAPHY, pp. 1-64.
p. 30, ¶3. Fitch's account book in coll. Hist. Soc. of Penna.
p. 32, ¶1. WHITTLESEY, pp. 98-101.
p. 34, ¶2. HISTORY, pp. 103-4.

CHAPTER III   TEXT NOTES

1. The Périers did not receive their exclusive privilege to pump water for Paris until October 25, 1776, and they did not actually organize a company until August 27, 1778. Even at the later date they failed to appreciate the advantages of a Watt engine, for when J. C. Périer went to England in 1779 it was with the intention of buying an atmospheric engine. During his stay in that mechanically advanced country, he finally became convinced of the superiority of the separate condensor. He ordered parts from Boulton and Watt. When they were delivered is not entirely clear, but the engine was not put in operation in Paris until July 1782, some five years after Jouffroy had come to Paris and the Périers had made their experiment with steam navigation. (Figuier, Louis, *Les Eaux de Paris*, Paris, 1862. *Mémoire sur les Eaux de Paris Presenté à la Commission Municipale par M. le Préfect de la Seine*, Paris, 1854. Muirhead, James Patrick, *The Life of James Watt*, N.Y., 1859. Dickinson, Henry Winram, *James Watt, Craftsman and Engineer*, Cambridge, Eng., 1936.)

2. Even authors who state that Jouffroy used a Watt engine show when describing the working of his machine that the injection water was thrown not into a separate vessel but into the cylinder itself. Jouffroy's son wrote: "A l'extrémité inférieure de les cylindres leurs fonds étaient réunis par une bôite de métal renfermant une toile ou tiroir et fermait alternativement le passage de la vapeur dans chaque cylindre, et celui de l'eau d'injection." He later states that at the same moment when steam entered one of the twin cylinders, the injection water was thrown into the other. (Jouffroy-d'Abbans, Achille-François, p. 18; see below.)

CHAPTER III   BIBLIOGRAPHY

French Experiments

Ducrest, Charles Louis, *Essai sur les Machine Hydrauliques*, Paris, 1777.
Figuier, Louis, *Les Merveilles de la Science*, I, Paris, 1867.
Jouffroy-d'Abbans, Achille-François, *Des Bateaux à Vapeur*, Paris, 1841.
Marestier, Jean Baptiste, *Mémoire sur Les Bateaux à Vapeur des Etats Unis d'Amerique*, Paris, 1824.
Nouvelle Biographie Générale, Paris, 1855-66.

William Henry

Harris, Alexander, *A Biographical History of Lancaster County*, Lancaster, 1872.
HISTORY, pp. 8, 35.
Jordan, Francis, *The Life of William Henry of Lancaster, Pennsylvania, 1729-1786*, Lancaster, 1910.
Lancaster County Hist. Soc. Papers, I, 1896-97, pp. 70-71; VI, 1901, pp. 61; XI, 1906, pp. 306-22; XVI, 1912, p. 156; XXVII, 1923, p. 91.
Lancaster Daily Express, Dec. 10, 1872. (This seems to be the source of the

erroneous story that Henry actually built a steamboat.)
ORIGINAL, pp. 1042, 1078.

CHAPTER IV   SOURCE REFERENCES

Quotations not otherwise referred to come from AUTOBIOGRAPHY, pp. 64-104.
p. 59, ¶1. WHITTLESEY, p. 100.

CHAPTER V   TEXT NOTE

1. Rumsey's pole boat was an attempt to imitate mechanically the common
method by which manpower was used to drive vessels up rapid rivers. Crews
of from four to ten men walked toward the sterns of their keel boats on
"running boards," pushing with their shoulders on poles set in the bottom of
the stream. Then while one or two men held the vessel stationary, the rest
lifted their poles, returned to the bow, and repeated the operation.
    Rumsey was not the first to attempt to make the current drive craft up-
stream. The Marquis of Worcester wrote in 1663: "I can make a vessel of
as great a burden as the river can bear to go against the stream, which
the more rapid it is, the faster it shall advance, and the moveable part that
works it may be by one man still guided to take advantage of the stream."
(Preble, George Henry, *A Chronological History of the Origin and Development of Steam Navigation*, Phila., 1895, p. 13.)
    Jonathan Hulls suggested that on shallow rivers setting poles might be
substituted on steamboats for paddle wheels.
    Fitch insisted that Rumsey's pole-boat scheme "was many years ago tried
on the river Schuylkill by a farmer near Reading, but without success."
(ORIGINAL, p. 1046.) Although Rumsey may well have conceived of the
idea for himself, the basic conception was undoubtedly a very old one.

CHAPTER V   SOURCE REFERENCES

p. 64, ¶2. Washington to Richard Henry Lee, Aug. 22, 1785: in Bacon-Foster,
Corra, *The Potomac Route to the West*, Wash., 1912, pp. 157-58.
p. 65, ¶1. Jefferson to Washington, Mar. 6, 1784: in Bacon-Foster, *op. cit.*, p. 128.
p. 65, ¶2. Washington to Jefferson, Mar. 29, 1784: in Bacon-Foster, *op. cit.*, pp.
129-30.
p. 67, ¶1. Washington's diary for Sept. 4, 1784: in Bacon-Foster, *op. cit.*, p. 133.
p. 67, ¶2. *Maryland Gazette*, June 19, 1784: in Gardiner, Mabel Henshaw, &
Gardiner, Ann Henshaw, *Chronicles of Old Berkeley*, Durham, N. C., 1928, p. 53.
p. 67, ¶3. Asbury, the Rev. Francis, *Journal*, N.Y., 1821, II, p. 53.
p. 67, ¶4. *Maryland Gazette*, June 13, 1784: in Gardiner, *op. cit.*, p. 52.
p. 69, ¶1. Dated Sept. 7, 1784: in Fitzpatrick, John C., editor, *The Writings of
George Washington*, Wash., 1931-41, XXVII, p. 468.
p. 69, ¶2. Note for Oct. 4, 1784: in Fitzpatrick, John C., editor, *The Diaries of
George Washington*, Bost. & N.Y., 1925, pp. 327-28.
p. 69, ¶3. TURNER, p. 15.
p. 70, ¶1. Affidavit of Michael Bedinger, Nov. 28, 1787: in TREATISE, pp.
1031-32. Washington to Thomas Jefferson, Nov. 22, 1787: in Fitzpatrick, *Writings, op. cit.*, XXIX, p. 319.
p. 70, ¶2. TREATISE, p. 1014.
p. 70, ¶3. John Marshall to Judge Muter, Jan. 7, 1785: in House of Representatives, 29th Cong., 1st session, *Committee Report 403*, Wash., 1846, pp. 23-24.
Rumsey to Washington, Oct. 18, 1784: in MARYLAND, pp. 14-15.
p. 72, ¶3. TREATISE, p. 1014. Deposition of Nicholas Orrick, May 19, 1788: in
REMARKS, p. 109.
p. 73, ¶1-2. Rumsey to Washington, Nov. 10, 1785: in MARYLAND, pp. 18-19.

p. 74, ¶2. Washington to Rumsey, June 5, 1785: in Fitzpatrick, *Writings, op cit.,* XXVIII, p. 160.

CHAPTER VI SOURCE REFERENCES

p. 75, ¶1-2. AUTOBIOGRAPHY, p. 109.
p. 76, ¶1. Phillips, Phillip Lee, *A Rare Map of the Northwest, 1785, by John Fitch, Inventor of the Steamboat,* Wash., 1916.
p. 76, ¶2. AUTOBIOGRAPHY, pp. 111-12. HISTORY, p. 1. ORIGINAL, p. 1078.
p. 77, ¶1. HISTORY, p. 2. AUTOBIOGRAPHY, p. 12.
p. 78, ¶3. ORIGINAL, p. 1041.
p. 78, ¶4. HISTORY, pp. 3, 115-16.
p. 79, ¶1. William C. Houston to Lambert Cadwallader, Aug. 25, 1785: in HISTORY, p. 4.
p. 79, ¶3-5. HISTORY, pp. 129-30.
p. 80, ¶1. HISTORY, p. 89.
p. 80, ¶2-p. 81, ¶1. HISTORY, pp. 6-7.
p. 81, ¶3. HISTORY, p. 8. WESCOTT, p. 132.
p. 82, ¶2. Fitch to Franklin, Oct. 12, 1785: in coll. Am. Philos. Soc.
p. 83, ¶1-3. HISTORY, pp. 8, 35. ORIGINAL, pp. 1042, 1078.
p. 84, ¶2-p. 85, ¶2. HISTORY, p. 9. Washington to Thomas Johnson, Nov. 22, 1787: in Fitzpatrick, *Writings, op. cit.,* XXIX, p. 320. ORIGINAL, p. 1043.
p. 85, ¶4. Washington to Johnson, *op. cit.*
p. 86, ¶1. Fitzpatrick, *Writings, op. cit.,* XXVIII, p. 374.

CHAPTER VII TEXT NOTES

1. As is to be expected, the idea of making a boat move by driving water out of its stern had been suggested many times. In 1730, for instance, John Allen not only recommended that a pump be used for this purpose, but remarked that it could be linked to a Newcomen engine. However, Rumsey was to state that the idea was altogether original with him; he did not borrow it from Franklin or anyone else.
   Pump propulsion is sometimes still used on lifeboats, as screws or wheels are likely to injure survivors swimming in the water.
2. The membership of Fitch's steamboat company seems to have shifted with considerable rapidity. BOYD (p. 153) gives the following list for April 1786: Richard Wells, merchant and later cashier of the Bank of North America; Benjamin Morris, retailer of wines and groceries; Joseph Budd, hatter; Magnus Miller, Israel Israels, John and Chamless Hart, Thomas Palmer, and Gideon Wells, merchants or tavern keepers; Thomas Say, gentleman; Thomas Hutchins, geographer general of the United States; Richard Stockton, lawyer; Doctors John Morris and Benjamin Say; Edward Brooks, ironmonger, and Stacy Potts, Quaker farmer.
   In the collection of the Historical Society of Pennsylvania there is a document dated April 19, 1786, containing the names of sixteen members of the company. Of these, the following are not in BOYD's list: Fitch and Voight; Benjamin Wistar; James Wilson, lawyer and statesman; Robert Scott, engraver; Samuel Wetherille, Jr., druggist; and James [?] Vaughan.
3. The Potomac Canal project proved so far beyond the engineering possibilities of the time that it was eventually abandoned.

CHAPTER VII SOURCE REFERENCES

p. 87, ¶2. Washington to Edmund Randolph, Sept. 16, 1785: in Bacon-Foster, *op. cit.,* p. 160. Rumsey to Washington, Dec. 17, 1787: in MARYLAND, p. 138.

p. 88, ¶1. Washington to Rumsey, July 2, 1785: in Fitzpatrick, *Diaries, op. cit.*, II, pp. 189-90.

p. 88, ¶2. Rumsey to Washington, Dec. 17, 1787: in MARYLAND, p. 138.

p. 89, ¶3. Affidavit of Francis Hamilton, May 17, 1788: in REMARKS, pp. 104-5.

p. 90, ¶1. TREATISE, p. 86.

p. 90, ¶3. HISTORY, p. 12. ORIGINAL, pp. 1044-45.

p. 91, ¶2-3. Franklin, "Letter to David Le Roy," in Bigelow, John, editor, *The Complete Works of Benjamin Franklin*, N.Y., 1888, IX, pp. 173-74. HISTORY, p. 8.

p. 92, ¶2. HISTORY, pp. 191, 132-33.

p. 92, ¶3. HISTORY, pp. 14-15, 130-31.

p. 93, ¶2. HISTORY, pp. 11-12, 130.

p. 93, ¶3. HISTORY, pp. 15-16.

p. 94, ¶1-2. HISTORY, pp. 201-3.

p. 95, ¶1. HISTORY, p. 19.

p. 95, ¶2. HISTORY, p. 21.

p. 96, ¶2. HISTORY, p. 22.

p. 97, ¶3. Barnes affidavit, Dec. 10, 1787: in TREATISE, p. 1029.

p. 98, ¶1. Hamilton affidavit, *op. cit.* Jefferson to Dr. Willard, Mar. 24, 1789: in Jefferson, Thomas, *Writings*, Wash., 1904, VII, p. 328.

p. 98, ¶2. Fitzpatrick, *Diaries, op. cit.*, III, p. 122.

p. 98, ¶3. Rumsey to Washington, Sept. 19, 1786: in MARYLAND, pp. 136-37.

p. 99, ¶3. Rumsey to Washington, Dec. 17, 1787: in MARYLAND, p. 140.

CHAPTER VIII   TEXT NOTES

1. Every engineering idea is likely to have a long history; Fitch's crank and paddle scheme is no exception. In 1678 Edward Bushnell described a similar device to be motivated by men turning a capstan.
2. WESTCOTT (pp. 183-85) gives the following list of members of the reorganized steamboat company; the numbers refer to the number of shares held. Samuel Vaughan, merchant, 1; Richard Wells, merchant, 1; Richard Wells, Jr., son of the preceding, 1; Gideon Hill Wells, merchant, 1; Benjamin W. Morris, wine merchant and grocer, 1; Joseph Budd, hatter, 1; Benjamin Say, physician, 2; Thomas Say, gentleman, 1; Richard Stockton, lawyer and statesman, 3; Magnus Miller, merchant, 1; John Morris, physician, 1; John and Chamless Hart, merchants, 1; Thomas Hutchins, geographer, 1; John Strother, protégé of Richard Stockton, 1; Israel Israels, innkeeper, 1; William Reubel, no information, 1; Edward Brooks, Jr., ironmonger, 1; Henry Toland, grocer, 1; Thomas Palmer, merchant, 1; Voight, 5; and Fitch, 13.

   Fitch tells us that some three years later, in 1790, the company was made up for the following members: Richard Wells; Benjamin Say; William Thornton, gentleman and practitioner of many arts; Thomas Say; Joseph Budd; Benjamin W. Morris; Israel Israels; Gideon Wells; Edward Brooks; John Hart, soldier; Magnus Miller; Samuel Vaughan; Henry Tolland; William Rubel; Wood Lloyd; Voight; and Fitch. Among these men the only ones who did not at some time withdraw or show great backwardness in paying levies were Richard Wells, Benjamin and Thomas Say, Edward Brooks, and Israel Israels. (HISTORY, p. 115.)

CHAPTER VIII   SOURCE REFERENCES

p. 100, ¶1-2. HISTORY, p. 22.

p. 101, ¶1. HISTORY, p. 23.

p. 102, ¶2. Voight, petition to Washington for appointment in mint, Jan. 5, 1791: in HISTORY, p. 221. Voight, petition to Pennsylvania Legislature, Sept. 6, 1788: in *Documentary History of the State of New York*, Albany, 1849, p. 1082.

p. 102, ¶3. *Freeman's Journal*, April 29, 1789: in Prime, Alfred Cox, *The Arts and Crafts in Philadelphia, Maryland and South Carolina*, Topsfield, Mass., 1929-32, II, p. 269.

p. 103, ¶1. WESTCOTT, p. 157. AUTOBIOGRAPHY, p. 114.

p. 103, ¶2. HISTORY, p. 196.

p. 103, ¶3. Bathe, Greville, *American Engineers Miscellany*, Phila., privately printed, 1938, p. 44.

p. 103, ¶4. HISTORY, p. 23.

p. 104, ¶2. Fitch to Franklin, Sept. 4, 1796: in WESTCOTT, p. 162.

p. 105, ¶2–p. 106, ¶1. AUTOBIOGRAPHY, p. 116.

p. 106, ¶3. Fitch to Potts, July 28, 1786, ms. in coll. N.Y. Hist. Soc.

p. 106, ¶4–p. 107, ¶1. Potts to Fitch, Sept. 2, 1786, ms. in coll. N.Y. Hist. Soc. HISTORY, pp. 40-41.

p. 107, ¶2-3. HISTORY, pp. 24-26.

p. 109, ¶1-2. *Columbian Magazine*, Jan. 1787.

CHAPTER IX   TEXT NOTES

1. All the lives of Fulton give the date of his father's death as 1768; this is a fallacy. Eleanore J. Fulton in her *An Index to the Will Books and Intestate Records of Lancaster County*, Lancaster, 1936, states that the elder Robert died intestate in 1774. This date is borne out by a letter in the Register's Office, Lancaster, from Mary Fulton, Sept. 16, 1774, in which she renounces administration of the estate of Robert Fulton, deceased, in favor of Henry Helm. In the same year, Helm appeared before the overseers of the poor, asking them to assume responsibility for Samuel Chapman, an eleven-year-old pauper who was in 1772 apprenticed to Fulton, to learn tailoring. The estate, Helm explained, had failed to bind him elsewhere, and did not have funds to continue his apprenticeship. (*Penn. Mag. of Hist. and Biog.*, 1880, IV, pp. 130-32.)

2. We are told that West's father was a near neighbor and friend of the elder Fulton; according to the travel conditions of the time, they lived two days' journey apart. A pair of canvases purporting to represent Robert's parents have come to light, signed "B. West 175—." The signatures cannot be authentic, since West's early work is never signed, since the canvases in question bear no relation to his style, and since the costumes of the sitters date well after West had gone to Europe, never to return. Fulton's sister was to marry West's nephew, but that was not till some years after Fulton had left Lancaster.

3. During his years as a miniature painter in Philadelphia, Fulton was an obscure artisan. There was no more reason why his sitters should record the name of the young man who painted their likenesses than there is for us to treasure the identity of the journeyman photographers who snap our portraits. And Fulton, following the custom of the time, did not sign his work.

   Years later, after he had become famous in another line, pictures by him took on a value that was entirely independent of their artistic merit. The temptation to attribute portraits to him became strong, not only for dealers but also for descendants. It is an axiom of "family tradition," that great source of error, that it strives for higher things. We all of us have maiden aunts who are convinced their line comes from all the kings of England. The same psychological process attributes ancestral portraits to well-known artists. We need not be surprised then that many pictures are ascribed to Fulton's Philadelphia period, that they are mutually contradictory, and that it is very difficult to be sure which, if any, are actually by his hand.

4. Later in the same year, on September 18, 1786, Fulton bought three lots in the town of Washington for a down payment of £15 and an agreement to pay £1.2/6 a year in perpetuity. The lots, which were given to his sisters,

seem to have been part of the same general family arrangement that resulted in the purchase of a farm for his mother.

CHAPTER IX   SOURCE REFERENCES

p. 111, ¶1. Account Books of James Fullton, in coll. Dr. John F. Fulton, New Haven.
p. 113, ¶1. Watson, John F., *Annals of Philadelphia and Pennsylvania*, Phila., 1857, II, p. 450.
p. 113, ¶3. Information in letter from Robert C. Latimer to author, Mar. 9, 1942.
p. 115, ¶2. DELAPLAINE, p. 201.
p. 116, ¶1. Prime, *op. cit.*, I, p. 42.
p. 118, ¶3. Dr. David Hosack to Colden, Jan. 1, 1817: in COLDEN, p. 262.
p. 118, ¶4. REIGERT, p. 40.
p. 119, ¶2. Renwick, James, "Life of Robert Fulton," in Sparks, Jared, ed., *The Library of American Biography*, X, Bost., 1839, p. 13.
p. 120, ¶1. *Penn. Packet*, June 5, 1786: in Prime, *op. cit.*, II, pp. 12-13. *Penn. Mag. of Hist. and Biog.*, Phila., 1899, XXIII, pp. 83-84.

CHAPTER X   SOURCE REFERENCES

p. 122, ¶2. HISTORY, p. 41.
p. 123, ¶1. HISTORY, pp. 41-42.
p. 123, ¶2–p. 125, ¶1. HISTORY, pp. 56, 42-45.
p. 126, ¶1. HISTORY, p. 47.
p. 126, ¶3. HISTORY, p. 47. Stiles, Ezra, *The Literary Diary of Ezra Stiles*, 1901, N.Y., III, p. 279.
p. 127, ¶2. HISTORY, p. 48.
p. 128, ¶1. TREATISE, p. 1016.
p. 129, ¶2. Barnes affidavit, Dec. 10, 1787: in TREATISE, p. 1029.
p. 129, ¶4. Account by A. R. Boteler, quoted in Beltzhoover, George M. Jr., *James Rumsey, the Inventor of the Steamboat*, West Vir. Hist. and Antiquarian Soc., 1900, pp. 16-18, based in part on letter from Henry Bedinger to Peter H. Cookus, May 12, 1836. Bedinger's ungarnished letter was published in House of Representatives, 29th Congress, 1st Session, *Committee Report 403*, Wash., 1846, pp. 10-13.
p. 131, ¶2. Certificates of Horatio Gates, the Rev. Robert Stubbs, etc., Dec. 3, 1787: in TREATISE, pp. 1020-23.
p. 132, ¶1. Certificates of Moses Hogf, John Morrow, Cornel Wynkoop, Benoni Swearingen, and James Swearingen, Dec. 13, 1787: in TREATISE, pp. 1022-23. *Virginia Gazette and Winchester Advertiser*, Jan. 11, 1788.

CHAPTER XI   TEXT NOTES

1. Rumsey had stated that during the fall of 1785 he had secured some copper work for his steamboat at Frederickstown and some brass cocks in Baltimore; Fitch tried to prove that this machinery was not made until the spring of 1786. Let us first examine the evidence concerning the Frederickstown work, which was done by Mathias Zimmers. I shall summarize the statements of each witness as given both in Fitch's publication and Barnes' reply.
   a. Elizabeth Zimmers, widow of Mathias, certified that no account book existed in which to ascertain the exact date that her husband had worked for Rumsey. She added that "to the best of my knowledge Michael Baltzel turned the works to finish the first machinery said Rumsey had of my husband." (ORIGINAL, p. 1068.) Later, at Barnes' request, Mrs. Zimmers signed another paper definitely stating that Rumsey had ordered his machinery in

November 1785. "The deponant likewise remembers of a certain gentleman of a certain spare, thin complexion, and black hair [Fitch], some time April last of this year 1788 asked her relative to the above subject, to which I answered in the manner herein recited." (REMARKS, p. 106.)

b. Frederick Tombough swore that he had been in partnership with Zimmers and had a blacksmith's shop next to Zimmers' coppersmith shop, and that he remembered that "some time in March 1786" Zimmers brought two copper pipes into his shop to have the seams fitted. He was told they were for Rumsey's steamboat. He knew of no other work done by Zimmers for Rumsey before this time. (ORIGINAL, p. 1067.)

c. Michael Baltzel, turner, swore that in March 1786 he made a wooden core on which Rumsey's copper works were to be rounded. (ORIGINAL, p. 1068.)

d. Jonathan Morris, innkeeper, was told at the end of March 1786 that Zimmers had begun some machinery for Rumsey's boat. (ORIGINAL, p. 1069.)

e. John Peters swore that he began to work as a journeyman for Zimmers at about the time his master started on Rumsey's copper work, namely March 1786. (ORIGINAL, p. 1069.)

f. Joseph Frymiller swore that he was apprenticed to Zimmers and had worked on Rumsey's machinery which was begun in the spring of 1786; "no part of the machinery was begun before." (ORIGINAL, pp. 1069-70.) Barnes secured two answering affidavits. Christopher Brudenhart swore that Fitch gave Frymiller half a dollar for his testimony and entertained him so well that when he returned to the shop Frymiller was drunk and stated that he would not mind taking oaths oftener "if he could always be so treated." Christopher Raborg agreed that Frymiller was groggy when he returned from the magistrate. (REMARKS, p. 111.)

g. Joshua Minshall, rival coppersmith, was "of opinion" that it was late spring or summer before Rumsey secured his work from Zimmers. (ORIGINAL, p. 1070.)

To summarize: Mrs. Zimmers definitely stated in her second affidavit that the machinery was ordered during November 1785. Joseph Frymiller swore that no machinery was made before the spring of 1786, but evidence was presented that he was drunk at the time he made out his affidavit. John Peters swore that Zimmers had begun some copper work for Rumsey in March 1786, but he was not in a position to know if this was the first work Zimmers had done for Rumsey. Frederick Tombough and Michael Baltzel claimed to have worked on machinery for Rumsey in March 1786, but neither stated categorically that this was the first machinery for Rumsey that Zimmers had undertaken. The evidence of Joshua Minshall and Jonathan Morris may be thrown out since it was either phrased uncertainly or based on heresay evidence. Let us note that unaided memory was involved in every case, there being no reference to written records. Add to this Rumsey's passion for secrecy, which would have made him do everything as quietly as possible, and we have an adequate explanation for the confusion. At best, Fitch demonstrated nothing except that Rumsey had had some copper work done in March 1786; he failed to prove that other copper work had not been delivered previously.

Fitch's other attempt to undermine Rumsey's chronology involved four large brass cocks which Rumsey claimed to have secured in Baltimore during the fall of 1785.

a. Christopher Raborg, brass founder, testified that Rumsey had said the cocks were for the warm springs at Bath. Raborg stated that he handed the job on to Charles Weir & Co., and that "said cocks I do believe were made in the fall of 1785, but have no charge made to ascertain the time with precision." (ORIGINAL, p. 1071.) The artisan later swore that he had been able to ascertain definitely that the cocks were made in September or October 1785. (REMARKS, p. 107.)

b. Charles Weir testified that he made the cocks for Raborg. "My books are destroyed, and I cannot exactly recollect the time of their being made, but am pursuaded it was early in the spring in the year 1786." At no other time did he make exactly four cocks for Raborg. (ORIGINAL, p. 1072.) Weir later swore that he had found a receipt which showed that he had delivered the cocks on or about October 15, 1785, and that he had been paid for them on October 17. (REMARKS, p. 108.)

c. Isaac Causten, Weir's partner, swore that his books had been destroyed, "but from some loose papers I found charged to Mr. Raborg on the company account on the 29th of March 1786 four brass cocks." They had at no other time made the exact number of four cocks for Raborg. (ORIGINAL, p. 1072.) Causten later swore that the cocks he had told Fitch about could not have been the right ones, for on further examining the books he found that the price charged did not agree with the amount Raborg paid. He was now convinced that the cocks under discussion were made at or about October 14, 1785. (REMARKS, pp. 108-9.)

Barnes presented the evidence of several more witnesses, but it was not needed; Fitch was not left a leg to stand on. In his manuscript history (p. 189) he receded to the position that the cocks could not have been for Rumsey's steamboat; they must have been for the warm springs.

2. Fitch claimed that in the papers he laid before the American Philosophical Society in September 1785 he had mentioned the possibility of boiling water in a pipe; this was three or four months before Rumsey, according to his own statement, started working on his pipe boiler. However, Fitch only used the pipe to heat the water before it flowed into a regular boiler, the object being to keep cold water from impeding the generation of steam. In May 1786 he showed his drawing to Voight, who "made an improvement upon it . . . in a few minutes after he examined my drawings." Timothy Matlock, an important political and philosophical leader, swore that in June 1786 Voight showed him and Nancarrow a draft of "a spiral tube for generating steam." When the two men of experience advised against using the revolutionary device that would certainly involve "difficulties and delays," Fitch and Voight continued to employ an old-fashioned boiler. (HISTORY, pp. 70, 158.)

However, on learning that Rumsey was on his way to Philadelphia and that this rival claimed an exclusive right to the pipe boiler, Voight made an entry of his boiler with the Prothonotary of the Court of Common Pleas, this being the manner in which books were copyrighted. Fitch gave Voight permission to do this in order to clear Voight's name of the charge that he had stolen the device. But Fitch could never be really content giving anyone else the credit for anything; soon he was arguing that although Voight had made the application, the basic idea was his. Yet he did not take the appliance very seriously. "It may be said," he wrote, "that this pipe boiler of mine is too trifling to deserve notice. I pray that my little pipe boiler may be left sacred to me, as trifling as it is." (HISTORY, p. 70.)

3. On May 15, 1788, the Rumsean Society comprised the following members; the numbers refer to the number of shares held. Benjamin Franklin, 1; General Arthur Sinclair, 1; the Rev. George Duffield, 1; William Bingham, 1; Benjamin Wynkoop, 20; the Rev. Samuel Magaw, 1; Myers Fisher, 1; William Barton, 1; Levi Hollingsworth, 2; John Wilson, 1; John Jones, 1; James Trenchard, 4; Joseph James, 2; Messrs. Reed and Ford, 1; Samuel Wheeler, 2; Richard Adams, 1; the Rev. Burgess Allison, 1; Myers Fisher for Robert Barclay, 1; Charles Vancouver, 1.

By September 23, the following additional men and firms had bought into the company: Woodrop and Joseph Sims, William Redwood and Son, Adam Kuhn, John Vaughan, John Ross, and William Turner.

4. A close friend of Franklin's, Vaughan had edited the only edition of Franklin's works to be published during their author's lifetime. He had, during the Revolution, been an active propagandist for the Americans, and during the peace negotiations of 1782 he had done important work as a mediator. Although married to the daughter of a prominent London merchant and engaged in his father-in-law's business, he was a radical who sympathized ardently with the French Revolution. In 1794 he was forced because of his heterodox views to flee England for Paris. Two years later he settled in the United States.

CHAPTER XI   SOURCE REFERENCES

p. 135, ¶1. Affidavits of Wm. Askew, Dec. 8, 1786 [1787?] and Henry Bedinger, Dec. 6, 1787: in TREATISE, pp. 1024-25.
p. 135, ¶2. TREATISE, pp. 1016-17.
p. 135, ¶3. TREATISE, p. 1020.
p. 135, ¶4. Rumsey to Washington, Mar. 24, 1788: in MARYLAND, pp. 142-43.
p. 136, ¶1. Rumsey to Morrow, Mar. 27, 1789: in MARYLAND, p. 272.
p. 136, ¶2. HISTORY, pp. 55, 53.
p. 137, ¶2. Crèvecoeur to M. le Duc d'Harcourt, Jan. 6, 1788: in Crèvecoeur, Robert de, *St. John de Crèvecoeur, Sa Vie et Ses Ouvrages*, Paris, 1883, p. 321.
p. 137, ¶3. Franklin to Crèvecoeur, Feb. 16, 1788: in Bigelow, John, ed., *The Complete Works of Benjamin Franklin*, N.Y., 1887-88, IX, p. 458.
p. 138, ¶4. ORIGINAL, p. 1064.
p. 139, ¶1. ORIGINAL, p. 1065.
p. 139, ¶2. REMARKS, p. 96.
p. 140, ¶2. HISTORY, p. 58.
p. 140, ¶3. Rumsey to Morrow, May 15, 1788: in W. & M., XXIV, p. 172.
p. 141, ¶2. Rumsey to Washington, May 15, 1788: in MARYLAND, p. 145.
p. 142, ¶2. Rumsey to Morrow, May 15, 1788: in W. & M., XXIV, p. 172.
p. 142, ¶3. Rush to Lettsom, May 4, 1788: in Pettigrew, Thomas Joseph, *Memoires of the Life and Writings of the Late John Coakley Lettsom*. Lond., 1817, II, pp. 430-31.
p. 143, ¶1. Franklin to Vaughan, May 14, 1788: in TURNER, p. 142. Rumsey to Washington, May 15, 1788: in MARYLAND, p. 146.
p. 143, ¶2-3. Rumsey to Morrow, May 15, 1788: in W. & M., XXIV, pp. 172-73.

CHAPTER XII   SOURCE REFERENCES

p. 144, ¶1. HISTORY, pp. 57-58.
p. 144, ¶2–p. 145, ¶1. HISTORY, p. 59.
p. 145, ¶2. Franklin to John Ingenhousz, Oct. 24, 1788: in Sparks, Jared, ed., *The Works of Benjamin Franklin*, Boston, 1836-40, X, p. 363.
p. 146, ¶1. WESTCOTT, p. 253.
p. 147, ¶1. REMARKS, p. 98.
p. 147, ¶2. *Documentary History of the State of New York*, Albany, 1849, pp. 1083-84.
p. 147, ¶3. TURNBULL, p. 100. Stevens to Rumsey, Sept. 5, 1788: in TURNBULL, pp. 101-2.
p. 148, ¶1. TURNBULL, p. 103.
p. 149, ¶1. AUTOBIOGRAPHY, p. 141.
p. 149, ¶2. HISTORY, pp. 62-63.
p. 150, ¶1–p. 151, ¶2. AUTOBIOGRAPHY, pp. 125-27.
p. 151, ¶3. HISTORY, p. 60.

CHAPTER XIII   SOURCE REFERENCES

p. 152, ¶2. Boulton and Watt to Mr. Handley, July 14, 1788: in TURNER, pp. 142-43.

p. 153, ¶1–p. 154, ¶4. Rumsey to Boulton and Watt, Aug. 6, 1788: ms. in coll. Penn. Hist. Soc.
p. 154, ¶5. Boulton to Watt, Aug. 14, 1788: in TURNER, p. 152.
p. 154, ¶6. Boulton to Watt, Aug. 15, 1788: in TURNER, p. 152.
p. 155, ¶1-3. Boulton and Watt to Rumsey, Aug. 14, 1788: in TURNER, pp. 150-51.
p. 155, ¶4–p. 156, ¶3. Boulton and Watt to Rumsey, Aug. 29, 1788: in TURNER, pp. 153-54.
p. 159, ¶1. Flexner, James Thomas, *America's Old Masters*, Viking, N. Y., 1939, pp. 216-17.
p. 160, ¶1. Taylor to Miller, Sept. 12, 1788: in *Great Exhibition of the Works of Industry of All Nations, 1851; Official Descriptive and Illustrated Catalogue*, supplementary volume, Lond., n.d., p. 1473.
p. 160, ¶2. Miller, Patrick, "A Short Narrative of Facts Relative to the Invention and Practice of Steam Navigation by the Late Patrick Miller," in *Edinburgh Philos. Mag.*, 1825, XXV, p. 85.
p. 161, ¶1. Symington, William, "Autobiography," in *Cassiers Mag.*, 1907, XXXII, p. 528.
p. 162, ¶1. Symington, *op. cit.*, p. 530.
p. 163, ¶2. Rumsey to Morrow, Jan. 1789: in House of Representatives, 29th Congress, 1st session, *Committee Report 403*, 1846, p. 30.
p. 164, ¶1. Rumsey to Edward Rumsey, Mar. 7, 1789: in House of Representatives, 27th Congress, 2nd session, *Committee Report 324*, 1842, p. 8.
p. 165, ¶1. Rumsey to George William West, Mar. 20, 1789: in MARYLAND, pp. 152-54.
p. 165, ¶2. Rumsey to Morrow, Mar. 27, 1789: in MARYLAND, pp. 272-73.
p. 166, ¶1. Jefferson to Dr. Willard, Mar. 24, 1789: in Jefferson, Thomas, *Writings*, Wash., 1904, VII, p. 328.
p. 166, ¶2. Rumsey to Morrow, Mar. 27, 1789: in MARYLAND, p. 272.
p. 166, ¶3. Rumsey to Morrow, April 2, 1789: in *Report 403, op. cit.*, p. 5.
p. 167, ¶1. Rumsey to Morrow, Aug. 4, 1789: in W. & M., XXV, p. 28. Rumsey to Jefferson, Sept. 8, 1789: in MARYLAND, p. 280.
p. 167, ¶2-4. Rumsey to Morrow, Aug. 4, 1789: in W. & M., XXV, pp. 28-30.
p. 168, ¶1. Rumsey to Morrow, Jan. 25, 1788 [1789?] in *Report 403, op. cit.*, p. 30. Rumsey to Morrow, Aug. 4, 1789: in W. & M., XXV, p. 31.
p. 168, ¶2. Rumsey to Jefferson, Sept. 8, 1789: in MARYLAND, p. 280.
p. 168, ¶3. Jefferson to Rumsey, Oct. 14, 1789: in Ford, Paul Leicester, ed., *The Writings of Thomas Jefferson*, N.Y., 1895, V, pp. 131-32.
p. 168, ¶4. Jefferson to William Short, April 27, 1790: in Ford, *op. cit.*, V, p. 165.
p. 169, ¶3. Miller, *op. cit.*, pp. 91-92. Symington, *Autobiography, op. cit.*, p. 530.
p. 170, ¶1. Miller to Taylor, Dec. 7, 1789: in Woodcroft, Bennet, *A Sketch of the Origin and Progress of Steam Navigation*, Lond., 1848, pp. 44-45.
p. 171, ¶1-4. Watt to Robert Cullen, April 24, 1790: in *Great Exhibition, op. cit.*, p. 1475.
p. 173, ¶1. Stanhope to Boulton and Watt, Oct. 23, 1789: in Gooch, S. W. and Gooch, G. P., *The Life of Charles, 3rd Earl of Stanhope*, Lond., 1914, p. 168.
p. 173, ¶2. Boulton and Watt to Stanhope, May 11, 1790: in Gooch, *op. cit.*, p. 169.
p. 174, ¶1–p. 176, ¶1. Rumsey to Morrow, Feb. 27, 1790: in TURNER, pp. 175-77.
p. 176, ¶2. Rumsey to Morrow [?], April 23, 1790: in *Report 403, op. cit.*, p. 31.
p. 176, ¶3. Rumsey to Morrow, Oct. 24, 1790: in *Report 403, op. cit.*, p. 32.

CHAPTER XIV   SOURCE REFERENCES

p. 178, ¶2. TURNER, pp. 124-25.
p. 178, ¶3–p. 180, ¶2. HISTORY, pp. 88-92.
p. 181, ¶1. HISTORY, p. 97.

p. 181, ¶2. HISTORY, p. 103.
p. 181, ¶3. HISTORY, p. 97.
p. 182, ¶1. HISTORY, pp. 98-100.
p. 182, ¶2. HISTORY, p. 100.
p. 183, ¶1. HISTORY, p. 101.
p. 184, ¶1-2. HISTORY, pp. 110-11.
p. 185, ¶1. HISTORY, pp. 111-13.
p. 185, ¶2. Thornton, William, *A Short Account of the Origin of Steamboats, Written in 1810 and Now Committed to the Press*, Albany, 1818, p. 5.
p. 186, ¶1. HISTORY, p. 117.
p. 188, ¶2. HISTORY, p. 205.

CHAPTER XV   TEXT NOTES

1. Fitch begged the Rev. Elihu Palmer to return to town, but, so the inventor wrote, "he not being such a veteran as myself was conquered on the first repulse, and I may say by the advance guard only of the broken Christians." (BOYD. p. 264.) After a period during which he practiced law, Palmer returned to the preaching of Deism in 1794. Making his headquarters in New York City, he became a national leader of the movement.
2. Voight's career from here on is full of interest, but it does not fall within the boundaries of this book. Although Rittenhouse held the position of director, Voight, as chief coiner and superintendent, was the active executive officer of the first mint in the United States. He is largely responsible for the coins produced in Philadelphia between his appointment on June 1, 1792, and his death at the age of seventy-one on February 7, 1814. To meet the requirements of the mint, he is said to have discovered in 1793 a new method of making steel. For a detailed account of his activities see Stewart, Frank H., *History of the First United States Mint*, n.p., 1924.

CHAPTER XV   SOURCE REFERENCES

p. 190, ¶1-5. WESTCOTT, p. 365.
p. 191, ¶2. HISTORY, p. 209.
p. 191, ¶3. Fitch to Gen. Gibson, n.d.: in WESTCOTT, p. 296.
p. 192, ¶1. HISTORY, pp. 212, 208-9.
p. 192, ¶2. HISTORY, p. 206.
p. 193, ¶4. AUTOBIOGRAPHY, p. 113.
p. 194, ¶1-2. AUTOBIOGRAPHY, pp. 120-21.
p. 195, ¶1. AUTOBIOGRAPHY, pp. 133-35.
p. 196, ¶1. AUTOBIOGRAPHY, p. 124.
p. 196, ¶2. HISTORY, p. 220. AUTOBIOGRAPHY, p. 113.
p. 197, ¶1. HISTORY, p. 230.
p. 197, ¶3. Fitch to Morris and Pollock, Feb. 26, 1791: in HISTORY, pp. 241-48.
p. 198, ¶1. Smith, Edgar Charles, *A Short History of Naval and Marine Engineering*, Cambridge, Eng., 1938, frontispiece.
p. 198, ¶4. HISTORY, p. 276.
p. 199, ¶1. AUTOBIOGRAPHY, p. 129.
p. 199, ¶2–p. 200, ¶1. AUTOBIOGRAPHY, pp. 130, 129, 131.
p. 200, ¶2. AUTOBIOGRAPHY, pp. 136-37.
p. 201, ¶2. HISTORY, p. 281.
p. 202, ¶1. HISTORY, pp. 292-93.
p. 202, ¶2. HISTORY, p. 296.
p. 203, ¶1-2. BOYD, pp. 249-50.
p. 203, ¶3. HISTORY, p. 310.
p. 204, ¶2. HISTORY, pp. 1-2.

p. 205, ¶1. AUTOBIOGRAPHY, pp. 136, 140-41.
p. 205, ¶3. Fitch to Jefferson, July 24, 1792: in WESTCOTT, p. 339.
p. 206, ¶1-5. BOYD, pp. 266-68.
p. 207, ¶5. WESTCOTT, pp. 337-39.

CHAPTER XVI   SOURCE REFERENCES

p. 208, ¶2. Rumsey to Dr. James McMechen, April 15, 1792: in W. & M., XXIV, p. 171.
p. 208, ¶3. Rumsey to Morrow, Jan. 5, 1791: in W. & M., XXIV, p. 245.
p. 209, ¶1-2. Rumsey to Morrow, Aug. 23, 1791: in W. & M., XXIV, p. 247. Rumsey to G. W. West, Sept. 12, 1791: in W. & M., XXIV, pp. 239-41.
p. 210, ¶1. Rumsey to G. W. West, Sept. 12, 1791: in W. & M., XXIV, pp. 239-41. Barnes to Morrow, Jan. 29, 1792: in W. & M., XXV, p. 33.
p. 210, ¶2-3. Rumsey to Morrow, Aug. 24, 1791: in W. & M., XXIV, pp. 249-50.
p. 211, ¶1-2. Rumsey to Morrow, Mar. 30, 1792: in W. & M., XXV, pp. 25-26.
p. 211, ¶3-p. 212, ¶2. Rumsey to G. W. West, Dec. 18, 1792: in *National Intelligencer*, Wash., Nov. 7, 1816.
p. 212, ¶3. R. C. Wakefield to G. W. West, Dec. 26, 1792: in *National Intelligencer, op. cit.*
p. 212, ¶5. *Gentleman's Magazine*, 1793, LXIII, p. 182.

CHAPTER XVII   TEXT NOTES

1. Pesce, whose scholarship is usually sound, linked Rumsey with Benjamin West as one of Fulton's two principal protectors, while Fulton's contemporary, Delaplaine (p. 204) states that Rumsey and Fulton were acquainted, adding, "perhaps it was from this connection that Mr. Fulton might have dated his confirmed and exclusive devotion to subjects of mechanical science." Preble (*op. cit.*, p. 21) writes: "A gentleman not many years ago had in his possession letters written by Rumsey in London, which mentioned his receiving frequent visits there from a young American studying engineering. . . . This young man was Robert Fulton."
    If Fulton had not already met Rumsey when he was at Bath in 1786, he could easily have been introduced to him by G. W. West, who was both Rumsey's intimate friend and a fellow-student of Fulton's at Benjamin West's studio. Rumsey seems to have been acquainted with several of the artists working there.
2. A report does exist that Fulton was employed by the Duke of Bridgewater to build an inclined plane for an underground canal at Walkden, near Manchester. This statement, admittedly based on hearsay evidence, is not borne out by the papers of the Bridgewater trustees, and the date given, 1794, seems several years too early for Fulton to be engaged in such an enterprise.
3. On February 24, 1796, Fulton wrote Mifflin asking for an exclusive right in Pennsylvania for his small canals.

CHAPTER XVII   SOURCE REFERENCES

p. 215, ¶1. Flexner, James Thomas, *America's Old Masters*, Viking, N.Y., 1939, p. 95.
p. 215, ¶2. Fulton to Mother, April 14, 1793: in DICKINSON, pp. 13-14.
p. 215, ¶3. George Sanderson to Fulton's Mother, July 25, 1788: in SUTCLIFFE II, pp. 39-40. Fulton to Mother, Jan. 20, 1792: in SUTCLIFFE II, pp. 49-51.
p. 216, ¶1. Fulton to David Morris, May 21, 1793: ms. in coll. Chicago Hist. Soc. Fulton to Joshua Gilpin, Nov. 20, 1798: in SUTCLIFFE I, p. 318.

p. 216, ¶2. Fulton to Mother, April 14, 1789: in Lee, Cuthbert, *Early American Portrait Painters*, New Haven, 1929, p. 301.

p. 216, ¶3. Fulton to Mother, Jan. 20, 1792, *op. cit.* Fulton to Mother, July 31, 1789: in SUTCLIFFE II, pp. 43-44.

p. 217, ¶1. Fulton to Mother, Jan. 20, 1792, *op. cit.* Fulton to Mother, June 14, 1790: in SUTCLIFFE II, pp. 34-35.

p. 217, ¶2. Fulton to Mother, Jan. 20, 1792, *op. cit.*

p. 218, ¶1. Engravings reproduced in DICKINSON, pp. 18, 20.

p. 218, ¶2. Fulton to Mother, Jan. 20, 1792, *op. cit.*

p. 219, ¶2. SUTCLIFFE I, p. 330.

p. 220, ¶3. Farington, Joseph, *The Farington Diary*, N.Y., 1923, II, p. 108. Fulton to David Morris. Sept. 12, 1796: in DICKINSON, p. 59.

p. 221, ¶2. Stanhope to Fulton, Oct. 7, 1793: in DICKINSON, p. 24.

p. 221, ¶3. Fulton to Stanhope, Nov. 4, 1793: widely printed.

p. 221, ¶4. Fulton to Boulton and Watt, Nov. 4, 1794: in SUTCLIFFE I, pp. 303-4.

p. 223, ¶2. Fulton, *A Treatise on the Improvement of Canal Navigation*, Lond., 1796, p. xi.

p. 223, ¶3. DICKINSON, p. 29.

p. 224, ¶1. Fulton to Owen, Dec. 26, 1794: in Owen, Robert, *The Life of Robert Owen*, Lond., 1857-58, p. 65.

p. 224, ¶2. Fulton to Morris, April 1, 1794: ms. in coll. Chicago Hist. Soc.

p. 226, ¶2–p. 227, ¶1. Fulton to Stanhope, Dec. 28, 1796: in DICKINSON, pp. 53-55.

p. 227, ¶2. Fulton to Washington, Sept. 12, 1796: in SUTCLIFFE I, p. 307.

p. 228, ¶1. Fulton to Owen, April 28, 1797: in Owen, *op. cit.*, p. 69.

p. 228, ¶2. Stanhope to Boulton and Watt, n.d.: in Gooch, S. W., and Gooch, G. P., *The Life of Charles, 3rd Earl of Stanhope*, Lond., 1914, pp. 180-81.

p. 228, ¶3. Fulton to Stanhope, May 12, 1796: in DICKINSON, pp. 49-50.

p. 229, ¶1. Strickland, Mary, *A Memoir of the Life, Writings, and Mechanical Inventions of Edmund Cartwright*, Lond., 1843, p. 182.

CHAPTER XVIII   SOURCE REFERENCES

p. 231, ¶3. BOYD, pp. 275-76.

p. 232, ¶1. Fitch to Thornton, Aug. 11, 1793: in BOYD, p. 277.

p. 233, ¶1. Fitch, *An Explanation for Keeping a Ship's Traverse at Sea by the Columbian Ready Reckoner*, Lond., printed and pub. by the author, 1793.

p. 234, ¶1. BOYD, pp. 284-85.

p. 235, ¶3–p. 236, ¶1. For accounts of Elijah Ormsbee see Dow, Charles H., *History of Steam Navigation between Providence and New York, 1792-1877*, N.Y., 1877. Hoopes, Penrose R., *Connecticut's Contribution to the Development of the Steamboat*, New Haven, 1936. Preble, George Henry, *A Chronological History of the Origin and Development of Steam Navigation*, Phila., 1895. Lincoln, Jonathan Thayer, "The Beginnings of the Machine Age in New England," in *New England Quarterly*, 1933, VI, pp. 716-32.

p. 236, ¶3. Morey to William A. Duer, Oct. 31, 1818: in Duer, William Alexander, *A Reply to Mr. Colden's Vindication of the Steamboat Monopoly*, Albany, 1819, p. xvi. (Much has been written about Morey and many elaborate claims have been made; this letter from the inventor himself gives the authentic story.)

p. 237, ¶1. STEVENS LETTER, p. 414.

p. 237, ¶3–p. 238, ¶1. Fitch to Stevens, June 20, July 9, July 27, 1795; Stevens to John Nicholson, April 19, 1795; Matthew Barton to Stevens, April 16, 1795: mss. in coll. Stevens Institute.

p. 238, ¶2. Hutchins, John, *Honor to Whom Honor Is Due*, broadside, Williamsburg, L.I., 1846. LIVINGSTON, p. 260.

p. 238, ¶3–p. 239, ¶3. Morey to Duer: Duer, *Reply, op. cit.*, pp. xvii, x.

p. 239, ¶5. Goodwin, Katherine R., and Duryea, Charles F., *Captain Samuel Morey, the Edison of his Day*, White River Junction, 1931.
p. 241, ¶2. WHITTLESEY, p. 146.
p. 241, ¶3–p. 243, ¶2. Robert Wickliffe to a Philadelphia friend, Nov. 12, 1855: in WESTCOTT, p. 363.

CHAPTER XIX   TEXT NOTE

1. Fulton wrote Joshua Gilpin on September 17, 1798, that his plans had been adopted for a canal from Paris to Dieppe and Cambrai. The statement must have been an exaggeration for we hear no more of this success.

CHAPTER XIX   SOURCE REFERENCES

p. 244, ¶1. Fulton to David Morris, May 21, 1793: ms. in coll. Chicago Hist. Soc.
p. 245, ¶2-6. Gontaut-Biron, Marie Joséphine Louise de Montaut de Navailles, duchesse de; *Mémoires de Mme. la Duchesse de Gontaut*, Paris, 1893, pp. 49-50. English translation of the above by Mrs. J. W. Davis, N.Y., 1894, pp. 63-65.
p. 247, ¶1. Barlow to Mrs. Barlow, Aug. 17 & 31, 1800: in Todd, Charles Burr, *Life and Letters of Joel Barlow*, N.Y. and Lond., 1886, p. 177.
p. 247, ¶2. Fulton to Stanhope, 1797: in PARSONS, p. 88. Fulton to Cartwright, Sept. 20, 1797: in Strickland, Mary, *A Memoir of the Life, Writings, and Mechanical Inventions of Edmund Cartwright*, Lond., 1843, pp. 140-41.
p. 247, ¶3. Fulton, "Thoughts on Free Trade": in COLDEN, pp. 24-25. Fulton, "Motives for Inventing Submarine Attack": in PARSONS, p. 54.
p. 248, ¶2–p. 251, ¶4. Principal sources for David Bushnell are: Abbot, Henry L., *The Beginnings of Modern Submarine Warfare under Capt.-Lieut. David Bushnell*, Willets Point, N.Y., 1881. *American Journal of Science*, April 1820. Bushnell, David, "General Principles and Construction of a Submarine Vessel," in *Trans. Am. Philos. Soc.*, IV, 1799. *Conn. Hist. Soc. Colls.*, II, 1870. Howe, Henry, *Memoirs of the Most Eminent American Mechanics*, N.Y., 1841. Johnston, Henry P., *Yale and Her Honor Role in the American Revolution*, N.Y., 1888. Thatcher, James, *Military Journal of the American Revolution*, Hartford, 1862. White, George, *Historical Collections of Georgia*, 3rd ed., N.Y., 1855.
p. 252, ¶1. Jefferson to Stiles, July 17, 1785: in Jefferson, *Writings, op. cit.*, V, p. 37.
p. 253, ¶2-3. Fulton to Directory (in French), Dec. 13, 1797: in PESCE, p. 168.
p. 254, ¶1. Duboc, Emile, "Comment la France Faillit Vaincre l'Angleterre," in *La Révue des Révues*, XVIII, 1896, p. 481.
p. 255, ¶2-4. Fulton to Napoleon (in French), May 1, 1798: ms. in coll. N.Y. Public Library.
p. 256, ¶2–p. 257, ¶2. Commission report (in French), Sept. 5, 1798: in PESCE, pp. 180-88.
p. 258, ¶1. Fulton to Barras (in French), Oct. 27, 1798: in DICKINSON, p. 89.
p. 258, ¶2. Joshua Gilpin to Stanhope, Aug. 28, 1798: in *Century Magazine*, LXXVI, 1908, p. 935. Fulton to Gilpin, Nov. 20, 1798: in SUTCLIFFE I, pp. 316-18.
p. 258, ¶3. Fulton to Cartwright, June 20, 1798: in Strickland, *op. cit.*, p. 146.
p. 258, ¶4. Thornton, William, *A Short Account of the Origin of Steamboats*, Wash., 1814, p. 17.
p. 259, ¶3. DICKINSON, p. 76.
p. 259, ¶4. Fulton to Mother, July 2, 1799: in SUTCLIFFE II, pp. 68-69.
p. 259, ¶5–p. 260, ¶2. Gontaut-Biron, *op. cit.*, p. 80. Davis translation, *op. cit.*, pp. 63-64.
p. 261, ¶1. Fulton to Ministre de la Marine (retranslated into English from a French trans.), Oct. 6, 1799: in PESCE, p. 190.

CHAPTER XX   TEXT NOTE

1. The son of a New York City shopkeeper, Roosevelt had shown an early interest in mechanical boats. In 1781 or 1782, so he stated in a petition to the Pennsylvania Legislature dated July 13, 1815, he had put in motion on a little brook a small boat, "or model of a boat, with vertical wheels over the sides, each wheel having four arms or paddles or floats, . . . and that these wheels being acted upon by hickory or whalebone springs propelled the model of the boat through the water through the agency of a tight cord passed between the wheels and being reacted upon by springs." Roosevelt was to use this experiment as the basis for his claim that he was the inventor of the paddle wheel. (Latrobe, John H. B., *A Lost Chapter in the History of the Steamboat*, Balt., 1871, pp. 14-15.)

CHAPTER XX   SOURCE REFERENCES

p. 262, ¶1. Act of N.Y. Legis., Mar. 27, 1798: in Duer, *Reply, op cit.*, p. 88.
p. 262, ¶2. LIVINGSTON, pp. 258-59.
p. 263, ¶1. Livingston to Roosevelt, Dec. 8, 1787: ms. in coll. N.Y. Hist. Soc.
p. 263, ¶2. Livingston to Roosevelt, Dec. 22, 1787: Charles Stoudinger to Roosevelt, Dec. 18, 1787, N.Y. Hist. Soc.
p. 263, ¶3. Stoudinger to Roosevelt, Dec. 29, 1787: N.Y. Hist. Soc.
p. 264, ¶1. Livingston to Roosevelt, Jan. 12, Feb. 22, May 12, 1798: N.Y. Hist. Soc.
p. 265, ¶1. Livingston to Roosevelt, Sept. 10, 1798: N.Y. Hist. Soc.
p. 265, ¶2. Roosevelt to Livingston, Oct. 21, 1798: N.Y. Hist. Soc.
p. 265, ¶3. LIVINGSTON, p. 259.
p. 266, ¶1. Livingston to Roosevelt, Feb. 23, 1799: N.Y. Hist. Soc.
p. 266, ¶3. TURNBULL, p. 75.
p. 267, ¶1. Stevens to Roosevelt, July 15, 1799: N.Y. Hist. Soc.
p. 267, ¶4. STEVENS LETTER, p. 419.
p. 268, ¶2-3. Bathe, Greville, and Bathe, Dorothy, *Oliver Evans*, Hist. Soc. of Penn., Phila., 1935.

CHAPTER XXI   TEXT NOTE

1. This detailed account of Fulton's submarine trip is largely reconstructed from the author's knowledge of how the *Nautilus* was built and how it was managed. Fulton's own account was very brief, reading as follows: "Le 28, je relâchai dans un petit port appelé Growan près d'Isigny, et à 3 lieues des îles Marcou. Le 29 commença l'equinoxe qui fut très-mauvais pendant 25 jours. Durant ce temps, j'essayai deux fois d'approcher de deux bricks anglias qui étaient mouillés près d'une des isles; mais deux fois, soit à dessein, soit hazard, ils mirent à la voile et s'éloignèrent. Dans une de ces tentatives, je demeurai pendant toute une marée de 6 heures absolument sous l'eau, ayant seulement pour prendre l'air un petit tube qui ne pouvait être apperçu à un distance de 200 toises." (Fulton to Citizens Monge and La Place, Nov. 7, 1800: in PESCE, p. 201.)

CHAPTER XXI   SOURCE REFERENCES

p. 270, ¶1-2. Forfait to Napoleon (in French), June 16, 1800: in *Am. Hist. Rev.*, 1933-34, XXXIX, pp. 491-92.
p. 271, ¶2-3. Fulton to Napoleon (in French), June 15, 1800: in *Am. Hist. Rev.*, *op. cit.*, p. 493.
p. 272, ¶2. Barlow to Fulton, Sept. 6 & 7, 1800: in Todd, Charles Burr, *Life and Letters of Joel Barlow*, N.Y. & Lond., 1886, pp. 181-82.

p. 274, ¶3. Captain S. H. Linzie to Admiralty Secretary, Sept. 21, 1800: in DICKINSON, p. 109.

p. 274, ¶4. PARSONS, p. 35.

p. 276, ¶2. Fulton to Gaspard Monge and Pierre-Simon La Place (in French), Sept. 20, 1801: in SUTCLIFFE I, pp. 84-88.

p. 277, ¶1. *Annual Register*, XLIV, 1802.

p. 277, ¶2. Fulton, ms. appeal to court, dated 1811: in coll. Marine Museum of the City of N.Y.

p. 278, ¶1-p. 279, ¶1. Symington, "Autobiography," *Cassiers Mag.*, pp. 530-33.

CHAPTER XXII   TEXT NOTE

1. Fulton wrote that two years after he had started his submarine experiments, he "was so well satisfied with my success and that everything which I had contemplated might be performed, that I wrote the Earl of Stanhope and gave him general ideas of my plan and experiments. . . . He became alarmed, and as we know spoke of it in the House of Lords." (Fulton, "Motives for Inventing Submarine Attack": in PARSONS, p. 55.)

CHAPTER XXII   SOURCE REFERENCES

p. 281, ¶2. Fulton, Robert, *A Treatise on the Improvement of Canal Navigation*, Lond., 1796, p. xi.

p. 281, ¶3. Fulton, notes on Desblanc's patent, 1802: in SUTCLIFFE I, pp. 328-29.

p. 282, ¶1. Fulton to Cartwright, Mar. 10, 1802: in Strickland, Mary, *A Memoir of the Life, Writings, and Mechanical Inventions of Edmund Cartwright*, Lond., 1843, p. 150.

p. 282, ¶2. DICKINSON, p. 214.

p. 282, ¶3. Fulton to Cartwright, Mar. 28, 1802: in Strickland, *op. cit.*, p. 152.

p. 283, ¶2. Barlow to Fulton, June 14, 1802: in Todd, *op. cit.*, p. 189.

p. 283, ¶4. Barlow to Fulton, July 18, Aug. 15, 1802: in Todd, *op. cit.*, pp. 197, 200.

p. 284, ¶1. Barlow to Fulton, July 18, July 6, 1802: in Todd, *op. cit.*, pp. 197, 190-91.

p. 284, ¶2. Barlow to Fulton, July 26, 1802: in Todd, *op. cit.*, p. 198.

p. 284, ¶3. Barlow to Fulton, May 20, 1802: in Todd, *op. cit.*, p. 185.

p. 285, ¶1. Barlow to Fulton, May 21, 1802: in Todd, *op. cit.*, pp. 186-87.

p. 286, ¶1. SUTCLIFFE I, pp. 117-22.

p. 286, ¶2. Fulton ms. dated Feb. 1813: in Miller, Peyton F., *The Story of Robert Fulton*, N.Y., 1908, p. 96.

p. 287, ¶1-p. 287, ¶3. Fulton to Citizens Molar, Bandell, and Montgolfier, Jan. 25, 1803: in SUTCLIFFE I, pp. 333-38.

p. 288, ¶2. Nathaniel Cutting to Ferdinando Fairfax, Dec. 5, 1814: in Thurston, Robert H., *Robert Fulton, His Life and Its Results*, N.Y., 1891, pp. 16-17.

p. 289, ¶1. Fulton to Boulton and Watt, Aug. 6, 1803: widely printed.

p. 290, ¶1. Fulton to Skipworth: in SUTCLIFFE I, pp. 147-48.

p. 290, ¶2. Desbrière, Edouard, *1793-1805; Projets et Tentatives de Débarquement aux Iles Brittanniques*, Paris, 1902, III, p. 331.

p. 291, ¶3. Dr. David Hosack to Colden, Jan. 1, 1817: in COLDEN, pp. 262-63.

p. 292, ¶2-3. Also published in *Recueil Polytechnique des Pont et Chaussées*, I, p. 82, Yr. XI.

p. 293, ¶2. Fontin, Paul, *Les Sous Marine a l'Angleterre*, Paris, 1902, p. 39.

CHAPTER XXIII   TEXT NOTES

1. In a letter to Mrs. Benjamin West, Oct. 16, 1805, Fulton admitted that the

attack had been a failure, but added it was magnified in the French press, "which seems to show that they were much frightened or that the public must be amused with a long story." (Ms. in coll. N.Y. Hist. Soc.)

2. After Fulton had returned to America, and when the War of 1812 was actually in progress, Jefferson endorsed Fulton's submarine schemes. The statesman had not, however, forgotten that Bushnell had preceded Fulton. On June 19, 1813, he wrote Matthew Carr criticizing Clarke, who had just published his naval history of the United States, for not mentioning Bushnell's *American Turtle.* "It was excellently contrived," Jefferson stated, "and might perhaps, by improvement, be brought into real use. I do not know the difference between this and Mr. Fulton's submarine boat." (Jefferson, *Writings, op. cit.,* XIII, p. 263.)

3. Colden (p. 57) wrote in 1817: "Mr. Fulton did not pretend to have been the first to have discovered that gunpowder might be exploded with effect under water; nor did he pretend to be the first who attempted to apply it as the means of hostility. He knew well what had been done by Bushnell in our revolutionary war. He frequently spoke of the genius of this American with great respect, and expressed a conviction that his attempts against the enemy would have been more successful if he had had the advantages which he himself derived from the improvements of nearly forty years in mechanics and philosophy." This generous statement, so at odds with the claims Fulton had made when in France and England, probably expresses what Fulton said after he had returned to America where there were many witnesses to Bushnell's experiments.

4. There are in the Fulton documents three different spellings of Dutch names that are so close to one another that they may all be variants of the same name. Colden refers to Fulton's backer as M. Vanstaphast, and he has been followed in this by most writers. The spelling I have used, Vanstappoit, comes from a letter from Fulton to Daniel Parker, written in Amsterdam on October 2, 1803. However, another letter of Fulton's has turned up, addressed to a Mr. and Mrs. Van Staphout in Amsterdam. Written on September 29, 1806, shortly before Fulton left London, this document makes it clear that the Van Staphouts did not even know Fulton had deserted France for England. Although Fulton summarizes his activities of the previous years, he makes no mention of any financial connection still pending with the Hollanders.

CHAPTER XXIII SOURCE REFERENCES

p. 294, ¶2–p. 295, ¶2. Fulton, "Motives for Inventing Submarine Attack": in PARSONS, pp. 55-56.

p. 296, ¶1. Fulton to Pitt, Aug. 9, 1805: in DICKINSON, p. 189.

p. 296, ¶3. Fulton to James Monroe, Nov. 3, 1803; Fulton to Boulton and Watt, Nov. 3, 1803: in *N.Y. Pub. Lib. Bull.,* XIII, 1909, p. 567.

p. 297, ¶2. Fulton, "Motives," *op. cit.,* in PARSONS, p. 59.

p. 298, ¶3. Fulton to Mr. Hammond, June 22, 1804: in PARSONS, pp. 96-97.

p. 300, ¶1. Fulton to Sir Howe Popham, June 30, 1804: in PARSONS, pp. 99-100.

p. 300, ¶2-3. Fulton's own account: in PARSONS, p. 101.

p. 301, ¶1. SUTCLIFFE I, pp. 117-22.

p. 301, ¶2. Fulton, Robert, *Torpedo War and Submarine Explosions,* N.Y., 1810, motto on flyleaf.

p. 302, ¶1. Fulton to Boulton and Watt, July 13, 1804: in DICKINSON, p. 170.

p. 302, ¶3. Hosack to Colden, Jan. 1, 1817: in COLDEN, p. 264.

p. 304, ¶4–p. 306, ¶3. *Cobbett's Political Register,* IV, Oct. 27, 1804, pp. 641-42.

p. 306, ¶4. Fulton, "Motives," *op. cit.*: in PARSONS, p. 62.

p. 306, ¶5. Photostat ms.: in Parson's coll., N.Y. Public Library.

p. 307, ¶1. Fulton to Pitt, July 18, 1805: in PARSONS, pp. 103-4.
p. 307, ¶3. Fulton, *Torpedo War*, *op. cit.*, pp. 18-19.
p. 308, ¶2. PARSONS, p. 90. DICKINSON, p. 194.
p. 308, ¶3. Sidney Smith to Viscount Castlereagh, Nov. 22, 1805: in Castlereagh, *Correspondence*, Lond., 1851, V, p. 131.
p. 309, ¶1-3. Fulton to Castlereagh, Dec. 13, 1805: in PARSONS, p. 105.
p. 309, ¶4–p. 310, ¶3. PARSONS, pp. 143-44.
p. 310, ¶4. Fulton to Pitt, Jan. 6, 1806: in Castlereagh, *op. cit.*, pp. 146-50.
p. 311, ¶2–p. 312, ¶1. Gontaut-Biron, *op. cit.*, pp. 106-7. Davis translation, *op. cit.*, p. 130.
p. 312, ¶2-3. Barlow to Fulton, May 3, 1806: in SUTCLIFFE I, pp. 168-70.
p. 313, ¶2-4. Fulton, "Notes on Observations of the Arbiters, Particularly Captain Hamilton and Sir Charles Blagden": in PARSONS, pp. 125-26.
p. 314, ¶2–p. 315, ¶2. Fulton, *Letters Principally to the Rt. Hon. Lord Grenville on Submarine Navigation and Attack, etc.*, Lond., Sept. 23, 1806, pp. vi, 31-34.
p. 315, ¶4. Fulton to Sir Charles Blagden and Captain Thomas Hamilton, Sept. 23, 1806: in Fulton, *Letters, op. cit.*, pp. 34-37.
p. 315, ¶5. Fulton to Barlow, Sept. 1806: in Todd, *op. cit.*, p. 209.
p. 316, ¶3. Fulton to Stanhope, Oct. 4, 1806: in DICKINSON, p. 203.

CHAPTER XXIV   TEXT NOTES

1. Colden gives another explanation for *The Steamboat*'s sudden stop. Fulton, he says, realizing that the water wheels were not correctly adjusted, ordered the halt so that he could lessen their diameter in such a manner that the buckets would take less hold on the water.
2. Wooden steam engine boilers were one of Livingston's proudest inventions; he even sold the idea to Roosevelt, who used such boilers on many of the stationary engines he built. In a wooden chest containing water, an iron furnace was placed, while metal flues carried the smoke several times through the water before it reached the chimney. The theory was that since wood is a less good conductor of heat than metal, its use would decrease fuel consumption. The flaw was that it was almost impossible to keep the boiler tight for any length of time.

CHAPTER XXIV   SOURCE REFERENCES

p. 318, ¶1. SUTCLIFFE I, p. 188.
p. 318, ¶2. Clarkson, Thomas Streatfield, *A Biographical History of Clermont*, Clermont, 1869, p. 135.
p. 318, ¶3. Fulton to Livingston, Aug. 10, 1808: in SUTCLIFFE I, pp. 197-99.
p. 321, ¶3–p. 322, ¶1. SUTCLIFFE I, p. 212.
p. 322, ¶4–p. 323, ¶1. Fulton to unknown friend, n.d.: in SUTCLIFFE I, pp. 202-3.
p. 325, ¶2. Recollections of Miss Helen Livingston: in *Century Mag.*, LIII, 1896, p. 179.
p. 325, ¶3. Fulton to editor of *American Citizen*, Aug. 20, 1807.
p. 326, ¶1. Fulton to unknown friend, *op. cit.*
p. 326, ¶3-4. Fulton to Barlow, spring 1807: in Todd, *op. cit.*, p. 233.
p. 328, ¶1. Account of Judge John Q. Wilson: in Munsell, J., *Annals of Albany*, VI, Albany, 1855, pp. 23-26.
p. 328, ¶3. Fulton to Livingston, Nov. 20, 1807: in SUTCLIFFE I, p. 259.
p. 329, ¶3. Renwick, James, "Life of Robert Fulton," in Sparks, Jared, ed., *The Library of American Biography*, X, Bost., 1839, p. 61.
p. 329, ¶4. SUTCLIFFE I, p. 276.
p. 331, ¶1. Charles Willson Peale to Fulton, Nov. 15, 1807: in *Penn. Mag. of Hist. and Biog.*, IX, 1889, p. 129.
p. 331, ¶3. COLDEN, pp. 217-20.

CHAPTER XXV   SOURCE REFERENCES

p. 334, ¶2. TURNBULL, pp. 238-55.

p. 335, ¶2-3. Log kept by Robert Livingston Stevens: in TURNBULL, pp. 275-78.

p. 336, ¶2-3. Fulton's ms. patent specification: in coll. Marine Museum of the City of N. Y.

p. 338, ¶2. Fulton to Monroe: in *Jour. Am. Hist.*, I, 1907, p. 427.

p. 339, ¶3. Fulton to Barlow, June 18, 1811: in SUTCLIFFE I, pp. 286-87.

p. 341, ¶2–p. 343, ¶4. Latrobe, John H. B., *The First Steamboat Voyage on Western Waters*, Balt., 1871.

p. 344, ¶2. Morrison, John H., *History of American Steam Navigation*, N.Y., 1903, p. 205.

p. 345, ¶2. Morrison, *op. cit.*, p. 207. Petersen, William J., *Steam Navigation on the Upper Mississippi*, Iowa City, 1937, pp. 68-74.

p. 346, ¶1. Fulton to West, July 12, 1813: ms. in coll. N.Y. Hist. Soc.

p. 346, ¶2. Ms. account in coll. N.Y. Hist. Soc. Miller, Peyton F., *The Story of Robert Fulton*, N.Y., 1908, p. 97.

p. 347, ¶1. Fulton to John DeLacey, Mar. 20, 1814: ms. in coll. N.Y. Hist. Soc.

p. 347, ¶2. Livingston to Stevens, n.d.: in TURNBULL, p. 305.

p. 347, ¶3. Fulton to Stanhope, Oct. 4, 1806: in DICKINSON, p. 203.

CHAPTER XXVI   TEXT NOTE

1. Fulton's style of painting after his return to America can be discussed with considerable assurance since pictures exist, both large oils and miniatures, whose history makes it certain that they are his work. These, however, are not the only pictures that are attributed to his later period. Hopeful owners have decided that almost any portrait with a steamboat in the background is a self-portrait of Fulton, while many stray canvases have gravitated to his name, some with elaborate inscriptions added by not too honest hands. If my discussion of his late work is less enthusiastic than the discussions of some critics, it is because I am convinced that the most accomplished pictures attributed to him are not by the same artist who painted the key pictures that are surely by Fulton. The portraits of Mr. and Mrs. Henry Eckford, for instance, are now generally agreed by experts to have little relation to his style, although many panegyrics have been based on them.

CHAPTER XXVI   SOURCE REFERENCES

p. 348, ¶2. Dyer, J. C., "Notes on the Introduction of Steam Navigation," in *Memoirs of the Literary and Phil. Soc.*, Manchester, 3rd ser., II, Lond., 1865, p. 292.

p. 349, ¶1. Fulton to Thomas Law, April 16, 1812: in *Bull. N.Y. Pub. Lib.*, XIII, 1909, p. 579.

p. 350, ¶1. Preble, George Henry, *A Chronological History of the Origin and Development of Steam Navigation*, Phila., 1895, pp. 85-86.

p. 354, ¶3. Fulton, *Torpedo War and Submarine Explosions*, N.Y., 1810, p. 38.

p. 355, ¶2. *Torpedo War, op. cit.*, p. 36.

p. 355, ¶3. Fulton to Stanhope, April 10, 1811: in DICKINSON, p. 247.

p. 356, ¶2. Rowbotham, W. B., "Robert Fulton's Turtle Boat," in *Proc. U. S. Naval Inst.*, LXII, 1936, p. 1748.

p. 357, ¶3. *Edinburgh Evening Courant*, Aug. 31, 1815: in DICKINSON, p. 265.

p. 360, ¶3. Fulton to John Hoge, Oct. 20, 1805: ms. in coll. Chicago Hist. Soc.

p. 361, ¶1. SUTCLIFFE II, pp. 190-91.

p. 362, ¶1. COLDEN, pp. 248-51.

p. 362, ¶2. Hosack to Colden, Jan. 1, 1817: in COLDEN, p. 265.

Index